GROUND COMBAT

GROUND COMBAT

PUNCTURING the MYTHS of MODERN WAR

Ben Connable

GEORGETOWN UNIVERSITY PRESS / WASHINGTON, DC

Library of Congress Cataloging-in-Publication Data

Names: Connable, Ben, author.
Title: Ground combat: puncturing the myths of modern war / Ben Connable.
Description: Washington, DC: Georgetown University Press, [2025] | Includes bibliographical references and index.
Identifiers: LCCN 2024015921 (print) | LCCN 2024015922 (ebook) | ISBN 9781647125417 (hardcover) | ISBN 9781647125424 (paperback) | ISBN 9781647125431 (ebook)
Subjects: LCSH: Combat—Case studies. | War—Case studies. | Military art and science—United States—Case studies.
Classification: LCC UA23 .C66 2025 (print) | LCC UA23 (ebook) | DDC 355.409/04—dc23/eng/20241015

LC record available at https://lccn.loc.gov/2024015921
LC ebook record available at https://lccn.loc.gov/2024015922

♾ This paper meets the requirements of ANSI/NISO Z39.48-1992 (Permanence of Paper).

26 25 9 8 7 6 5 4 3 2 First printing

Printed in the United States of America

Cover design by Nathan Putens
Interior design by Westchester Publishing Services

CONTENTS

List of Figures vii
List of Tables ix
Preface xi
Acknowledgments xv

Introduction 1

1 American Forecasts of War and Ground Combat 20

2 World War II Ground Combat Case Examples 56

3 World War II Ground Combat Characteristics 78

4 Interval Cases, 1945–2002 103

5 Interval-Period Ground Combat Characteristics 129

6 Modern Ground Combat from 2003 through 2012 154

7 Modern Ground Combat from 2013 through 2022 181

8 Observed Characteristics of Modern Ground Combat 212

9 Conclusions on Ground Combat and on War 252

Appendix: Methodology and Source Insights 285
Selected Bibliography 295
Index 317
About the Author 329

FIGURES

I.1	Observation Interval, Lead Interval, and Forecast Time	7
3.1	U.S. Army Infantry Brigade in World War I	79
8.1	Total Ground Combat Case Count by Region, 2003–2022	213
8.2	Total Case Count by Aggregated Region per Five-Year Period	214
8.3	Total Ground Combat Case Count by Country, 2003–2022	214
8.4	Competitor Types, Aggregated, 2003–2022	216
8.5	Terrain Frequency, 2003–2022	217
8.6	Infantry Weapons Frequency, 2003–2022	219
8.7	Infantry Movement, Tactics, Other, 2003–2022	220
8.8	Observed Infantry Drone Use, 2003–2022	220
8.9	Ground Indirect-Fire Use Frequency Other than Infantry Mortars, 2003–2022	225
8.10	Ground Indirect-Fire Use Frequency over Time Other than Infantry Mortars	226
8.11	Light Armed and Armored Vehicles and Tank Frequency, 2003–2022	230
8.12	Light Armed and Armored Vehicles and Tank Frequency over Time	230
8.13	Manned Aircraft Frequency, 2003–2022	234
8.14	Manned Aircraft Frequency over Time	234
8.15	Drone Use Overall, 2003–2022	237
8.16	Drone Use over Time	238
9.1	Observation Interval, Lead Interval, and Forecast Time	275

TABLES

I.1	Levels of Conflict, Type, Units, and Relative Duration	2
I.2	Case Distribution by Time Period	10
2.1	Twenty World War II Ground Combat Cases, 1942–1945	58
4.1	Twenty-Five Interval Cases from 1945 through 2002	104
6.1	Case Frequency by Period	155
6.2	Cases by Country, 2003–2007	156
6.3	Cases by Country, 2008–2012	166
7.1	Cases by Country, 2013–2017	182
7.2	Cases by Country, 2018–2022	195
8.1	U.S. Army Infantry Weapons and Drones from WWII to Early 2020s	223
8.2	Comparative Approximate Tank Losses across Four Historic Cases	232
8.3	Recurrence of Characteristics in Modern Cases over Time, 2003–2022	244
9.1	U.S. Army Prioritized Criteria for Ground Combat Vehicle Design	265

PREFACE

Military professionals generally accept a tenet of war attributed to Prussian soldier-scholar Carl von Clausewitz: War is thought to have a universal and unchanging nature and also a constantly changing character. Putting aside for now the surprising likelihood that Clausewitz never made this clear distinction, there is broad consensus that war is naturally violent and chaotic. Sharper splits in opinion emerge when it comes to war's ostensibly changing character. Soldier-poet Archilochus's metaphor of the hedgehog and the fox helps frame two archetypal positions on this difficult issue: A hedgehog is confident, single-minded, and declarative, while a fox is more willing to equivocate in the absence of clear evidence.

I shifted between these two roles over thirty-five years of practice and scholarship and settled out as a fox. That choice puts me at a permanent disadvantage in the fast-moving, high-stakes policy world. In military and policy briefing rooms, clarity and boldness sell while equivocation leaves audiences frustrated and combative. Confident declarations about the character of war are embraced and applied to shape trillions of dollars in defense spending. Bold, declarative confidence is particularly useful in capturing the imagination of senior military leaders, many of whom have an abiding dislike of unsurety.

Confidence is convincing, but these hedgehog-like declarations about warfare slant toward absolutism and fearmongering. In particular, dramatically technophilic and technophobic descriptions of modern warfare find fertile ground among North Atlantic Treaty Organization (NATO) leaders. I describe in this book some of the tech-centric character-of-war visions that have driven defense investment, strategy, and even battlefield tactics in global instances of ground combat. Plenty of anecdotal evidence might indeed mitigate toward these visions. But examination of tech-centric characterizations and forecasts lays bare essential flaws.

Ahistoricism and lack of empiricism render most of these claims unsound. Crystal-clear characterizations of war that tend to fixate senior policymakers and military leaders too often derive from strongly held opinions built without adequate consideration of objective evidence. To be fair, the well-structured evidence needed to generate more comprehensive empirical results is surprisingly lacking in the public domain. This gap in structured knowledge has left the study of war stuck in a figurative rut.

Academia is ill-prepared to mount a rescue. At least in the American academy, the study of war has come to be regarded as unsavory. War is now primarily studied as a distasteful social and political phenomenon rather than as essential history. Residual military-focused history programs and isolated professors generate important individual case studies or historiographies. But for the most part these do not account in detail for the grand scope of warfare as it is constantly practiced from place to place around the world.

Absent the needed empirical, longitudinal analyses of the global practice of combat, grand visions of clean, orderly, and mechanistic war take hold. War's most frustrating if unevenly occurring commonalities—chaos, friction, uncertainty, and risk—are imagined away. And so technical dominance is forecast with tantalizing clean-war imagery and demands for exquisitely expensive investments.

Even after these bold forecasts repeatedly fail to bear out in the real world, challenges to high-concept technophilia are commonly dismissed. Skeptics of technical revolution are rudely equated with fanatical Neo-Luddites, carrying forward ahistorical misperceptions of Luddism.

At the other pole, skeptics of high-concept futurism take an equally personalized, ahistorical, and therefore generally unhelpful approach to the characterization and forecasting of war. More traditionally focused colonels and generals are too ready to label innovation advocates as self-satisfied iconoclasts. As I show in chapters 1 and 9 of this book, their equally aggressive critiques feed into an essentialist and dualistic debate with no viable middle ground. In keeping with our essentialist times, what should be a thoughtful, evidence-driven dialectic reads more like an angry TikTok beef.

This is in great part a communal failure of epistemology, or the way in which we seek and organize our knowledge and compare opinion to observable fact. Our epistemic failures have left us vulnerable to the most hyperbolic technical forecasts.

I conducted the research presented in this book to help address these problems. I entered into this project aware of at least some of my own biases. Most notably: While a parade of senior military officers and theoreticians from the late 1800s to the mid 2020s have argued that novel technologies and tactics periodically render historical lessons and traditional military power less relevant or even fully irrelevant, I had observed nothing of the sort.

While my experiences in war have been limited, I witnessed firsthand both the shining promise and gritty failures of technology in ground combat. The 1991 Gulf War is frequently held out as a case study to support high-technology explanations and forecasts of war, and particularly of ground combat.

In the meta explanation of the Gulf War, Western satellites, drones, and precision-guided munitions crushed the low-tech Iraqi Army in record time and with limited and generally inconsequential ground fighting. My experience as a scout machine gunner crossing into Kuwait with the First Marine Division was far more traditional. While jets and drones flew overhead, I saw men riding in old-fashioned trucks and tanks move against each other in the smoke and fog to shoot it out with chaos and intensity that would be familiar to any World War II Desert Rat.

Just over a decade later, in 2003, I returned to combat in Iraq as an intelligence officer. I had full access to all of the coalition's battlefield information systems as we pressed north from Kuwait toward Baghdad and then to Tikrit. Drone feeds were on constant display, our highest-technology aircraft flew sorties overhead, and we killed Iraqis wholesale.

But still, the war primarily was a slugfest between soldiers with rifles, cannons, rockets, and mortars, all of which differed little from those employed in World War II by the grandfathers of these modern soldiers. Computer systems in our command post faltered, leaving us to track our forces and those of the enemy with old-fashioned grease pencils on acetate maps. Technology was useful, but it was no panacea.

These collective experiences, and my later research on both of these wars and others at the RAND Corporation from 2009 through 2021, led to a rather obvious but important going-in proposition for this project: Descriptions of war should not be mutually exclusive. Essentialist interpretations of the character of war—either as clean, ethereal competitions between high-tech machines or as traditional, face-to-face combat between tough men with guns—did not appear to stand up even to a cursory examination of the historical record. Being a fox on this issue made sense. It also made good sense to try to do something useful to help bridge this epistemic gap.

So, building on the work of experts like Paddy Griffith (*Forward into Battle*, 1990) and Stephen Biddle (*Military Power*, 2004), I conducted an inductive large-batch, or large-*n* study of ground combat battle cases to provide military professionals, analysts, and policymakers with an enduring and practical dataset in order to help improve historical knowledge and our understanding of war.

My research coincided with Russia's accelerated invasion of Ukraine in early 2022. I was able to compare and contrast this relatively well recorded war both with previous Ukraine cases (2014–2021) and with all the other simultaneously occurring global cases of ground combat. In parallel with many other analysts around the world, I spent hours each day sunk into Ukraine war videos, combatant interviews, news reports, social media posts, and expert analyses. Teamed with colleagues who were on the ground in Ukraine, I co-led primary-source battle research. As I absorbed the deluge of evidence from the front, I also closely followed the excited debate over the meaning of the Ukraine war to characterizations and forecasts of modern combat.

In the opening days of the invasion, as lightly armed Ukrainian infantry appeared to rebuff the Russian war machine with Javelin missiles and drones, excited technophiles declared final proof that the age of robotic warfare had arrived. Then, as the war settled into something resembling twentieth-century-style mechanized infantry, armor, and artillery combat across vast trench networks, the champions of more traditional perspectives on warfare—war as grinding, face-to-face position and attrition—reveled in a bit of schadenfreude. As I studied sixty-one Ukraine War battles (2014 to the end of 2022) in detail, I found no irrefutable proof to support either of these most staunchly dichotomous perspectives. I saw instead complexity, variation, and a good measure of unsurety in the publicly available data.

War erupted in Gaza in late 2023 as I was finishing this manuscript. While it occurred after my basic research concluded, I saw in the months of fighting that followed the October 7 attacks similar ground combat characteristics to those I observed across the hundreds of other cases recorded in my ground combat database. As with many of the other cases from high-profile wars in Afghanistan, Iraq, Nagorno-Karabakh, and Ukraine (and others), the Gaza War—really, a contiguous ground combat battle—captured the immediate attention of the community of analysts. It rightly should be studied in depth and within its immediate sociopolitical context. But like all the various battles in Ukraine, it also must be considered, compared, and contrasted as only one case of many occurring around the world and over time.

I started this project in August 2022 with a generous yearlong grant from the Smith Richardson Foundation and the Naval Postgraduate School Foundation. I hope the detailed, large-*n* case study approach, the database, and my informed subjective observations will inspire others to confront our epistemic challenges head-on and to define and describe present and future war in ways that are progressively more realistic, practical, and empirically defensible. A Microsoft Excel database of these coded cases is available on three websites: https://benconnable.com, https://groundcombat.org, and https://ground-combat.com.

ACKNOWLEDGMENTS

Smith Richardson Foundation made this work possible with their generous yearlong grant. Todd Lyons and the staff at the Naval Postgraduate School Foundation facilitated the grant, and Todd (a former Marine Corps colleague) was an enthusiastic supporter of my work. Another fellow Marine, Matt Jones, provided me with the kind of blunt feedback I needed to stay on track as I brainstormed my approach and conclusions; I continue to enjoy our debates over military history, Marine Corps policy, and wargaming. My colleague Dan Byman at Georgetown University helped me obtain the services of research assistants Dalya Berkowitz and Genny Chekerdjian, both of whom provided essential support during the data gathering phase of this project. I am particularly grateful to Oleksandra (Sasha) Titorova, my research support colleague on the Ukraine War cases. Sasha conducted her research from the greater Kyiv area with spotty internet and phone connections while continuing to work as a journalist. She also is a colleague on a project I co-led on the Battle for the Irpin River, data from which helped feed this study. For that effort, Sasha and my colleagues James Sladden and Liam Collins walked battlefields in northern Ukraine and interviewed Ukrainian soldiers and civilians about the conduct of the early phase of that war. James Lacey served as one of my peer reviewers. Jim's insights helped me effectively streamline important sections in the book. Thank you to my editor Don Jacobs and to the Georgetown University Press for working with me to publish this manuscript.

Finally, thank you to my family for putting up with my virtual absence as I worked long days and nights to bring this project to fruition. My son, Aram, provided feedback on each chapter draft. His measured enthusiasm and occasionally sharp critique gave me welcome breaks in writing and forced me to rethink more than a few key sections of this book. I was proud and honored to receive his insights.

Introduction

Ground combat is *the violent combined-arms engagement between two or more military forces on land.*[1] My purposes in this book about ground combat are to leverage new, modern battle data to help fill a major gap in Western military history; to improve military forecasting; and in turn to improve tactics, strategy, and innovative approaches to military force design.[2]

In the chapters that follow I set a baseline description of twenty cases from World War II and twenty-five more in the interim period between 1946 and 2002, identifying both continuities and changes relevant to modern ground combat in the twenty-first century. I derive my key findings from over 400 global battles that took place between 2003 and 2022, a period I describe here as the modern era of ground combat.

Think about ground combat as the point at which military forces collide on land. It is the violent tactical application of what the British Army refers to as land warfare.[3] Broadly, land warfare is a form of war fought primarily by ground-bound forces vying for control over physical terrain and populated areas.[4] Land warfare is then in turn an aspect of *war* writ large.

Ground combat is described in terms of narrowly focused skirmishes or battles. Land war is described in terms of campaigns, or a series of battle strung together over time. *War* writ large includes naval, air, and space combat; coalition building; industrial production; and other high-level factors. Table I.1 below puts these relative descriptions in order from the ground up.[5]

Characterizing warfare at any of these levels generally is a high-stakes gamble. Military leaders and policymakers continually struggle to characterize ground combat and broader instances of global warfare so they can improve tactics and make smart, practical investments in military technology and manpower.[6] Top-level American military doctrine (*Joint Warfighting*, 2023) tells us these assessments guide strategic decision-making: "A critical task for senior national and military leaders is to anticipate the character of war that might

Table I.1. Levels of Conflict, Type, Units, and Relative Duration

Ground combat	Tactical	Skirmish	Smaller units and/or no ground taken
		Battle	Larger units and/or ground seized
Land war	Tactical-Strategic[1]	Campaign	A series of interconnected battles
War	Strategic	War[2]	All aspects of power over time

[1] *This is often referred to in Western military writings and doctrine as the operational level of war. However, in contemporaneous discourse this term is contested. Readers partial to the term "operational level of war" should insert it here.*

[2] *There may be a better term than* war *for this purpose. Debate over terminology at this level of analysis exceeds the aims of the present research.*

occur. That judgment should inform the political decision to fight or to take any action that could lead to war."[7]

So it follows that leaders who can find a way to characterize and then forecast more accurately have a better chance of winning future wars and also of avoiding the sometimes existential consequences of defeat. In practice these investments boil down to often enormously costly bets on inherently uncertain futures.[8] Given the stakes, one might assume there are highly structured methods driving this process.

Sadly, that is not the case. As of the mid 2020s, the most influential characterizations and forecasts of war have often been driven by subjective interpretations of selected cases and emerging, unproven technical trends rather than by more objective analysis.[9] This is particularly true for descriptions of ground combat, which is the most common aspect of modern war.

Terms like *the character of war* are themselves undefined or, worse, assumed to be self-defining (i.e., the character of war is the character of war).[10] When experts say or write "the character of war," it is not clear if they are referring to the character of all wars, of some wars but not others, or only of the most high-technology instances of warfare between military superpowers.[11] Implied in the term itself—the character of war—is that someone has divined a universal character of all war. I attack this implication head-on in the chapters that follow.

Lack of clear definition opens the door to excited and arguably unprovable claims that have direct impact on policy and military operations. For example, *Joint Warfighting* offers no definition of the character of war but still makes this dramatic claim: "In 2023, we are witnessing an unprecedented fundamental change in the character of war, and our window of opportunity to ensure we maintain an enduring competitive advantage is closing."[12] Absent a clear definition of *the character of war*, this statement amounts to a strongly expressed but ephemeral opinion.

Worse still, the etymology of the commonly used terms *nature of war* and *character of war* may be widely confused and abused; see chapter 9 on this point. Until these terms are better understood, all subjective or objective efforts to describe the changing character of war—including statements like the one cited above in a top-level Western military publication—are hollow. As I describe below, the concept and practice of *forecasting* are equally muddled.[13]

SUBJECTIVE OPINIONS ON WAR: INTERESTING, USEFUL, AND INADEQUATE

Subjective expert opinions on war are useful because they stimulate debate.[14] Personalized characterizations and forecasts of war have some value as long as they are not taken at face value. Unfortunately, military leaders searching for clarity in the fog of war sometimes are too eager to accept forceful arguments presented by well-known experts. These experts too often get it wrong. They are rarely held to account after the fact.

Rupert Smith's *The Utility of Force* (2007) probably is the best-known contemporaneous case in point. Smith is a deservedly well-respected general whose opinion should be thoughtfully engaged. But the provocative opening paragraphs of his characterization and forecast of land war were so spectacularly wrong that they deserve partial recapitulation here: "War no longer exists. Confrontation, conflict and combat undoubtably exist all around the world . . . and states still have armed forces which they use as symbols of power. Nonetheless, war as cognitively known to most non-combatants, war as a battle in a field between men and machinery, war as a massive deciding event in a dispute in international affairs: such war no longer exists."[15]

Smith went on to argue that tank battles were a thing of the past and would not be likely to occur again because they were impractical. No kind of "industrial war" was even feasible.[16] Given that I am writing this book with the benefit of hindsight, looking back over the large-scale ground battles and land wars that have since been fought in Yemen, Syria, Libya, Iraq, Sri Lanka, Ethiopia, Nagorno-Karabakh, Ukraine, and elsewhere, calling Smith out may seem obtuse.[17] But if we are to improve our understanding of war, we must hold to account influential generals who write about the character of war and in turn influence the following generations of military professionals and policymakers with their opinions.[18]

Sometimes a lone expert does get it right and in turn helps foster needed innovation.[19] For example, in the early 1920s, U.S. Marine officer Earl H. "Pete" Ellis traveled to Micronesia to examine Imperial Japanese military capabilities and to help the Marine Corps conceptualize ways to operate in the Pacific theater.[20] Working mostly on his own and deriving insights from personal observation, Ellis accurately forecast that the Japanese would attack to seize control of the many island chains in the Western Pacific and that they would start their campaign by trying to destroy American military power using airstrikes. Ellis's foresight drove Marine Corps force design for advanced base operations that helped prepare the Corps for World War II. That innovation seeded Marine Corps operational concepts one hundred years into the future.[21]

Still, relying on people like Ellis to get it right is an awfully risky way to bet on national security. How could we ever know *why* Ellis was right if there was no structured process behind his forecast? How could we replicate his approach without relying on arbitrary hope that the next expert would also have good intuition?

More structured alternatives abound.[22] At least in the United States, some of these efforts remain hidden behind walls of government secrecy or are so laden with formulae and jargon that they never gain traction.[23] Stephen Biddle found a good middle-ground approach with his 2004 examination of military force and the changing character of war.

BIDDLE'S CALL FOR IMPROVEMENT AND THE NEED FOR MILITARY HISTORY STUDIES

Biddle did not fill the gap between comprehensive evidence and subjective opinion in *Military Power*. He did provide a useful model, formula, historical analysis, and a small-*n* (small-batch) study of land warfare.[24] Biddle also made two arguments about the changing character of war that influenced my research.

First, he described the collective academic and military efforts to characterize and forecast war as an inadequate and tangled mess. Lack of effective methods had led directly to recurring misperceptions about war. For instance, Arab armies reportedly decimated Israeli tank units in the 1973 Yom Kippur War using early 1960s-era Malyutka anti-tank guided missiles.[25]

Driven by personalized interpretations of this single ground combat case, some experts concluded that tanks were "doomed" on the modern battlefield. Yet, according to Biddle and other historians, less than twenty years later American M1 Abrams tanks dominated the Gulf War battlefield in Iraq in the face of these same Malyutkas and even more advanced threats.[26]

Biddle also drew conclusions from his structured analysis about the changing character of war, and particularly land war and ground combat. He found that recurring forecasts of revolutionary change were repeatedly wrong. Specifically, proponents of the Revolution in Military Affairs (RMA)—a central subject in chapters 1 and 9 of this book—continually and enthusiastically misjudged the prospective impact of technology on the character of war and also on the ostensibly unchanging nature of war.

Looking forward from 2004, Biddle argued that there was no evidence of a "looming discontinuity" that might dramatically alter the ways in which ground combat services like the U.S. Army and Marine Corps might fight.[27] Instead, "The technological changes that were most often cited [in the RMA] as revolutionary—the increased lethality of precision guided weapons, the increased range of deep strike air and missile systems, and the increased ability to gather and process information—are all extensions of very longstanding trends. Militaries have been forced to cope with steadily increasing lethality, range, and surveillance capabilities for fully a century now; these are hardly sudden developments posing fundamentally new problems."[28]

These last thoughts are, of course, Biddle's own personalized interpretation of the historical record.[29] As with Smith and any other top expert, his ideas also should be actively engaged but not taken at face value. Biddle acknowledges this point by shaming the military analysis community over the long-standing vacuum of empirical research on the character of war and by calling for further work. With fortuitous timing, the University of Oxford had just been funded to help fill this gap.[30]

Between 2003 and 2024 (ongoing) Oxford's Changing Character of War Centre generated a body of work on the eponymous subject. It typically has explored a middle ground between evolution and revolution, choosing a dialectic approach rather than championing any decisive position. In 2011 Hew Strachan and Sibylle Scheipers made a strong case for the role of detailed and exhaustive historical analysis in the pursuit of better characterizations and forecasts of war. This is a brief but important quote from their book *The Changing Character of War*: "The historians [in the program] argued that we could not identify change if we did not have the historical awareness which enabled us to recognize continuity."[31]

In other words, historical analysis is the foundation of any good and reasonable effort to characterize and forecast war and to better appreciate the amplitude of past and likely future change. Renowned British historian Michael Howard had firmly established this necessity in his classic 1961 article "The Use and Abuse of Military History." Howard wrote that military professionals must study the history of war in width, depth, and context to master their craft and avoid the pitfalls of inadequate historical investigation.

Specifically to my purposes Howard argued: "First, [the military professional] must study in *width*. He must observe the way in which warfare has developed over a long historical period. Only by seeing what does change can one deduce what does not; and as much can be learned from the great 'discontinuities' of military history as from the apparent similarities of the techniques employed by the great captains through the ages."[32]

This need to study military history to effectively prepare for and practice war is a broadly accepted truism that, as we will see in chapter 1, is too often applied to at least American military policy with slipshod and disingenuous interpretations. Instead of objectively applying historical lessons in a structured and linear pathway from history to present to future, some prominent military forecasters cherry-pick confirmatory historical examples, skip over confounding cases, and make strong arguments about the character of war driven primarily by declarative force and with the imprimatur of personal reputation and position. In other words, they hedgehog it.

While objective study of military history is a prerequisite for good forecasting, a good understanding of history alone is insufficient to objectively describe and forecast the character of ground combat, land war, or strategic war. It is a logical fallacy to argue that historical trends dictate future events. For complex human interactions like war, good trend forecasting requires thoughtful multidisciplinary analysis and then only in the end some informed subjective judgment.

Ultimately, the idea is not to remove subjectivity from the process—this would be an impossibility—but to better frame its value and narrow its inherent vagaries. Sound, objective scientific method is needed to help build the structured baseline from which military leaders and policymakers can develop improved understanding of war and then make good judgments about the future. In 1975 two Soviet military scientists offered an interpretation of military characterization and forecasting that, while far from ideal, at least provides a good description of the process and a starting point for improvement.

FORECASTING IN MILITARY AFFAIRS

Many of the assumptions and central arguments in Yuri Chuyev and Yuri Mikhaylov's *Forecasting in Military Affairs* (1975) are debatable.[33] Certainly, few Western military experts in the 2020s would pay heed to the boilerplate praise of Vladimir Lenin common to Soviet-era military writing.[34] Soviet authors embraced the existence of military revolutions without debate, but as Biddle, Colin S. Gray, and others have argued, their existence is at least debatable.[35]

And readers with even a remote appreciation for the chaos and uncertainty of armed conflict would be skeptical of the Soviet belief that cold quantification would slice through the fog of war to generate anything close to a mathematically accurate forecast of future conditions. It is doubtful any of these Soviet methods were ever tested in full under real-world conditions. Yet given all of these caveats, Chuyev and Mikhaylov—for simplification here, the Soviets—still wrote one of the better and more enduring books on military forecasting.

The best way to make practical use of *Forecasting in Military Affairs* is to ignore the propaganda and the attempts to apply mathematical formulae and focus in on the straightforward descriptions of the forecasting process.[36] The

Soviets start by describing the uncertainty that lies at the heart of all forecasting. They make a seemingly obvious but crucial point about this uncertainty: It affects "the process being forecast in the past, present, and future."[37] In other words, imperfect knowledge of the past and present is intrinsic and just as detrimental to accuracy as the necessarily imperfect knowledge of the future. Historical knowledge is essential, but we must remind ourselves that it, too, is imperfect and can mislead if not carefully gathered, studied, and interpreted.

The Soviets go on with other simple but foundational statements and arguments: Forecasts are to some extent both objective and subjective.[38] More objective forecasts are more scientifically sound. Increasing objectivity in turn decreases subjectivity.[39] More scientifically objective forecasts will not necessarily be accurate, but they may be somewhat *more* accurate and, at the very least, will be less subject to manipulation.[40]

Forecasts may also be qualitative or quantitative, or a mix of both. There is nothing inherently better about qualification or quantification as long as the methods are scientific.[41] Given the Soviet focus on quantitative methods, this is a remarkable acknowledgment with broad implications for the analysis and assessment of war.[42]

Good military forecasts have two central components. They accurately describe (1) a future condition occurring in (2) a period of time that is precise enough to help inform policy choices. Accurately forecasting near-term events is generally easier than accurately forecasting distant events. The Soviets offer a generally acceptable bounding of short-term, medium-, or mid-term, and long-term forecasts to help differentiate timelines and policy challenges:

Short-term:	Present to five years
Mid-term:	Five years to ten years
Long-term:	Beyond ten years[43]

They also describe time marks and intervals to help guide the linear process from historical analysis to present trend analysis to forecast. The *observation interval* is the relevant period of history up to the time the forecast is made. The *lead interval* is the period from the present to the *forecast time,* which is the anticipated moment of the condition or event. Figure I.1, below, depicts these concepts:

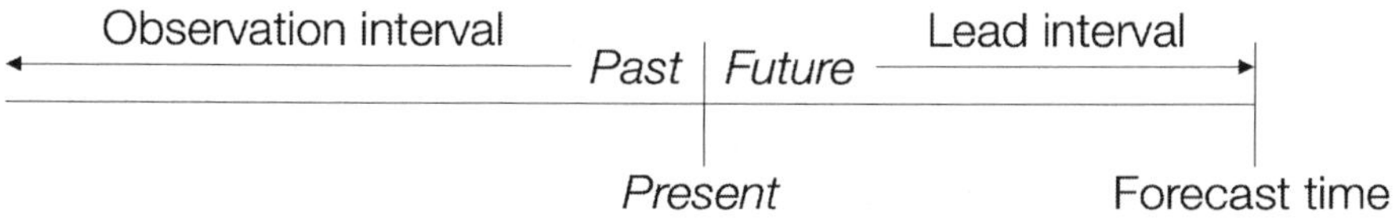

FIGURE I.1. Observation Interval, Lead Interval, and Forecast Time

These intervals and marks—observation interval, present, lead interval, and forecast time—can be generally understood as history, present, and future. Here is the Soviets' idea of timelines and intervals summed up in a simplified dualism: Thorough forecasts of the near future built from objective historical analysis of the past are, as a general rule, more likely to be accurate than forecasts of the long-term future built from shallow, subjective historical analysis.

I wrote above that subjective opinion was inadequate to understand and forecast war *and* that it also is inseparable from the most objective scientific method; even the very process of crafting a forecasting process requires exercising informed, and ideally expert, opinion. Expert opinion is the necessary subjective component of forecasting.

Indeed, there is inherent value in experience, wisdom, and *coup d'oeil,* or a quick and holistic appreciation of a complex military problem.[44] Canonical works that apply subjective interpretation to the nature and character of war including Clausewitz's *On War,* Sun Tzu's (Sun Zi's) *The Art of War,* Antoine-Henri Jomini's *Summary of the Art of War,* and Ardant du Picq's *Battle Studies* are essential reading; collective knowledge on war cannot be left to scientists.[45] Expert opinions—including those drawn from canonical literature on land war—are necessary. They should inform but not drive forecasting. With good historical analysis and characterizations of the present, expert opinion may turn out to be the least important input.

ADDING HISTORICAL OBJECTIVITY THROUGH GROUND COMBAT CASE STUDIES

If the subjective expert opinions of experienced senior generals like Rupert Smith are not to be absorbed as holy writ, then certainly mine hold no greater weight. I neither expect nor hope that any reader will accept my interpretation of the historical record or thoughts on ground combat without question. That said, I do not cop out. In chapter 1 I offer an incisive critique of American efforts to characterize and forecast war, and in chapter 9, I fire some evidence-driven broadsides.

But this book is primarily intended to summarize my inductive large-*n* (large-batch) case study of modern ground combat. Ideally it will feed relatively more objective evidence into what the Soviets called the observation interval, or the historical period before any characterization or forecast is made. I summarize the cases in subsequent chapters, and I am making the Ground Combat Database, Version 1 (GCD-V1) a public resource for further analysis.

All types of historical study are valuable and necessary. All types of historical evidence should be gathered and different methods applied to feed a holistic understanding of war. Every after-action report, historical book, interview, video, article, annotated map, scientific study, and so on adds prospective value. Following this holistic and comparative approach for case studies, detailed single cases and small-*n* studies should be accompanied by large-*n* studies that rope in tens, hundreds, or even thousands of cases.[46]

There are obvious trade-offs between these approaches. A single case or smaller batch of cases allows for more patient and thorough data gathering and provides far greater insight into each case. Larger batches allow for broader scope but necessitate quicker and therefore shallower analyses of each case. I selected the large-batch method for reasons I describe in the appendix, none of which obviate the need for single case histories or smaller-batch studies.

WHAT ABOUT SEA AND AIR COMBAT?

A large-batch study of all types of tactical military combat—land, air, sea, space—would help further holistic knowledge of war. But while water covers over 70 percent of the Earth's surface, and while the total volume of air and space dwarfs the Earth's physical ground surface coverage, land warfare is still by far the most prolific type of conflict.[47] Prospects for future sea-centric and air-centric wars certainly exist. But since the end of World War II, unique instances of both ship-versus-ship and aircraft-versus-aircraft combat appear to have declined precipitously in frequency and scale.[48] Instances of ground combat are continual with a high frequency of incidence and are also continuous as a feature of human interaction. And perhaps more importantly for my purposes, I am personally interested in ground combat. Having a sustained interest in the subject matter helps prevent burnout when studying nearly 600 unique cases.

OVERVIEW OF METHODOLOGY

The appendix in this book describes my research methodology. Briefly, in mid August 2022 I began a mostly inductive case study and coding process of ground combat skirmishes and battles between the early phases of World War II and the end of 2022, with a focus on twenty-first-century warfare. I used World War II as a baseline, then examined changes from World War II through the end of 2022, and then focused my research on what I blocked out as the modern period of ground combat: early 2003 through my data collection end point in late 2022.

As I went through all of these cases, I paid particular attention to the introduction and impact of technology. American characterizations and forecasts of war tend to be tech-centric. In chapter 1 I describe a continual fifty-year, decade-by-decade American effort to characterize war in terms of competitive technical advantage. Precision-guided munitions, sensors, drones, and robotics are described as revolutionary, changing both the character and the ostensibly

Table I.2. Case Distribution by Time Period

Period	Coded	
1942–1945	20	
1946–2002	25	
2003–2022	**423**	Out of 548 identified

immutable nature of war. At least as of late 2024, these depictions are for the most part driven by deeply personalized interpretations of warfare. By coding for technology in the ground combat cases, and by conducting supplementary research, I hope to provide some objective evidence and a new perspective on this contentious issue.

Table I.2 depicts the total number of cases examined, coded, and not coded across each of the three time periods I examined: (1) during World War II; (2) interim period from World War II through the end of 2002; and (3) 2003 through the end of 2022. World War II and interim period cases were exemplary of type. I attempted to code all publicly available modern cases but only found sufficient evidence to code 423 out of the 548 I was able to identify. That left 125 modern cases from 2003 to 2022 investigated, recorded in the database, but not coded.

CASE CRITERIA AND COMBINED ARMS DEFINED

This project started with a series of questions and categories of information about ground combat.[49] Many of the cases I studied (e.g., Al-Mosul Iraq 2016–2017) were large-scale battles not suitable to disaggregation. But in order to cast the widest possible net for case selection and to create the broadest possible understanding of ground combat, I set minimalist case criteria:

1. Minimum of platoon strength (about twenty-five to forty people) on both sides
2. Combined arms employment by both sides

Setting a minimum unit size on both sides helped eliminate counterterror raids and other minor gunfights.[50] My criteria imply that all of the cases from World War II to 2022 recorded in the database including battles between insurgents and counterinsurgents, and even between two or more insurgent groups, are conventional warfare cases. This is a contestable point that I return to throughout the book. Use of the term *combined arms* opens up another prospective debate. The Marine Corps offers a rather clear and well-tested description:

> Combined arms is the full integration of arms in such a way that to counteract one, the enemy must become more vulnerable to another. We pose the enemy not just with a problem, but with a dilemma—a no-win situation.... An example of the concept of combined arms at the very lowest level is the complementary use of the automatic weapon and grenade launcher within a fire team. We pin an enemy down with high-volume, direct fire of the automatic weapon, making him a vulnerable target for the grenade launcher. If he moves to escape the impact of the grenades, we engage him with the automatic weapon.[51]

With this example, Marine Corps doctrine sets what is probably the lowest possible tactical bar for combined arms at the four-man fire team using light machineguns and grenade launchers. There was no possibility of scoping every case of combat at this level, so I raised the bar slightly to at least the combined platoon-level use of rifles and small knee mortars or light indirect-fire rockets.[52] Given the extensive number of prospective cases with groups like the Islamic State in Syria and Iraq, I also left open the inclusive combination of rifles and suicide bombing attacks; see chapters 6–8 and the appendix and database for more explanation.

WHAT ABOUT INTANGIBLE FACTORS LIKE WILL TO FIGHT?

This work focuses on tangible factors in war: technology, equipment, terrain, soldiers, observed behaviors, and so on. It does not account for the essential intangible factors in war, including leadership, adaptability, training, and the will to fight.

Most Western military doctrine is derived from Carl von Clausewitz's *Vom Krieg*, or *On War*.[53] Clausewitz defined war as a contest of opposing human wills. Specifically, he wrote that "War is thus an act of force to compel the enemy to do our will."[54] Violence is therefore a means to destroy enemy forces in order to (or at the very least also to) break their will to fight.[55] American ground force doctrine places great significance on the importance of human will.

Both the U.S. Army and Marine Corps describe will to fight as one of the most, or the single most, important factors in warfare. Army doctrine describes war as a "fundamentally human clash of wills," and the Marine Corps' capstone doctrine lays the same foundation: "The essence of war is a violent struggle between two hostile, independent, and irreconcilable wills, each trying to impose itself on the other.... Appreciating this dynamic interplay between opposing human wills is essential to understanding the fundamental nature of war."[56]

I generally agree with this perspective and have written extensively about the impact of will to fight in land warfare.[57] But the purposes of this book are to describe the ways in which military forces fight in ground combat and to understand the pace of historical changes in the forms of land warfare, not to explore *why* combatants fought or to ascribe success or failure to any material or human input. Any future holistic study of combat power, or combat effectiveness, must incorporate at least a fighting force's physical capabilities like weapons and equipment and intangible factors like leadership, adaptability, training, and the will to fight.[58]

INNOVATE OR DIE?

Debate over the so-called character of war often centers on the merits of innovation. If the character of war is constantly changing, then continual innovation is ostensibly essential to maintain technical-tactical overmatch. But innovation is one of those terms used in military circles without adequate consideration for its true meaning or subtle vagaries. Broadly, it is the application of new ideas to improve a capability or process. Michael Horowitz and Shira Pindyck define innovation from a broad literature review as *changes in the conduct of warfare designed to increase the ability of a military community to generate power.*[59]

My old RAND Corporation colleague Adam Grissom distilled perhaps the most useful, and certainly one of the most widely used, description of military innovation, setting three prerequisites:

(1) It changes the manner in which military formations function in the field;
(2) it is significant in scope and impact, and;
(3) it achieves some kind of improved military effectiveness.[60]

Given these three prerequisites, it is hard to argue that a military innovation is anything other than an unalloyed good. Thus rhetorically armed, the most fervent innovation advocates tell us that we must "innovate or die," often while gleefully skewering naysayers and mild skeptics alike.[61] Prima facie, any innovation that fulfilled all three requirements might indeed be good. Who wouldn't want a positive, practical, broad-based change that increases effectiveness? However, this inherently optimistic use of *innovation* has allowed it to settle into the Western military lexicon in ways that may in fact be insidious.[62]

It is quite possible to apply the first two parts of this formula—to innovate, or propose and enact ideas that have significant, direct, and broad impact on ground combat operations—and also *not* achieve some kind of improved military effectiveness. Any given innovation might not really be needed to overmatch adversary forces; oft-used innovation terms like *overmatch* or *dominance* are ill-defined and relative standards with no clear or provable benchmarks.

In fact, it also would be possible to innovate and in doing so actually reduce military effectiveness even in those units directly affected by the innovation. For example, American soldiers employing the first version of the M-16 rifle in the Vietnam War probably did not feel particularly enthusiastic about that military-wide ground combat innovation as they struggled to fight with poorly designed and, far too often, jammed and nonfunctional weapons.[63] Since the term "combat effectiveness" also is undefined (see chapter 9), the only practical way to debate the effectiveness of an innovation is after it has been tested in many battles. This makes innovation look more like a submission to chance than an unalloyed good.

And as useful as the various distilled definitions have been to the study of innovation, they generally do not account for another prospective and more immediate downside.[64] Politicians can raise new funds to pay for new weapons and forces, but innovations often require roughly equivalent cutbacks somewhere else.[65] Perhaps the best example of innovation trade-offs for modern ground combat is the U.S. Marine Corps' Force Design 2030, a subject in chapters 1 and 9 of this book. Marine leaders made cuts from their own forces and systems to pay for innovations in missile and data technologies, and so on. Those bets may yet prove wise, but I find that they have almost certainly created worrying gaps in Marine ground combat capability.

In light of these significant risks—uncertain improvement and the possibility of dangerously degrading the force—innovation takes on more anodyne meaning. Instead of an invigorating, barrier-shattering mechanism for unalloyed good, innovation really is just a functional process with inherent risks and trade-offs. Reluctance to innovate is a risk, and excessive enthusiasm for innovation is a risk.

As with any functional process applied to a complex and inherently uncertain human endeavor like ground combat, innovation benefits from ever-more-objective, empirical, and to the greatest extent possible, comprehensive historical understanding. Innovation risks are exaggerated when history is ignored or picked over for its narrowest and least defensible lessons. I immediately pick up this thread in chapter 1.

STRUCTURE OF THIS BOOK

Through the remainder of this book, I build a case for more objective and inductive case research on war and specifically, ground combat. I start in chapter 1 with a straightforward critique of American character-of-war descriptions and forecasts over the past fifty years (late 1960s through the early 2020s). This analysis points to the need for more objective research.

In the core chapters that follow I offer a progressive chronology of case histories and analysis of evolutionary ground combat developments, starting with a baseline assessment of World War II in chapters 2 and 3, interluding cases from 1945 to 2002 in chapters 4 and 5, and progressing in five-year increments from 2003 through 2022 in chapters 6 and 7. Throughout this book I present descriptive summaries of forty-four cases of ground combat.

In each of these core chapters—2 through 7—I give a general description of the cases, provide coded findings from that period (i.e., what did the coding reveal about ground combat), present exemplary case narratives, and offer some insights into the availability and use of technology. In chapter 8 I provide overall findings from the study, focusing on describing ground combat as it appears in the cases. In chapter 9 I conclude with insights for policy and recommendations for further research, and specifically for use of the database that I am releasing as a companion to this book.

The single appendix describes the case methodology, addresses the epistemological challenges that plague efforts to characterize and forecast war, and raises serious concerns about the ephemeral nature of knowledge in the digital world. Selected references conclude the book.

NOTES

1. This is my working definition of ground combat. It appears that no formal definition is applied by the U.S. military as of late 2024, though various definitions were used to determine the roles of women in the armed services from the mid 1990s through the late 2010s. See, for example, U.S. Department of Defense, *DOD Dictionary of Military and Associated Terms,* electronic manual, November 2021, https://jcs.mil; U.S. Marine Corps, *MAGTF Ground Operations,* MCWP 3–10 (Washington, DC: Headquarters, U.S. Marine Corps, April 2018); and U.S. Army, *Operations,* ADP 3–0 (Washington, DC: Headquarters, Department of the Army, October 2017). The United Kingdom's Joint Doctrine defines land "combat force elements" like armor and infantry units but not their role in applying combined arms. UK Ministry of Defence, *UK Land Power,* Joint Doctrine Publication 0–20, 6th ed. (Shrivenham, UK: Development, Concepts and Doctrine Centre, 2023), 43.
2. A Microsoft Excel database of these coded cases will be disseminated in parallel with the publication of this book. It will be available at https://benconnable.com, https://groundcombat.org, and https://ground-combat.com.
3. Forces engaged in ground combat often receive some kind of support from the air and sea. As long as the purpose of the fighting is land based, and the air and sea actions are supporting land forces, then the definition of ground combat still obtains.
4. For a more thorough description of land warfare see UK Ministry of Defence, *Land Operations,* AC 71940 (Wiltshire, UK: Land Warfare Development Centre, 2017).

5. Jehuda Wallach offers a good description of the post-Clausewitz German interjection of the operational level of war into this framing: Jehuda L. Wallach, *The Dogma of the Battle of Annihilation: The Theories of Clausewitz and Schlieffen and Their Impact on the German Conduct of Two World Wars* (Westport, CT: Greenwood Press, 1986), 11. Antulio J. Echevarria II writes about a Clausewitzean distinction between war and warfare. The U.S. Marine Corps offers a decent explanation of these levels of conflict in its late-1990s doctrinal publication series. See Antulio J. Echevarria II, *Clausewitz and Contemporary War* (Oxford, UK: Oxford University Press, 2007), 57; U.S. Marine Corps, *Tactics*, MCDP 1–3 (Washington, DC: Headquarters, U.S. Marine Corps, July 1997); U.S. Marine Corps, *Campaigning*, MCDP 1–2 (Washington, DC: Headquarters, U.S. Marine Corps, August 1997); U.S. Marine Corps, *Strategy*, MCDP 1–1 (Washington, DC: Headquarters, U.S. Marine Corps, November 1997).
6. Forecasts of war also shape military-industrial-base investments, and, perversely, military industry can shape forecasts of war to fit profit objectives. This issue is relevant to the present discussion but falls slightly outside the bounds of this book.
7. U.S. Joint Chiefs of Staff, *Joint Warfighting*, Joint Publication 1, Vol. 1 (Washington, DC, August 27, 2023).
8. See Robert A. Johnson, "Predicting Future War," *Parameters* 44, no. 1 (Spring 2014).
9. See the next section in this chapter and chapter 9 for more detail. Others have drawn similar conclusions. See, for example, Paddy Griffith, *Forward into Battle: Fighting Tactics from Waterloo to the Near Future* (Wiltshire, UK: Crowood Press (1981/1990)), chapter 1.
10. I present many examples of this vagary throughout the book. For a quick example see this official U.S. Army monograph. It repeatedly refers to the nature and character of war without defining either term. U.S. Army, *The Operational Environment and the Changing Character of Warfare* (Fort Eustis, VA: Training and Doctrine Command, October 7, 2019).
11. Similar issues apply to the term *nature of war*. See chapter 9 for more on this topic.
12. U.S. Joint Chiefs of Staff, *Joint Warfighting*, Joint Publication 1, Vol. 1 (Washington, DC, August 27, 2023), i.
13. There are no clear, universal definitions of the terms forecast or prediction. Debate over their meanings centers on whether an event is expected at a specific or in a general time frame in the future, and on the degree to which the term suggests perfect or imperfect accuracy.
14. See, for example, Mick Ryan, *War Transformed: The Future of Twenty-First Century Great Power Competition and Conflict* (Annapolis, MD: Naval Institute Press, 2022).
15. Rupert Smith, *The Utility of Force: The Art of War in the Modern World* (New York: Alfred A. Knopf, 2007).
16. Smith, *Utility of Force*, 3.
17. Certainly, Smith is not alone. Other examples are listed in chapter 1. Contemporaneous reviews of Smith's work were mostly laudatory, perhaps reflecting the tired, mid-Iraq War, counter-intervention zeitgeist of the mid 2000s. See, for example, William Grimes, "Why the Strongest Armies May Lose the Newest Wars," *New York Times*, January 18, 2007; Robert Bolia, "The Utility of Force: The Art of War in the Modern World," *Naval War College Review* 59, no. 2 (Spring 2006), 169–170.

18. In a 2023 article, Eliot Cohen argued that experts and policymakers are rarely, if ever, held to account for bad forecasting. See Eliot A. Cohen, "Beware the False Prophets of War," *Atlantic Online*, September 11, 2023, https://theatlantic.com.
19. For more on forecasting, see Philip E. Tetlock, *Expert Political Judgment: How Good Is It? How Can We Know?* (Princeton, NJ: Princeton University Press, 2006); David R. Mandel and Alan Barnes, "Accuracy of Forecasts in Strategic Intelligence," *Proceedings of the National Academy of Sciences* 111, no. 30 (July 29, 2014), 10984–10989; Philip E. Tetlock and Dan Gardner, *Superforecasting: The Art and Science of Prediction* (New York: Random House, 2015); et al.
20. For more on Ellis, see Dirk Anthony Ballendorf, "Earl Hancock Ellis: A Marine in Micronesia," *Micronesian Journal of the Humanities and Social Sciences* 1, no. 1–2 (December 2002), 9–17; and "Lieutenant Colonel Earl H. Ellis," online biography, U.S. Marine Corps, https://usmc.mil.
21. U.S. Marine Corps, *Advanced Base Operations in Micronesia*, Fleet Marine Force Reference Publication 12–46 (Washington, DC: Headquarters, U.S. Marine Corps (1921/1992)).
22. See, for example, Olaf Helmer-Hirschberg, *Analysis of the Future: The Delphi Method* (Santa Monica, CA: RAND Corporation, 1967).
23. I led or participated in several of these efforts while serving as an intelligence officer in the 2000s and while working at the RAND Corporation from 2009 through 2021.
24. Stephen Biddle, *Military Power: Explaining Victory and Defeat in Modern Battle* (Princeton, NJ: Princeton University Press, 2004). Biddle draws on an older battle database called CDB90—one of only two I was able to identify in my research—which he and coauthor Stephen Long write about in Stephen Biddle and Stephen Long, "Democracy and Military Effectiveness: A Deeper Look," *Journal of Conflict Resolution* 48, no. 4 (2004), 525–546. See the appendix of this book for more on CDB90.
25. The Malyutka is still in service in many countries in 2024. For more on this system, see Chris McNab, *Sagger Anti-Tank Missile vs M60 Main Battle Tank: Yom Kippur War 1973*, ebook (Oxford, UK: Osprey, 2018); and "9K11 Malyutka (AT-3 Sagger) Russian Anti-Tank Guided Missile (ATGM)," U.S. Army Worldwide Equipment Guide, n.d., U.S. Army, https://odin.tradoc.army.mil.
26. Biddle, *Military Power*, 2. The debate over the value of the tank in ground combat is, of course, ongoing in late 2024. See chapters 4 and 5 for more on the Gulf War, ATGMs, and M1 tanks.
27. Biddle, *Military Power*, 197.
28. Biddle, *Military Power*, 197. He reiterates these points in the context of the Ukraine War in Stephen Biddle, "Back in the Trenches: Why New Technology Hasn't Revolutionized Warfare in Ukraine," *Foreign Affairs*, August 10, 2023, https://www.foreignaffairs.com.
29. Biddle was also not the only one to make these observations about the RMA or other characterizations and forecasts. See chapter 9 for a fuller discussion on this point.
30. The Changing Character of War Centre, or CCW, was established in 2003.
31. Hew Strachan and Sibylle Scheipers, eds., *The Changing Character of War* (Oxford, UK: Oxford University Press, 2011), 7.

32. Michael Howard, "The Use and Abuse of Military History," *Parameters* 11, no. 1 (1981), 9–14, 14.
33. Canada Secretary of State Department, trans., *Forecasting in Military Affairs: A Soviet View*, by Yuri V. Chuyev and Yuri B. Mikhaylov (Moscow: 1975), distributed by the U.S. Government Printing Office, Washington, DC, referred to in further citation as Chuyev and Mikhaylov, *Forecasting*, 1975.
34. Chuyev and Mikhaylov, *Forecasting*, 1975, and other sources.
35. Chuyev and Mikhaylov, *Forecasting*, 1975. See chapter 9 for more on Colin Gray's insights on the RMA.
36. For reflections see, for example, Clint Reach et al., *Russian Military Forecasting and Analysis: The Military-Political Situation and Military Potential in Strategic Planning* (Santa Monica, CA: RAND Corporation, 2022); Timothy L. Thomas, "Russian Forecasts of Future War," *Military Review*, May–June 2019, 84–93; Jacob W. Kipp, *The Methodology of Foresight and Forecasting in Soviet Military Affairs* (Fort Leavenworth, KS: Soviet Army Studies Office, 1987).
37. Chuyev and Mikhaylov, *Forecasting*, 1975, 6.
38. I am intentionally skipping over their definitions of prediction, forecasting, forecast, and a forecasting system. These are simple and useful but distracting and not inherently right or wrong. Chuyev and Mikhaylov, *Forecasting*, 1975, 8.
39. This is not necessarily a zero-sum, one-for-one trade-off.
40. Chuyev and Mikhaylov, *Forecasting*, 1975, 6–8, and other pages. The last point on manipulation is my extrapolation from the original translated text.
41. Chuyev and Mikhaylov, *Forecasting*, 1975.
42. See Ben Connable, *Embracing the Fog of War: Assessment and Metrics in Counterinsurgency* (Santa Monica, CA: RAND Corporation, 2012).
43. Chuyev and Mikhaylov, *Forecasting*, 1975, 14. Variations on these timelines are limitless and subjective.
44. Western military professionals generally attribute this term to Carl von Clausewitz, author of *Vom Krieg*, or *On War*, a core text in professional education curricula. A more thorough etymology can be found in Lorraine Daston, "The Coup d'Oeil: On a Mode of Understanding," *Critical Inquiry* 45, no. 2 (Winter 2019), 307–331. Daston attributes its origin to French military officer Jean-Charles Folard; Daston, "Coup d'Oeil," 313.
45. Historians have generally settled on the conclusion that Sun Tzu did not exist as one person. See Toshi Yoshihara, "Sun Zi and the Search for a Timeless Logic of Strategy," in *The New Makers of Modern Strategy*, ed. Hal Brands (Princeton, NJ: Princeton University Press, 2023), 67–90, and Antulio J. Echevarria II's chapter on Jomini in the same volume.
46. See, for example, Michael Brecher, "International Studies in the Twentieth Century and beyond: Flawed Dichotomies, Synthesis, Cumulation: ISA Presidential Address," *International Studies Quarterly* 43, no. 2 (June 1999): 213–264.
47. During my initial research and throughout my case study work over the course of one year, I examined and looked for instances of distinct sea and air conflict divorced from ground combat cases. I found some off the waters of Sri Lanka and in the skies over Ukraine, but not enough to constitute an equivalent portion of a large database including ground combat.
48. In the absence of a full accounting of such cases, this unfortunately is a subjective assessment.

49. In other words, I personally selected them based on my research objectives and literature review. I then added categories and factors as they appeared. The database contains the full list of categories (e.g., infantry, artillery, cyber) and factors (e.g., T-60-series tanks employed).
50. See the appendix, Methodology.
51. U.S. Marine Corps, *Warfighting*, MCDP-1 (Washington, DC: Headquarters, U.S. Marine Corps, 1997), 94–95.
52. I argue this point based on my survey of available data and also on the varying uses of grenade launchers. As a former automatic grenadier (Mk-19 Mod 3 40mm), I can attest to the fact that grenade launchers are often used for direct fire, not indirect fire. A knee mortar is a handheld mortar usually of small caliber in relation to other mortars, typically 2-inch or ~51mm. In contrast to grenade launchers, mortars are almost always employed as indirect fire weapons.
53. Carl von Clausewitz, *On War*, trans. J. J. Graham (1873); or Carl von Clausewitz, *On War*, ed. and trans. Michael Howard and Peter Paret (Princeton, NJ: Princeton University Press, 1976). Also see Beatrice Heuser, *Reading Clausewitz* (London: Pimlico, 2002); and Christopher Bassford, *Clausewitz in English: The Reception of Clausewitz in Britain and America, 1815–1945* (Oxford, UK: Oxford University Press, 1994).
54. Heuser, *Reading Clausewitz*, 84.
55. See chapters 1 and 9 for more on Clausewitz.
56. U.S. Army, *Operations*, ADP 3–0 (Washington, DC: Headquarters, Department of the Army, November 2016), 1–4; and U.S. Marine Corps, *Warfighting*, 3–4.
57. See, for example, Ben Connable et al., *Will to Fight: Analyzing, Modeling, and Simulating the Will to Fight of Military Units* (Santa Monica, CA: RAND Corporation, 2018); and Ben Connable, *Iraqi Army Will to Fight: A Will-to-Fight Case Study with Lessons for Western Security Force Assistance* (Santa Monica, CA: RAND Corporation, 2022).
58. Many other factors should also be included. See chapter 9 on the terms *combat power* and *combat effectiveness*.
59. Michael C. Horowitz and Shira Pindyck, "What Is a Military Innovation and Why It Matters," *Journal of Strategic Studies* 46, no. 1 (2022), 1–220, 99.
60. Adam Grissom, "The Future of Military Innovation Studies," *Journal of Strategic Studies* 29, no. 5 (2006), 905–935, 907.
61. The term "innovate or die" has unclear origins and probably should be treated as a cultural cliché. It appears frequently in American business literature. There is a common crossover between business innovation literature and military innovation advocacy. See Robert Iger, *The Ride of a Lifetime: Lessons Learned from 15 Years as CEO of the Walt Disney Company* (New York: Random House, 2019); and Robert G. Spulak Jr., *Innovate or Die: Innovation and Technology for Special Operations* (MacDill Air Force Base, FL: Joint Special Operations University, December 2010).
62. The idea that innovation is not, in fact, an unalloyed good emerges in some of the major works on the subject by Barry Posen, Allan Millett and Williamson Murray, etc. Also on this subject see Kendrick Kuo, "Dangerous Changes: When Military Innovation Harms Combat Effectiveness," *International Security* 47, no. 2 (Fall 2022), 48–87.

63. For more on the initial introduction of the M-16, see Bob Orkland and Lyman Duryea, *Misfire: The Tragic Failure of the M16 in Vietnam* (Mechanicsburg, PA: Stackpole Books, 2019); and Omar Burleson, "Special Subcommittee on the M-16 Rifle Program" (Washington, DC: U.S. Government Printing Office, 1967).
64. Also see works by Theo Farrell, Williamson Murray, MacGregor Knox, Allan R. Millet, Frans Osinga, Terry Terriff, Stephen P. Rosen, Barry Posen, Frank Hoffman, Eliot Cohen, Keith B. Bickel, Paddy Griffith, James A. Russell, et al., cited in Grissom, 2006, and also in Ben Connable, "Warrior-Maverick Culture: The Evolution of Adaptability in the U.S. Marine Corps" (doctoral thesis, King's College London, 2016).
65. Kuo describes downsides of innovation in periods when commitments exceed capabilities. Kuo, "Dangerous Changes."

ONE

American Forecasts of War and Ground Combat

In this chapter I describe and critique some of the most important and influential American characterizations and forecasts of land war over fifty years, starting from the late 1960s and working up through the early 2020s. I begin with the often overlooked military-technical revolution forecast delivered by William C. Westmoreland to the U.S. Congress in late 1969 and conclude with the most recent characterizations and forecasts guiding American military transformation in the early 2020s.

Strongly worded subjectivity and what MacGregor Knox and Williamson Murray describe as "an astounding lack of historical consciousness" dominate American military forecasting.[1] Exploring and understanding the real-world impact of these often impassioned characterizations of warfare are essential to improving the use of objective historical evidence in support of Western military policymaking and innovation.

History rarely occurs in neat decade-by-decade blocks, but it reads better that way. I therefore added some artificiality by breaking this chapter out into separate decade-focused sections. The reader will see the generally decennial sine wave of prognostication on the character and future of war. This ten-year increment also correlates to the Soviet medium-term timeline, which generally correlates to American conceptions of medium-term, or mid-term, forecasting. It is a practical horizon: A ten-year interval is neither so short that it is made irrelevant by the temporally uneven process of military innovation, nor so long into the future that it reads like fantastical science fiction.

This book is about ground combat *and* about the ways in which experts characterize and forecast war. While I focus in this chapter on the American ground combat services—the Army and the Marine Corps—I explore a range of strategic, technical, naval, and air war projections that influenced American military spending over this half-century period. All of these directly influenced contemporaneous ground combat capabilities and tactics, and they all culminated in extraordinary changes in Marine Corps ground combat force design in 2020.

I also make reference in each section to the many ground combat skirmishes and battles that were by oversight or by purpose ignored as policymakers embraced subjective opinions and invested trillions of dollars.

WESTMORELAND, 1970–1980

Fairly or not, William C. Westmoreland will be remembered primarily for his leading role in America's strategic catastrophe in Vietnam in the 1960s.[2] Yet instead of fading away after his post-Tet Offensive return from Vietnam, Westmoreland was elevated to chief of staff of the Army and made responsible for manning, training, and equipping the vast bulk of America's ground combat forces. In his new role he fixed on the idea of radically changing the Army to realize a high-technology vision of future warfare.

On October 14, 1969, Westmoreland testified before Congress on this vision.[3] He briefly traced his understanding of the evolution of ground combat from the Napoleonic Wars to Vietnam. He argued that innovation risks taken with tanks in World War I paid tactical dividends on the battlefield in World War II. Then he described a revolution in land warfare under way in Vietnam as part of an accelerating curve of military transformation, with the mobility of the helicopter and advanced sensors reshaping the way land wars could and should be fought.

Westmoreland centered his case on a forecast of the mid future derived from his personalized interpretation of military history. He made his claims with unswerving confidence: "Comparing the past few years of progress with a forecast of the future produces one conclusion: We are on the threshold of an entirely new battlefield concept."

Building on his central argument, he then painted a picture of a new American Army reshaped by advanced technology and, with this powerful new technical advantage, dominating ground combat: "On the battlefield of the future, enemy forces will be located, tracked, and targeted almost instantaneously through the use of data links, computer assisted intelligence evaluation, and automated fire control. . . . I see battlefields or combat areas that are under 24-hour real or near real time surveillance of all types. I see battlefields on which we can destroy anything we locate through instant communications and the almost instantaneous application of highly lethal firepower."[4]

First-round kill probabilities on this future battlefield would be nearly certain. Large ground forces would be obsolescent. Army tactical teams would be reorganized not to fight ground battles but to locate and channelize enemy forces so they could be destroyed by advanced precision-guided munitions.

Shunting aside prospective skeptics, Westmoreland argued this automated battlefield capability could, with the right investments, be achieved in ten years.

Over the ensuing decade—1970 to 1980—the United States and Western allies made extraordinary investments and advances in battlefield surveillance and precision-strike technology.[5] Reconnaissance satellites proliferated.[6] The first global positioning system (GPS) satellites were launched.[7] New precision weapons and munitions, including the Paveway II laser-guided bomb and the TOW missile, increased both in type and inventory volume.[8] The U.S. Navy and the Air Force experimented with unmanned aircraft, including in 1971 a drone that could fire a guided missile at ground targets.[9] The Defense Advanced Research Projects Agency (DARPA) developed stealth technology, advanced cruise missiles, and the communications networks needed to bring Westmoreland's land-warfare vision to life.[10]

Still, by the end of the 1970s the forecast vision of the automated battlefield had not materialized. As a land forces service chief, Westmoreland could not compel the air and sea forces to reorganize to achieve his objectives. Despite many technical advances, military forces in the late 1970s looked very much like the military forces in the late 1940s. Even Army force design stayed centered on big divisions with lots of ground combat power.[11]

In his report to Congress in 1972, Westmoreland reiterated the need for a fully automated battlefield but described only incremental, evolutionary investments in systems to improve communication, detection, targeting, and fires.[12] Several of these named systems, including the disposable M72 anti-tank rocket, remain in service in the 2020s.

Americans did not fight in any major land wars in the late 1970s. Global instances of ground combat in the late 1970s between China and Vietnam at Lang Son and Lao Cai, at the battle of Masawa in Eritrea, Jinja in Uganda, and the battle at Kolwezi in Zaire, and others were similar to battles fought a decade earlier.[13] Neither American nor global ground combat forces significantly changed. Westmoreland may have projected a future battlefield that might one day be realized, but at the very least he misjudged the pace of competitive global innovation and the degree to which advanced technologies might be leveraged to realize ground combat dominance.

STARRY, 1980–1990

An automated battlefield may not have been realized within Westmoreland's forecast ten-year time horizon, but similar characterizations of ground combat reemerged. During the late 1970s the Soviets had internalized their mid-1960s interpretation of military-technical revolution in which advanced sensors and precision-guided munitions would clear the fog of war and allow an advanced military force to dominate near-future battlefields with high-tempo reconnaissance-strike operations against, primarily, land forces.[14] Soviet forecasting would later stimulate the 1990s-era American pursuit of the RMA.

While Soviet military writers leaned forward, the U.S. Army temporarily pumped the brakes on high-tech ground combat forecasting. Through the late 1970s and into the early 80s, Army General Donn A. Starry and his staff formulated AirLand Battle, a doctrine anchored in the Clausewitzean language of uncertainty, chaos, and the centrality of the human in war.[15]

Starry's descriptions of near-future conflict were influenced by emerging maneuver warfare advocates who were pushing what they believed to be Clausewitz's first-principle edicts on the nature of war.[16] Throughout the 1980s, maneuver warfare—a fluid, chaos-embracing, human- and tactics-focused theory of warfare derived primarily from *On War*—would serve as a conceptual counterpoint to the RMA.

Starry's work anchored the central dialectic in American military discourse over the nature and character of land warfare and, inclusively, ground combat. His acceptance of uncertainty and chaos drove AirLand Battle's human-centric admonitions.[17] Starry and his staff wrote: "Commanders will find it difficult to determine what is happening [in land war]. Small units will often have to fight without sure knowledge about their force as a whole. Electronic warfare, vulnerability to command and control facilities, and mobile combat will demand initiative in subordinate commanders.... The fluid nature of modern war will place a premium on leadership, unit cohesion, and effective, independent operations."[18]

Starry argued that land war was not only naturally uncertain and chaotic, but that it was also inherently idiosyncratic.[19] He at least implied that it was not possible to draw practical, universal conclusions from the collective history of warfare to characterize modern and near-future war. AirLand Battle represented a purposeful break from "active defense," a mid-1970s doctrine driven by force ratio and weapons effectiveness calculations intended to defeat a notional Soviet Blitzkrieg-style penetration in Eastern Europe; ironically even the Soviets may not have believed such an attack was feasible at the time.[20]

In writing *AirLand Battle*, Starry placed less emphasis on force calculations and technology than his predecessors. But while his doctrine may have been a diversion from contemporaneous mechanistic, technology-centric concepts, it was no more empirical or objective than any preceding American military narrative.

Along with *AirLand Battle*, the Army also published *AirLand Battle 2000*, a twenty-year forecast of the character of ground combat and a roadmap for Army technology investment, force design, and operational art. The core of this forecast projected Starry's original vision decades ahead. In this mid-to-distant future, a hostile electronic environment and enemy recon-strike capabilities would compel American ground combat forces to operate independently rather than in hierarchical division structures. Borrowing from early maneuverist writings, Army forecasters argued that decision-making tempo and the speed of information would be essential to success in future war.[21] Technology would play an important but still supporting and nonrevolutionary role in future ground combat.[22] *Airland Battle 2000* set something of a middle ground between Starry's more traditional view and Westmoreland's proposed techno-war.

At least in the Western military perspective, two major ground combat events bookended the AirLand Battle period.[23] In 1982 Argentina invaded the Falkland Islands and the United Kingdom responded by dispatching a long-range amphibious force that fought its way inland over several weeks of intensive combat.[24] And in 1990 Iraq invaded Kuwait and the United States led a coalition to expel the Iraqis in an intensive monthlong air campaign and a four-day land war.[25]

Both of these wars centered on traditional ground forces augmented by advanced technologies like Milan antitank missiles and Paveway II laser-guided bombs in the Falklands, and thermal sights, drones, and stealth aircraft in Kuwait and Iraq. Fought approximately a decade apart, the Falklands War and the Gulf War heated up the debate between experts who perceived war as unswervingly gritty, human-centric, and uncertain, and those who perceived an inevitable technical revolution emerging through the smoke of the modern battlefield.

Proponents of revolutionary military change saw promise and wasted opportunity in both of these wars. Technophilic interpretations of the Gulf War accelerated arguments for improved systems and recon-strike capabilities. In particular, two future U.S. defense secretaries, Ashton Carter and William J. Perry, coauthored a think-tank report in 1992 arguing that the American recon-strike capabilities in the Gulf War were revolutionary and that they granted the United States at least a decade of undenied global military dominance.[26] Other advocates would argue that more absolute and perhaps lasting supremacy could be achieved.

MARSHALL AND KREPINEVICH, 1990–2000

Andrew W. Marshall led the U.S. Office of Net Assessment from 1973 through his passing in 2015. Marshall generally is credited with conceptualizing and championing the revolution in military affairs.[27] Under his guidance, military historians, political scientists, and technical experts across the defense scientific community expanded on the concept of military-technical revolution to further what was, in effect, Westmoreland's original vision for land warfare:

a networked system of military sensors and precision-guided munitions that would allow the United States and its allies to achieve something close to total military dominance.[28]

One document clearly lays out the military revolution in theory and intended praxis. Retired U.S. Army officer Andrew Krepinevich led Marshall's original investigations of Soviet military forecasting and in 1992 published his findings in *The Military-Technical Revolution: A Preliminary Assessment*.[29] Krepinevich ascribes the idea of a military-technical revolution to Soviet writing in the 1980s.[30] He never offered a clear definition (see chapter 9 of this book for more on this point) but wrote that revolutions occur when new technologies are integrated into military systems and combined with new operational concepts.[31] Together these technologies and concepts alter the character and *nature* of warfare so they both have to be reimagined.[32]

Krepinevich makes a good and often overlooked argument about counterrevolutionary tactical measures in ground combat. He believed tank-heavy ground forces like those of the Soviet Army would inevitably respond to proposed Western recon-strike dominance by hugging NATO forces at close range and by applying effective countermeasures that would then require development of ground combat counter-countermeasures.[33] This probably would feed an endless cycle of technical and operational measure and countermeasure. Krepinevich's points on tanks and technical countermeasures are front and center in the 2020–2024 debate over the Marine Corps' Force Design 2030 and the emerging lessons from the war in Ukraine.[34]

But Krepinevich did not equivocate when it came to describing warfare and advocating revolutionary change. In fact, his analysis reads far more like a sales pitch for the RMA than it does an analysis of Soviet military theory. Like Donn Starry, Krepinevich borrowed some language (e.g., center of gravity) from maneuver warfare advocates. But he characterized war as a mechanical interaction between networked system-of-systems rather than as the kind of chaotic, uncertain, and fundamentally human struggle enshrined in Western military doctrine.[35] To drive home this motif, he used *system* or *systems* 225 times in fewer than sixty pages of text.

Whether or not they were fantastical, these systems-centric arguments were at least fairly straightforward. Other essential language in *Military-Technical Revolution* was more problematic. Perhaps most importantly, Krepinevich's tortured employment of the term *revolution* lay bare a fundamental challenge in military characterizations and forecasts that Biddle highlighted in *Military Power* (2004).[36] In broad terms, change can occur relatively more quickly or relatively more slowly.

As commonly understood, evolutionary change occurs gradually along a gentle grade or curve. Revolutionary change signals a sharp, definitive, and observable break with the past. But Krepinevich wrote, with original emphasis: "*What is revolutionary is not the speed with which the change takes place, but rather the magnitude of the change itself.* At some point the cumulative effects of technological advances and military innovation will invalidate former conceptual frameworks by bringing about a fundamental change in the nature of warfare."[37] So by Krepinevich's definition, highly impactful military revolutions could take place gradually over many decades, or even centuries. The machinegun offers a good example for this case.

Arguably, the concept of the machinegun was first introduced as the organ gun in the 1300s, evolved to the Puckle gun in the 1710s, then to the Gatling gun in 1860s, and eventually to the Maxim gun in the 1880s.[38] The Maxim gun and other machineguns like the French Hotchkiss were used in combat in the Boer War, the Spanish-American War, and the Russo-Japanese War. In Krepinevich's framing, the revolution of the repeating direct-fire projectile weapon (eventually, the machinegun) took place over about fifty years, from Gatling gun to World War I, and then dramatically revolutionized ground combat in 1914.[39]

This loose interpretation of revolutionary timelines allows RMA advocates to lead policymakers and generals on a perpetual military-technical dragon chase.[40] If a revolution can take decades, and we never quite know where we are on the revolutionary grade or curve, then there is always reason to promise more and better tech return in the next investment cycle.

Note also that Krepinevich argued that revolutionary technical change would alter the nature of war itself, not just its character. This implied that if the revolution could be realized, then war could be controlled and dominated with minimal risk by the side fastest to adapt.[41] Dramatic claims and implications like this captured the imagination of contemporaneous leadership and continue to influence ground combat concepts today.

While Krepinevich ultimately diverted from the traditionalist leanings of maneuver warfare advocate William S. Lind, he shared Lind's fixation with World War II-era German military-technical innovations and the Blitzkrieg.[42] He admiringly described the German Army as the dominant land warfare force from 1939 to 1942.[43] Krepinevich and coauthor Barry Watts also fixated on the Blitzkrieg in their biography of Marshall.[44]

For his part, Lind was infamous for wearing historically accurate German officer uniforms to official events at the U.S. Marine Corps base at Quantico, Virginia. His fellow enthusiasts pushed books extolling German ground combat art into the hands of American military officers.[45] Between the maneuverists and revolutionaries, Germanophilia dominated American military discourse on land warfare and ground combat during the 1990s.[46]

In their peculiar collective fixation with Wehrmacht military culture and a reconceptualized historical ground combat event—Operation Barbarossa—both camps revealed an essential belief that tactical-technical solutions to war's diverse and vexing challenges existed just over a revolutionary horizon. In their minds, Germany's total defeat in World War II derived therefore not from any inherent weakness in the concept and technologies of the Blitzkrieg but from the lack of political will and resources to apply the concept and technologies to their fullest potential. Essentially, if only Nazi dictator Adolf Hitler had been a better wartime leader, lightning war would have worked. Therefore, if American political leaders could embrace maneuver warfare or the military-technical revolution or both, at the very least land warfare (and therefore ground combat) dominance could be achieved.

These maneuverist and revolutionary interpretations of Barbarossa and of many essential writings on war were selective and, in many cases, spurious.[47] Wehrmacht worship and forecast conceptualizations of immaculate systemic dominance frequently were backed by cherry-picked quotes and questionable historical characterizations of war.[48] For their parts, Krepinevich and Lind strongly implied that battles, and particularly ground battles, might even be won without fighting if sufficient technical dominance, "shock and awe," or a brilliant Blitzkrieg-type maneuver could be achieved.

This was a prima facie interpretation of Sun Tzu's fifth-century BCE writings reinforced by dubious ideas proposed by B. H. Liddell Hart in the twentieth century, several of which I describe in chapter 9.[49] Tantalizing belief in the idea of winning wars without fighting, or at least of winning with very limited risk and loss, would feed and in turn be fed by creeping risk aversion in the American policy and military communities through the early 2020s.[50]

Krepinevich, Lind, and other ardent proponents of revolution and maneuver followed the pattern established by Westmoreland and Starry: They selected from the canon to create a compelling, personalized, yet ultimately unsubstantiated narrative.[51] Absent evidence-driven counterarguments, these narratives influenced future cycles of American military investment.[52]

As Krepinevich's and Marshall's arguments took hold across the Department of Defense, Army leaders increasingly adopted the language of military-technical revolution. The Army's AirLand Battle 2000 morphed into AirLand Battle Future, then to the Army After Next, and eventually to the Army Objective Force in the early 2000s.[53]

In parallel and in contrast the Marine Corps embraced maneuver warfare. Three successive Marine Corps commandants, with the support of influential general Paul K. Van Riper, centered the Marine Corps on an explicitly Clausewitzean and therefore human-centric theory of land warfare and ground combat.[54] In the early 2020s, both retired commandant Charles C. Krulak and Van Riper would reemerge to play controversial roles in the debate over the Marine Corps' Force Design 2030 and the character of modern ground combat.

OWENS, 2000–2010

During the 1990s, the United States and its allies fought in the Balkans, the Russians fought two major wars in Chechnya, and combined-arms battles took place around the world in Pakistan, Ethiopia-Eritrea, Sri Lanka, Nagorno-Karabakh, Afghanistan, Mali, Somalia, and elsewhere.[55] Technology had varying impacts and influence on the outcome of all of these events, but the visions laid out by Westmoreland and Krepinevich still had not been realized by 2000. Nor had any war arisen that might allow critics of the RMA to offer strong rhetorical challenges. Maneuver warfare effectively remained an isolated Marine Corps dogma.[56] So, throughout the 1990s, talk of military revolution crowded out all other characterizations and forecasts of war.[57] This all culminated with the publication of *Lifting the Fog of War* by Bill Owens.[58]

As a retired senior admiral and former vice chairman of the U.S. Joint Chiefs of Staff, Owens wielded significant influence within the Department of Defense.[59] He had been a leading proponent of military-technical revolution while serving in the Pentagon and had helped guide hundreds of billions of dollars in military-technical investment. Owens continued to press his case after retirement while working in the defense industry. In his book *Lifting the Fog of War,* he radically personalized war characterizations and forecasting, abandoning any of the restraints that had at least to some extent tempered the language of his predecessors.

Owens dutifully reflected on what had by the late 1990s become a path-dependent regurgitation of ostensibly successful technical-tactical revolutions. He handpicked quotes and aphorisms from Napoleon and Clausewitz and paid brief homage to the Wehrmacht. Owens called the Blitzkrieg a "successful military strategy," missing a number of misperceptions and key points brushed over by both maneuverists and revolutionaries throughout the 1980s and into the 2020s: Putting aside the unpleasant whiff of Nazi-era military fetishism associated with this recurring and virtually undiluted praise, it is almost willfully ahistorical.

Interlude: Debunking the Blitzkrieg

Studying and even appreciating the military organization and tactical acumen of an adversary is warranted and, to a measured extent, wise. Fervently praising and seeking to emulate an adversary the United States and its allies defeated in absolute terms eight decades ago—using their own remarkably un-Blitzkrieg-like methods—is nonsensical. It is time to expunge the deeply embedded Blitzkrieg myth from American military professional discourse on war.

Chief of the interwar German land forces Hans von Seeckt generally is given credit for building the army that became the Wehrmacht and for designing what later was described as Blitzkrieg.[60] The concept emerged from von Seeckt's fixation with the tactical maneuvers applied in the 216 BCE Battle of Cannae and the limited German encirclements or breakthroughs against the Russians at Tannenberg (1914), at Gorlice–Tarnów (1915), and against British forces during the 1918 Kaiserschlacht counteroffensive in the First World War.[61]

While German officers' interwar adoption of fleetingly advanced technology temporarily amplified their ground combat power, their tactical concepts were unimaginative. Von Seeckt's conceptualization could be summed up as aggressive, fast-moving penetration or outflanking to achieve the annihilation of an enemy's military force; see Cannae, 216 BCE.[62]

It is not clear that von Seeckt even widely employed the term *Blitzkrieg*. It probably was an ex post fabrication by social scientist Fritz Sternberg.[63] In his 1938 *Germany and a Lighting War*, Sternberg appears to have at least popularized Blitzkrieg—a word the Nazi dictator Hitler himself abjured and is said to have called "very stupid"—and presciently argued it would fail.[64]

German deep-strike maneuver operations did not generate success in either world war. Not one of the frontline encirclements or penetrations that inspired von Seeckt had led to or even correlated with a German strategic victory in World War I. Germany's 1918 penetrations in the Kaiserschlacht counteroffensive contributed to the same kind of overextension that undermined the Wehrmacht on the eastern front in World War II.[65] German ground combat forces raced forward, stretching their logistics lines and exposing their flanks. This left them most vulnerable when they were also most exhausted.

In the words of historian Michael Geyer, the deep-penetration tactics described as Blitzkrieg were a "make-believe spectacle" that in their fantastical technical-tactical overreach ultimately contributed to Nazi Germany's existential defeat in 1945.[66] Clausewitz had warned against such overextension in *On War*.[67] And still these critiques do not touch on the relative weaknesses of the adversaries the Wehrmacht faced in the opening phases of World War II.

Early Wehrmacht successes from 1939 through 1941 were achieved by a professional force led by a number of combat-experienced veteran officers fielding mostly modern armor and aircraft against ill-prepared, outgunned, and in some cases outmanned Polish, French, and Soviet armies (and others). In Poland in 1939 the Germans attacked a thinly spread and off-guard ground combat force.[68] The Poles fought at perhaps a 10:1 troop disadvantage against the Wehrmacht and, toward the end of the monthlong campaign, also fought simultaneously against the Red Army that fielded perhaps hundreds of thousands of troops, approximately 4,000 tanks, and 2,000 combat aircraft.[69]

Still, armed with a grab bag of infantry weapons, horseback cavalry, dated artillery pieces, WWI-era anti-tank rifles, and paltry armored forces, the Poles blunted several German attacks (e.g., Mokra, Mlawa) and even successfully counterattacked at the Bzura River before succumbing to combined German and Soviet pressure. In one month of ground combat in Poland, Germany reportedly suffered over 40,000 casualties and lost one in four tanks that were either destroyed or put out of action.[70]

French and Red Army forces were far superior in number to the Poles, and they were relatively better equipped. However, neither force presented the kind of challenges the Wehrmacht would face as early as 1942 at Moscow and Stalingrad, or in North Africa. As the later-war period suggests, early-war outcomes might have been far different against better-prepared and more capable foes. So even if one accepts at face value Max Hastings's provocative 1985 argument that German soldiers were inherently better and more lethal than Allied soldiers, it does not follow that the Blitzkrieg was a brilliant warfighting revolution.[71]

Von Seeckt's real success came not from revolutionizing warfare but from building a new modern army of professional officers and noncommissioned officers out of the cataclysmic end of the First World War. Relative Wehrmacht combat power applied against weaker, ill-prepared foes highlighted the importance of routinely updating weapons and equipment to at least match prospective adversaries; measure and countermeasure. Blitzkrieg raised important questions about relative combat power and will to fight. Any further extrapolation is at the very least questionable.

Therefore, advocating for current policy based on the unchecked assumption that the Blitzkrieg was a brilliant revolution is illogical. It should not be used to justify any modern innovation or force design or validate any contemporary buzzword concept like shock and awe.

Yet as I later note later in this chapter and in chapter 9, Owens would not be the last to praise the Blitzkrieg in modern Western military literature. His writing fits within a general personalized analytical approach to war characterization that is neatly (if perhaps not unimpeachably) warned off by Richard M. Swain, the former director of the U.S. Army's Combat Studies Institute: "History misapplied is worse than no history at all."[72]

Back to Owens, 2000–2010

Building from his distorted historical references, Owens primarily advanced Krepinevich's 1992 arguments regarding systemic warfare: Achieving the revolution meant establishing full-spectrum dominance through exquisite system-of-systems.[73] He doubled down on prospective outcomes. For sea, air, and integrated ground combat, nearly absolute military control could be achieved by linking together sensors that would provide uninterrupted, precise, and accurate knowledge of the location of all friendly and enemy forces anywhere within an imagined subsurface to thermosphere cube, with each face of the cube measuring 4,000 square miles.[74] Military commanders thousands of miles away from the battle would be able to press buttons and almost instantly demolish enemy tanks, artillery, and infantry before the hapless enemy soldiers realized they were being targeted.

Owens proposed that with perfect knowledge, immediate and perfectly relayed information, and weapons with instant responsiveness and near-perfect accuracy, ground combat as I define it here—violent, combined-arms engagements by land forces—would almost certainly be unnecessary. The nature of war would be altered to the point that it would not even be a feasible undertaking for any of America's prospective adversaries.[75] This was consummate hedgehoggery. In his contemporaneous review of *Lifting the Fog of War*, Eliot Cohen summarized Owens's rhetorical approach: "He writes not as an evaluator of an unfolding phenomenon but as a prophet who articulates a Truth and heaps derision on unbelievers."[76]

Owens suggested the RMA might be achieved with heavy investment in additional technology. Systems relevant to ground combat include the Javelin anti-tank missile; Joint Direct Attack Munition (JDAM) guided bombs; moving-target indicator technology to find ground targets on a cluttered battlefield; and the Army Tactical Missile System (ATACMS), a ground missile that can target enemy land forces nearly 200 miles away, almost a full length of Owens's proposed 200-by-200-mile domination cube.[77]

Approximately one year after the publication of *Lifting the Fog of War*, Al Qa'ida attacked the United States. The United States then invaded and occupied Afghanistan and less than two years later invaded and occupied Iraq. Throughout the 2000s, perhaps hundreds of billions of U.S. dollars would be invested in primarily land warfare operations, weapons, and equipment, including advanced drones with ground-strike capabilities, radars, electronic warfare tools, and a wide array of precision munitions intended to help lift the fog of war and gain battlefield dominance.

The United States and allied Western military forces had ample opportunity to build, buy, test, and refine advanced precision systems and use them against tactically and technologically inferior ground opponents in every type of terrain and weather. Money flowed and the pace of technical innovation accelerated. The 2000s offered remarkable opportunities to at the very least realize a revolution in ground combat.

Yet still, by 2010—ten years after Owens's ten-year forecast and forty years after Westmoreland's original ten-year forecast—the revolution remained beyond reach. Krepinevich's accurate warnings of counterrevolutionary adaptation in ground combat played out in places like the Korengal Valley and Sangin in Afghanistan, and in Baghdad, Ramadi, and Mosul in Iraq.

As they had done in the Vietnam War, technically inferior ground forces denied American overmatch through ambush and by employing low-tech weapons like improvised explosive devices (IEDs), highly mobile mortars and light rocket systems, and the venerable machinegun. Aerial drones and even tower and balloon-mounted multispectral camera systems were in high demand in Iraq and Afghanistan, but there were never enough of these assets to see, let alone understand and help affect, the whole battlefield even within the confines of a single small city or rural area.[78]

For ground combat forces, Iraq and Afghanistan produced more frustration than revolution. The Army's RMA-centered Objective Force concept, published in 2001, was derailed by operational realities. Instead of reshaping its ground forces for networked high-order conventional war against a near-peer adversary like Russia or China, the Army had to reshape its ground combat brigades for irregular conflict.[79]

And in order to realize the Objective Force and a ground combat revolution, the Army had tried to build the Future Combat Systems (FCS).[80] If it had been implemented, the FCS would have represented a culmination of the revolutionary vision: a fully networked, globally transportable system-of-systems including ultramodern fighting vehicles, robotic ground vehicles, drones, sensors, and missiles.

Instead, in 2009 FCS was cancelled with an ~$18 billion investment in ground combat innovation effectively wasted.[81] High-flying concepts like giant quad-copters designed to carry a heavy main battle tank proved to be technically infeasible. Pristine network designs that looked impressive in artistic renderings proved to be all but impossible to assemble and sustain in the real world. Collapse of FCS was an opportunity to shift course toward a more evidence-driven approach to war characterization, forecasting, and force design. But if that opportunity was recognized by anyone in the Pentagon, it was not taken.

CSBA, THE AIR FORCE, AND THE NAVY, 2010–2020

Failure of these ground combat forecasts to materialize in either Iraq or Afghanistan, or in any of the other ground battles fought around the world between 2000 and 2010, did not deter RMA advocates.[82] If ground combat could not carry the revolution forward, then air and sea combat might offer a more effective channel. So, while the Army and Marine Corps were tangled up with the land wars in the Middle East and South Asia, the military-technical revolution was recast for the air-and-sea-centric Pacific theater.[83]

Military experts at the Center for Strategic and Budgetary Assessment (CSBA), including Krepinevich and future deputy secretary of defense Robert O. Work, helped establish the forward-leaning concepts of AirSea Battle.[84] Work would go on to champion the Third Offset, an updated twist on the RMA. Both of these concepts—AirSea Battle and Third Offset—would directly influence Army forecasts and redesign, and the Marine Corps' radical approach to ground combat force design in the years just before Russia invaded Ukraine in 2022.

Through the mid to late 2000s, Air Force and Navy leaders eager to demonstrate their services' value were ready customers for any characterization and forecast of war centered on the air and sea domains. They almost certainly were active partners with CSBA forecasters, particularly given Work's back-and-forth duties at the Pentagon.

Between 2003 and 2010, Krepinevich, Work, Jan van Tol, Watts, and others published a laddered series of arguments building to what would become *AirSea Battle,* the Navy and Air Force answer to Starry's ground combat-centric doctrine of the early 1980s. These papers were fortuitously timed to culminate as President Barack H. Obama's administration began pursuing a strategic pivot away from the dissatisfying Middle East land wars toward a potentially more straightforward military problem in East Asia.

The AirSea Battle series started with *Meeting the Anti-Access and Area-Denial Challenge,* which described a world in which the United States would be increasingly unable to project global air, sea, or ground combat power due primarily to adversary advanced missile capabilities.[85] Krepinevich, Watts, and Work did not disappoint the Wehraboos, describing the German Blitzkrieg as "stunningly successful" in a cursory historical review.[86] Overall, though, the narrative deemphasized ground combat in favor of air and sea warfare.

This was an understandable omission given the vast expanse of the Pacific Ocean and the relative absence of terrestrial ground, an essential component of ground combat. The authors described several advanced technologies, including rail guns, directed-energy weapons, Comanche helicopters, and remote underwater vehicles as potentially revolutionary.[87] They forecast near-future war with dire warnings. Failure to invest in these technical revolutions would be a "huge gamble" with implied existential consequences; innovate or die.[88]

In 2007 Krepinevich and Work published an even more thorough argument for revolutionary change, albeit with similar objectives. *A New Global Defense Posture for the Second Transoceanic Era* argued that a new threat era had emerged with the impending rise of China and the dissolution of American global dominance.[89] The Blitzkrieg was relegated to a footnote, replaced center stage by China's efforts to build an anti-access and area-denial zone in the East and South China Seas. Work was made undersecretary of the Navy in 2009 and was therefore well positioned to push the China threat and this air-sea concept in the Pentagon.

In 2010 Krepinevich and his CSBA colleague Jan van Tol culminated the pivot-to-Asia series with *Why AirSea Battle?* and *AirSea Battle: A Point-of-Departure Operational Concept.*[90] They both reiterated the anti-access, area-denial argument and advocated a new strategy centered on the Air Force and Navy. Both papers made only passing reference to the Marine Corps and the Army since ground combat did not figure in to the characterization of the air-sea-centric anti-access, area-denial environment or strategy.[91]

At the same time, Marine and Army leaders were so absorbed in Iraq and Afghanistan that they did not fully appreciate the growing momentum behind AirSea Battle and strategic reorientation away from the Middle East. While they were busy fighting two ground wars and supporting global counterterrorism operations, the White House, the Pentagon, and the think-tank world had recharacterized warfare in a way that threatened ground combat concepts and budgets. Circa 2012, with the surge in Afghanistan over, Iraq temporarily in the rearview mirror, AirSea Battle on the rise, and the White House's pivot to Asia underway, it might be fair to say that American ground force leaders panicked.[92]

Both the Marine Corps and the Army quickly responded with their own recharacterizations and force redesigns. It was fairly easy for the Marine Corps to adjust. With *Expeditionary Force 21* and a following series of distributed maritime concepts, the Marines accepted the new A2/AD paradigm and "re-blued," or recentered on amphibious operations and away from ground campaigning, just as they had after the wars in Korea and Vietnam.[93] Perhaps sensing impending encroachment from the Army, the Marines emphasized in bold print their dominion over all things amphibious.[94] They embraced the anti-access, area-denial problem but did not yet fixate on China as a pacing threat.[95]

By contrast, the relatively ground-bound Army took the pivot to Asia as an immediate and existential threat from its long-standing parochial rivals in the Marine Corps.[96] During the early to mid 2010s, Army leaders pushed hard to justify their ground combat capabilities in the Pacific air-sea domain. The fastest way to renewed relevance was back through the RMA, which was effectively relabeled as *multi-domain operations.*[97]

Army generals leaned hard into high-concept, high-tech visions. In 2018 the commanding general of the Army's new Futures Command suggested the multi-domain operations concept was desirably "infeasible," or so impossibly forward leaning that it would impel revolutionary change.[98] Undeterred by the jarring collapse of FCS, the Army renewed experimentation with high-tech armored vehicles, advanced robotics, artificial intelligence, and cloud computing.[99] Army leaders reenvisioned ground combat primarily in terms of anti-access, area-denial, long-range missile fights with China while deemphasizing the reemerging Russian threat in Europe.[100]

At least by the end of the 2010s, none of these investments had radically changed either the American military as a force or the way in which it prepared for war. A full fifty years after Westmoreland's ten-year ground combat revolution forecast, thirty years after Krepinevich's initial interpretation of the military-technical revolution, and two decades after Owens's ten-year forecast, global warfare may have evolved but it had not yet evinced the revolutionary character described in *AirSea Battle* or multi-domain operations.

Extraordinarily destructive, often large-scale ground battles fought in Libya, Syria, Yemen, Iraq, Ukraine, the Caucuses, South Sudan, Afghanistan, Myanmar, Mali, and Somali appeared to have limited influence on American characterizations and forecasts of ground combat. In some cases, what appeared to be high-technology successes from these battles were cherry-picked to further the case for near-future revolution.[101] Throughout the 2010s the belief that technology could dramatically alter both the character and nature of land war persisted and spawned more grandiose visions.

WORK, MILLEY, AND MCCONVILLE, 2020 ONWARD

Robert Work helped foster these visions. Writing from the Center for New American Security in January 2014—just months before being appointed as deputy secretary of defense, the second-ranking official in the Pentagon—Work coauthored *20YY: Preparing for War in the Robotic Age*.[102] In it he described a "deeper revolution" afoot in unmanned systems that would move the United States beyond the guided munitions era and into the "Robotic Age."[103]

Work's use of "20YY" in the title of this report was openly intended to avoid having to deal with what he and his coauthor called the "needless debate" over one of the two central requirements in effective forecasting: timing.[104] In keeping with previous revolutionary forecasts, this one also came with a clear warning: Failure to embrace the envisioned Robotic Age would put "tomorrow's U.S. military at unnecessary risk."[105] In other words, innovate or die.

Work's 2014 paper laid the foundation for the Third Offset, which would in turn shape the enormously influential 2018 National Defense Strategy and subsequently the structural changes in Army and Marine Corps ground combat forces.[106] *Offset* is a conceptual term used to characterize technical-military methods applied to rebalance uneven combat power.[107] Applying this high-concept framing, nuclear weapons allowed the United States to offset Soviet ground combat power advantages in the 1950s and 1960s. Then American precision munitions ostensibly offset Soviet power in the 1970s and 1980s. Looking forward, artificial intelligence and robotics would, according to Work, be the "technological sauce" that would offset the Russians and, primarily, the Chinese through the twenty-first century.[108]

Like Owens and arguably like Krepinevich, Work saw the contemporary battlefield not as chaotic and primarily human-centric but as a neat structure of systems, linear planes, and three-dimensional schematics, much like a multilevel chess board.[109] In 2016 he described a battle network of grids, emphasis added here on the word *effects*, a common orienting term in military-technical-revolution literature: "Now, a battle network is a very simple concept. First of all, you have a sensor grid. . . . Then you have a command, control communications and intelligence grid. . . . And the final thing you have is an effects screen. And then the effects grid is the thing that actually achieves *effects* on battlefields."[110]

When retired U.S. Marine Corps General James N. Mattis took control of the U.S. Department of Defense in 2018 he gently off-ramped this kind of high-concept, military-technical, system-of-systems language.[111] Mattis, an infantry officer with a grounding in the more traditional literature of land warfare, was never a fan of the RMA. In fact, he had previously attempted to kill some military uses of the word *effects* in the 2000s.[112] But the idea of a China offset made its way front and center into the 2018 defense strategy.[113] And shepherded by Chairman of the Joint Chiefs of Staff Mark A. Milley, both the Army and Marine Corps pressed ahead with the characterizations and forecasts of war spelled out in Work's forward-leaning vision.[114]

As Army chief of staff from 2015 to 2019, Milley intersected with Robert Work in the Pentagon and oversaw the Army's development of the multi-domain operations concept. In 2016 Milley argued that the character of war was undergoing a "fundamental, profound and significant change."[115] Over the next several years he became one of the foremost proponents of the idea that the character of war was rapidly changing and that investment in revolutionary technology was required to keep the United States in a position of relative battlefield advantage.[116]

Milley was appointed chairman in 2019. In 2020 he publicly stated: "I would argue that today [we] are in the middle of a fundamental change in the character of war."[117] He often repeated this belief and was echoed by other officers.[118] Milley actively supported both Army and Marine Corps ground combat force innovations to keep ahead of these presumably fundamental changes.[119]

In 2021 Army Chief of Staff James C. McConville moved to actualize Milley's character-of-war concepts in *Army Multi-Domain Transformation*.[120] McConville warned in this top-level concept paper that American military overmatch was fleeting and that "bold transformation" driven by cutting-edge technology procurement was needed to achieve what he called *decision dominance*. This was another new term that seemed to merge maneuver warfare (OODA-loop) tempo and RMA full-spectrum dominance concepts.[121]

New Army advances would be made through the Regionally Aligned Readiness Modernization Model, or ReARMM: "ReARMM addresses the problem of [operational tempo] while providing a path for the Army transition from *evolutionary modernization*—incremental capability improvements to existing platforms—to *revolutionary modernization* that skips generations of capabilities to achieve transformational change and meet future challenges."[122]

It was not clear which generations of capabilities would be skipped, but it was clear that at this point in the early 2020s the Army had fully re-embraced the bleeding-edge interpretation of the military-technical revolution. McConville's verbiage brought the Army's ground combat characterization and forecasting full circle, all the way back to Westmoreland's foundational 1969 vision.

But while both Milley and McConville may have wanted to see the Army break away from Starry's 1980s-era Russia-Europe-centric framing of ground war and toward high-tech missile wars with China, Russia's actions in Ukraine from 2014 onward inexorably drew the Army back to its relatively traditional Cold War ground combat roots. The U.S. Marines had no such anchor weighing them down in Europe. While the Army planned a pivot to Asia and revolutionary force redesign, the Marine Corps made it happen.

BERGER, 2020 ONWARD

General David H. Berger took over as the Marine Corps' commandant in 2019. Building from *Expeditionary Force 21* and iterations of the late-2010s expeditionary advanced base operations (EABO) concept, Berger radically reshaped the Marine Corps to meet the directives spelled out in Mattis's defense strategy.[123] There were no equivocations about reorienting toward the China pacing threat or about the shift away from land warfare.

In his 2019 planning guidance, Berger made clear his intent to tune the whole Marine Corps toward defeating global anti-access, area-denial threats to American power projection: "We will build one force—optimized for naval expeditionary warfare in contested spaces, purpose built to facilitate sea denial and assured access in support of the fleets. That single purpose-built force will be applied against other challenges across the globe; however, we will not seek to hedge or balance our investments to account for those contingencies."[124]

Berger firmly believed that the marines needed to finalize their stuttering shift away from army-centric ground combat toward blue water amphibious operations.[125] He laid out a revolutionary new approach in *Force Design 2030*, an actualization of his planning guidance. Berger then swiftly executed that plan before it could be derailed by budgeteers or critics. It was a bold move for even a four-star service chief, and it stirred plenty of controversy, all of which is immediately relevant to modern character-of-war and forecasting debates.[126]

Berger's new force design started with the same characterization of modern warfare underlying AirSea Battle and the Third Offset. *Force Design 2030* described "unrelenting increases" in the range, accuracy, and lethality of modern weapons, and warned that China and other powers would try to use these long-range weapons to deny American access to important sea lanes of communications and littorals.[127] In order to operate in this new threat environment, the Marine Corps needed to acquire high-technology capabilities including long-range missiles, advanced unmanned systems, modern electronic warfare assets, and smaller, stealthier watercraft.[128] And to free up money and resources to make room for this new technology, the Marine Corps would have to divest some of its traditional ground combat capabilities.

Based on the stated assumptions about the rapidly changing character of war, Berger cut several of the Marine Corps' twenty-seven infantry battalions, trimmed each of the remaining battalions by nearly a fifth of their overall manpower, eliminated most of the Corps' cannon artillery batteries, halved the number of amphibious vehicle companies, and sharply cut manned aircraft that were long considered central to the Marines' signature air-ground task forces.[129]

Perhaps most controversially, Berger eliminated all of the Corps' tanks.[130] He summed up his reasoning on tanks in a short paragraph: "We have sufficient evidence to conclude that this capability [tanks], despite its long and honorable history in the wars of the past, is operationally unsuitable for our highest-priority challenges in the future. Heavy ground armor capability will continue to be provided by the U.S. Army."[131]

Tanks were eliminated from the Marine Corps inventory almost at once, and many artillery pieces were quickly moved into storage. Marines trained to operate tanks and artillery were shuttled into other jobs or even transferred to the Army.[132] These big cuts came before most of the high-tech equipment replacements could be acquired and even before some of the new technologies were available for full experimentation.

In a May 2022 update to the force design, the Marine Corps acknowledged that new precision fires, targeting sensors, vehicles, and missile systems would not be fully operational until well into the mid to late 2020s, or even by 2030. Delays in technology fielding compounded the already significant risks Berger had assumed for the Corps.

By mid 2022 an unprecedented and explosive public debate had erupted over *Force Design 2030*. A group of retired Marine Corps generals, including at least one former commandant, publicly attacked Berger's plan.[133] They argued that a myopic focus on China, divestiture of core ground combat power—tanks and some cannon artillery and infantry—and a reliance on as-yet unproven, untested, and in some cases aspirational technologies had gutted the Marine

Corps' traditional role as a global force in readiness. Berger remained mostly above the fray, but his proxies fought back hard.[134]

What might have been a thoughtful behind-closed-doors discussion about the character of war escalated into a public and sometimes personalized spat.[135] In May 2022 Robert Work joined Dov S. Zakheim onstage to argue with retired Marine generals Paul Van Riper and Anthony Zinni, both of whom were adamantly opposed to the new force design. Work, who was a retired Marine Corps colonel in addition to being a former deputy secretary of defense, likened the flaring debate over Berger's plan to a custody battle between grandparents and parents over a "beloved child," with Van Riper and Zinni et al. battling Work, Zakheim, and Berger.[136]

Work's employment of this infantilizing metaphor, and the emotional critiques that helped instigate its use, marked an unfortunately temporary low point in the increasingly personalized debate over the character of war and the future of American ground combat capabilities. Professional dialectic had devolved into unseemly diatribes between hedgehogs.

As commandant, Berger probably had every statutory right to drive radical change through *Force Design 2030*.[137] But he repeatedly chose to brand his characterization of war and his solutions as personalized choices. He and his staff offered thin public evidence of objective analysis to justify big decisions like divesting tanks and artillery.[138] Fairly or not, the official structured analyses on the force redesign conducted after Berger issued his planning guidance in 2019 looked as if they had been contrived to justify what was by then a top-down fait accompli.

Van Riper, Zinni, and other critics also chose to personalize and publicize their own vitriolic characterizations, all of which were driven by even less evidence of objective historical or trend analysis. In any event, this was a poor state of affairs for the Marine Corps and for the strategically important efforts to characterize and forecast war.

WAR CHARACTERIZATION AND FORECASTING: A POOR STATE OF AFFAIRS OVERALL

This is not to say there was any observable decline in the quality of American descriptions and forecasts of ground combat or war writ large in the fifty years between 1970 and 2020. Instead, it was clear that throughout this period the most important observations—the ones that helped to drive defense plans and force designs—remained stubbornly subjective despite the ready availability of more objective methods.[139]

Clear signs of path dependence emerged in the selected historic cases that recurred in nearly every published forecast cited above. Readers could count on obligatory references to Napoleon, Clausewitz, Sun Tzu, the Blitzkrieg, the 1973 October War, and then later the 1991 Gulf War and the 2003 Iraq invasion. But the same readers were unlikely to see any references to contradictory theories or cases. This abuse of the historical record was fed in part by the scientific community's failure to provide better-structured and more compelling collective, global, case-and-trend evidence. It points to a disturbing failure to address challenges with science consumption in at least the U.S. Department of Defense.

Throughout this fifty-year period, thousands of models, war games, case studies, and other data fed into descriptions and forecasts across the lower echelons of the defense community. Some were good, others were less helpful.[140] And just as history alone cannot dissipate the fog of war, models, games, and simulations have a specific and limited use.

A few of the good and of the less helpful examples bubbled their way up to where, at least in my reading of the cited record, they were ignored, retailored, or picked over to justify the subjective analyses and outlooks of senior leaders. Sometimes games and sims were disingenuously crafted to prove rather than test or exercise a theory.[141] Millennium Challenge 2002 (MC2002) is probably the best-known manipulation of war-gaming and computer simulation in recent American military history.[142]

Building from the RMA writings of the 1990s, the Department of Defense constructed MC2002 as a massive integrated game, sim, and live exercise event that was explicitly intended to showcase advanced and transformational technologies. Officials brought in Paul Van Riper to play the red force, or bad guys, to give the impression that this scripted event was really a free-play test of the RMA concept.

When Van Riper derailed the whole game by sinking the U.S. Navy's imaginary ships and trying to shoot down the Marines' new tilt-rotor aircraft, the game runners simply reset everything to make it look more like the showcase for advanced military tech it was intended to be.[143] Even though he wasn't allowed to sink the imaginary ships, Van Riper spoke up in public and sank the game's reputation. Retrospectively, MC2002 is generally considered a travesty.

Millennium Challenge may or may not stand as an iconic insult to military professional integrity and judgment, but even the most realistic war games and simulations still have limited value in characterizing and forecasting war. No matter how well-thought-out they might be, models are just models, games are just games, and simulations of combat are basically just models and games on screens.[144] All are useful for thinking through complex problems and new technology employment. None are inherently accurate, objective, or predictive.

For example, through at least 2024 many human-in-the-loop simulations and games like Unified Challenge and Unified Quest have helped Army leaders think through multi-domain operations challenges.[145] But it would be a crime against logic to suggest they validated the MDO concept. Games also were used tack a veneer of validation on the failed Future Combat System program.

In an ex post examination of FCS, RAND Corporation analysts wrote: "Wargames are good at identifying issues for resolution, but they cannot be taken as validation of concepts. The original intent of the wargames leading up to the FCS program was to highlight issues. But that intent was lost along the way, and the importance and interpretation of wargame events took on much larger meaning in the Army's concept formulation, solidifying the concepts into Army thinking without the due diligence necessary."[146]

Army use of war-gaming and computer simulation to ostensibly validate FCS in the late 1990s echoes in the Marine Corps' use of gaming to validate Force Design 2030. Tabletop games generated useful discussion to inform the Corps' major changes to its ground combat forces. Because games are just games and not dependable replications of the real world, these games proved nothing about the viability of new technologies or about the character of current or future war.

But in the original *Force Design 2030* (2020), Berger wrote that his participation in war games over the course of five years convinced him that the Marine Corps needed to undergo revolutionary change.[147] Whether or not they helped Berger think through specific design problems, these games never should have had so much influence on multibillion-dollar, life-and-death decisions about American ground combat capabilities.[148]

With the exception of Don Starry's *AirLand Battle* and some of the more reasonable interpretations of maneuver warfare, all of these American force design debates from 1970 through the early 2020s revolved around the advent and promise of mostly conceptual revolutionary technology. In its various incarnations, the idea of the military-technical revolution drove the subjective American descriptions of current and future war, and particularly of land war and ground combat.

A recurring theme emerged in the early RMA writings, from Westmoreland in 1969 to Owens in 2000: Authors promised a technical revolution that would change not just the character but also the ostensibly immutable nature of war.[149] Revolution could be achieved within about ten years. Failure to invest in the revolution would lead to disaster. After about forty years of failed forecasting, authors like Work (2010s) kept the promises and dire warnings but overtly dropped the anticipatory timelines.

Without timelines—what the Soviets would call the *forecast time*—these American military projections were untethered from any type of reasonable comparative process. They slipped away from the necessarily liminal gray space between hard knowledge and subjective foresight and moved closer to a deeply personalized idiom.

This has been an admittedly harsh review. Any one of these aforementioned proponents could, of course, be the next Pete Ellis, the Marine Corps major who forecast the Japanese attacks in the Pacific. Any or all of them—Westmoreland, Krepinevich, Owens, Work, Milley, Berger, et al.—may have been right about everything except perhaps most of the dire existential warnings through at least the early 2020s; military catastrophe had not befallen the United States despite its failure to achieve the RMA.

Even if it turns out they are objectively wrong, the earnest desire of these military leaders and policy advocates to innovate and improve American fighting power is, at least from an American perspective, laudable. Improvement comes not from shutting down these kinds of forward-leaning thinkers but from providing them with a structured process and evidence they can work from so they can be both more universally trusted and, ideally, more accurate.

The next chapters and companion database to this book seek to provide a solid body of evidence to support this improved process. They focus on ground combat and will be more immediately relevant to soldiers, marines, and special operations ground officers around the world. But they can help form a baseline for a better overall understanding of the character of land war and war writ large.

NOTES

1. MacGregor Knox and Williamson Murray, *The Dynamics of Military Revolution, 1300–2050* (New York: Cambridge University Press, 2001), 5.
2. For more on the debate over Westmoreland's legacy, see Lewis Sorley, *Westmoreland: The General Who Lost Vietnam* (New York: Houghton Mifflin Harcourt, 2011), 99–105; and Gregory A. Daddis, "Review Essay on Lewis Sorley's Westmoreland: The General Who Lost Vietnam," *Parameters* 41, no. 3 (2011). Also see Westmoreland's own book: William C. Westmoreland, *A Soldier Reports* (Garden City, NY: Doubleday, 1974). In this book he barely touches on modernization.
3. William C. Westmoreland, "New Developments in Ground Warfare," congressional testimony, in U.S. Senate, Volume 115 of the Congressional Record, Part 22 (October 16, 1969), 30348–39349.
4. Westmoreland, "New Developments," 30349.
5. Critics of U.S. defense spending in (particularly) the early 1970s would describe these investments as inadequate. See, for example, Colin S. Gray and Jeffrey G. Barlow, "Inexcusable Restraint: The Decline of American Military Power in the 1970s," *International Security* 10, no. 2 (1985), 27–69.
6. See the five-volume history of satellites published by the National Reconnaissance Office (NRO), https://www.nro.gov.
7. See chapter 5 for more on GPS.
8. John T. Cornell, "The Emergence of Smart Bombs," *Air & Space Forces Magazine*, March 1, 2010. For a good, dependable weapons systems reference, see the U.S. Army's Worldwide Equipment Guide (WEG).

9. This was the Ryan Aeronautical Model 234A. David Axe, *Drone War Vietnam* (Yorkshire, UK: Pen & Sword Military, 2021), 129.
10. Defense Advanced Research and Projects Agency, *DARPA: 50 Years of Bridging the Gap* (2016, https://www.darpa.mil), ebook.
11. There were of course variations in form, but they were generally inconsequential and temporary. The shift to the Pentomic Division, a unit with five fighting elements instead of three, is a good case in point. See John B. Wilson, *Maneuver and Firepower: The Evolution of Divisions and Separate Brigades* (Washington, DC: U.S. Army Center of Military History, 1998). A shorter but equally useful history can be found in Richard W. Kedzior, *Evolution and Endurance: The U.S. Army Division in the Twentieth Century* (Santa Monica, CA: RAND Corporation, 2000).
12. William C. Westmoreland, *Report of the Chief of Staff of the United States Army, 1 July 1968 to 30 June 1972* (Washington, DC: Department of the Army, 1977), chapter IX.
13. I coded Lang Son 1979 as an interim period case. For more on these battles, see Edward C. O'Dowd, *Chinese Military Strategy in the Third Indochina War: The Last Maoist War* (New York: Routledge, 2007); Xiaoming Zhang, *Deng Xiaoping's Long War: The Military Conflict between China and Vietnam, 1979–1991* (Chapel Hill: University of North Carolina Press), 2015; Tom Cooper and Adrian Fontanellaz, *Ethiopian-Eritrean Wars: Volume 1, Eritrean War of Independence, 1961–1988* (West Midlands, UK: Helion, 2018) ebook; Tom Cooper and Adrian Fontanellaz, *Wars and Insurgencies of Uganda 1971–1994* (West Midlands, UK: Helion, 2016), ebook; Thomas P. Odom, *Shaba II: The French and Belgian Intervention in Zaire in 1978* (Fort Leavenworth, KS: Combat Studies Institute, 1993); Daniel Kowalczuk, *Operations "Leopard" and "Red Bean"—Kolwezi 1978: French and Belgian Intervention in Zaire* (West Midlands, UK: Helion, 2019), ebook.
14. See the remainder of this chapter and chapter 9 for more on the military-technical revolution. For an overview see Mary C. FitzGerald, *Marshal Ogarkov and the New Revolution in Soviet Military Affairs* (Alexandria, VA: Center for Naval Analyses, 1987).
15. I refer here to Carl von Clausewitz's *Vom Krieg* (*On War*), which still serves as a foundation for Western military theory and doctrine in the early 2020s. See Bassford, *Clausewitz in English*; Heuser, *Reading Clausewitz*; U.S. Joint Chiefs of Staff, *Doctrine for the Armed Forces of the United States*, Joint Publication 1 (Washington, DC: Chairman of the Joint Chiefs of Staff, 2017). Various translations of *On War* are cited later in this book and in the bibliography.
16. See references in *Press On!*, below.
17. *AirLand Battle* also integrates advanced technology concepts and calls for the kind of semi-independent operations described in some future forecasts of war, including the U.S. Marine Corps' Force Design 2030. See chapter 9 for more.
18. By "he" I mean Starry and his staff writers. U.S. Army, *Operations*, Field Manual 100–5 (Washington, DC: Headquarters, U.S. Army, 1982), I-3.
19. Starry had risen through the ranks mostly as a traditional Cold War armor officer, and his later writings (see Sorley, *Press On!*, 2009, cited below) make clear his appreciation for advanced technology. But his experience as a ground combat commander in Vietnam guided his general understanding of land warfare. See Mike Guardia, *Crusader: General Donn Starry and the Army of His Times* (Havertown, PA: Casemate, 2018); and Lewis Sorley, ed., *Press On! Selected Works*

of General Donn A. Starry, Volume I (Fort Leavenworth, KS: Combat Studies Institute Press, 2009).

20. See John L. Romjue, *From Active Defense to AirLand Battle: The Development of Army Doctrine 1973–1982* (Fort Monroe, VA: U.S. Army Training and Doctrine Command, June 1984).
21. The idea that it is beneficial to outthink and outpace adversaries was not a revolutionary one even in the 1970s. John R. Boyd wrote about the OODA (observe-orient-decide-act) loop that would anchor maneuver warfare concepts through the 1980s and into the late 1990s. It emerges as *tempo* in Marine Corps doctrine. The term *OODA loop* is still used frequently in U.S. military circles. See Robert Coram, *Boyd: The Fighter Pilot Who Changed the Art of War* (New York: Hachette, 2002); Stephen Robinson, *The Blind Strategist: John Boyd and the American Art of War* (Dunedin, New Zealand: Exisle, 2021); Frans Osinga, *Science, Strategy and War: The Strategic Theory of John Boyd* (Delft, The Netherlands: Eburon Academic, 2005); U.S. Marine Corps, *Warfighting.*
22. The word *revolutionary* appears twice in *AirLand Battle 2000,* both referring briefly to the perceived information revolution that was trending in the early 1980s.
23. These two events were not at all representative of all ground combat during this decade. See the next section for more, including focus on the Iran-Iraq War, the Soviet-Afghan War, the Sri Lankan civil war, Grenada, Panama, Angola, and others.
24. I believe the best Falklands War resource is the three-part documentary series sponsored by the UK Army. As of early May 2023 it could be found on YouTube. Part one was available at https://www.youtube.com/watch?v=hw-Jupy_PMk.
25. For a quick review of forces and timeline, see Joseph P. Englehardt, *Desert Shield and Desert Storm: A Chronology and Troop List for the 1990–1991 Persian Gulf Crisis* (Carlisle Barracks, PA: Strategic Studies Institute, 1991).
26. Ashton B. Carter, William J. Perry, and John D. Steinbruner, *A New Concept of Cooperative Security* (Washington, DC: Brookings Institution, 1992). Thomas A. Kearney and Eliot A. Cohen (along with the rest of the Gulf War Air Power Survey team) offered a more nuanced analysis and gently criticized Carter, Perry, and Steinbruner for overstating their case. Andrew W. Marshall served on the Air Power Survey review committee. Marshall would go on to enlist Cohen's aid in examining the RMA. Thomas A. Kearney and Eliot A. Cohen, *Gulf War Air Power Survey: Summary Report* (Washington, DC: U.S. Department of the Air Force, 1993).
27. The specific term *revolution in military affairs* appeared in at least the 1975 English-language, U.S. military translation of *Forecasting in Military Affairs,* probably verbatim in other Soviet writings, and as early as the 1950s in other works (see chapter 9 of this book for more details and references). See chapter 9 for use of related language dating back to the late 1800s. Andrew Krepinevich and Barry Watts, *The Last Warrior: Andrew Marshall and the Shaping of Modern American Defense Strategy* (New York: Basic Books, 2015). Also see Dimitry (Dima) Adamsky, "The Two Marshals: Nikolai Ogarkov, Andrew Marshall, and the Revolution in Military Affairs," in *The New Makers of Modern Strategy,* ed. Hal Brands (Princeton, NJ: Princeton University Press, 2023), 895–917.

28. For more on the RMA, see chapter 9 and, for example, Bill Owens and Ed Offley, *Lifting the Fog of War* (Baltimore: Johns Hopkins University Press, 2000); Arthur K. Cebrowski and John H. Garstka, "Network-Centric Warfare—Its Origin and Future," *Proceedings* 124, no.1 (January 1998); Frederick W. Kagan, *Finding the Target: The Transformation of American Military Policy* (New York: Encounter Books, 2006); Knox and Murray, *Dynamics of Military Revolution*; and others.
29. Andrew F. Krepinevich Jr., *The Military-Technical Revolution: A Preliminary Assessment* (Washington, DC: Center for Strategic and Budgetary Analysis, 1992).
30. For references to Soviet military writing on the subject, see Thomas W. Wolfe, *Evolution of Soviet Military Policy* (Santa Monica, CA: RAND Corporation, 1968); and John Erickson, "Détente, Deterrence, and 'Military Superiority': A Soviet Dilemma," *The World Today* 21, no. 8 (August 1965), 337–345. Related terms like revolution in military science appear in other Soviet writings. For example, V. Sokolovakiy and M. Cherednichenko, "Revolution in Military Science, Its Importance and Consequences, Military Art on a New Stage," *Krasnaya Zvezda*, no. 203 (1964), 2–3, translated and published by the U.S. Air Force Systems Command, Wright-Patterson Air Force Base, Ohio (1964).
31. Krepinevich lists past military-technical revolutions in the American Civil War, World War I, and World War II. Machineguns, combustion engines, and radios were all, in Krepinevich's interpretation of history, revolutionary technical triggers. Krepinevich, *Military-Technical*, 4–5.
32. Krepinevich, *Military-Technical*, 3.
33. The term *reconnaissance-strike complex*, or recon-strike complex, described the Soviet military-technical revolution version of what Krepinevich and, later, parts of the Department of Defense would describe as reconnaissance-surveillance-targeting-acquisition (RSTA), or the networked sensor-shooter system that constituted the core of the RMA. See Krepinevich, *Military-Technical*, 8; Larry A. Brisky, "The Reconnaissance Destruction Complex: A Soviet Operational Response to Airland Battle," *Journal of Soviet Military Studies* 3, no. 2 (1992), 296–306; Milan Vego, *Recce-Strike Complexes in Soviet Theory and Practice* (Fort Leavenworth, KS: Soviet Army Studies Office, 1990).
34. These issues are addressed later in this chapter and in chapter 9. See David H. Berger, *Force Design 2030* (Washington, DC: Headquarters, U.S. Marine Corps, March 2020).
35. For example, he refers to the center of gravity, an emerging term adopted by maneuver warfare advocates like William S. Lind and John R. Boyd, and cites the same military theorists frequently referred to by Lind, Boyd, and others, including J. F. C. Fuller and B. H. Liddell Hart. Krepinevich, *Military-Technical*, 33, and others.
36. Krepinevich, *Military-Technical*, 1, 3–5, and other sections in the report. His descriptions are matched by other proponents (e.g., Kearney and Cohen, *Air Power Survey*) and by some more objective observers of the debate. They are not, however, universally accepted.
37. Krepinevich, *Military-Technical*, 3.
38. I drew from Griffith, *Forward into Battle*; Will Elsbury, "The Machine Gun: Its History, Development and Use: A Resource Guide" (Washington, DC: U.S. Library of Congress, 2022); Paul Wilcock, "The Armoury of His Grace the Duke of Buccleuch and Queensberry," *Armour* 9, no. 2 (2013), 181–205; An Instructor, *Complete*

Guide to the Hotchkiss Machine Gun (London: Gale and Polden, n.d.); Paul Cornish, *Machine Guns and the Great War* (South Yorkshire, UK: Pen & Sword Military, 2009); and other books on weaponry.

39. Krepinevich, *Military-Technical,* 4.
40. Merriam-Webster online dictionary (https://www.merriam-webster.com) defines a revolution as "a sudden, radical, or complete change." There are many ways to interpret each of these conditions or to interpret them collectively; this dictionary definition offers little clarification.
41. This last implication is my interpretation of Krepinevich's writings in this 1992 report and in those that followed. See the remainder of this chapter for additional evidence.
42. Blitzkrieg is German for *lightning war.* For more on Lind, see William S. Lind, *Maneuver Warfare Handbook* (New York: Routledge, 1985); and Robinson, *Blind Strategist.*
43. Krepinevich, *Military-Technical,* 4. He devotes a full chapter to praising the Blitzkrieg in his 2023 book on military innovation: Andrew F. Krepinevich Jr., *The Origins of Victory: How Disruptive Military Innovation Determines the Fates of Great Powers* (New Haven, CT: Yale University Press, 2023), chapter 7.
44. The authors mention the Blitzkrieg ten times and describe it as a concept that revolutionized land warfare. Even Marshall was enamored of purported Wehrmacht land warfare ingenuity, asking at one point if the Soviets could pull of a Blitzkrieg against NATO. Krepinevich and Watts, *Last Warrior,* 180 and 194.
45. I was witness to some of these appearances. Lind wore German uniforms to various training events and to the mess night for my Basic Officers Course class in 1995. At the latter event he took the opportunity to make an uninvited toast to the Nazi Operation Barbarossa. On readings, for example, Bruce Gudmundsson's *Stormtroop Tactics* made a number of Marine Corps reading lists and was available for sale at the base exchange. Bruce I. Gudmundsson, *Stormtroop Tactics: Innovation in the German Army, 1914–1918* (New York: Praeger, 1989).
46. Less kindly, and perhaps unfairly depending on context and perspective, someone applying the Urban Dictionary to this fixation might use the term *Wehraboo,* or a person who fervently believes the Wehrmacht to have been the greatest fighting force in recorded history.
47. Stephen Robinson and Cathal J. Nolan offer the most cutting and, I believe, the best interpretations of Blitzkrieg. See Robinson, *Blind Strategist,* and Cathal J. Nolan, *The Allure of Battle: A History of How Wars Have Been Won and Lost* (Oxford, UK: Oxford University Press, 2017), chapter 13.
48. See Robinson, *Blind Strategist,* for more on their insights.
49. Sun Tzŭ, *The Art of War,* trans. Lionel Giles (1910), attributed to Sun Tzŭ in approximately fifth century BCE. See chapter III, Attack by Stratagem. For comparison see the Roger T. Ames more detailed and compelling translation: Sun Tzu, *The Art of War,* trans. Roger T. Ames (1993), in Caleb Carr, ed., *The Book of War: Sun-Tzu The Art of Warfare & Karl von Clausewitz On War* (New York: Random House, 2000), 78. Hans Delbrück wrote what probably is the definitive discourse on the need to seek or avoid battle. See Hans Delbrück, *The Dawn of Modern Warfare,* trans. Walter J. Renfroe (Westport, CT: Greenwood Press, 1985), 293–318. This is also a central theme in Nolan, *Allure of Battle.*
50. I return to this important point in chapter 9.

51. One could argue that Clausewitz took this same personalized approach, rendering his works equally suspect. Jehuda Wallach identified references to 130 separate campaigns in *On War*, which to some extent would help alleviate this perception. But volume alone does not necessarily elevate cherry-picking to empirical process. Wallach, *Dogma of Battle*, 10.
52. See the footnote above on RMA literature.
53. Mark Hanna, *Task Force XXI: The Army's Digital Experiment* (Washington, DC: National Defense University, 1997); Stephen Silvasy Jr., "AirLand Battle Future: The Tactical Battlefield," *Military Review* 71, no. 2 (1991), 2–12; "AirLand Battle Future: The Other Side of the Coin," *Military Review* 71, no. 2 (1991), 13–24; John Matsumura, Randall Steeb, Thomas Herbert, Scot Eisenhard, John Gordon, Mark Lees, and Gail Halverson, *The Army after Next: Exploring New Concepts and Technologies for the Light Battle Force* (Santa Monica, CA: RAND Corporation, n.d.); Robert H. Scales, "Forecasting the Future of Warfare," *War on the Rocks*, April 9, 2018; U.S. Army, *Concepts of the Army Objective Force*, white paper (Washington, DC: Department of the Army, 2001).
54. For more on the development of maneuver warfare in the Marine Corps and of *warfighting*, see Connable, *Warrior-Maverick*, 145–151; G. I. Wilson, Michael D. Wyly, William S. Lind, and Bernard E. Trainor, "The 'Maneuver Warfare' Concept," *Marine Corps Gazette* 65, no. 4 (1981), 49–54; Kevin R. Clover, "Maneuver Warfare: Where Are We Now?," *Marine Corps Gazette* 72, no. 2 (1988), 54–99; Terry Terriff, "'Innovate or Die': Organisational Culture and the Origins of Maneuver Warfare in the United States Marine Corps," *Journal of Strategic Studies* 29, no. 3 (2006), 475–503; Robinson, *Blind Strategist*.
55. These include sometimes heavy combined-arms engagements at or around Kupres in Bosnia-Herzegovina, Shusha in Nagorno-Karabakh, Grozny in Chechnya, Cenapa Valley on the Peru-Ecuador border, Tskhinvali in Georgia, Koshare in Serbia, Mogadishu in Somalia, Ain Defla in Algeria, Amran in Yemen, Weli Oya and Mullaitivu in Sri Lanka, Lisne Lekh in Nepal, Walikale in the Democratic Republic of the Congo, and Badme on the Eritrea-Ethiopia border, among many others.
56. Army leaders adopted some elements of maneuver warfare into their doctrine and training, including the idea of mission-type orders ("mission command") and adaptability. But the Marine Corps embraced the concept in both term and intent. Whether or not they practiced maneuver warfare is a question to be decided elsewhere.
57. Influence of the RMA on U.S. military concepts and strategies was made clear in *Joint Vision 2010* and *Joint Vision 2020*, both published before the 2003 Iraq war. U.S. Joint Chiefs of Staff, *Joint Vision 2010* (Washington, DC, 1998); U.S. Joint Chiefs of Staff, *Joint Vision 2020* (Washington, DC, 2000). Also see Michael L. Brown and Tammy M. Furrow, *"Revolution in Military Affairs Conference," Report on the Conference Conducted at the Strategic Assessment Center, 12–13 November 1996* (McLean, VA: Science Applications International Corporation, 1997); John Arquilla and David Ronfeldt, *In Athena's Camp: Preparing for Conflict in the Information Age* (Santa Monica, CA: RAND Corporation, 1997); Charles J. Dunlap, "Joint Vision 2010: A Red Team Assessment," *Joint Forces Quarterly*, no. 17 (Autumn-Winter 1997–1998), 47–49; and other widely available material. For more Blitzkrieg fixation, see James R. FitzSimonds and Jan M. Van Tol, "Revolutions in Military Affairs," *Joint Forces Quarterly*, no. 4 (Spring 1994), 24–31.

Counterarguments emerged but gained less traction. See, for example, Michael E. O'Hanlon, "Beware the 'RMA'nia!,'" *Brookings Institution* (September 9, 1998).

58. Owens wrote the book with the help of Ed Offley, but these are his ideas and many parts are written in the first person. Bill Owens, with Ed Offley, *Lifting the Fog of War* (Baltimore: Johns Hopkins University Press, 2000).
59. Also see James R. Blaker, *Transforming Military Force: The Legacy of Arthur Cebrowski and Network Centric Warfare* (Westport, CT: Praeger Security International, 2007).
60. For critiques of the modern interpretation of Blitzkrieg, see Jürgen Förster, "From 'Blitzkrieg' to 'Total War': Germany's War in Europe," in *A World at Total War: Global Conflict and the Politics of Destruction, 1937–1945*, eds. Roger Chickering, Stig Förster, Bernd Griener, Christof Mauch, and David Lazar (Cambridge, UK: Cambridge University Press, 2004), 89–107; and Robert A. Doughty, "Myth of the Blitzkrieg," in *Challenging the United States Symmetrically and Asymmetrically: Can America Be Defeated?*, ed. Lloyd J. Matthews (Carlisle Barracks, PA: Strategic Studies Institute, July 1998), 57–79. For a detailed analysis of von Seeckt's interwar activities and concept development, see James S. Corum, *The Roots of Blitzkrieg: Hans von Seeckt and German Military Reform* (Lawrence: University of Kansas Press, 1992).
61. This view emerges primarily from my reading of Corum's analysis of the genesis of the Blitzkrieg concept, and specifically of von Seeckt's concept development process in Corum, Walter Goerlitz's *History of the German General Staff, 1657–1945*, and to some extent in S. J. Lewis's *Forgotten Legions*; Lewis had a broader focus. Corum, *Roots of Blitzkrieg*; S. J. Lewis, *Forgotten Legions: German Army Infantry Policy 1918–1941* (New York: Praeger, 1985); Walter Goerlitz, *History of the German General Staff, 1657–1945*, trans. Brian Battershaw (Lucknow Books, 2015/1953), ebook. Also see Nolan, *Allure of Battle*, 413–419.
62. Alfred von Schlieffen, *Cannae* (Fort Leavenworth, KS: Command and General Staff School Press, 1931). No individual translator is identified in this publication.
63. Sternberg has also been described as an economist. S. J. Lewis offers up a fascinating etymology of the word *Blitzkrieg* in a detailed footnote, tracing its emergence or at least common usage from Sternberg's 1938 treatise to a 1939 English-language newspaper article warning of a possible "lighting war" in Europe. Lewis, *Forgotten Legions*, 45.
64. Fritz Sternberg, *Germany and a Lighting War* (London: Faber and Faber, 1938). The Hitler quote is from Förster, "From 'Blitzkrieg,'" 90, citing three sources. The translated quote is: "I have never used the word Blitzkrieg because it is a very stupid word." In the same cited discussion he reluctantly associates the word with Operation Barbarossa, ex post.
65. For a good analysis of the factors contributing to the failure of the 1918 offensive, see Wallach, *Dogma of Battle*, 191–193.
66. Michael Geyer, "Restorative Elites, German Society, and the Nazi Pursuit of War," in *Fascist Italy and Nazi Germany: Comparisons and Contrasts*, ed. Richard Bessel (Cambridge, UK: Cambridge University Press, 1996), 134–164, 142.
67. On this point see Wallach, *Dogma of Battle*, Book One, and particularly pages 21, 23–25.
68. For details on this campaign see Robert Forczyk, *Case White: The Invasion of Poland, 1939* (Oxford, UK: Osprey, 2019); Roger Moorhouse, *Poland 1939: The*

Outbreak of World War II (New York: Basic Books, 2020); Steven J. Zaloga, *Poland 1939: The Birth of Blitzkrieg* (Oxford, UK: Osprey, 2002); and Nolan, *Allure of Battle*, 420–425.

69. Forczyk, *Case White*, 296, appendices, and other pages; Zaloga, *Poland 1939*, 153.
70. Forczyk, *Case White*, 324–325.
71. Max Hastings, "Their Wehrmacht Was Better Than Our Army," *Washington Post* (May 4, 1985). Hastings cited unspecified analysis by Trevor N. Dupuy.
72. This is not necessarily true—total rejection of history might in fact be worse in practice—but it is at the very least an apt warning. See von Schlieffen, *Cannae*, preface.
73. I am skipping over the adoption of the term *transformation* and other buzzwords to avoid adding more jargon to this already compressed narrative. See Donald H. Rumsfeld, "Transforming the Military," *Foreign Affairs* 81, no. 3 (May–June 2002), 20–32.
74. He describes a 200 × 200-mile surface plane that would ostensibly follow the Earth's curvature, but he expounds on this image toward a three-dimensional space later on the page. See Owens and Offley, *Lifting the Fog*, 14–15, and other pages.
75. When *Lifting the Fog of War* was published, there was some debate as to whether Owens had chosen to be intentionally hyperbolic to gather attention or if he genuinely believed in these absolutist descriptions. See, for example, Eliot A. Cohen, "Lifting the Fog of War by William A. Owens, Ed Offley," *Foreign Affairs* 79, no. 4 (July–August 2000), 154.
76. Cohen, "Lifting the Fog."
77. Owens and Offley, *Lifting the Fog*, 148 and 237–240.
78. These included the General Atomics MQ-9 Reaper and MQ-1 Predator drones, and the Ground-Based Operational Surveillance System (G-BOSS) and Rapid Aerostat Initial Deployment (RAID) tower, and other technical systems frequently referred to in open sources.
79. U.S. Army, *Objective Force*.
80. For information on FCS, see for example, Andrew Feickert, *The Army's Future Combat System (FCS): Background and Issues for Congress* (Washington, DC: Congressional Research Service, 2009); Paul L. Francis, *Defense Acquisitions: The Army's Future Combat Systems' Features, Risks, and Alternatives*, testimony (April 1, 2004); and U.S. Congress, *The Army's Future Combat Systems Program and Alternatives* (Washington, DC: Congressional Budget Office, 2006).
81. All issues with FCS are presented in detail in Christopher G. Pernin, et al., *Lessons from the Army's Future Combat Systems Program* (Santa Monica, CA: RAND Corporation, 2012).
82. Other battles include but are by no means limited to Bukavu in the Democratic Republic of the Congo, Khara Army Base in Nepal, N'Djamena in Chad, Maroun al-Ras in Lebanon, Muhamalai Defensive Line in Sri Lanka, Jowhar in Somalia, Sa'ada in Yemen, Loe Sam in Pakistan, and Myawaddy-Three Pagodas Pass in Myanmar.
83. Jan Van Tol and other experts, including Mark Gunzinger and Jim Thomas, were also instrumental in building these cases.
84. Work was also a retired colonel in the U.S. Marine Corps with twenty-eight years of service.
85. Andrew Krepinevich, Barry Watts, and Robert Work, *Meeting the Anti-Access and Area-Denial Challenge* (Washington, DC: Center for Strategic and Budgetary

Assessments, 2003). The term *anti-access and area-denial,* or A2/AD, was already in use at least in the U.S. Navy. The word *missile* appears 199 times in this ~100-page report.

86. Krepinevich, Watts, and Work, *Anti-Access, Area Denial,* 8.
87. Krepinevich, Watts, and Work, *Anti-Access, Area Denial,* 58, 63, 73, 75, and other pages.
88. Krepinevich, Watts, and Work, *Anti-Access, Area Denial,* iv.
89. Andrew Krepinevich and Robert O. Work, *A New Global Defense Posture for the Second Transoceanic Era* (Washington, DC: Center for Strategic and Budgetary Assessments, 2007).
90. Andrew F. Krepinevich, *Why AirSea Battle?* (Washington, DC: Center for Strategic and Budgetary Analysis, 2010); and Jan van Tol, Mark Gunzinger, Andrew Krepinevich, and Jim Thomas, *AirSea Battle: A Point-of-Departure Operational Concept* (Washington, DC: Center for Strategic and Budgetary Analysis, 2010).
91. Van Tol et al. wrote in a footnote: "The arguments in this section largely concern the Air Force and the Navy, since these are the two Services whose integrated operations in the Western Pacific theater lie at the core of an AirSea Battle concept. However, they may also be applicable in many cases to the Army and the Marine Corps as well." Van Tol et al., *AirSea Battle,* 112.
92. This last point is subjective. It reflects my observation based on contemporaneous engagements with Pentagon-level staffs from both services, building from my experiences on active duty in the U.S. Marine Corps through 2009. Also see "Fact Sheet: Advancing the Rebalance to Asia and the Pacific," press release, The White House, November 16, 2015; Kenneth G. Lieberthal, "The Pivot to Asia," *Brookings Institution,* December 21, 2011, https://www.brookings.edu; and Janine Davidson, "The U.S. 'Pivot to Asia,'" *American Journal of Chinese Studies* 21, special issue (June 2014), 77–82.
93. U.S. Marine Corps, *Expeditionary Force 21,* concept paper (Washington, DC: Headquarters, U.S. Marine Corps, 2014).
94. U.S. Marine Corps, *Expeditionary Force,* 6. While the Marine Corps is generally considered to be the service primarily responsible for amphibious warfare as directed by the U.S. National Security Act of 1947, as amended, the Army has used and retains a sizable amphibious fleet.
95. U.S. Marine Corps, *Expeditionary Force,* 9–10. The term *pacing threat* would emerge in the late 2010s to describe the primary challenge all U.S. military services would focus on as they designed, manned, trained, and equipped their forces.
96. This is an informed subjective observation based on extensive interactions with various parts of the Army headquarters staff throughout the 2010s, as well as a reading of contemporaneous literature. Also see Michael E. O'Hanlon, "How Big an Army Does the United States Need?," *Brookings Institution* (November 15, 2013).
97. For example, U.S. Army, *The U.S. Army in Multi-Domain Operations 2028* (Fort Leavenworth, KS: U.S. Army Training and Doctrine Command, December 6, 2018).
98. These comments were made by then-Lieutenant General Eric J. Wesley on December 4, 2018, at the Association of the United States Army (AUSA) conference on

multi-domain operations, starting at 9:18 in the video of the conference posted on YouTube entitled "AUSA 2018 CMF 8 Multi-Domain Operations."

99. See Timothy M. Bonds, et al., *What Role Can Land-Based, Multi-Domain Anti-Access/Area Denial Forces Play in Deterring or Defeating Aggression?* (Santa Monica, CA: RAND Corporation, 2017); Rachael Jeffcoat, "Army Conducts 1st RIMPAC Joint Live-Fire Sinking Exercise as Multi-Domain Task Force" (U.S. Indo-Pacific Command, July 25, 2018); C. Todd Lopez, "For Contingencies in Indo-Pacom, Army Will Serve as 'Linchpin' for Joint Force," *DOD News*, December 1, 2021, https://www.defense.gov; Eric Setzekorn, "Taiwan and the U.S. Army: New Opportunities amid Increasing Threats," *Military Review*, September–October 2020, 44–53; John Grady, "SECARMY Wormuth Pitches Army's Next Role in the Western Pacific," *USNI News*, December 2, 2021, https://news.usni.org; Andrew Feickert, *The Army's Ground Combat Vehicle (GCV) Program: Background and Issues for Congress* (Washington, DC: Congressional Research Service, March 14, 2014).
100. This was a matter of emphasis, not binary distinction. Army leaders did put additional resources into the European theater, and ground combat leaders in Europe made significant adjustments to rebuild conventional capabilities withered during irregular warfare operations.
101. I address this approach in the following section and in chapter 9.
102. Robert O. Work and Shawn Brimley, *20YY: Preparing for War in the Robotic Age* (Washington, DC: Center for New American Security, January 2014).
103. Work and Brimley capitalized Robotic Age. I leave it capitalized here without implication.
104. "We call this the '20YY' regime to avoid needless debate over what decade or year [this revolution] might occur." Work and Brimley, *20YY*, 6. Work and Brimley offer a tone-box analysis of the terms military-technical revolution, revolution in war, revolution in warfare, and revolution in military affairs. Work and Brimley, *20YY*, 9.
105. Work and Brimley, *20YY*, 6.
106. See Gian Gentile, Michael Shurkin, et al., *A History of the Third Offset, 2014–2018* (Santa Monica, CA: RAND Corporation, 2021). For the National Defense Strategy, or NDS, see U.S. Department of Defense, *Summary of the 2018 National Defense Strategy of the United States of America* (Washington DC, 2018).
107. Then-Secretary of Defense Harold Brown and his director for defense research and engineering (and future secretary of defense) William J. Perry conceived of and acted as proponents of the offset strategy starting in 1977. See Edward C. Keefer, *Harold Brown: Offsetting the Soviet Military Challenge, 1977–1981* (Washington, DC: Office of the Secretary of Defense, 2017).
108. See Gentile et al., 2021.
109. Hans Delbrück offers a fairly direct counter: "War is no chess game; it is a struggle of physical, intellectual, and spiritual forces." Delbrück, *Dawn of Modern Warfare*, 376.
110. Robert O. Work, "Remarks by Deputy Secretary Work on Third Offset Strategy," transcript from a speech delivered in Brussels, Belgium, U.S. Department of Defense (April 28, 2016, https://www.defense.gov).
111. Work left the federal service in 2017 but continued to write about military-technical revolutions. For example, Robert Work, James A. Winnefeld Jr., and

Stephanie O'Sullivan, "Steering in the Right Direction in the Military-Technical Revolution," *War on the Rocks*, March 23, 2021, https://warontherocks.com.

112. I refer here to Effects-Based Operations, or EBO, a component concept of the RMA. As the commander of the now-defunct Joint Forces Command, Mattis attempted to shift the U.S. military away from the word *effects* and from other EBO terminology and thinking. James N. Mattis, "USJFCOM Commander's Guidance for Effects-based Operations," *Parameters* (Autumn 2008), 18–25. I have written somewhat extensively about EBO. See Ben Connable, *Embracing the Fog of War: Assessment and Metrics in Counterinsurgency* (Santa Monica, CA: RAND Corporation, 2012), and other works available at www.rand.org.
113. U.S. Department of Defense, *National Defense Strategy*.
114. There were continuing references to Third Offset in service writing years after Work's retirement. For example, Eric P. Hilner, "The Third Offset Strategy and the Army Modernization Process," *Center for Army Lessons Learned*, May 2019, https://usacac.army.mil.
115. Mark A. Milley, quoted in Rick Maze, "Radical Change Is Coming: Gen. Mark A. Milley Not Talking about Just Tinkering around the Edges," *AUSA.org*, December 13, 2016, https://www.ausa.org.
116. See, for example, Daisy Thornton, "Army Trying to Keep Up with 'Changing Character of War,'" *Federal News Network*, June 25, 2018, https://federalnewsnetwork.com; Arpi Dilanian and Matthew Howard, "The Number One Priority: An Interview with Gen. Mark Milley," *U.S. Army*, November 4, 2019, https://www.army.mil; Mark A. Milley, "Strategic Inflection Point: The Most Historically Significant and Fundamental Change in the Character of War Is Happening Now—While the Future Is Clouded in Mist and Uncertainty," *Joint Forces Quarterly*, no. 110 (3rd Quarter 2023, 2023), 6–15; and many other publicly available sources.
117. Mark A. Milley, quoted in John Grady and Sam LaGrone, "CJCS Milley: Character of War in Midst of Fundamental Change," *U.S. Naval Institute News*, December 4, 2020.
118. For example, Navy Captain Gerard Roncolato wrote: "War is changing at a dramatic rate and scope." Chairman of the Joint Chiefs of Staff Joseph F. Dunford wrote: "Over the past two decades . . . the pace of change and modern technology, coupled with shifts in the nature of geopolitical competition, have altered the character of war in the 21st Century." Army General Randy A. George stated: "The character of war has changed over the last two years." Gerard Roncolato, "The Character of War Is Constantly Changing," *Proceedings* 148, no. 5 (May 2022); Joseph F. Dunford, "The Character of War and Strategic Landscape Have Changed," *Joint Forces Quarterly*, no. 89 (2018), 2–3; Zach Sheely, "Senior Army Leader Lays Out His Vision, and How Guard Fits," press release, National Guard Bureau, August 21, 2023, https://www.nationalguard.mil.
119. In late 2022 Milley stated: "We are under a very fundamental change in the character of war . . . that country that innovates the most will have a decisive advantage at the beginning of a war." Mark A. Milley, televised appearance, CNBC Television, November 10, 2022, https://www.cnbc.com.
120. James C. McConville, *Army Multi-Domain Transformation: Ready to Win in Competition and Conflict*, Chief of Staff Paper #1 (Washington, DC: Headquarters, Department of the Army, March 16, 2021).

121. McConville, *Army Multi-Domain*, preface.
122. U.S. Army, *Army Multi-Domain Transformation: Ready to Win in Competition and Conflict* (Washington, DC: Chief of Staff of the Army, March 16, 2021), 23.
123. He made this point directly: "Broadly speaking, our future force must align to the NDS." U.S. Marine Corps, *Force Design*, 4. The Marine Corps published an EABO manual in 2021, reiterating character-of-war assumptions laid out in *Force Design 2030*. U.S. Marine Corps, *Tentative Manual for Expeditionary Advanced Base Operations* (Washington, DC: Headquarters, U.S. Marine Corps, February 2021).
124. See David H. Berger, *Commandant's Planning Guidance: 38th Commandant of the Marine Corps* (Washington, DC: Headquarters, U.S. Marine Corps, July 15, 2019).
125. Fairly or not, the first-person writing in *Force Design 2030* made it read as Berger's personalized reimagining of the Marine Corps. Issues with this personalization would come back to annoy if not haunt him just months after the plan's release. Many of the salient points in *Force Design 2030* were written in the first person.
126. For early critiques see, for example, Mark F. Cancian, "The Marine Corps' Radical Shift toward China," Center for Strategic and International Studies, March 25, 2020; Dan Gouré, "Force Design 2030: USMC Innovation or Dissolution?," *Defense .info*, April 2, 2020, https://defense.info; Jim Webb, "The Future of the U.S. Marine Corps," *National Interest*, May 8, 2020, https://nationalinterest.org.
127. U.S. Marine Corps, *Force Design*, 2.
128. U.S. Marine Corps, *Force Design*, 1–2, with details spelled out throughout the paper.
129. U.S. Marine Corps, *Force Design*, 7. An infantry battalion typically had about 900 Marines.
130. Many observers—I include myself in this camp—found the sharp reduction in artillery assets to be more controversial. But the tank decision gained the most public attention.
131. U.S. Marine Corps, *Force Design*, 8.
132. For example, Gina Harkins, "Marine Corps to Shut Down, Cut Back 7 MOSs as the Force Prepares for Change," Military.com, May 27, 2020, https://www.military .com; and Chad Garland, "'Marines Make Excellent Soldiers': Over Half a Marine Tank Company Just Joined the Army National Guard," *Stars and Stripes*, September 16, 2020, https://www.stripes.com. An MOS is a military occupational specialty, which is a code assigned to all U.S. service members based on their specific roles and training.
133. For example, Paul K. Van Riper, "The Marine Corps' Plan to Redesign the Force Will Only End Up Breaking It," *Task & Purpose*, April 20, 2022, https:// taskandpurpose.com; Charles Krulak, Jack Sheehan, and Anthony Zinni, "War Is a Dirty Business. Will the Marine Corps Be Ready for the Next One?" *Washington Post*, April 22, 2022, https://www.washingtonpost.com; Paul Van Riper, "This Is the Marine Corps Debate We Should Be Having," *Marine Corps Times*, December 7, 2022, htts://www.marinecorpstimes.com; Paul K. Van Riper, "Jeopardizing National Security: What Is Happening to Our Marine Corps?," *Military Times*, March 21, 2022, https://www.militarytimes.com; among others articles and blog posts. Some of the original maneuver warfare advocates and authors also attacked the plan. See, for example, Gary Wilson, William A. Woods, and Michael D. Wyly,

"Exchanging a Force-in-Readiness for a Force-in-Waiting," *Fabius Maximus*, September 18, 2022, http://fabiusmaximus.com.

134. For example, Gina Harkins, "Top Marine General Hits Back at Critics Who Say the Corps' New Force Redesign Plan Is Too Focused on China," *Military.com*, June 3, 2020.
135. For more on the debate, see Worth Parker, "How the Marine Corps Went to War with Itself over the Next War," *Task & Purpose*, June 13, 2022.
136. Robert O. Work, quoted in "On the Future of the Marine Corps: Assessing Force Design 2030," transcript of an online event, Center for Strategic and International Studies, Washington, DC, May 16, 2022, https://www.csis.org, 4. Pages are not numbered, so this is the fourth page including the title page.
137. See 10 U.S. Code § 8043—Commandant of the Marine Corps, U.S. law.
138. This is an important point that I revisit in the conclusion.
139. With the exception of *Force Design 2030*, most of these documents were aspirational rather than directive. Most of the described visions did not come true.
140. For example, see Ben Connable et al., *Modeling, Simulation, and Operations Analysis in Afghanistan and Iraq: Operational Vignettes, Lessons Learned, and a Survey of Selected Efforts* (Santa Monica, CA: RAND Corporation, 2014).
141. For more on these points, see Jacquelyn Schneider, "What War Games Really Reveal: Outcomes Matter Less Than Who Pays and Who Plays," *Foreign Affairs*, December 26, 2023.
142. For the best analysis of this event see Micah Zenko, "Millennium Challenge: The Real Story of a Corrupted Military Exercise and Its Legacy," *War on the Rocks*, November 5, 2015. Also see U.S. Joint Forces Command, *MC02 Final Report* (Norfolk, VA, 2002); Joe Galloway, "Rumsfeld's War Games," Military.com, April 26, 2006; Francis Horton, "The Lost Lesson of Millennium Challenge 2002, the Pentagon's Embarrassing Post-9/11 War Game," *Task & Purpose*, November 6, 2019; Elaine M. Grossman, "Unintended Lesson of Millennium Challenge?," *Inside Missile Defense* 8, no. 20 (October 2002), 3–5.
143. Zenko, "Millennium Challenge," and other references to this exercise cited herein. To be fair to the game runners, some glitches in the computer system also informed the reset, but the ex post explanations of the decision left an unfavorable impression.
144. I make this argument as a researcher who has led modeling, gaming, and simulations research for a range of U.S. Government sponsors for over a decade.
145. "Unified Quest," *Stand-To!*, September 24, 2016, https://www.army.mil; Todd South, "Massive Simulation Shows the Need for Speed in Multi-Domain Ops," *Army Times*, September 12, 2019, https://www.armytimes.com; Jon Harper, "Just In: Army Struggling to Simulate All-Domain Warfare," *National Defense*, October 18, 2021, https://www.nationaldefensemagazine.org; Sydney J. Freedberg Jr., "Army Multi-Domain Wargame Reveals C2 Shortfalls," *Breaking Defense*, September 12, 2019, https://breakingdefense.com; and other sources cited in chapter 9.
146. Pernin et al., *Future Combat Systems*, xviii.
147. He wrote: "Those war games helped shape my conclusion that modest and incremental improvements to our existing force structure and legacy capabilities would be insufficient to overcome evolving threat capabilities, nor would they enable us to develop forces required to execute our approved naval concepts." U.S. Marine Corps, *Force Design*, 3. In the 2022 update the Marine Corps promised to make

these games more transparent for the general public. U.S. Marine Corps, *Force Design 2030 Annual Update* (Washington, DC: Headquarters, U.S. Marine Corps, May 2022), 6.

148. For more on war games and *Force Design 2030,* see Benjamin Jensen, "The Rest of the Story: Evaluating the U.S. Marine Corps Force Design 2030," *War on the Rocks,* April 27, 2020.
149. It was easy to shift between these terms since both are ill-defined.

TWO

World War II Ground Combat Case Examples

I have identified two important problems with the way we understand war as it is practiced on land: First, there is inadequate understanding of the varying breadth of ground combat as it has been practiced around the world, and particularly in the first part of the twenty-first century. Second, there is inadequate empirical evidence to show how ground combat and land warfare—and perhaps even war writ large—have actually changed over time.

In this chapter I set a foundation to help solve these problems, building the historical baseline for the investigation of modern ground combat cases that follows. These mid-twentieth-century cases also start to outline the complexity and diversity of the range of combat typologies and characteristics present even within a single (albeit massive) war.

Why does World War II provide the best historical baseline to help understand modern ground combat? World War II was the first large-scale conflict to showcase all of the tactics, techniques, and technologies that would influence global ground combat in the first part of the twenty-first century. It is generally considered the first war in which combined-arms combat was widely and consistently employed by all combatants at nearly all levels of command.[1] Given the central importance of combined-arms tactics to my working definition of ground combat, common use of combined arms is requisite for a solid research baseline.

The scope and scale of the fighting in World War II also allowed for the best possible survey of cases, technology employment, and the emerging development of new technologies—including the first combat use of drones—that anchored the contentious debates over military revolutions that emerged over the following half century. It is therefore the only reasonable baseline for an examination that follows. However, I see nothing revolutionary in World War II ground combat. I purposefully trace what I see as the evolution of both tactical and technical characteristics that emerged in some cases well before World War II, leading to a continuing evolutionary track described in chapters 4–9.

I reviewed and coded twenty exemplary, nonrepresentative baseline cases of World War II battles and integrated these cases with a broader review of the secondary source literature on the characteristics of World War II ground combat. I used cases that touch on a diverse set of combat characteristics from different theaters, at varying scales, in different types of terrain, and so on. Each case had to be:

(1) a ground combat engagement involving at the very least a platoon of infantry on each side employing basic combined arms, like mortars and rifles together;
(2) roughly representative of a diversity of terrain and climate, including urban, plains, rivers, jungles, islands, desert, ice and snow, and so on to reveal how both terrain and climate might affect combat;
(3) roughly representative of a range of different military forces—American, German, UK and Commonwealth, Canadian, Soviet, Japanese, Polish, Chinese, Italian, Australian—to highlight diversity and similarities in ground combat approaches; and
(4) roughly representative of a diversity of combat type, including infantry only, armor heavy, amphibious, airborne, and so on. I also weighted selection toward the tail end of the war (1944–1945) in order to set a clearer end-of-war baseline.

I do not present the aggregated results of all the coding here. These cases are nonrepresentative and might be misleading without further context. I return to the coding process in the chapters on modern ground combat and in the appendix.

WORLD WAR II GROUND COMBAT CASES, 1942–1945

These twenty cases start in chronological order at Tatsinskaya Soviet Union in 1942 and progress through Medicina Italy in 1945. All descriptions, references, and codes are presented in the database, and the full case list is provided below and in the accompanying database. From these twenty coded cases I selected ten—Ortona, Changde, Monte Altuzzo, Leopold Canal, Peleliu, Warsaw, Tarakan, Mutanchiang, Hill 170, and Medicina—to help describe the varying characteristics of ground combat in different World War II theaters, with different military forces, and applying different tactics, equipment, and weapons, all of which evolved at varying pace from the start to the end of the war. Table 2.1, below, lists the twenty World War II cases:

Table 2.1. Twenty World War II Ground Combat Cases, 1942–1945

Tatsinskaya Soviet Union 1942	Leopold Canal Belgium 1944	Okinawa Japan 1945
Ortona Italy 1943	Walcheren Holland 1944	Meitkila Burma 1945
Prokhorovka Soviet Union 1943	Aachen City Germany 1944	Tarakan Borneo 1945
Guadalcanal 1943	Saipan 1944	Mutanchiang China 1945
Changde China 1943	Peleliu 1944	Hill 170 Burma 1945
Monte Altuzzo Italy 1944	Bastogne Belgium 1944	Medicina Italy 1945
Saint-Lô France 1944	Warsaw Uprising Poland 1944	

Context for each case is necessarily limited: The purpose of this book is to focus on the fighting, not on the political, strategic, or operational context that forced the two combatants together. Key references are cited for further reading. Each case starts with a location, a list of combatants, bounding dates, and a footnote of key sources.[2] All cases are presented as they appear in the cited sources; deeper research into each case would necessarily reveal a somewhat different narrative.

ORTONA, ITALY, 1943[3]

Location: Ortona, Sicily, Italy
Combatants: Canada and the Allied armed forces versus Germany
Dates: December 10–December 28, 1943

As part of the Allied push up the eastern coast of Sicily in late 1943, the Canadian 1st Infantry Division (Reinforced) attacked through the German 90th Panzergrenadier Division and the 1st Parachute Division in and around the town of Ortona.[4] Exhausted by a tough opposed river crossing during the tactical approach to the town, the Canadian armor-infantry teams had to push through dug-in German infantry, armor, artillery, and anti-tank guns positioned in a 200-yard wide gulley west of Ortona that afforded an almost perfect defensive line. German heavy artillery rounds and Nebelwerfer rockets slammed into the Canadians, stalling their attack. The Canadians tried again, reinforced by tanks, but this attack also stalled in a minefield covered by heavy German defensive fires.

German infantry-armor teams executed several local counterattacks under the cover of blanketing artillery and mortar barrages. A hasty Canadian combined-arms defense stalled the Germans. Over the next few days on the roads leading into Ortona, the two sides pushed back and forth, with Canadian M-4 Sherman tanks dueling German Panzer Mark IIIs and IVs, while tanks from both sides were being picked apart by anti-tank guns and short-range rockets. Infantry struggled to find covered approaches, engaging in heavy rifle and machinegun skirmishes often within grenade range. Artillery fire was relentless: In just one day of the battle, the Royal Canadian Horse Artillery fired 5,938 rounds at the defending Germans; probably tens of thousands of rounds were fired overall.[5] Eventually the 90th Panzergrenadiers were so worn down that they all but collapsed, ceding the defense to the German 1st Parachute Division who had dug themselves into the urban terrain of Ortona. German defenders rubbled the streets to deter armored advances and set up deadly kill zones with overlapping anti-tank guns, machineguns, anti-tank mines, flamethrowers, snipers, rockets, mortars, and light artillery.

Tight urban terrain and the dense stone walls of some buildings prevented the Canadians from using their superior firepower—tanks, artillery, and bombers—to compel a German withdrawal from a reasonable distance. Instead, they had to fight for each street and each building, engaging German infantry at close range with cannons, rifles, submachineguns, pistols, grenades, and knives. Hand-to-hand combat was commonplace as the Canadians cleared each building in turn, working their way down boulevards and alleys, smashing and pushing the Germans in front of them as they went. Heavy anti-tank guns were brought up in an effort to reduce dense stone and brick walls. Thousands of rounds of explosives were used to smash defensive positions and kill German soldiers. Germans counterattacked when they could, infiltrated at night, and fought hard, but eventually they were defeated. From the start of the battle in early December through the end of the month, thousands of Canadians and Germans were killed and wounded. The battlefield was littered with burned-out tanks and trucks from the edge of the Moro River to the far end of Ortona city.

Observations and insights from Ortona, Italy, 1943. With some exceptions, nearly all types of ground combat weapons, equipment, munitions, and both ground and aviation fire support were employed by both sides at Ortona; this was an extended, intensive combined-arms battle. Flanking attacks and counterattacks were routinely attempted, but assaults were mostly straightforward armor-infantry-artillery slugfests in both directions. Neither ground nor aviation reconnaissance by either side effectively spotted or tracked enemy forces. Anti-tank guns and rockets were highly effective against tanks and light armor, but the shaky mechanical reliability and limited range of the Allied PIAT launcher reduced its usefulness. Terrain, ground cover (vegetation), and built-up areas effectively dictated engagement ranges, benefited the defenders, and limited weapons effectiveness, forcing infantry into close-quarters battle.

Changde, China, 1943[6]

Location: Changde, Hunan, China
Combatants: Republic of China and Japan
Dates: November 23–December 20, 1943

Five Japanese infantry-heavy divisions under the 11th Army, reinforced with artillery and armor, attacked to clear defending Chinese 6th Army forces from the Hunan plains and the city of Changde (or Changte, 常德). They converged from multiple directions to pin the defenders and choke off avenues for Chinese maneuver or escape. Japanese forces engaged across the Yangtze River and over rugged mountainous terrain, extending their lines of communication toward the city. Chinese troops withdrew and then, centering their defenses on the 57th Division, put up a fierce resistance around and within Changde. Japanese troops attacked overland with integrated tank support, moving on foot and on horseback. Infantry charged in mass waves into Chinese guns on several occasions. They also conducted a sustained and opposed amphibious attack across Dongting Lake and up the Yuan River, pushing troop transports onto the shores east of the urban areas while under heavy fire.

Air support played a crucial role for both sides, with U.S. fighters and bombers of the 14th Air Force providing close-air support for the 57th Division, dropping supplies, and disrupting the amphibious assault. American P-40 fighter-attack aircraft destroyed tens of sampans and larger boats, killing scores of Japanese infantrymen. In turn, Japanese aircraft bombed Chinese troops and engaged in intensive dogfights with the Americans over the city and the nearby plains to gain air superiority. Both sides lost aircraft as they attempted to support their respective ground forces. For various reasons, the American air support was curtailed just as the Chinese 3rd and 10th Divisions were racing up to relieve the beleaguered 57th, which was about to collapse.[7] There also were indications the Japanese had used chemical weapons against the Chinese defenders during the initial attacks on the plains and at the edge of the city. On December 3, the city fell.[8] Only about 400 troops from the 8,000-man 57th Division made it out alive after high-intensity street fighting with cannons, machine-guns, and blades of various types.

Japanese infantry held Changde for six days as the Chinese counterattacked through surrounding villages and farmland. American B-25 bombers unleashed continual high-explosive and incendiary strikes on the defending Japanese troops, softening them up and at least contributing to their decision to withdraw. Pressing forward under heavy artillery and air support, Chinese troops of the 3rd and 10th Divisions had decimated Japanese supporting divisions on the suburban outskirts and plains, so by the time the Japanese withdrew they were able to effectively walk in and reclaim the now almost flattened city. Reported total Chinese casualties were at least 7,500 dead or captured; this probably was a low count. Japanese official records list 1,274 dead and 2,977 wounded Japanese soldiers through December 24, 1943.

Observations and insights from Changde, China, 1943: As with Ortona, these were large-scale, combined-arms battles across varying terrain. The Japanese had to fight over mountains and across water gaps—lake and river—and then into the dense urban environment, all in the course of one tactical movement and under intensive aerial bombardment. They conducted their amphibious assault as a matter of course, not as any kind of special naval infantry activity; this dynamic of routine amphibious assault replays throughout the cases.

Combat ranges extended out across the plains to probably over 500 meters, and then contracted violently as the Japanese concentrated their infantry wave assaults and pressed into the city. Once inside the urban terrain, the rifle, machinegun, anti-tank gun, knee mortar, and sometimes knives and swords, dominated the fighting, with visibility probably limited to individual streets and alleys. Aerial observation helped both sides to identify large troop movements, particularly given the fairly open terrain and the lake crossing. But relaying that information to ground commanders was at least on the American-Chinese side a time-consuming and inefficient process. Japanese use of horse cavalry, and their loss of over 2,000 horses, stands out as a rare regressive nineteenth-century moment in World War II ground combat.[9] Another key figure from the Japanese account of the battle stands out: They self-reported 11,812 soldiers as "sick," which constitutes about a full division of infantry.[10]

Monte Altuzzo, Italy, 1944[11]

Location: Florence Province, Italy
Combatants: United States versus Germany
Dates: September 10–17, 1944

In an effort to break through the German Gothic Line, which generally ran along the Apennines Mountains in northern Italy, the U.S. Army 85th and 91st Divisions attacked into the defending German 4th Parachute Division (Reinforced). Steep mountainous terrain forced the attackers up narrow roads and directly into the guns of a well-prepared defense. The Germans had accurately forecast the attack route and emplaced layers of interlocking machineguns, anti-tank guns, mortars, artillery, and concrete pillboxes overlooking minefields and barbed wire, behind which they set in a series of defensive trench lines along military crests. Heavy pine tree growth concealed many of the German defensive positions, making it difficult for the Americans to find a good avenue of approach and to target the defenders with their own artillery and mortars.[12]

American infantry regiments in the main effort were backed by a wide array of fire support ranging from 105mm pack howitzers to 240mm howitzers, as well as Sherman M4-variant tanks and M-18 tank destroyers. However, they conducted their initial push up Monte Altuzzo with no preparatory fires. Given the steep and heavily wooded terrain on parts of the mountainside, infantry frequently had to trudge up into fairly close range before they could spot and engage most of the German defensive positions. In other places they had to cross wide open fields, uphill, under the direct observation of German machine gunners positioned on the slopes above. Terrain forced a full regimental attack to be distilled into a series of fierce engagements between infantry platoons using every natural rise and dip in the ground, every tree and rock, to hide and conceal movement. The American assault slowed.

Then the artillery joined in. Chemical units fired concealing smoke while thousands of artillery rounds splashed up and down the mountainside, including into the Germans' rear area to disrupt their command, control, and logistics. An entire American infantry battalion advanced in a linear formation in a daring night frontal assault. Under withering machinegun and mortar fire, they moved uphill but again stalled.

The Germans wasted no time looking for advantage, counterattacking after a short barrage of 50mm mortar fire.[13] They made repeated assaults with mortars, grenades, and submachineguns, moving downhill to break up the American attack and force them back down the mountain. But the Germans, too, were stopped. British fighter-bombers joined in and began strafing and bombing the German trenches and gunlines, wreaking havoc and helping the American infantry to retake the initiative.[14] At the end of the battle, both American divisions coordinated for a final push, driving the exhausted Germans from the peak and cracking open the Gothic Line for follow-on attack.

Observations and insights from Monte Altuzzo, Italy, 1944. Steep, wooded terrain with gullies, streams, and hillocks all but prevented the Americans from making good use of their armor. This put the defending German light infantry on an equivalent footing with the Americans, who were already at a significant disadvantage attacking uphill, frequently at night, and into prepared fires.

While American aerial reconnaissance was able to pick out and target the most obvious defensive positions like those on denuded crests, they could not see through the trees to spot most of the concealed direct-fire weapon emplacements that probably caused most of the American casualties. Nor could the intelligence teams accurately describe the micro-terrain—the minor rises and drops in slope, rock outcrops, streambeds, and berms—that could mean the difference between a successful covered infantry assault and a massacre. Infantry platoons had to send out reconnaissance squads to feel their way forward and, in most cases, to be shot at in order to fix the enemy for assault. Artillery fire, long-range tank fire, and aerial attacks were essential to overall success, but they were not clearly decisive. This was primarily an infantry battle.

Leopold Canal, Belgium, 1944[15]

Location: Sint-Laureins, Belgium
Combatants: Canada and Allied armed forces versus Germany
Dates: October 6–13, 1944

As part of the broader campaign to seize the Scheldt Estuary and open the Port of Antwerp to Allied logistics ships, the Canadian 3rd Infantry Division attacked to cross the Leopold Canal and to defeat or drive off the defending German 64th Infantry Division. The Germans had spent considerable time and effort digging in to the far side of the canal and had backed their frontline positions with heavy artillery, all types of mortars, and direct-fire cannons. Prior to the attack the Canadians used loudspeakers in an effort to trick the Germans into thinking they were facing a much larger force; this had limited effect. Canadian planners also tried to catch the Germans by surprise, eschewing preliminary bombardment on this full-division defensive belt and relying instead on an interesting improvisational weapon to crack open a far beachhead: They lined up Wasp light-armored vehicles that launched flaming jellied gasoline in arcs across the canal and into the German trenches.

This tactic momentarily stunned the Germans. Napalm burned and killed some of them, but they recovered and focused their guns on the Canadians attempting to cross the narrow waterway. German machinegun fire and artillery laced into the leading Canadian brigades and pinned them on the bank once they had crossed. As at Ortona, minor dips and rises in terrain that were effectively imperceptible on tactical maps gave the defender significant advantages: The earthen bank of the canal acted like an engineered defensive berm, preventing direct Canadian cannon fire from the near bank from hitting key defensive positions. By surviving the flame attack and responding with their own heavy fires, the Germans set the conditions for aggressive counterattacks. German infantry pressed forward to break up the beachheads and to push the Canadians back across the canal. But at this point Canadian and supporting Allied heavy artillery concentrated to smash the German infantrymen as they uncovered from their trenches and bunkers.

Nothing was settled with this rapid back-and-forth along the canal bank. The Canadians were pinned for five days as the Germans counterattacked repeatedly, sometimes every two hours.[16] As at Ortona, hand-to-hand combat was commonplace. Both sides kept up continuous bombardment with artillery, and the Canadians called in Allied air support. German troops benefited from their pre-dug covered positions, while the Canadians desperately scraped their way into the mud to protect against shelling. On the fifth day the Canadians sent in their reserve and attacked into the German defenses at the nearby town of Moershoofd. They shelled the town with 25-pounder artillery and then pressed in behind 2-inch mortars, machinegun, and direct rocket fire from infantry PIATs. After about another day of fighting they had secured a defensible far-side beachhead for onward operations.

Observations and insights from Leopold Canal, Belgium, 1943. Combat at the canal was straightforward slaughter dished out primarily by men with rifles, knives, machineguns, flamethrowers, mortars, and artillery tubes. Failure to initiate the assault with a heavy bombardment probably cost the Canadians many casualties and allowed the Germans to regroup from the rather successful surprise flame attack. This failure to sufficiently reduce the enemy's prepared earthen and concrete defenses recurs in the next case (Peleliu 1944), which poses a somewhat different problem: how to deliver effective preparatory fires on engineered defensive positions in dense coral rock.

Opposed river crossing operations are always hazardous, even at relatively narrow gaps (probably about 75 feet at the Leopold Canal crossing point), and basic weapons like machineguns and mortars can be devastating to exposed infantry in small boats. And as the Canadian infantry found on the far bank, holding a narrow beachhead requires considerable resources and will. Attackers are at a disadvantage when they are consolidating on an objective, and even more vulnerable when their back is to water. Aerial observation was probably quite helpful for Canadian and Allied artillery, but given the tight quarters, artillerymen on both sides probably didn't need too many targeting cues to kill the enemy.

Peleliu, Palau, 1944[17]

Location: Peleliu, Palau
Combatants: United States versus Japan
Dates: September 15–November 27, 1944

The First Marine Division, reinforced, conducted an amphibious attack to seize the island of Peleliu from the Japanese 14th Infantry Division (Reinforced) as part of the larger campaign to defeat the Japanese Empire throughout the Pacific Ocean island chains.[18] Two preinvasion miscalculations would cost the Marines dearly.[19] First, U.S. Navy planners incorrectly believed that less than three days of shelling and aerial bombardment would eliminate the Japanese defenses. This turned out to be woefully inadequate, particularly considering the Japanese had prepared nearly bombardment-proof shelters. Second, intelligence terrain analysis described the island as "low-lying" when in fact it rose up to 260 feet, a significant enough height to drastically alter the characteristics of small unit infantry combat. As the Marines moved to shore in their landing craft, hidden Japanese coastal guns opened up and nearly demolished the opening assault wave. Nearly all eighteen Sherman tanks with the assault waves were hit by shells, but only three were destroyed, still allowing the Marines decent mobile firepower ashore.[20]

Even with tanks and well-rehearsed infantry-armor-artillery teaming, Peleliu was a nasty slog that would quickly shatter the vaunted First Marine Regiment.[21] Japanese soldiers fought tenaciously from caves, fighting holes, and bunkers dug into the coral rock high ground overlooking the landing beaches and, further inland, many of the approach lanes across the island. When the Marines managed to get off the beaches and assault the main airfield, they had to attack across open ground swept by Japanese direct and indirect fire and then defend against a well-coordinated and professional infantry-armor counterattack. Marine Sherman tanks and rocket assaulters caught the Japanese Type-95 light tanks from the flanks, while machine gunners, riflemen, and mortarmen killed the advancing infantry.

Marine units then pushed into the Umurbrogol Pocket, a deadly natural rock bowl ringed by interlocking Japanese defenses. They fought uphill into intense and often close-range machinegun and rifle fire. American artillery, mortars, and close-air support rocket and bomb attacks had minimal impact on the dug-in Japanese defenders; most had to be blasted out with rockets, grenades, tank cannons, demolition charges, and flamethrowers. Throughout the slow advance across the island, hidden Japanese artillery, heavy mortars, and anti-tank guns that had not been spotted by repeated reconnaissance sweeps harassed and killed the attacking infantry. Eventually the Marines and soldiers from the U.S. Army 81st Division secured all of Peleliu and its keys. The Japanese garrison was almost entirely destroyed with nearly 7,000 probably killed, while the Americans took over 2,700 killed.

Observations and insights from Peleliu, 1944. There were few options for tactical maneuvers or flanking attacks due to the restricted terrain, so core combined-arms skills and teamwork were essential to tactical success on Peleliu. Both sides practiced excellent infantry-armor teaming, though the Japanese assault across open ground in daylight with thinly armored vehicles was ill-advised.

Peleliu highlighted the limitations of even high-volume expert fire support in the face of a thinking and resourceful adversary fighting from favorable terrain, and particularly from terrain that was resistant to even accurate high-explosive attacks. American warships and aircraft operating unopposed against targets on a small island denuded of concealing vegetation were still unable to knock out most Japanese positions due to the pre-assault engineering preparations and the rocky ground.[22] Japanese engineering on Peleliu had been specifically accelerated as a countermeasure to superior American firepower observed in previous battles. Intensive daytime heat caused a good number of casualties among the Americans and degraded their ability to conduct extended offensive combat.

Warsaw, Poland, 1944[23]

Location: Warsaw, Poland
Combatants: Polish anti-occupation forces versus Germany
Dates: August 1–October 2, 1944

Well over 20,000 Polish Resistance fighters conducted a coordinated, preplanned uprising against occupying German Wehrmacht battlegroups of about equal troop strength but fielding far superior equipment, weapons, and fire support. Most of the Poles were armed with a mix of bolt-action rifles, captured submachineguns, and some light machineguns. They also used Molotov cocktails, grenades, PIAT anti-tank launchers, a few anti-tank guns and howitzers, some flamethrowers, and a handful of captured tanks and assault guns.[24] German soldiers were armed with the most advanced infantry weapons of the era, all calibers of mortars including heavy siege weapons, artillery, Nebelwerfer rocket launchers, tanks, assault guns, antiaircraft cannons capable of firing directly into Polish fighters, and close-air support bomb and gun runs. The Germans also had remote-controlled explosive ground drones that they used to destroy Polish fighting positions, and SturmPanzer IV and Sturmtiger assault guns; the massive Sturmtiger had a 380mm direct-fire rocket launcher that destroyed entire buildings in Warsaw.[25]

Given this imbalance in firepower, the Poles still attacked the Germans across the city. They began with ambushes and ground assaults to seize and then hold city blocks against the inevitable German counterattack. Lightly armed irregular infantry built up barricades of rubble to block or channel Wehrmacht vehicles into places where they could be destroyed by Molotov cocktails or the few anti-tank guns and rockets available to the Resistance. Snipers positioned on high points behind the barricades shot down into the advancing German infantry with good effect, at least during the initial counterattack. In the first few days of the battle there were intense close-range fights at the barricades, with frequent hand-to-hand action as the Germans attempted to press forward.[26] They were repelled in their initial assaults. Wehrmacht reports from the battle described low will to fight among their own troops as a serious impediment to success.[27]

Probably due in great part to the wavering dedication of their infantry, German leaders pulled back their troops, called in armored reinforcements, and crushed the defenders under the weight of thousands of high-explosive shells and aerial bombs. With effective air superiority—the Resistance shot down just a few attacking aircraft with antiaircraft artillery fire—Stuka dive-bombers attacked Polish defenses with near impunity. Lighter explosive shells proved insufficient to destroy urban defenses in the early attacks, so the Germans emphasized the use of 240mm mortars, 380mm rockets, and large aerial bombs to bury Resistance fighters under collapsing buildings. Infantry pushed forward into the burning and pancaked residential and commercial areas of the city, breaking the residual positions. Despite Soviet efforts to reinforce the Poles through airdrops, the Germans secured the city.

Observations and insights from Warsaw, Poland, 1944. While I do not specifically address will to fight in the case studies and coding (see explanation the introduction), this is one of those cases where it is an unavoidable factor. Wehrmacht infantry, including Schutzstaffel (Waffen-SS) units that had been murdering Polish civilians prior to the uprising, had little interest in brutal urban infantry combat. In contrast, the resistance fighters engaged a superior force and held their ground even under intense bombardment and with little chance of tactical success. The combination of these two human factors—the low will to fight of the German troops and the high will to fight of the Poles—combined to influence a German shift from infantry assault to destruction by fire.

Large parts of the city were crushed by the army ostensibly intent on holding it as German territory. Urban terrain channelized armor, reducing its effectiveness in the early parts of the battle, but tanks and assault guns proved more useful in leveling buildings from a distance. About eighty Goliath ground drones were employed with some good effect, but the Poles disabled a number of them by blowing up their command wires with grenades. In a few cases they were able to detonate the drones next to their controllers with devastating results.[28]

Tarakan, Borneo, 1945[29]

Location: Tarakan, North Kalimantan, Borneo
Combatants: Australian-led Allied coalition versus Japan
Dates: May 1–June 24, 1945

Australian forces were given the order to secure Tarakan Island to prevent the Japanese from using its oil production facilities and to support the broader effort to secure Borneo. The reinforced Australian 26th Brigade of just over 11,000 troops attacked a combined Japanese force made up of the 455th Battalion and the 2nd Naval Garrison Force.[30] Defending troops were belted in behind a ring of manmade obstacles backed by infantry positions and antiaircraft guns, and with a series of fallback positions in the jungle and on the nearby high ground. Heavy pre-landing bombardment from ships and strategic bombers smashed the Japanese-held airfield and some of the defensive positions around the landing beach. Australian troops moved to shore in a mix of landing craft that also brought in tanks and artillery. Aside from some brief exchanges of fire, the landing was unopposed; Japanese troops pulled back to more defensible positions. A beachhead was established in short order.[31]

However, as the Australians moved off the beach they began to run into stiffer resistance. Japanese troops holed up in concrete bunkers and had to be blasted out with explosives. Infantry reinforced by tanks moved out to clear the airfield and were met by long bursts from a Japanese 25mm antiaircraft gun interlocked with supporting machinegun fires. Minefields slowed movement further as Japanese 20mm cannons joined in the fight. Australian infantry pressed forward with flamethrowers and light infantry weapons into trenches ringed with razor wire. In parallel, Australian commandos pushed up to the heavily wooded Tarakan Hill, where they discovered concrete pillboxes and a tunnel system the Japanese were now using for defense. Tanks had to be called up to blast the tunnels with explosive shells. Japanese troops conducted night counterattacks but were repulsed.

Over the next few weeks, the Australians continued to push forward under cover of supporting fires, including bomber sorties, naval gunfire, and 25-pounder artillery that had been brought in from the sea. They made extensive use of mortars to support frontline troops, taking advantage of the weapons' high angle of attack in the dense terrain. Japanese defenders fought from bunker after bunker, trench line after trench line, falling back into increasingly unforgiving terrain along a razorback ridge. Infantry clashes were nearly continuous and at close range, sometimes with knives. Working from the captured airfield, P-38 Lightning fighter-bombers dropped napalm to burn the Japanese out of their positions on the ridge. Infantry worked closely with tanks to direct cannon fire straight into the entrenchments. Fighting went on like this through early June when the Australians pushed the remaining Japanese across the island and began to mop up. The attacking force had used more than 50,000 artillery and mortar rounds and over 850,000 rounds of small arms ammunition.[32]

Observations and insights from Tarakan, Borneo, 1945. Pre-landing bombardment took the Japanese aircraft out of the fight and probably destroyed some surface positions, but bombardment was less effective against the concrete defensive positions, trenches, antiaircraft guns, or the will to fight of the Japanese soldiers and naval infantrymen. Once the Australians pushed out from the airfield, Tarakan turned into an infantry brawl.

Australian infantry-armor teaming allowed for steady progress even in the face of heavy defenses, but most of the bunkers, trenches, and concrete pillboxes had to be cleared out by Bren guns, grenades, .303 rifles, flamethrowers, and knives. Aerial observation appears to have had limited success pinpointing Japanese defenses through the tree canopy, and the poor bombing accuracy (even by the typically more accurate, low-flying P-38s in some cases) reduced the value of Australian supporting fires. Mortars played a significant role in this battle, and both sides made good use of direct-fire antiaircraft artillery against opposing infantry.

Mutanchiang, China, 1945[33]

Location: Mutanchiang, China
Combatants: Japan versus the Soviet Union
Dates: August 12–16, 1945

Japanese First Area Army forces, reinforced by local Chinese militia, attempted to slow or stop the Soviet (Red Army) Fifth Army and 1st Red Banner Army around the city of Mutanchiang as part of the larger Soviet offensive to drive the Japanese out of Manchuria. Japanese forces had built up extensive linear fortifications along the border in anticipation of an eventual offensive. The Soviet main effort consisted of a motorized rifle division with Su-76 self-propelled guns, a brigade of tanks, and heavy artillery backed by divisions of additional infantry, armor, and mobile guns.[34] Muddy, forested terrain on the border forced the Soviets to leapfrog their infantry and tanks back and forth at what must have been a frustrating pace for the Soviet commanders. Even with the fortifications and terrain, Soviet forces smashed through the border fortification line in short order and ripped open a 35-kilometer gap for the follow-on echelon forces.[35]

Once into the plains west of the border line, attacking commanders stressed tempo, maximizing the speed of their armor units with mobile artillery in support. They made extensive use of combined multiple-launch rocket and artillery strikes to soften up Japanese defenses. Infantry were frequently used to mop up the flanks after tank units had punched through point objectives. As the Soviets pressed forward, the Japanese collapsed inward toward the city, attempting to use the Mutanchiang River as a final defensive line to their west and wooded and mountainous areas in the east to canalize Soviet forces into their relatively far less mobile infantry-heavy forces. The Japanese were able to put up stiff resistance and execute local counterattacks at places like Taimakou on a ridgeline east of Mutanchiang City.[36] But without adequate anti-armor capabilities like wheeled anti-tank guns and effective infantry rockets, and without their own organic tank-heavy forces, there may have been little chance their static defenses or counterattacks could have done more than slow Soviet advance toward the city.

Eventually the Soviet armor-infantry forces reached the perimeter line that the Japanese First Area Army had established around Mutanchiang City. Remnants of two Japanese divisions defended against the Soviet 1st Red Banner Army moving in from the north and the 5th Army moving in from the east. Soviet infantry passed through the vanguard armor brigades and moved into the urban terrain under cover of heavy artillery and rocket fire, seizing the city and demolishing the defending Japanese divisions. The defenders suffered almost total local defeat, while Soviet forces may have lost as many as 10,000 dead and 600 tanks in the overall Manchuria campaign.[37] At least in readily available sources, there are insufficient reliable records on dead and wounded in the specific battles near and within Mutanchiang.

Observations and insights from Mutanchiang, China, 1945. Soviet commanders had come to rely heavily on their artillery and armor on the eastern front, and they applied what they believed to be proven tactics against the Japanese around Mutanchiang. They only slowed down and allowed their infantry to probe forward when the terrain absolutely prevented open-field running by their T-34 tank units backed by equally mobile self-propelled artillery and rockets. Terrain slowed them again on the ridges east of the city, and light urban infrastructure eventually forced a shift to infantry attack.

The Soviets may not have applied the most advanced infantry-armor teaming tactics in the fight for the city, particularly given what appeared to be a separation between their armored brigades and infantry divisions. Lack of sufficient anti-armor capabilities, including a decent infantry anti-tank rocket, probably cost the Japanese significant casualties. Order of battle for the Soviet forces showed extensive antiaircraft capabilities. But the cited analyses do not give much credit to close-air support in this campaign. It is not clear if the Soviets' excellent ground-attack aircraft like the Ilyushin Il-2 made a significant contribution to the fight.[38]

Hill 170, Burma, 1945[39]

Location: Near Kangaw, Burma
Combatants: British-led Commonwealth forces versus Japan
Dates: January 22–31, 1945

As part of a broader push by the Indian XV Corps to seize Kangaw, Burma, British, West African, and Indian regular forces and British commandos—3 Commando Brigade and parts of 5 Commando Brigade—conducted a surprise amphibious landing. They came ashore on a beach near Hill 170, which dominated the terrain on the approach to Kangaw. Royal Air Force bombers laid a smoke screen to cover the landing, and the troops pushed ashore through muddy terrain to establish a beachhead.[40] Commando units took the lead with Indian M4-variant Sherman tanks providing fire support. Rough, rocky terrain, some dense vegetation, and small hills made rough going for the foot-mobile infantry, and heat and diseases began to inflict casualties before the first serious engagements with the defending Japanese 54th Division.

Commando units leapfrogged forward and eventually took up positions at the base and along one slope of Hill 170 and another nearby hill. The Japanese immediately tried to push them back, dropping in 75mm artillery and mortars before charging forward in a repeated series of infantry assaults. At one point in the battle, they may have charged into the commando lines on the swampy plains below Hill 170 with as many as 500 troops. British commanders called in their own fires from artillery, mortars, and supporting Sherman tanks and were able to kill many of the Japanese before they reached the hasty defensive positions. But a good number of Japanese infantrymen pushed through to engage in close-range combat with rifles, pistols, and hand grenades.

Japanese suicide attackers carrying bamboo poles with explosive charges and incendiary devices were able to knock out at least one Sherman. Fighting became so desperate that at one point a British soldier took to firing a 2-inch mortar from his hip directly into the onrushing attackers.[41] Over the course of a very busy day, the commandos and Japanese troops attacked and counterattacked up and down the slopes of Hill 170 and across the flat terrain at the base of the hill. Both sides expended grenades and small-arms ammunition at an almost unsustainable rate as they clung to the bare outcroppings and fought for control of the Japanese trench lines. Indian armor pushed through the Japanese delaying lines to provide the British commandos with enough support to finish off the remaining defenders. This forward element of the Japanese 54th Division was effectively destroyed.

Observations and insights from Hill 170, Burma, 1945. It is difficult to kill what cannot be seen. The British use of air-dropped obscurant smoke during the amphibious landing is a good example of what was a common practice throughout most of World War II: Smoke would be delivered by both specialized and regular units as an integral part of an attack.[42] Even the best-prepared defensive fires are degraded when the gunners cannot see the enemy. Smoke is notoriously difficult to deliver on target in a timely manner, and shifting winds can suddenly unmask attackers in open ground, but obscuration often was an infantryman's best friend in the attack.

Ammunition supply to forward troops and armor is always a challenge during even a deliberate advance. It is hard to predict how much ammunition, food, water, and other staples need to be pushed forward or held in reserve at any point in time. At Hill 170, British ammunition shortages could have been disastrous if reserves had not moved forward just at the right moment. Being able to sustain combined-arms combat for extended periods of time probably is just as important as being able to bring an effective combination of weapons to bear at a given place and point in time.

Medicina, Italy, 1945[43]

Location: Medicina, Italy
Combatants: UK Commonwealth forces versus Germany
Dates: April 15–16, 1945

During the final push up the coast of Italy shortly before German capitulation, the British 14/20th King's Hussars and the 43rd Brigade of the 6th Gurkha Rifles, supported by flanking New Zealand and Polish forces, attacked through the defending elements of the German 4th Parachute Division and a brigade of Italian paratroopers in the town of Medicina. Attacking troops operated as part of a mechanized infantry battle group, moving on Kangaroo armored personnel carriers in line with M4 Sherman tanks and supported by organic self-propelled field artillery.[44] Flat, marshy terrain broken up by small rivers and irrigation ditches channelized and slowed the attackers. German paratroopers had prepared thin linear defense lines along the ground to the southeast of the town, backed by Pak 40 75mm anti-tank guns, 88mm dual-purpose guns, modified StuG-43 assault guns, some tanks, lots of mortars, and artillery.[45]

Before the attackers could punch into Medicina, they had to cross one of several narrow rivers that ran perpendicular to the line of advance. On April 15, the Hussars and Gurkhas pushed across the Sillaro River but were blanketed by indirect fire from German mortars and artillery; they had to withdraw under pressure. They tried again with a night river crossing early on the morning of the 16th, grabbed a toehold on the opposite bank, and then managed to throw a mobile bridge over the river. Mechanized infantry and armor then pushed across and prepared for the assault into the town. While the allies moved through a vineyard into the attack position, German direct fire destroyed two advancing tanks that had advanced with insufficient infantry support. German infantry destroyed a third British tank with a rocket launcher before Gurkhas pressed forward, dismounted from their Kangaroos, and cleared out the defenders with rifles.[46]

After capturing the vineyard, the UK troops leaned on the speed of their mechanized forces to push directly into the town. Speed of attack shocked the German defenders, who managed only to destroy the leading Sherman before falling back into the town. About a company of mechanized infantry teamed with Shermans forced their way through the urban terrain, attacking directly into the loosely prepared defenses. German and Italian troops brought a Stug-43 and a pair of 88mm guns to bear in direct-fire mode, but the Shermans destroyed the assault gun and shot the crews off the 88s before the guns could be fired. Infantry attacked house-to-house, in some cases engaging in hand-to-hand combat. Gurkhas pushed on past the Shermans, and in one case a Gurkha soldier killed a German Panzerschreck anti-tank rocketeer with a kukri knife.[47] Despite some late-arriving German reinforcements, UK infantry-armor teams cleaned out the remaining defenders with sometimes intensive close-quarters combat.

Observations and insights from Medicina, Italy, 1945. Any kind of water barrier, or in modern Western military parlance, "wet gap," can pose serious problems for ground combat attackers. Even the narrow rivers southeast of Medicina required a dangerous crossing operation exposing the attacking troops to observation and fires. Combined-arms fire covering wet-gap crossings can be particularly lethal if it is well coordinated. At least through the end of World War II, there were no technical solutions to the wet-gap problem; they just had to be crossed with risk and hard work. Obscurant smoke and supporting fires are generally helpful as well.

And at Medicina the advancing Sherman tanks outpaced their accompanying infantry on several occasions. Failure to stay abreast was disastrous for at least one tank team at the vineyard southeast of the town, though in a few cases the forward-leaning tanks were devastating to defenders in the urban terrain. Both armor and infantry were reportedly more effective together. The Gurkha kukri knife attack on the German anti-tank soldier is perhaps an overly dramatic example of infantry protecting tanks, but it is still a good one.

WORLD WAR II GROUND COMBAT AND THE CHARACTER OF WAR

Given all of these narratives, and the rest of the well-recorded histories covering land warfare from 1939 through 1945, what was the character of ground combat in World War II? Instead of looking ahead for my answer, I ask the reader to pause here and consider the enormity of this question. It ostensibly requires an aggregation, summation, and distillation of all combat actions across all theaters of war for the entire conflict from at least the initial phase of the German strategic offensive through Victory in Japan Day in August 1945.[48] These case summaries above barely scratch the surface in terms of variation across ground combat actions in World War II.

This returns us to a central epistemological challenge with all characterizations of war, specifically applied to World War II ground combat: What do we mean by World War II ground combat? Are we trying to characterize all ground combat in World War II, perhaps by averaging everything together? Or are we characterizing only the highest-order, most modern types of ground combat like the Battle of the Bulge and not smaller battles like the fight for Hill 170 in Burma?[49] Should we have different characterizations for different types of World War II ground combat, perhaps one for large-scale desert war, one for urban skirmishes, and so on? I see no good answer to these questions as they apply to World War II, only subjective interpretation and personal preference. Neither of these advances objective knowledge or adds empiricism to forecasts of future ground combat.

In the absence of a concise and definitive answer to the question, What is the character of World War II ground combat?, I offer some observations in chapter 3. There were tactics, techniques, weapons, vehicles, munitions, technologies, and other factors—*characteristics*—that were important in many skirmishes and battles even if they do not together provably constitute a singular character of ground combat in World War II. All of these characteristics were also important elements of the historical baseline, or observation interval, leading up to the 2003–2022 case results in chapters 6 through 9.

NOTES

1. This is a subjective conclusion. World War I could also serve as a good baseline. Combined arms were certainly employed in many battles in the First World War. However, in World War I fires commonly were delivered as a prelude or accompaniment to maneuver and not coordinated by the forwardmost tactical leaders in direct support of ongoing ground combat.
2. For more on sourcing, see the appendix.
3. Sources for this case included G. W. L. Nicholson, *Official History of the Canadian Army in the Second World War, Volume II, The Canadians in Italy 1943–1945* (Ottawa: Queen's Printer and Controller of Stationary, 1956); Mark Zuehlke, *Ortona: Canada's Epic World War II Battle* (Vancouver: Douglas & McIntyre, 1999); Shaun R. G. Brown, "'The Rock of Accomplishment': The Loyal Edmonton Regiment at Ortona," *Canadian Military History* 2, no. 2 (1993): 11–24; G. C. Case, "Trial by Fire: Major-General Christopher Vokes at the Battles of the Moro River and Ortona, December 1943," *Canadian Military History* 16, no. 3 (2007): 13–28; "'Battle of Ortona 1943' Parts 1 and 2, video documentary, From the Battlefields," From the Battlefields (FTB), September 22, 2021, YouTube video; "Canadian Army Newsreel: Battle of Ortona," archival newsreel, Canadian Army Film Unit, 1940–1946, YouTube video.
4. This case does not include the Moro River crossing on the approach to the city.
5. Zuehlke, *Ortona*, 218.
6. Including Supreme Commander for the Allied Powers to the Japanese Government, *Army Operations in China: December 1941–December 1943*, translated Japanese Army monograph (1943); U.S. Air Force, *The Changteh Campaign of*

October–December 1943, historical monograph (14th Air Force Headquarters, May 1945); James C. Hsiung and Steven I. Levine, eds., *China's Bitter Victory: War with Japan, 1937–1945* (Routledge, 1992); "HD Historic Archival Stock Footage WWII—Chinese Troops Drive Japs [sic] from Changteh," archival newsreel, Military Newsreels 1944, no. 5, YouTube video; Battle of Changde, https://baidu.com.

7. U.S. Air Force, *Changteh Campaign*, 32.
8. U.S. Air Force, *Changteh Campaign*, 34.
9. Supreme Commander for the Allied Powers to the Japanese Government, *Army Operations*, 121.
10. Supreme Commander for the Allied Powers to the Japanese Government, *Army Operations*, 121.
11. Including Charles B. MacDonald and Sidney T. Mathews, *Three Battles: Arnaville, Altuzzo, and Schmidt* (Washington, DC: U.S. Army Center of Military History, 1993); U.S. Army, *Battle Analysis: The Battle of Monte Altuzzo, Offensive, Deliberate Attack, Mountain 85th and 91st Infantry Divisions, Sept 1944* (Fort Leavenworth, KS: Combat Studies Institute, 1984); U.S. Army, *5th Army History* (Washington, DC: Government Printing Office, 1945); Christian Jennings, *At War on the Gothic Line: Fighting in Italy, 1944–45* (New York: Thomas Dunne Books, 2016).
12. MacDonald and Mathews, *Three Battles*, 103–140.
13. MacDonald and Mathews, *Three Battles*, 156.
14. MacDonald and Mathews, *Three Battles*, 165.
15. Including Mark Zuehlke, *Terrible Victory: First Canadian Army and the Scheldt Estuary Campaign: September 13–November 6, 1944* (Vancouver: Douglas and McIntyre, 2007); Graham A. Thomas, *Attack on the Scheldt: The Struggle for Antwerp 1944* (South Yorkshire, UK: Pen and Sword Books, 2017); "Battle of Leopold Canal, Parts 1–3," video interview with Clifford Chadderton, Government of Canada, Report No. 188, https://www.canada.ca; Report No. 188, "Canadian Participation in the Operations in North-West Europe, 1944, Part VI: Canadian Operations, 1 Oct-8 Nov: The Clearing of the Scheldt Estuary," official history, Government of Canada, https://www.canada.ca; "The Clearing of the Scheldt Estuary and the Liberation of Walcheren 2 October—7 November 1944," official historical record (UK Government (n.d., https://assets.publishing.service.gov.uk)); Kristian Harris, "Chaos on the Canal: An Examination of the Algonquin Regiment at the Battle of the Leopold Canal," thesis (Ontario: Nipissing University, July 2022); Gerald Rawling, *Cinderella Operation: The Battle for Walcheren 1944* (London: Cassell, 1980).
16. See "Leopold Canal," Canadiansoldiers.com, n.d.
17. Including Frank O. Hough, *The Assault on Peleliu* (Washington, DC: U.S. Marine Corps History Division, 1950); Gordon D. Gayle, *Bloody Beaches: The Marines at Peleliu* (Washington, DC: U.S. Marine Corps History Division, 1996); Bill D. Ross, *Peleliu: Tragic Triumph* (New York: Random House, 1991); "'Fury in the Pacific' WWII Battle of Peleliu 1944 Marianas Island Campaign (print 2) 22234," archival newsreel, U.S. Army, Navy, and Marine Corps, 1944, licensed by Periscope Film, YouTube video; "U.S. Marines Intense Combat Footage Battle of Peleliu and Ngesebus Island WW2 w/Sound," archival newsreel, undated, YouTube video; "Marine Combat on 'Bloody Nose Ridge' in the Pacific's Battle of Peleliu with Frank Pomroy," video interview with archival newsreel footage, American Veterans Center,

undated, YouTube video; Eugene B. Sledge, *With the Old Breed: At Peleliu and Okinawa* (Novato, CA: Presidio Press, 1981).

18. The U.S. Army 81st Infantry Division was held in reserve but wound up playing an important role in the battle when the 1st Marine Regiment had to be pulled off the front line. The 81st took over the mopping-up phase of the battle from the 1st Division staff.
19. Hough, *Assault on Peleliu,* 14–15, 24–25.
20. Hough, *Assault on Peleliu,* 37.
21. Hough, *Assault on Peleliu,* 25–29.
22. There were effectively no threats to American warships and aircraft operating around and above Peleliu, so the crews could focus their efforts on fire support without distraction or serious risk.
23. Including Charles River Editors, *The Warsaw Uprising of 1944: The History of the Polish Resistance's Failed Attempt to Liberate Poland's Capital from Nazi Germany* (2016), ebook; Alexandra Richie, *Warsaw 1944: Hitler, Himmler, and the Warsaw Uprising* (New York: St. Martin's Press ebook, 2013); J. K. Zawodny, *Nothing but Honour: The Story of the Warsaw Uprising, 944* (Stanford, CA: Hoover Institution Press, 1978); Warsaw Uprising 1944, http://www.warsawuprising.com.
24. For example, see Richie, *Warsaw 1944,* 198. The Poles also employed captured German anti-tank rockets during the battle, but not in significant quantities.
25. Richie, *Warsaw 1944,* 416.
26. Richie, *Warsaw 1944,* 399.
27. Richie, *Warsaw 1944,* 408.
28. See Richie, *Warsaw 1944,* 54, 340, 416–417, 441, 520, 562, and 783.
29. Including David Dexter, *Australia in the War of 1939–1945, Series 1: Army, Volume VI, The New Guinea Offensives* (Canberra: Government of Australia, 1963); Christopher Somerville, *Our War: How the British Commonwealth Fought the Second World War* (London: Weidenfeld & Nicolson, 1998); Gavin Long, *Australia in the War of 1939–1945, Series 1: Army, Volume VII, The Final Campaigns* (Canberra: Government of Australia, 1963); "Australian Soldiers Fire as They Advance on Tarakan Island in Borneo, Indonesia Dutch East Indies, HD Stock Footage," archival newsreel, CriticalPast, undated, YouTube video.
30. Long, *Australia in the War,* 407–408.
31. The rest of this section is drawn from Long, *Australia in the War,* 415–451.
32. Long, *Australia in the War,* 447, footnote.
33. Sources for this case include Japanese Imperial Army, *Record of Operations Against Soviet Russia, Eastern Front (August 1945),* captured military document (published by Headquarters, Army Forces Far East, 1945); David M. Glantz, *August Storm: The Soviet 1945 Strategic Offensive in Manchuria* (Fort Leavenworth, KS: U.S. Army Command and General Staff College, 1983); "Battlefield—Manchuria: The Forgotten Victory—Part 1," video documentary, *The War Channel,* April 25, 2020, YouTube video; Lilita I. Dzirkals, *"Lightning War" in Manchuria: Soviet Military Analysis of the 1945 Far East Campaign* (Santa Monica, CA: RAND Corporation, 1976).
34. Glantz, *August Storm,* 51.
35. Glantz, *August Storm,* 115.
36. Glantz, *August Storm,* 120.

37. Japanese Imperial Army, *Record of Operations,* 69. Casualty counts cited here are estimates.
38. Records show 1,137 aircraft flying in support of the Soviet 1st Red Banner Army, 5th Army, and 25th Army in the Manchuria campaign. Glantz, *August Storm,* 42.
39. Including James Luto, *Fighting with the Fourteenth Army in Burma* (South Yorkshire, UK: Pen & Sword Books, 2013); S. Woodburn Kirby, *The War against Japan: Volume IV—The Reconquest of Burma* (London: Her Majesty's Stationary Office, 1968); Donovan Webster, *The Burma Road* (New York: Farrar, Straus, and Giroux, 2003); Lucy Betteridge-Dyson, "A Brief History of 44 Royal Marine Commando at the Battle of Hill 170," online article (September 2, 2020, https://royalmarineshistory.com); "1 Commando, War Diary of Hill 170," http://www.commandoveterans.org.
40. Kirby, *War against Japan,* 220–224.
41. This paragraph and specific reference to the 2-inch mortar are drawn from the Commando Veterans website, official timeline, and narrative of the battle.
42. Smoke can also be employed in the defense, typically to confuse attackers or to conceal a withdrawal or local counterattack.
43. Including James Lunt, *Jai Sixth! 6th Queen Elizabeth's Own Gurkha Rifles 1817–1994* (London: Leo Cooper, 1994); J. G. H. Corrigan, "The Battle of Medicina," online article, https://www.6thgurkhas.org; "The Battle of Medicina—The 14/20 Hussars and Gurkhas in Italy," video podcast, WW2 TV, May 14, 2021, YouTube video.
44. The Kangaroo is an ad hoc armored personnel carrier (APC) made by removing the turret from a Sherman tank and adding an open-top troop compartment, or by removing the gun component from an M7 Priest with the same troop modifications up top. For a Canadian take on the Kangaroo, see John R. Grodzinski, "'Kangaroos at War': The History of the 1st Canadian Armoured Personnel Carrier Regiment," *Canadian Military History* 4, no. 2 (1995): 43–50.
45. Reports on German tanks in this battle are conflicting. There are sources that refer to Panthers, MkIVs, and Tigers.
46. This narrative is drawn primarily from the 6th Gurkha's official account and the 14/20 Hussars documentary.
47. Corrigan, "Battle of Medicina." For more on the Panzerschreck, see chapter 4, "Anti-Armor weapons."
48. Some experts might argue that this period should include the Japanese invasion of China and other pre-1939 operations.
49. The Battle of the Bulge, or German Ardennes Offensive, was a large-scale battle between the peak high-technology American armed forces and the peak high-technology German armed forces from December 1944 through January 1945. See, for example, Hugh M. Cole, *The Ardennes: Battle of the Bulge* (Washington, DC: Center of Military History, 1993).

THREE

World War II Ground Combat Characteristics

How can we set the World War II ground combat baseline? The research questions posed in the introduction can be summed up to help guide this effort: At least in the coded cases, what weapons, equipment, and munitions did both sides employ? How were the two sides organized for ground combat, and what kinds of tactics did they employ? These descriptions, which include some important prewar historical tracing, also feed directly into the debate over the existence of military-technical revolutions affecting ground combat. All of these are derived from the case studies listed in chapter 2 and from a review of other cited secondary sources.

LOW-LEVEL INTEGRATED COMBINED ARMS

While all combatants used combined arms throughout the First World War, World War II was really the first war in which combined arms were used in all battles with few exceptions, also in many skirmishes, and at all levels of tactical scale.[1] Mortars and machineguns were ubiquitous in nearly all infantry units in all armed forces, reflecting a gradual shift away from World War I-era separate heavy weapons units like machinegun battalions and toward integrated combined-arms firepower at the company level, or at units of between about 80 and 140 soldiers.[2] This drive toward lowest-level integrated direct and indirect fire capability had become the gold standard for infantry design by the end of the war.

For example, the U.S. Army's expeditionary infantry forces in World War I generally were organized at the brigade level, with the early-war brigade consisting of about 8,000 soldiers and later-war brigades manned at about 5,500 soldiers.[3] Most of the infantry brigades that saw action in Europe in World War I had a three-company machinegun battalion, and later versions had a light mortar and a 37mm light artillery platoon assigned to each regiment.[4] This

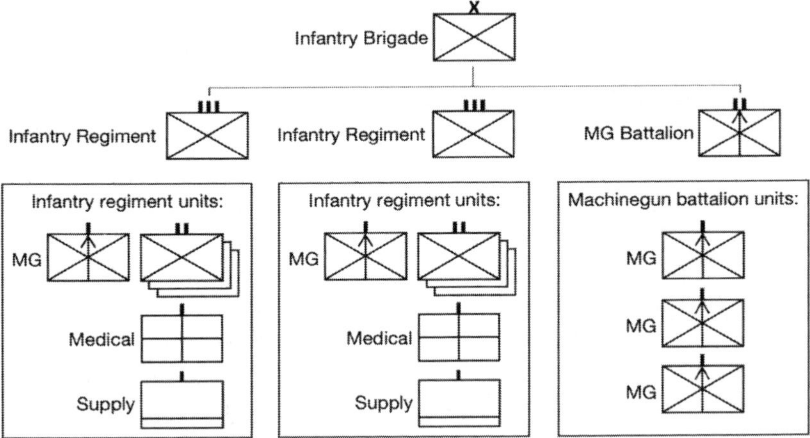

FIGURE 3.1. U.S. Army Infantry Brigade in World War I
Note: This figure is derived from McGrath, 2004, 34. Each unit (brigade, regiment, battalion, company) is depicted as a rectangular block. An "x" above a unit marker denotes a brigade, three lines a regiment, two lines a battalion, and one line a company. Crossed lines within a unit marker denote an infantry unit. The addition of an upward arrow to an infantry unit denotes a machinegun (MG) unit. A perpendicular cross denotes a medical unit, and a single low line denotes a supply unit. In this formation, each infantry battalion had four subordinate rifle companies. This figure does not include small headquarters and ordnance units depicted in the original graphic in McGrath, 2004.

meant that frontline infantry commanders who wanted heavy fire support to integrate with their organic rifle fire needed to borrow it from their higher-echelon commanders. Riflemen and junior officers down at the company level of organization would view machineguns and mortars as add-on capabilities, not integral combined-arms tools.[5]

This all changed through the first years of World War II. By 1940, Army infantry battalions were given their own 81mm mortars and heavy machineguns, and each infantry company was given its own 60mm mortars and medium machineguns.[6] This meant that a U.S. Army infantry company commander in World War II was capable of employing combined arms with no additional support, and he could also attach his organic mortars to lower-level platoons of thirty to forty soldiers to give them their own combined-arms capability. These organic indirect- and direct-fire weapons allowed for shifts in tactics to more dispersed operations, giving infantry companies some capability to independently attack and defend. With considerable variation, other military forces also pushed indirect-fire capabilities down to lower-echelon commanders. This basic U.S. Army structure has remained relatively consistent for both Army and Marine Corps infantry units through the mid 2020s.

ARMOR

Tanks are the mechanical heroes of the Blitzkrieg story that captivated so many of the American military experts and forecasters I took to task in chapter 1. While tanks may have fallen out of favor with some experts in the 2020s, they have played an unavoidably important role in ground combat for over a century, most notably in Ukraine from 2014 through at least 2024. All land armies designed and employed their own tanks before and throughout World War II, and large parts of the American, British, German, Japanese, and Soviet military-industrial bases were given over to producing more and better tanks, more and better explosive and kinetic shells to penetrate the armor of enemy tanks, and—as we shall see below—more and better ways to keep tank-heavy forces from overwhelming the infantry in ground combat.

Well over 200,000 tanks were produced by all combatant countries through 1945.[7] It really takes a daylong tour through the sprawling Tank Museum at Bovington Camp, England, to gain a full appreciation for the wide varieties of armored vehicles designed, tested, and employed in ground combat through World War II. There were the tiny Italian Carro Armato L6/40s with their paper-thin armor and peashooter 20mm autocannons, the workhorse Soviet T-34s, American Shermans, British Matildas, Japanese Type-97s, and German Panzer Mark IVs, and then the heavier tanks adapted to survive on an increasingly lethal battlefield: the German Tiger II, the Soviet KV-85, the American M-26 Pershing, and others.[8]

In parallel to the development of what are generally called main battle tanks, several countries fielded assault guns like the German Sturmgeschütz III.[9] These were designed specifically to provide infantry with *mobile protected firepower*, a genericized 2020s-era term generally intended to describe infantry-support vehicles; see the section "Infantry-Armor Teaming" below.

Tanks are loud, consume sometimes enormous amounts of fuel, require extensive maintenance, and are no good in heavy mud or very dense or steep terrain. But all these tanks added at least three characteristics to World War II ground combat: (1) They allowed battlefield commanders to quickly move heavy direct-fire weapons over rough ground into places of tactical advantage; (2) they reduced risks to friendly infantry advancing under fire; and (3) they often instilled fear in enemy troops to help erode their will to fight. Tanks were invaluable assets for the Soviet divisions operating on the plains outside Mutanchiang city and for the Canadian infantry advancing through the streets of Ortona. In other cases, they probably were the wrong tool for the job or just poorly employed; the 1944 British tank disaster in Northern France during Operation Goodwood is a latter case in point.[10] Chapters 5–9 show the tank's sometimes unsung, sometimes overstated, but generally enduring role in more modern ground combat.

VEHICLE-BORNE INFANTRY

Tanks alone cannot hold ground once it is captured. All of these relatively fast-moving tank units required infantry that could keep pace on the steppes of Russia and Manchuria, across the vast rolling deserts of North Africa, through the French and Italian farmlands, and across the Rhineland. Trucks allowed for what is generally called *motorized* infantry movement. Soldiers mounted up into unarmored transport trucks and drove through relatively safe rear areas until they reached the rearmost part of the front lines, dismounted, and then walked into battle. If the trucks moved too close to the front, they would be wiped out by enemy artillery, tanks, or even by light infantry. Understandable risk calculus prevented motorized infantry from moving alongside tanks into combat. Tank units backed by truck-borne infantry had to move in stutter steps, reducing their ability to outmaneuver the enemy. Lightly armored infantry carriers would at least allow infantry to move closer to the front lines or even to attack across open terrain in line with tanks.[11] Increasingly heavy dependence on tanks through World War II drove the development of *mechanized* infantry tactics and the technical development of the *armored personnel carrier* (APC) and the *infantry fighting vehicle* (IFV).[12]

Arguably, the German Wehrmacht and the U.S. Army made the biggest strides toward the development of mechanized infantry forces and tactics before and through World War II.[13] In the years leading up to American entry into the war in 1941, the U.S. Army experimented with truck and half-track integration into an armor division to form a combined armor-infantry organization.[14] Commander of the U.S. Army's tank forces Adna R. Chaffee Jr. rebuilt the existing 4th Armored Division—the same lineal division that would later serve as the testbed for the Army's 1990s-era Task Force XXI military-technical revolution experiment—as an armored infantry unit.[15] In 1940 the 4th Division of less than 15,000 soldiers had over 2,700 vehicles including more than 600 infantry half-tracks.[16] These were lightly armored trucks with wheels in the front and tracks in the rear to improve rough terrain mobility and to keep pace with the division's tanks.

The 4th mechanized armor-infantry division played a key role in the encirclement of the French city of Nancy in 1944.[17] At this late point in the war the division had been modified from the experimental early-war structure. It fielded about 11,000 troops, 263 light and medium tanks, 54 organic self-propelled M-7 artillery pieces—more on these vehicles in the "Artillery" section below—and hundreds of half-tracks to move its three mechanized infantry battalions.[18] As the mechanized 3rd German Panzergrenadier Division counterattacked against Army forces north of the city, the 4th Division cut south, using the speed of its mechanized infantry battalions to interdict some of the retreating German troops.[19] An Army report on the battle for Nancy stated that this was "one of the few historical examples that shows American mechanized forces waging war in accordance with the tenets of AirLand Battle."[20] Whether or not this was objectively true, combining tanks with mechanized infantry was a well-tested concept by the end of the war. Infantry-armor teaming also advanced as a ground combat technique.[21]

INFANTRY-ARMOR TEAMING

Infantry-armor teaming is a technique employed by both foot-mobile and vehicle-borne infantry. Sometimes referred to as armor-infantry teaming, this is the integration of tanks or lighter armored vehicles like assault guns—mobile protected firepower—with foot soldiers to advance through difficult terrain like city streets or defended cave networks like those found on Peleliu in 1944. Infantry troops move forward and clear terrain while the accompanying tanks provide the kind of heavy firepower the soldiers could not hope to carry or drag along on their own. If the infantry can keep enemy soldiers from bringing anti-tank weapons to bear, then the armor can give their own infantry a significant direct-fire advantage by blasting apart pillboxes and suppressing enemy soldiers with mounted machinegun fire. At least in close terrain, armor and infantry generally work better together than apart: Tanks working alone often are killed by infantry anti-armor weapons, and infantry working alone often suffer heavy casualties without mobile protected firepower.

Given the pervasive threat from infantry-armor teams and also from large tank formations like those employed by the Germans during the initial phase of the war in Europe, there was urgent need for reliable anti-armor capabilities at the outset of the war. Some detail on the development of anti-armor weapons is necessary to help set this World War II baseline of ground combat characteristics, but also to help frame the early 2020s debates over the role and value of armor, rockets, and missiles in ground combat.[22]

ANTI-ARMOR WEAPONS

Anti-armor weapons emerged shortly after the first tank saw action in World War I.[23] Krepinevich might describe this as an example of the metronomic exchange of military-technical innovation and counter-innovation during war. Armor on the first tanks was capable of stopping basic rifle and machinegun bullets. World War I-era anti-tank rifles like the Mauser 1918 T-Gewehr were capable of punching through the relatively thin armor of these first battle tanks, and rifles like the 14mm Boys and the 20mm Finnish Lahti L-39 saw continuing service through World War II and beyond.[24] But anti-tank rifle rounds lost power at extended ranges and were generally less capable of penetrating the increasingly thick armor of contemporaneous World War II-era battle tanks like the Panzer Mk IV or the British Mk IV Churchill. Hand-drawn or towed anti-tank guns proliferated and were made increasingly powerful over the course of the war, but they were cumbersome and their crews were vulnerable to rifle and machinegun fire.[25] Shoulder-fired rockets offered a good alternative source of anti-tank firepower.

The United States is largely credited with the design and employment of the first effective, mass-produced anti-tank rocket, the M1A1 Bazooka. Military rocket technology had evolved gradually from the earliest Chinese employment of incendiary rockets in at least the fourteenth century at the Siege of Souzhou (1366), through the employment of the Congreve indirect-fire rocket in the Anglo-Mysore Wars (1767–1792) and the Crimean War (1853–1856), through to Robert H. Goddard's prototype infantry rocket launcher in 1918.[26] Max Von Foerster developed the cavity charge explosive effect in 1883, which over several decades of international experimentation was developed into the modern shaped-charge warhead.[27]

Both components for the anti-armor rocket—the rocket and the shaped-charge warhead—existed at least by 1935. American experimentation with both technologies continued through the interwar period. But investment in new military production had lagged in Europe and the United States in the 1930s. No country had developed a viable mass-produced anti-tank rocket by the start of World War II. Then in 1941 U.S. Army officers watched the tank-heavy Wehrmacht advance through Poland and the Western Soviet Union. They quickly focused resources on developing countermeasures.

American weapons designers paired the rocket and shaped-charge warhead in the 2.36-inch M1A1, which was eventually replaced by a more powerful 3.5-inch rocket. Japanese designers did not build a viable anti-tank rocket until the end of the war and never put one into production.[28] The Germans developed the Raketenpanzerbuchse (Panzerschreck) and Panzerfaust, and the British and Commonwealth forces developed and employed the PIAT.[29] All of these Allied and Axis weapons gave infantry the ability to destroy tanks, partially resetting an early-war imbalance in power between infantry and armor. And all of these designs served as templates for the important rockets and missiles that would follow, including the Soviet RPG-7 rocket and the Soviet Malyutka and Kornet anti-tank guided missiles, the British NLAW rocket, the French Milan anti-tank missile, and the American M-72 LAAW rocket, BGM-71 TOW missile, and then the Javelin fire-and-forget anti-tank missile popularized in the 2022– Ukraine War.[30]

ARTILLERY

From at least the early twentieth century, artillery generally was considered to be a ground-fired smooth-bore or rifled weapon using powder charges to launch an explosive projectile in an indirect arc.[31] The term *artillery* is also frequently used to describe indirect-fire ground-to-ground rockets like the ubiquitous Katyusha (later Grad) multiple-launch rocket systems developed in the early part of World War II. Albert Manucy starts his book on the history of artillery with two sentences that drive right to the heart of the debate over military-technical revolutions and ground combat: "To compare a Roman catapult with a modern trench mortar seems absurd. Yet the only basic difference is the kind of energy that sends the projectile on its way."[32]

The explosion of the mortar round at the far end of its parabola also differentiates it from a solid catapult shot. But Manucy was suggesting that it is more important to think about the intended purpose of the tool of war than it is to think about its transient form. The point of artillery is to loft a projectile from one point on the ground to strike an enemy target at a distant point on other ground. Artillery is relatively more effective when it can loft that projectile further, more accurately, with fewer seconds between shots, and with relatively more devastating effect at the point of impact.

In purely technical terms, artillery technology clearly evolved from about the fourth-century BCE to what was comparatively far more devastating form by the end of World War II. A Roman onager swing-arm catapult probably could launch a ~60 pound stone capable of cracking a wall about 1,000 meters away, while a World War II-era American M1 240mm howitzer could launch a 360-pound high-explosive shell capable of knocking down a building out to more than 16,000 meters.[33] This is a dramatic difference in capability achieved through creeping, centuries-long evolutionary change: The need to strike an enemy from a distance led to progressive global innovations that over the course of about fifteen centuries gradually improved artillery range, accuracy, reloading speed, and impact damage.

All armies in World War II made liberal use of artillery, sometimes employing just one or two tubes or rocket launchers in smaller engagements and at other times employing quantities of artillery exceeding those used in iconic World War I battles like the Somme. British preparatory fires at the Somme in 1916 reportedly consisted of 1,537 artillery pieces. British artillerymen launched approximately 3,526,000 rounds at the German defenders over several months.[34] By comparison, Soviet commanders at the 1945 battle for Seelow Heights directed several thousand artillery pieces and rocket launchers to reportedly fire well over one million rounds at German defenders in one day, and the Germans shot right back with their own massive barrages.[35] Intensive artillery employment at both of these battles—the Somme in 1916 and Seelow Heights in 1945—was impressive. But while these attacks were quite dramatic, they did not generate their intended outcomes.

At the Somme in World War I, German defenders well accustomed to heavy artillery barrages and had dug deep bunkers, built impressive concrete emplacements capable of shrugging off even heavy artillery strikes, and in had general designed their fortifications to withstand exactly the kind of shelling the British dished out.[36] German defenders weathered the bombardment and on the first day of infantry advances at the Somme, British infantry suffered approximately 57,470 total casualties including over 19,000 dead.[37] At Seelow Heights in World War II, German defenders well accustomed to Soviet doctrine—smash and advance—had dug impressive trench lines but left little to chance: They withdrew their troops to rearward positions during the bombardment and then moved back up as soon as the shelling had ended.[38] The poor Soviet troops moving across the Oder River on the first day were stopped cold with heavy losses.[39]

Both the Somme and Seelow Heights cases reinforce Manucy's point regarding function over form. Despite important advances in accuracy and responsiveness, the fundamental point of artillery remained consistent from World War I through the end of World War II: Launch a shell from one point on the ground to another to harm enemy troops and their equipment.[40] Naturally, the enemy on the receiving end of the shells had little interest in their own destruction, so they took countermeasures like adding layers of physical protection, hiding themselves from observation, and moving out of the way of the shells.

Even significant World War II-era advances in technique and technical capability like increasing accuracy, improved aerial spotting, and radio direction targeting did not endow artillery-launched explosives with magical powers of destruction. What artillery did provide was *responsive* and *repeatable* firepower for ground combat forces. Self-propelled artillery like the M7 Priest, a 105mm howitzer mounted on a lightly armored tracked carriage, added responsive mobile firepower to fast-moving ground combat organizations like the 4th Armored Infantry Division.[41] Repeatability, or the ability to apply indirect fire over and over again for months on end, became a critical issue in 2020s-era debate over supporting fires.

CLOSE-AIR SUPPORT

Aircraft also played an essential ground combat support role in many—perhaps most—ground combat battles throughout World War II, including at Seelow Heights. As ground force leaders were improving their teaming with ground armor, many also improved their coordination with close-air support aircraft that employed machineguns, automatic cannons, unguided bombs, and unguided rockets to destroy enemy fortifications, armor, infantry, and supporting mortars and artillery.[42] When this kind of firepower is provided directly in support of ground forces engaged in direct-fire combat, it is referred to as close-air support, or CAS. Typically, strikes are called in by an observer with a radio working from the ground or from another aircraft who spots the enemy and talks the attacking aircraft on to the target using visual cues. In World War II these cues were usually nearby prominent terrain features like crossroads or hilltops, or some kind of signaling smoke. Cueing would evolve after World War II to include laser designators and other technology.

However, while close-air support tactics and technologies improved from 1939 through 1945, throughout the war a great number of global ground attack missions were tailored for *interdiction* missions. These typically are strikes against enemy rear-area units, airfields, or supply lines not in direct support of ground combat forces. Even when their general mission was to support ground troops, aircraft in all of the Allied and Axis militaries frequently operated not as an integrated combined-arms air-ground team but as independent air units ranging out over the battlefield looking for more distant targets. For example, while the Soviets arguably had one of the best ground attack aircraft in the war, the Il-2 Sturmovik, they did not clearly fly their Il-2s in close tactical support of, or under the control of, low-level ground commanders who were in direct contact with German ground forces.[43] Even if Red Army commanders had wanted to tie their attack aircraft more closely to their ground forces, their lack of sufficient and effective aircraft radios—and particularly the very-high frequency (and newer ultrahigh-frequency) radios that worked best for ground-air coordination—all but prohibited close teaming.[44]

By contrast, U.S. Marine Corps units built on their interwar experiences with close-air support in the Dominican Republic, Nicaragua, and elsewhere to establish what was at the very least one of the tightest air-to-ground support relationships of any fighting organization in World War II.[45] By late 1944, Marine forward air controllers routinely radio-directed the ground attacks of Marine aviators flying F4-variant Corsair fighter-bombers for pinpoint gun, rocket, and bomb attacks in direct support of ground troops. Marine Corps technical radio design and procurement were tailored for clear and reliable ground-air communication; technical acquisition followed tactical adaptation.

Even so, these Marine Corps missions represented what must have been a tiny fraction of overall aviation missions conducted in all ground combat actions from 1939 through 1945; they were not universally representative.[46] By the end of the war, most global infantry and armor forces tied up in a ground fight probably could not count on responsive or reliable close-air support.[47] This critical gap would narrow gradually for some armies over the following decades and, by the 2000s, would come to include the increasingly routine incorporation of drones.

DRONE OVERVIEW

All types of drones, including fixed-wing aircraft, rotary-wing aircraft, ground vehicles, and both surface and subsurface naval vessels, figure prominently into the changing-character-of-war debate through the mid 2020s. For the sake of simplicity, a military drone is any kind of remotely controlled or autonomous vehicle designed to carry out combat or support missions including reconnaissance, kinetic strike, or suicide attacks in which the drone is destroyed along with its explosive payload.[48] While the Germans and other powers produced and employed thousands of remote-controlled ground drones during the war, in general neither air nor ground drones figured prominently in World War II ground combat. Drone capabilities and tactics did, however, continue to evolve through the mid 1940s toward important ground support roles in the early 1980s and into the early 2020s.

Aerial Drones

Early experimentation with aerial drones started in 1908 with Albert L. Stevens's design for a controllable airship.[49] By the time World War I was in full swing, design of new airships, glide bombs, and remote-controlled aircraft accelerated and effectively culminated in the successful testing of the American Kettering Bug and the Italian Crocco Telebomb in 1918.[50] Both of these were described as aerial torpedoes, or what today are called kamikaze or suicide drones.

Neither the Kettering Bug nor the Telebomb were used in combat in World War I, but aerial drone experimentation and even some limited production continued through the interwar period. In 1929 the British successfully flew a Larynx suicide test drone into an inert naval target.[51] In 1940 Italian air crews attempted a live operational attack against British shipping with a Marchetti SM.79 Sparviero propeller plane. Fortunately for the British sailors, the Italian drone veered off course and crashed in the nearby mountains.[52]

While the Italian attack failed, the U.S. Navy successfully employed television-guided drone bombers to attack Japanese ships anchored near the island of Bougainville in the Pacific Ocean.[53] Surviving camera footage of test bomb runs against abandoned Japanese ships shows sailors guiding the drones from what look like a primitive version of a modern drone video control station.[54]

In 1944 U.S. Army Air Corps pilots flew a television-guided PB4Y Liberator suicide drone packed with high explosives directly into a German base at Heligoland in the North Sea. An American observer at the airborne television control station recalled the drone making its final attack run on the German barracks and fuel farm below: "In my television screen several miles away at about 5,000 feet, I could see trees, streetcars, automobiles, windows in barracks, an airfield complete with airplanes and the enemy running by the hundreds to take cover. . . . The control pilot [in the] mother plane guided the drone as if he were in it, straight toward the airfield. . . . I watched the hit. . . . It was the largest explosion I had ever seen."[55]

The Germans built two versions of the Mistel-series production drones, one an unproven air-to-air fighter and another a suicide bomber, and they flew a handful of successful drone combat missions. They also fitted a camera to a drone for successful reconnaissance use.[56] In 1945 the German Luftwaffe planned a 100-drone suicide Mistel attack—what might today be called a drone swarm attack—with accompanying bombers carrying their own radio-controlled glide bombs.[57] Bad weather repeatedly delayed the attack, and eventually the launch sites were overrun by enemy ground forces, ending the Luftwaffe's experiment with drone warfare. Despite some limited success, none of these international programs (or the many others not listed here) were in any way integrated into ground combat operations by the end of the war.

Ground Drones

Remote-control ground vehicle development paralleled aerial drone programs. The first viable designs emerged right before World War I, and testing of "land torpedoes" continued through the end of ground combat operations in 1918. These tracked explosive robots were controlled by wires or radio signals and intended to destroy enemy obstacles like barbed wire or even manned fortifications. None were ever successfully employed in combat in World War I, but like the Kettering Bug and the Crocco Telebomb they paved the way for interwar development and eventual combat use in the 1940s. The Soviets experimented with a number of remote-controlled tanks, but the Germans put the greatest effort into developing ground drones for combat employment.

German engineers designed two categories of ground drone for use in World War II: (1) land torpedoes, or ground suicide drones; and (2) mine-clearing drones. The most successful of these were the Borgward and Goliath tracked vehicles, both of which were employed extensively in ground combat.[58] World War II-era electronics generally were too fragile to allow for reliable use in a tracked ground drone, so their limited success was relative to a significant number of technical and tactical failures. Many of the ground drones broke, exploded before reaching their targets, failed to detonate, were shot by opposing infantry, or were blown apart by opposing force artillery.

Wehrmacht troops that had access to the Borgwards and Goliaths still made good use of both the suicide and mine-clearing variants, integrating them into assault plans when they were available. Goliaths were small enough to be lashed to the backs of tanks and piggybacked into battle, where they were then offloaded and used to destroy obstacles and bunkers. In 1942 the Germans also retrofitted captured Allied tracked vehicles with remote controls and explosives, successfully detonating them against Soviet positions near Sevestopol. In one engagement, ad hoc German ground drones cleared a minefield lane, killed Soviet soldiers in a trench line, destroyed several bunkers and an ammunition storage point, and were then successfully employed in urban combat against Soviet riflemen.[59] German troops also used Goliath mines in the 1944 Warsaw Uprising, one of the cases I coded for this book. Overall, probably thousands of German ground drones were employed in combat in World War II.[60]

PRECISION-GUIDED MUNITIONS

Suicide drones are a type of precision-guided munition, or PGM. Therefore, early drone development also was early PGM development, and the suicide-drone examples above count as examples of precision munitions in combat. Usually when military experts talk about these kinds of munitions, they mean air-delivered guided bombs or missiles launched from airplanes or from ground stations. The German V-1 and V-2 missiles are probably the best-known examples of guided munitions in World War II. Both were preprogrammed guided missiles capable of long-range flight. The V-1 was launched from both aircraft and ground platforms, while the larger V-2 was a ground-only system.

Germany probably manufactured about 30,000 of the more effective and deadly V-1s and launched over 10,000 of them at London as strategic terror weapons.[61] If the V-1s were ever used to directly support ground combat forces, those events were not well recorded. In any event, the V-1's relatively poor accuracy when compared to radio-controlled suicide drones like the U.S. Navy's TDR-1 or the German Mistel—measured in miles rather than in meters—and the inability to reprogram the missiles in flight rendered them all but useless in a fluid ground combat situation.

The U.S. Army Air Corps attempted to rectify these accuracy and responsiveness problems by adding radio control guidance to their version of the German V-1, the JB-2. Ground-tracking radar could have been used to guide the missile onto target from up to 100 miles away, but tests were disappointing and the tactic was never employed in combat.[62] The Americans did fire several preprogrammed JB-2s in combat against the Germans with accuracy and impact results similar to those of the German V-1s being fired in the opposite direction. Like the V-1s, the JB-2s also had no real utility in ground combat. But both munitions, the V-1 and the JB-2, served as a technical baseline for later guided missile development that would have sometimes significant impact on ground combat involving military forces with advanced technologies.[63]

Glide bombs designed during World War II also had limited immediate impact on ground combat but set a foundation for rapid post-war technical improvements that would feed directly into the late twentieth and early twenty-first-century debates over the ostensible recon-strike revolution. The Germans, Japanese, and Americans experimented with glide bombs, which in this early design phase were bombs with movable fins dropped from aircraft and guided to their targets by radio or television control.[64]

Germany designed and employed the radio-controlled PC 1400 X (Fritz-X) and used two of them to sink the Italian capital battleship *Roma* in 1943.[65] The United States put a few GB-4 television-guided glide bombs to use in the European theater.[66] Designers also experimented with early versions of fire-and-forget bombs and seeker bombs, which scanned for and then homed in on radar signatures. All of the radio-guided versions of these weapons were vulnerable to electronic jamming, a basic technical countermeasure that would feature prominently in the Ukraine War over seventy years after the end of World War II.[67]

OTHER WORLD WAR II TECHNOLOGY AND TECHNIQUES RELEVANT TO GROUND COMBAT

Many other technological advances, and attendant development of new battlefield techniques, characterized at least some ground combat actions in World War II. Many of them set important comparative baselines for the postwar cases. This is a brief survey of advances that recurred in the shifting characteristics of observable ground combat through the early 2020s, order not implying relative significance:

Infrared and thermal scopes. With some notable exceptions, darkness typically slowed ground combat through at least the end of World War II.[68] Flares could illuminate a battlefield but would give away both friendly and enemy movements. Any ability to see through darkness would therefore give significant advantage, allowing tactical movements at night and opening new opportunities for surprise attack, or improved defense against night attack. Infrared technology experiments ran from the early 1800s, and basic infrared devices were used during World War I.[69] Specific infrared night-vision technology was envisioned and tested in the 1920s.[70] Early devices were adopted for military use by the Germans in the 1930s and employed in limited quantities in ground combat in American sniper scopes and German tank sights, but both saw only limited use in World War II.

Wireless communication. Near-instant two-way, mobile radio communication gave ground combat commanders the ability to direct their forces without the kind of potentially lethal delays common in most nineteenth-century warfare. It allowed for ground-to-air directions, the control of naval gunfire, and other support.[71] Longer radio ranges allowed for more distributed force design—smaller, more independent units—and dispersed tactics across a larger battlefield. Radio communications also created vulnerabilities: They could be intercepted or jammed, and radiolocation could help enemy forces pinpoint transmitters and kill friendly soldiers.[72] Between 1945 and the early 2020s, wireless communication would evolve to include satellite and microwave transmission, cellular telephones, data transfer, global positioning, and other technologies.

Electronic warfare. Histories of electronic warfare through World War II focus almost exclusively on air and naval warfare.[73] Combatants in aircraft, on ships, and at ground stations fought each other for control of the electromagnetic spectrum in the air and over water.[74] There is far less focus on ground combat applications, but ground uses emerged in parallel. Ground transmitters and receivers in all major armies were used to jam enemy ground force transmissions and to track and target enemy troop movements. For example, in their opening ground offensive, the Germans were able to track French troops landing on Walcheren Island and later in the war track British ground force movements in Norway and North Africa.[75]

Naval gunfire support. Ships have trained their mounted weapons on enemy positions ashore for centuries, and dedicated fire-support ships (e.g., floating batteries) were employed by naval forces from at least the mid 1800s.[76] British Royal Navy vessels bombarded shore positions and broke up Turkish counterattacks in support of the Gallipoli amphibious landings in World War I.[77] In World War II, techniques like two-way radio communication and aerial target spotting improved the responsiveness, accuracy, and lethality of naval gunfire. Parallel technical advances like improved gun range and accuracy, deck-mounted siege rockets, and radar-directed fires would also make naval gunfire more responsive and deadly by the end of the war. During World War II, British, American, Japanese, and other navies would fire tens of millions of shells in support of ground combat operations around the world.[78]

Aerial observation. Readers will see a clear theme here: A need for support is identified, experimentation follows, and in fits and starts over decades or centuries, capabilities are improved. Ground combatants have long sought to spot and track enemy ground forces over low-lying visual obstructions like trees and hills. Better observation comes from achieving greater heights, better angles of view, longer viewing distances, more survivable observation assets, and the ability to quickly and reliably transmit observations to friendly commanders. Balloons were used for early aerial reconnaissance, probably first by the French at the Second Battle of Fleurus in 1794 and later during the siege of Paris, then by the Americans in their 1860s Civil War.[79]

Balloons remained in service through and well beyond World War II, but winged aircraft proved far more effective in most situations. Fixed-wing manned aircraft observation and photography were employed extensively from the middle part of World War I, and aerial observation was fully integrated into larger-scale ground combat operations like those at Medicina in 1945. Observation planes including the Soviet Po-2, Japanese D4Y Suisei, American L-4, and modified fighters and bombers would all support ground forces by spotting troop movements, transmitting targets for artillery and naval gunfire, etc.[80]

Helicopters. Basic rotary-wing aircraft theories and designs are centuries old (e.g., Leonardo da Vinci's famous fifteenth-century drawing of an aerial gyroscope), but experimental helicopters did not emerge until about the early 1920s.[81] Functional helicopters were tested in the early years of World War II and put into limited production.[82] They all suffered from design limitations, most of which would be gradually ironed out through the second half of the twentieth century. During World War II the Americans, Germans, and British developed and employed a limited number of helicopters in anti-submarine, rescue, transport, and observation roles.[83] They had effectively no impact on ground combat in any theater. However, even this limited operational experience established a baseline for rapid development of helicopter technology through the 1950s, particularly in support of U.S. Marine Corps operations in the Korean War (1950–1953).

Antiaircraft defenses. Ground forces can be spotted, tracked, attacked, and destroyed by aircraft, so ground combat units need antiaircraft defenses to keep enemy planes and drones off their backs. The first dedicated antiaircraft guns probably did not appear until early in World War I. These early versions were simply artillery pieces and machineguns modified for improved elevation.[84] Dedicated systems were quickly designed and employed as the air threat took on greater significance, and by the end of World War I about 1,000 total aircraft may have been shot down by ground fires.[85] By the end of World War II, antiaircraft artillery (AAA) was well advanced, with radio proximity fuses, radar direction finding, and guns capable of ranging over 32,000 feet in ceiling.[86] Most importantly for ground combat forces, mobile air defense guns were designed and fully integrated into ground unit design.[87] What is typically called "short-range air defense," or SHORAD, evolved as a technique, a doctrine, and as a technology to the point that it was generally considered as essential as tanks or logistics.[88]

Flame weapons. Some military technologies evolved toward wider and more effective use during World War II, while others reached at least a temporary peak of employment. Fire inflicts terrible wounds, terrifies, and destroys, so—divorced from moral and ethical considerations tied with its use—it is an excellent tool for ground combat.[89] Historic uses of flame weapons precede the Common Era, while the man-portable flamethrower was first employed against ground troops in World War I. Man-portable, vehicle-borne, and air-delivered flame weapons and munitions were widely employed in all theaters in World War II, often to great effect. The Churchill Crocodile tank could launch a concentrated jet of jellied gasoline about 100 meters into enemy trenches and bunkers, terrifying and incinerating enemy troops.[90] However, most military forces had removed flame weapons from their inventories by the early 1980s.[91] They were still used less frequently thereafter.[92]

Chemical, biological, and radiological weapons. Despite prewar conventions against the use of chemical weapons, most combatants employed them with zeal through World War I.[93] The horrors of chemical wounds and deaths through 1918 mitigated strongly against their use on the battlefield in World War II.[94] However, the Japanese employed chemical munitions in a number of ground combat battles, particularly against the Chinese; they reportedly did so at Changde in 1942.[95] Japanese forces also employed biological weapons against Chinese civilians. While the war between Japan and the Allied Powers was effectively ended by the strategic employment of atomic weapons in 1945, there was no battlefield use of nuclear or radiological weapons in ground combat in World War II.

Rifles. Machineguns are lethal, but they are generally used to suppress enemy troops so friendly infantry can both move and deliver accurate rifle fire. Ground combat forces started using shoulder-fired gunpowder weapons in the sixteenth century. These evolved from short-range smoothbore guns to rifles that imparted a spin on bullets to significantly increase accuracy and range. Infantry rifles are relatively more useful when they can seriously wound or kill an enemy soldier with fewer rounds, with more accuracy, at longer ranges, and with less time needed to reload between shots.

Effective, mass-produced shoulder-fired rifles were integrated into most large-scale ground combat forces by the end of the nineteenth century. Infantry rifles in World War I like the Russian Mosin-Nagant M1891 could be used to kill an enemy soldier at 500 meters using only iron sights, but they were heavy, slow to reload, and had limited magazine capacity.[96] Repeating rifles like the American M-1 Garand proliferated early in World War II, and by the end of the war all forces were moving toward faster-firing weapons with larger magazines.[97] Scopes were still tools for specialists; riflemen had to direct their fire with the naked eye.

GROUND COMBAT INSIGHTS FROM WWII

Modern descriptions of the character of ground combat and more generally of war are all explicitly or implicitly anchored in the historical narrative of World War II. There is no avoiding the massive, yearslong clash of tens of millions of people using every tool at their disposal to terrify, break, crush, burn, lacerate, and puncture the flesh of their enemies. The term *conventional war* was given indelible meaning primarily by the large-scale engagements of combined-arms ground forces sweeping over empty deserts and steppes to engage each other with integrated fires from rifles, machineguns, cannons, mortars, artillery, rockets, flamethrowers, and aerial bombs.

Across the world, this ideation of *war* has been driven home through the postwar torrent of books, movies, television series still being produced in the 2020s. It is no wonder the path-dependent explanations of the ground combat interval period—the historical precedent to all modern descriptions and forecasts—are tied to the big, set-piece battles like the second battle of El Alamein in 1942 and later, the 1991 Gulf War and the 2003 invasion of Iraq.

Certainly, there is much to learn about ground combat from the set-piece battles of World War II. All the basic characteristics of modern ground combat were established or cemented on these battlefields. With a few potentially important exceptions like stealth technology, satellite communication, and artificial intelligence, every type of weapon, munition, vehicle, aircraft, tactic, technique, and procedure employed in early 2020s ground combat has some lineal precedent dating back to at least the mid twentieth century and frequently to the turn of the century or earlier.

For example, a modern British Challenger 2 tank is clearly an evolutionary descendant of the World War I Mark 1 and the World War II-era Churchill. Modern MQ-9 Reaper drones that feature prominently in the debate over military-technical revolutions are clear evolutionary decedents of the 1910s Kettering Bug and the U.S. Navy's mid-century TDR-1. And the new U.S. Army M7 service rifle, introduced in 2023, has the same basic functions as a sixteenth-century musket or a World War II-era M1 rifle: An infantryman points or aims the weapon, squeezes a trigger, and with lethal intent launches a direct-fire projectile toward an enemy soldier.[98] So, World War II ground combat was not always novel. But it was perhaps the single greatest showcase of all of these building-block characteristics of ground combat. It therefore rightfully recurs in our historical narrative.

However, as I show in the following chapters, fixation on the big World War II conventional ground battles has also done some harm to our collective ability to describe and forecast war. Popularized big World War II battles like the epic desert combat between British-led Allied forces and the Axis at El Alamein or the U.S. Marine Corps assault against dedicated Japanese defenders at Iwo Jima leave little room in the public imagination—or even in collective expert knowledge—for the thousands of smaller battles and skirmishes that took place in the shadows or across the less studied periphery.

Simple arithmetic ensures that most Western military officers will be far more familiar with the massive 1944 D-Day landings than they will with the lesser-known Battle for Hill 170 in Burma; there simply aren't enough hours in a human life to study all of these battles with equal and dedicated focus. Cultural filters narrow perspectives even further. For example, Chinese military officers probably are far more likely than their Western counterparts to be intimately familiar with the battle of Changde.

How, then, can we describe the character of World War II ground combat? Should it be defined by an aggregation of the big battles? If so, then at very least all global battles of similar scale should be included, Changde alongside El Alamein, and others. Should different types of big battles be characterized, like desert armor combat and mountain infantry combat? If World War II revealed anything about modern warfare, it is that terrain influences and in some cases dictates engagement ranges and the types of weapons that can be effectively brought to bear against the enemy. Sweeping division-level armor movements were not feasible in the island jungles of Guadalcanal in 1942, and heavy artillery was less effective against soldiers in rocky caves than against those on open grasslands. Terrain is therefore a good character-of-war differentiator.

But so then is scale: Different things happen when two infantry divisions of 15,000 soldiers reinforced by armor and aircraft fight each other and when two regular infantry platoons of thirty-five riflemen and light machine gunners go head to head. Varying availability of technology across national armies can affect the way battles play out. Another characterization of war might therefore be needed for different levels of conflict, different types of terrain, differing technology, and so on. Scratch the surface of this simple question, "What is the character of World War II ground combat?," and it quickly becomes clear that there is no good universal answer. The epistemology of the problem—the way we organize our understanding and existing knowledge—should at least give pause to anyone pursuing a definitive answer.

At least the basic building blocks for analysis of World War II battles are readily available. There typically are dozens of books published for every major battle. Most of the minor battles fought by major armies—the Germans, British, Americans, and to a lesser extent the Italians, Soviets, and Japanese—are recorded in official reports and narrow historical books that can be found online with a quick search and deep pockets for ebook purchases.

Thousands of skirmishes probably went unrecorded and are lost to history, but there is more than enough material to get a good sense of World War II ground combat at all levels, in all types of terrain, with different combatants, and with all different types of weapons, munitions, vehicles, and techniques. In terms of available scholarship and information on ground combat, World War II is a gold mine. After World War II, our collective understanding of global ground combat worsens unevenly but for the most part progressively by the decade.

NOTES

1. The Battle of Cambrai in World War I is often referred to as a representative case of combined-arms land warfare, with tanks, artillery, infantry, and aircraft working together to push through German defenses.
2. Machinegun battalions were still employed throughout World War II, though guns were also provided organically to infantry units. The British Army employed a machinegun battalion through at least 1944. For example, see George T. Raach, *A Withering Fire: American Machine Gun Battalions in World War I,* 2015, ebook; and "The Vickers Machine Gun and the Manchester Regiment," *Museum of the Manchester Regiment,* n.d., https://vickersmg.blog.
3. John J. McGrath, *The Brigade: A History, Its Organization and Employment in the US Army* (Fort Leavenworth, KS: Combat Studies Institute Press, 2004), 32–34; John B. Wilson, *The Evolution of Divisions and Separate Brigades* (Washington, DC: Center of Military History, 1998), 50; Virgil Ney, *Evolution of the U.S. Army Infantry Battalion: 1939–1968* (Fort Belvoir, VA: Technical Operations, Incorporated Combat Operations Research Group, October 1968), 7–8; Steven E. Clay, *U.S. Army Order of Battle, 1919–1941* (Fort Leavenworth, KS: Combat Studies Institute Press, 2010), 196–197.
4. McGrath, *The Brigade,* 33–34.
5. Light automatic magazine-fed weapons like the French Chauchat and M1918 Browning Automatic Rifle (BAR) were widely used in infantry line units, but these were not technically machineguns. See Chris Gentry, "Use of Machine Guns in First Army during World War I," *Over There,* no. 8 (March 2018).
6. Wilson, *Evolution of Divisions,* 144; and Ney, *Evolution of Infantry Battalion,* 68. Army infantry companies in 1942 had two organic .30 caliber machineguns, three 60mm mortars, and eleven Browning Automatic Rifles (BARs), which were the precursor to the 5.56mm Squad Automatic Weapon (SAW) employed in Iraq and Afghanistan, the newer 5.56mm M-27, and the 6.8mm M-250 SAW replacement issued to U.S. Army units starting in early 2024.
7. Mark Harrison, ed., *The Economics of World War II: Six Great Powers in International Comparison* (Cambridge, UK: Cambridge University Press, 1998), 18. This data only covers the period from 1942 through 1944, and it only accounts for production by six countries. Other countries also produced tanks, though in relatively lesser quantities. Also see David E. Johnson, *Fast Tanks and Heavy Bombers: Innovation in the U.S. Army, 1917–1945* (Ithaca, NY: Cornell University Press, 2013).
8. There are many references for World War II-era armored vehicles. See, for example, The Smithsonian, *Tank: The Definitive Visual History of Armored Vehicles* (London: DK, 2017); U.S. War Department, *Handbook on German Military Forces,* TM-E 30–451 (Washington, DC, March, 1945); U.S. War Department, *Soldier's Guide to the Japanese Army* (Washington, DC: Military Intelligence Service, 1944).
9. Another class of vehicles were generally referred to as tank destroyers. Examples include the German Panzerjäger series and the American M10 Gun Motor Carriage. These were light vehicles with heavy cannons capable of moving quickly and destroying opposing tanks. Original Allied versions were intended to provide quick reaction forces in depth behind friendly lines to blunt enemy breakthroughs, but they were commonly used on the front lines.

10. Operation Goodwood was a British armor offensive intended to help push out of the Caen area and through to southern France. See Christopher Dunphie, *The Pendulum of Battle: Operation Goodwood—July 1944* (South Yorkshire, UK: Leo Cooper, 2004).
11. See Wolfgang Schneider, *Panzer Tactics: German Small-Unit Armor Tactics in World War II* (Guilford, CT: Stackpole Books, 2000). Schneider describes armor-infantry integrations and also infantry-armor teaming; see below in this section. Also see Gordon L. Rottman, *World War II US Armored Infantry Tactics* (Oxford, UK: Osprey, 2011).
12. Generally, an APC is a lightly armored vehicle that is treated like an armored truck, designed to move infantry into combat, while an IFV is designed to allow infantry to fight straight through an enemy defense while mounted. In practice there is little to clearly differentiate APCs from IFVs. APCs like the M113, developed in the postwar period, were commonly used as IFVs or even as light tanks in the Vietnam War, while IFVs like the BMP and the Bradley could be used as troop transports in some instances.
13. The British, Soviets, Canadians, and to some extent the Japanese and U.S. Marine Corps also employed mechanized infantry formations.
14. The Wehrmacht Panzergrenadiers are probably the more popularized mechanized infantry units in World War II. The Wehrmacht, British Army, and U.S. Army examples are most useful here.
15. Wilson, *Evolution of Divisions*, 150. See Hanna, *Task Force XXI*, for a summary of that unit.
16. Wilson, *Evolution of Divisions*, 150. Gordon Rottman (Rottman, *Armored Infantry Tactics*, 14–17) offers significantly different numbers.
17. Christopher R. Gabel, *The 4th Armored Division in the Encirclement of Nancy* (Fort Leavenworth, KS: Combat Studies Institute, April 1986).
18. Gabel, *4th Armored Division*, 1–2. Gabel also notes that the division typically had standing attachments of 155mm towed artillery, M-18 tank destroyers, antiaircraft artillery, and others.
19. Gabel, *4th Armored Division*, 15–16.
20. Gabel, *4th Armored Division*, foreword.
21. In some Western forces, a tactic is a combat action taken by a military unit to gain advantage over another unit; a technique is a practiced method applied by a military unit to accomplish a narrow task within a tactical movement; and a procedure is a typically fixed technical process that can be applied in or out of combat.
22. In military context, a rocket is typically an unguided self-powered munition using some kind of exhaust-jet propulsion, while a missile is a rocket guided by a command wire, an inertial navigation system, or by more modern technology (e.g., Javelin fire-and-forget). Some projectiles like the PIAT are launched by a spring or a small booster charge rather than exhaust jet but are typically referred to as rockets.
23. The first example of counter-innovation might be the German armor-piercing K-bullet, which was designed to be fired from a standard Mauser bold-action rifle.
24. See Sami Korhonen, "The Battles of the Winter War: Anti-tank Weapons Used by the Finns in the Winter War, Part II," online article, n.d., http://www.winterwar.com.

25. For example, see Steven J. Zaloga, *US Anti-tank Artillery 1941–1945* (Oxford, UK: Osprey, 2005).
26. See Tonio Andrade, *The Gunpowder Age: China, Military Innovation, and the Rise of the West in World History* (Princeton, NJ: Princeton University Press, 2016); Gordon L. Rottman, *The Bazooka* (Oxford, UK: Osprey, 2012); J. G. Benton, *Ordnance and Gunnery* (New York: D. Van Nostrand, 1862); David A. Clary, *Rocket Man: Robert H. Goddard and the Birth of the Space Age* (New York: Hachette, 2003).
27. See Donald R. Kennedy, *History of the Shaped Charge Effect: The First 100 Years*, presentation at the 100th Anniversary of the Discovery of the Shaped Charge Effect by Max Von Foerster, Schrobenhausen, West Germany, September 20–22, 1983.
28. The Japanese experimented with the Type 4 70mm anti-tank weapon, which was a bipod-mounted weapon fired using a mortar-like charge rather than like a typical rocket. There is a photograph and description of a launcher at the U.S. National Air and Space Museum website, https://airandspace.si.edu.
29. See U.S. War Department, *German Military Forces*; and U.S. War Department, *German and Japanese Solid-Fuel Rocket Weapons* (Washington, DC: Military Intelligence Division, n.d.).
30. All of these systems will be referenced later in this section or in chapters 4–9.
31. Artillery terminology is complex and sometimes contested. The terms *gun*, *howitzer*, *cannon*, and *rifled breech-loader* are all commonly used. Generally, there are smoothbore weapons with shorter ranges and longer-range weapons with rifling in the barrel that imparts a spin on the projectile, increasing its accuracy. Both types can be used in direct fire as needed, and often are. I am not including mortars up to 120mm in this category since mortars are typically employed by infantry as integrated combined-arms weapons. Artillery should also include heavy mortars when they are used in formations, like the Wehrmacht's Heavy Mortar Battalions in World War II or perhaps organized modern Russian employment of a battery of 2S4 Tyulpan (Tulip) 240mm mortars.
32. Albert Manucy, *Artillery through the Ages* (January 30, 2007), 5, ebook.
33. Data on the onager is drawn from a variety of sources, none of which are convincing in their accuracy. Suffice it to say, catapults are less effective than field guns. Data on the M1 howitzer comes from U.S. War Department, *240-mm Howitzers M1918M1 and M1918M1A1, 240-mm Howitzer Carriage 1918A2, and Transport Wagons M4 and M5*, TM 9–340 (April 6, 1944). Also see Boyd L. Dastrup, *King of Battle: A Branch History of the U.S. Army's Field Artillery* (Fort Monroe, VA: U.S. Army Training and Doctrine Command, 1992).
34. Mark Adkin, *The Western Front Companion* (London: Aurum Press, 2013), Kindle, locations 1554 and 11359. Also see Paddy Griffith, *Battle Tactics of the Western Front: The British Army's Art of Attack 1916–1918* (New Haven, CT: Yale University Press, 1994). Griffith weaves the story of the Somme throughout the book, so readers cannot be directed to any specific pages. It is highly unlikely the number of shells was exactly 3,526,000, so this is necessarily a rounded estimate.
35. Exact data on artillery use at Seelow Heights is harder to nail down due to the scope of the battle. It could be narrowed to one reinforced Soviet division attacking a German regiment, or it could be expanded to include large parts of the front on either side. Historian Antony Beevor lists 8,983 artillery pieces available to

the Soviets for this battle and 1,236,000 shells fired on the first day alone. Antony Beevor, *The Fall of Berlin 1945* (Penguin Books, 2020), 316, ebook. Also see the official Soviet take on the battle in Soviet General Staff, *The Berlin Operation 1945*, ed. and trans. Richard W. Harrison (West Midlands, UK: Helion, 2016).

36. See Paddy Griffith's descriptions of the artillery employment and German preparations in Griffith, *Battle Tactics*, 148, 149, 157–159, and others.
37. The UK Imperial War Museum lists these casualty figures. Also see Griffith, *Battle Tactics*, 3. Griffith does not refer to a specific source. Doubtless the official counts are available in archives.
38. See Beevor, *Fall of Berlin*, 319–325 and others; and Soviet General Staff, *Berlin Operation*.
39. This is an illustrative example, not an argument for causality.
40. There are also specialized nonlethal artillery shells including smoke and illumination rounds. But the vast majority of artillery rounds fired in all wars in the twentieth and twenty-first centuries have almost certainly (absent empirical evidence) been filled with explosives or deadly chemicals.
41. For more on the M7, see Steven J. Zaloga, *M7 Priest 105mm Howitzer Motor Carriage* (Oxford, UK: Osprey, 2013).
42. Guided weapons were also employed but in such limited quantities that they are not relevant to general characteristics of World War II ground combat. See the sections on drones and precision-guided munitions below.
43. See Kenneth R. Whiting, "Soviet Air-Ground Coordination, 1941–1945," in *Case Studies in the Development of Close Air Support*, ed. Benjamin Franklin Cooling (Washington, DC: U.S. Air Force Office of Air Force History, 1990), 115–142; D. Klaus Uebe, *Russian Reactions to German Airpower in World War II*, captured military document (Maxwell Air Force Base, AL: Aerospace Studies Institute, July 1964); Oleg Hoeffding, *Soviet Interdiction Operations, 1941–1945* (Santa Monica, CA: RAND Corporation, 1970); E. R. Hooton, *War over the Steppes: The Air Campaigns on the Eastern Front, 1941–45* (Oxford, UK: Osprey, 2016).
44. Hooton, *War over the Steppes*, 21–22.
45. See U.S. Marine Corps, *An Annotated Bibliography of the United States Marine Corps' Concept of Close Air Support* (Washington, DC: Headquarters, U.S. Marine Corps Historical Branch, 1968); Hough, *Assault on Peleliu*; Stephen M. Fuller and Graham A. Cosmas, *Marines in the Dominican Republic 1916–1924* (Washington, DC: Headquarters, U.S. Marine Corps History and Museums Division, 1974); Charles W. Boggs Jr., *Marine Aviation in the Philippines* (Washington, DC: Headquarters, U.S. Marine Corps Historical Division, 1951); and Edward C. Johnson with Graham A. Cosmas, ed., *Marine Corps Aviation: The Early Years 1912–1940* (Washington, DC: Headquarters, U.S. Marine Corps History and Museums Division, 1977).
46. For more on U.S. sortie evidence, see the Theater History of Operations (THOR) dataset, https://data.world.
47. For more on teaming, see Daniel R. Mortensen, *A Pattern for Joint Operations: World War II Close Air Support in North Africa* (Washington, DC: Center of Military History, 1987), 22.
48. There also are nonexplosive kinetic drones that damage or destroy their target by delivering blunt or edged force at a pinpoint location.

49. This section is derived primarily from H. R. Everett's encyclopedic history of early to mid-twentieth-century drones: H. R. Everett, *Unmanned Systems of World Wars I and II* (Cambridge, MA: MIT Press, 2015). Other sources referenced and cited are Kenneth P. Werrell, *The Evolution of the Cruise Missile* (Maxwell Air Force Base, AL: Air University Press, 1985); and Katherine Fehr Chandler, "Drone Flight and Failure: The United States' Secret Trials, Experiments and Operations in Unmanning, 1936–1973" (thesis, University of California, Berkeley, 2014).
50. Everett, *Unmanned Systems*, 253–260.
51. Everett, *Unmanned Systems*, 292–293.
52. Everett, *Unmanned Systems*, 318.
53. Everett, *Unmanned Systems*, 321–337.
54. See "U.S. Navy WWII TDR-1 Drone Operational Tests in South Pacific 30772," U.S. Navy, Periscope Film, YouTube video; and "Did You Know Assault Drones Were Used in WWII?," *Smithsonian Channel*, YouTube video.
55. Quoted in Everett, *Unmanned Systems*, 363. Original citation is M. McDonnell, "The Armed Robots," *Naval Aviation News* (January 1973), 8–13.
56. Everett, *Unmanned Systems*, 347–354.
57. Robert Forsyth, *Mistel: German Composite Aircraft and Operations 1942–1945* (Manchester, UK: Crecy, 2021).
58. Everett, *Unmanned Systems*, 461–490.
59. Everett, *Unmanned Systems*, 479.
60. See the sections in Everett, *Unmanned Systems*, on both the Borgward and Goliath.
61. Werrell, *Cruise Missile*, 60.
62. Werrell, *Cruise Missile*, 66.
63. See Everett, *Unmanned Systems*, for what may be the closest thing to a comprehensive accounting of testing and design efforts.
64. For more on the development of glide bombs, see Everett, *Unmanned Systems*, 371–391.
65. Samuel J. Cox, "H021-1: *Fritz-X*—The Dawn of Precision-Guided Warfare," Naval History and Heritage Command, September 2018, https://www.history.navy.mil.
66. See "GB-4 2000 Lb. Television Glide Bomb," declassified program report, U.S. Army Air Corps (October 1, 1945).
67. For example, Everett, *Unmanned Systems*, 353.
68. For examples of some of these exceptions, see Claude R. Sasso, *Soviet Night Operations in World War II* (Fort Leavenworth, KS: Combat Studies Institute, 1982).
69. This history is compiled in Andreas T. Haka, "Thermography," book chapter, in *Between Making and Knowing: Tools in the History of Materials Research*, eds. Joseph D. Martin and Cyrus C. M. Mody (Singapore: World Scientific, 2020), 539–552.
70. For more on night-vision development, see Nkolika O. Nwazor and Stella I. Orakwue, "A Review of Night Vision Technology," *Australian Journal of Science and Technology* 4, no. 1 (March 2020), 265–269.
71. The U.S. Army Signal Corps published a good, digestible history of communications in two forms: George Raynor Thompson and Dixie R. Harris, *The Signal Corps: The Outcome (Mid-1943 through 1945)* (Washington, DC: U.S. Army Center of Military History, 1991); and "Radio History: Signal Corps 1860–1976 Communications Technology, Radar, Electronics Training," YouTube video.

72. See the next subsection and Thompson and Harris, *Signal Corps*, for more on electronic warfare. Interception is generally referred to as communications intelligence when used for direction finding or signals intelligence when used to intercept the content of messages. For more, see Albert Praun, *German Radio Intelligence* (U.S. Department of the Army, Office of the Chief of Military History, 1950); Jeffrey S. Harley, "Reading the Enemy's Mail: Origins and Development of U.S. Army Tactical Radio Intelligence in World War II, European Theater of Operations" (thesis, U.S. Army Command and General Staff College, 1993); and James L. Gilbert and John P. Finnegan, eds., *U.S. Army Signals Intelligence in World War II: A Documentary History* (Washington, DC: U.S. Army Center of Military History, 1993), 179–195.
73. See Alfred Price, *Instruments of Darkness: The History of Electronic Warfare 1939–1945* (Yorkshire, UK: Frontline Books, 2022/1967).
74. See the Crypto Museum website for more, https://www.cryptomuseum.com.
75. Praun, *German Radio Intelligence*, 16, 24, 26, 32, 43, 64.
76. For example, see Anthonie van Dijk, "The Mysterious Floating Batteries of the Royal Netherlands Navy," *Warship International* 25, no. 3 (1998), 229–238.
77. David Stevens, "Naval Gunfire Support at Gallipoli," online article, Royal Australian Artillery History Organization (n.d., www.artilleryhistory.org).
78. See Donald M. Weller, *Naval Gunfire Support of Amphibious Operations: Past, Present, and Future* (Arlington, VA: Universal Systems, 1977); Harold A. Bivins, *An Annotated Bibliography of Naval Gunfire Support* (Washington, DC: U.S. Marine Corps Historical Division, 1971).
79. See Amrom H. Katz, *Some Notes on the History of Aerial Reconnaissance (Part I)* (Santa Monica, CA: RAND Corporation, April 1966). Also see James B. Campbell, "Origins of Aerial Photographic Interpretation, U.S. Army, 1916–1918," *Photogrammetric Engineering & Remote Sensing* (January 2008), 77–93; Peter W. Mead, *Eye in the Air: History of Air Observation and Reconnaissance for the Army 1785–1945* (London: HMSO, 1983).
80. For example, Edgar F. Raines Jr., *Eyes of Artillery: The Origins of Modern U.S. Army Aviation in World War II* (Washington, DC: U.S. Army Center of Military History, 2000); Mike Pietrucha, "Airpower Orphans, Part II: Whatever Happened to Liaison Aircraft?," *War on the Rocks* (August 26, 2019); Herbert P. LePore, "Eyes in the Sky: A History of Liaison Aircraft and Their Use in World War II," *Army History*, no. 17 (Winter 1990–1991), 30–39.
81. J. Gordon Leishman, *A History of Helicopter Flight*, online paper, derived from J. Gordon Leishman, *Principles of Helicopter Aerodynamics* (New York: Cambridge University Press, 2000).
82. U.S. Marine Corps aviators employed the Pitcairn OP-1 autogyro in Nicaragua in 1932 with limited success. An autogyro is a propeller-driven aircraft with an unpowered overhead rotor that provides lift derived from the plane's forward momentum. See Eugene W. Rawlins, *Marines and Helicopters: 1946–1962* (Washington, DC: U.S. Marine Corps History and Museums Division, 1976), 1.
83. Other countries including Canada and the Soviet Union employed autogyros during World War II.
84. See Kenneth P. Werrell, *Archie to SAM: A Short Operational History of Ground-Based Air Defense* (Maxwell Air Force Base, AL: 2005), 2.
85. Aggregated claims drawn from Werrell, *Archie to SAM*, 3.

86. For example, the U.S. 90mm Mark 1 AAA gun could fire a shell to about 32,000 feet above the ground. Werrell, *Archie to SAM*, 26.
87. For example, in the Soviet Manchuria offensive in 1945, the Japanese employed the 22nd Field Antiaircraft Artillery Unit with seven battalions of guns, three battalions of searchlights, and over ten independent gun companies, while the Soviets employed entire antiaircraft artillery divisions under most of their army groups, and in this case another antiaircraft artillery regiment under the 17th Army. Glantz, *August Storm*, 179–203.
88. Readers familiar with the lapse in Western ground combat force air defenses in the 2000s will raise an eyebrow here.
89. For example, John W. Mountcastle, *Flame On: U.S. Incendiary Weapons, 1918–1945* (Mechanicsburg, PA: Stackpole Books, 1999); David W. Van Wyck, "Beyond the Burn: Studies on the Psychological Effects of Flamethrowers during World War II," *Military Medical Research* 7, no. 8 (2020), 1–8.
90. David Fletcher, *Churchill Crocodile Flamethrower* (Oxford, UK: New Vanguard, 2007).
91. In 1983, a United Nations protocol banning flame weapons went into effect.
92. I track the use of some flame weapons in more contemporary cases, including the Russian employment of thermobaric rockets in Chechnya, Syria, and Ukraine.
93. See the 1874 International Declaration Concerning the Laws and Customs of War, Article 13(a), and the Hague Convention of 1899 and 1907, available online, https://www.denix.osd.mil/rcwmprogram/history/.
94. Because it is not immediately relevant to ground combat, I am not taking into account the Nazi employment of chemical gas to murder millions of civilians. These horrors are well recorded and indisputable.
95. For more on Japanese chemical and biological weapons employment, see Walter E. Grunden, "No Retaliation in Kind: Japanese Chemical Warfare Policy in World War II," and Jeanne Guillemin, "The 1925 Geneva Protocol: China's CBW Charges against Japan at the Tokyo War Crimes Tribunal," book chapters, in *One Hundred Years of Chemical Warfare: Research, Deployment, Consequences*, eds. Bretislav Friedrich, Dieter Hoffmann, Jürgen Renn, Florian Schmaltz, and Martin Wolf (Springer Open, 2017), 259–288, ebook.
96. Bill Harriman, *The Mosin-Nagant Rifle* (Oxford, UK: Osprey, 2016).
97. For more on the M1, see U.S. War Department, *Basic Field Manual, U.S. Rifle, Caliber .30, M1* (Washington, DC: Government Printing Office, 1940).
98. For more on the M7, see for example, "Army Awards Next Generation Squad Weapon Contract," press release, U.S. Army Public Affairs, April 19, 2022, https://www.army.mil.

FOUR

Interval Cases, 1945–2002

After World War II, the ground combat experience quickly decentralized away from binary Axis versus Allies industrial land war to far more diffuse examples and even more widely varied forms. Cold War proxy fighting among the United States, Soviet Union, China, and both NATO and Warsaw Pact nations ensured a steady supply of small arms, tanks, artillery, rockets, attack aircraft, and other implements of war to militaries around the world. Each individual combatant organization, like the Yemen Arab Republic ground forces (1962–1970 North Yemen Civil War) and the Afghan Mujaheddin (1979–1989 Soviet-Afghan War), took these ground combat tools and adapted them for their own local terrain, enemies, and their particular style of fighting.

Many of the mid-1940s–1990s conflicts are referred to as irregular wars, insurgencies, or civil wars. All these terms are subjective and have loose meaning even in the oppressive lexical confines of the American Department of Defense. No matter which term is applied to a conflict, anything other than straightforward conventional land war between two nation-state armies is generally excluded from character-of-ground-combat debates.[1] Big battles in the Korean War, in the Arab-Israeli Wars, and to a lesser extent the Iran-Iraq War, frequently make the cut. Yet even a cursory examination of 1945–2002 cases commonly referred to as *irregular* reveals often large-scale battles between mechanized combined-arms forces employing some of the most modern weapons, munitions, and equipment then available. For example, see the Battle of Cuito Cuanavale, Angola (frequently referred to as the African Stalingrad) below.

INTERVAL CASES

I applied the same case selection criteria as I applied to the World War II cases—combined-arms skirmish or battle, diversity of terrain and climate, different

Table 4.1. Twenty-Five Interval Cases from 1945 through 2002

Inchon-Seoul South Korea 1950	Xuan Loc Vietnam 1975	Afabet Eritrea 1988
Dien Bien Phu Indochina 1954	Lang Son Vietnam 1979	Battle of the Tawakalna Iraq 1991[2]
Mitla Pass Egypt 1956	Paquisha Ecuador-Peru 1981	Shusha Nagorno-Karabakh 1992[3]
Ia Drang Valley Vietnam 1965	Goose Green Falklands-Malvinas 1982	Kupres Bosnia-Herzegovina 1992[4]
Plaman Mapu Malaysia 1965	Beqa'a Valley Lebanon 1982	Grozny Chechnya 1994
Hue City Vietnam 1968	Al-Faw Iraq 1986	Cenapa Peru-Ecuador 1995[5]
Hilli-Bogra Bangladesh 1971	Sate-Kandev Pass Afghanistan 1987[1]	Koshare Serbia 1999
Chinese Farm Egypt 1973	Fada Chad 1987	
Kifangondo Angola 1975	Cuito Cuanavale Angola 1987	

[1]*Afg = Afghanistan*
[2]*Battle of the Tawakalna Division*
[3]*Shusha Nagorno-Karabakh*
[4]*Kupres Bosnia-Herzegovina*
[5]*Cenapa Valley on the Peru-Ecuador border*

military forces, variety of combat types—and added in global variation. In other words, I tried to pick examples from around the world to highlight not just similarities and diversity in combat style but also to highlight the cases themselves. Some of these, like the battle of Inchon and Seoul in the Korean War and Ia Drang Valley in Vietnam, will be familiar to military professionals and even nonexperts with basic interest in military history.

Others, like the combined-arms battle at Kifangondo in Angola (1975), Paquisha along the Ecuador-Peru border (1981), and Afabet in Eritrea (1988), are less familiar or even unknown to many Western military professionals. This does not, of course, make them any less relevant to the study of military history. One purpose in highlighting these cases is to spark interest and encourage Western students of land war and ground combat to seek insight outside the familiar canon. Table 4.1 lists the twenty-five 1945–2002 cases.

All twenty-five of these cases are important to understand the wide variety of ground combat characteristics relevant to the 1945–2002 period. These ten descriptive examples are not even representative of the twenty-five coded cases, but they are sufficient to drive the analysis of ground combat forward in the following chapters: (1) Inchon-Seoul South Korean 1950; (2) Ia Drang Valley Vietnam 1965; (3) Hilli-Bogra Bangladesh 1971; (4) Xuan Loc Vietnam 1975; (5) Beqa'a Valley Lebanon 1982; (6) Al-Faw Iraq 1986; (7) Cuito Cuanavale Angola 1987; (8) Battle of the Tawakalna Iraq-Kuwait 1991; (9) Shusha Nagorno-Karabakh 1992; and (10) Cenapa Valley Peru-Ecuador 1995.[2]

Inchon to Seoul, Korea, 1950[3]

Location: Inchon to Seoul City, South Korea[4]
Combatants: United States (UN) versus the Democratic People's Republic of Korea (DPRK)
Dates: September 10–28, 1950

In a bold effort to isolate all of the DPRK forces in South Korea, the U.S. First Marine Division (Reinforced) with attached U.S. Army forces conducted an amphibious landing at Inchon on the coast west of the capital, Seoul.[5] A layered naval and air fire support plan pinned the defending North Korean troops while the Marines plowed ashore.[6] Navy cruisers poured thousands of high-explosive shells into Wolmi-do island just offshore from the landing beaches. As the landing craft moved closer to shore, destroyers closed in and kept up a continuous stream of 5-inch and 40mm shells, and heavy machinegun fire. Marine F-4 Corsair fighter-bombers saturated Wolmi-do with napalm.

Shallow-keel rocket ships then moved up and launched about 1,000 indirect-fire rockets at high angle onto the defenders and then added to the close-range orchestra of fire with their own deck-mounted cannons and machineguns. Marine infantry and M-26 Pershing tanks landed and poured on their own organic direct and indirect fires. Ground liaison teams refined the accuracy of both close-air support and naval gunfire support with radioed directions.[7]

Marine forces quickly moved inland from the Inchon beachhead to sustain their momentum against the surprised North Korean defenders. As they advanced in column toward Seoul, a reinforced platoon of DPRK T-34 tanks attempted to counterattack without infantry or antiaircraft support; they were decimated by Marine F-4s dropping napalm and firing rockets. Another North Korean counterattack, this time with supporting infantry, drove right into an infantry-armor ambush. Marines used machineguns, rifles, both light and heavy bazookas, recoilless rifles, and M-26 90mm tank rounds to decimate this DPRK mechanized team.

The attack toward Seoul then advanced through hilly terrain defended by more alert and aggressive troops. Ground combat devolved into an increasingly linear, frontal series of assaults and counterattacks as the Marines closed in on the city. Employing both Marine and supporting U.S. Army LVT amphibious tractors, the joint American units crossed the Han River in stride under heavy combined-arms fire and moved into the urban terrain.[8]

Just before the Marines could execute their night attack into the city, the North Koreans attempted a daring counterattack with T-34 tanks and mounted infantry. They were chewed up by the rockets and cannons of the Marine units already crouched in their attack positions. The Marine attack then commenced with a heavy rolling barrage of artillery and continuous air support. Infantry-armor teams on both sides continued to engage at close range, with Marine flame tanks burning many of the DPRK infantry out of their positions.

Mortars and high-angle artillery played a key role in suppressing the defenders so the infantry-armor teams could advance through the streets. Frequently, tanks engaged tanks in the urban terrain and on the surrounding hills, with Marine rocket and recoilless rifle teams chiming in to help give their M-26s tactical advantage. Amphibious tractors were used as armored personnel carriers, and one version with a 75mm howitzer was used as an infantry fighting vehicle. After a grueling combined-arms push using all available weapons, vehicles, and munitions, the city was secured.

Observations and insights from Inchon to Seoul, Korea, 1950. Successfully putting troops ashore during an opposed amphibious assault requires extensive preparation, intelligence gathering, and supporting fires. Lessons from World War I and World War II errors at Gallipoli and Peleliu (etc.) were fed directly into the Inchon landing plan. Preparatory fires continued unabated and probably increased in volume—albeit with smaller-caliber munitions—as the landing force moved ashore. None of these bombardments achieved magical effects: Even close-range direct precision fires from 5-inch guns had to be followed up with repeated salvos and suppressing fire from heavy machineguns and direct-fire antiaircraft cannons as the Marines moved ashore.

Defending forces both at Inchon and on the drive toward and through Seoul frequently continued to fight despite heavy bombardment, requiring enormous volumes of fire to sustain infantry-armor advances. The North Korean counterattacks reinforced the importance of infantry-armor teaming at the lowest possible tactical level of organization. By most measures, the Marine Corps' M-26 tanks were technically superior to the DPRK T-34s.[9] But knocking out even these older Soviet tanks sometimes required repeated on-target 90mm shots. Having Marine riflemen and machine gunners strip away DPRK infantry and adding infantry anti-tank rockets to each tank fight gave the Marines a strong competitive advantage.

Ia Drang Valley, Vietnam, 1965[10]

Location: Ia Drang Valley, Republic of Vietnam
Combatants: Democratic Republic of Vietnam versus the United States
Dates: November 14–18, 1965

During the broader contest over control of Pleiku Province, Republic of Vietnam in 1965, the U.S. Army First Battalion, Seventh Air Cavalry Regiment (1/7) conducted a heliborne assault into a landing zone at the base of the Chu Pong mountain range. Their objective was to engage one of two People's Army of Viet Nam (PAVN) regiments—the 33rd and 66th—operating in the area and to degrade their combat power with combined arms attacks.[11] After short preparatory fires by supporting 105mm artillery against suspected targets, a handful of UH-1 helicopters landed the first wave of Americans into a small clearing at the base of the mountain range. Initial surprise caused by the sudden appearance of the helicopters threw the defending PAVN soldiers on the back foot. This allowed for a second wave of helicopters to approach as the 9th Battalion of the North Vietnamese 66th regiment, sitting in laager just up the mountainside, mobilized for the concentrated infantry assaults that followed.

Once the two sides were fully engaged, the battle devolved to a series of intensive small-unit infantry engagements at the platoon and company level. North Vietnamese forces outnumbered the Americans and controlled the high ground above the landing zone. They used their advantage in elevation and clear sightlines to bring down effective rocket, mortar, recoilless rifle, and heavy machinegun fire onto the American troops. Helicopters flying combat support and firing into the PAVN units with machineguns and rockets were frequently taken under heavy machinegun fire. A fire-support officer attached to the 1/7 battalion headquarters, and also the company commanders at the point of contact, called in mortar fire, artillery fire, helicopter gun runs, and airstrikes throughout the battle.

Even with these intensive supporting fires, on the first day PAVN infantry managed to overrun part of the American line and cut off an entire platoon. However, as further American reinforcements landed by helicopter, the combination of supporting arms and intensive ground fire eventually wore down the 9th Battalion and the 7th Battalion, the latter of which had been thrown into the line on the second morning of the battle. The North Vietnamese were forced to withdraw.

This did not end the fight. While the attacking American battalion, 1/7, was withdrawn from the battlefield by helicopter, the reinforcing battalions, 2/5 and 2/7, made a foot movement in column through dense wooded terrain to their extraction point at Landing Zone (LZ) Albany. Bad luck struck 2/7 on its way to

Albany when it accidentally ran into the PAVN 66th Regiments' 8th Battalion. The North Vietnamese got the jump on the Americans and attacked them just as they had become strung out in a long column and were exposed with inadequate flank protection. Well aware of the American advantage in supporting arms, the 8th Battalion commander ordered his infantry to move in tight to the American lines so they could not make best use of their artillery and airstrikes. The North Vietnamese were partly successful, inflicting heavy casualties on the Americans with rifles, machineguns, and mortars. But eventually, the artillery and airstrikes took their toll on the attackers. The battle effectively ended when the Americans reinforced their shaky perimeter with fresh infantry and the PAVN withdrew.

Observations and insights from Ia Drang, Vietnam, 1965. Three characteristics are highlighted in the first part of this battle, the fight at LZ X-Ray. Mass and concentration of infantry forces mattered for both attackers and defenders. The Americans were at their most vulnerable with the fewest number of troops on the ground: Fewer troops meant fewer rifles, more space for the PAVN to maneuver, and fewer tactical options for the defenders in the face of concerted attack.[12] Elevation gave at least a technical advantage to the PAVN, and if they had had better antiaircraft artillery and missiles, they might have been able to isolate the first American waves on the small landing zone below the dominant terrain.

And at LZ X-Ray, professional ground-air coordination by trained support officers allowed for precision fire support in the close-quarters fight. At the battle for LZ Albany, the North Vietnamese commander's order to hug the American forces to limit their supporting arms was a good example of the tactical adaptation to an adversary's technical advantage. The North Vietnamese and others learned how to apply human behavioral changes to diminish the technical advantage of American fire support.

Hilli and Bogra, Bangladesh, 1971[13]

Location: Hilli and Bogra, Bangladesh
Combatants: India versus Pakistan
Dates: December 10–18, 1971

During the Bangladesh war for liberation, Pakistani Border Guards and the 205th Infantry Brigade supported by tanks and artillery defended the border town of Hilli and the route southeast from the border. Their mission was to prevent the Indian 202nd and 304th Mountain Brigade Groups from seizing the vital road and rail hub at Bogra. Pakistani troops had dug in along the border behind a line of mines, wire obstacles, and water gaps covered by interlocking direct fire from concrete bunkers and all supported by mortars and artillery. Indian forces kicked off with artillery preparation and then moved forward in a night assault. They were slowed by the heavy defenses, and some of the supporting Indian T-55 tanks became stuck in thick mud. Close-range infantry combat ground down the advancing Indians, who at some points were forced into hand-to-hand combat.

Pakistani troops counterattacked around Hilli and the nearby town of Morapara, employing PT-76 amphibious tanks to take back lost ground from the Indian troops. A stalemate ensued for about two weeks while action progressed on the flanks. On December 10, Indian forces renewed their ground assault around Hilli and managed to clear out the bunker complexes with direct tank fire and infantry assaults. Indian forces then consolidated and moved toward Bogra with Gurkha Rifle units in the lead supported by PT-76 and T-55 tanks from the 69th Armored Regiment. Gurkha units moved on foot, employing infiltration tactics to get in close to the defending Pakistani infantry and whenever possible to engage in close-range fighting, with Indian artillery holding back any counterattackers. Pakistani defenders used recoilless rifles and machineguns to peel away leading elements of the attacking Indian columns, but eventually they were driven back from their positions to Bogra.

Indian troops advanced on Bogra from three axes, with their own PT-76 tank teams cutting off the town from the south and the Gurkha infantry moving through to clear. Approximately 1,500 Pakistani troops from a mix of units, including a brigade headquarters element, defended Bogra in depth through the urban area. A rolling artillery barrage preceded the Indian dismounted infantry advance, but as in most urban fights close-range infantry fighting dominated. A Gurkha officer recalled, "Our best weapons were small arms, grenades, and 3.5 inch and 57mm rockets. Everyone carried Molotov cocktails." Indian troops also called in lighter 75mm artillery but found that these smaller-caliber cannons did little damage to the buildings from which the Pakistani troops were fighting. Progress was slow, but eventually the last defenders were encircled and they made the decision to surrender, ending the battle.

Observations and insights from Hilli and Bogra, Bangladesh, 1971. Once again, high explosives were no technical cure-all for well-prepared defenses. Concrete bunkers along the border defensive line allowed the Pakistani troops to hold off the attacking Indian forces until they could muster their own infantry-armor counterattack. However, bunkers also anchored the defenders in place, making them easier to spot, target, outflank, and eventually overrun with sufficient firepower and aggression. Both sides made extensive use of recoilless rifles, which are basically long-range bazookas on tripods, employing them to destroy opposing armor moving in column down hardball roads and to break through layered sandbagged positions.[14]

A postwar Indian assessment noted several lessons worth learning from the Hilli fight, including: Interlocking fires in difficult terrain make for good defenses; decentralized execution, flexibility, bravery, leadership, and initiative are essential to success; use the right tools for the job (PT-76s were more nimble than T-55s in marshy terrain); and "the morale of the troops is contingent on the cause."[15] At least from this singular perspective, the troops who cared more fought harder.

Xuan Loc, Republic of Vietnam, 1975[16]

Location: Xuan Loc, Republic of Vietnam[17]
Combatants: Democratic Republic of Vietnam versus Republic of Vietnam
Dates: April 9–15, 1975

During the final North Vietnamese offensive into South Vietnam, the Army of the Republic of Vietnam (ARVN) 18th Division, reinforced by some regional militia and a battalion of rangers, defended the vital road junction at the town of Xuan Loc.[18] An entire North Vietnamese corps consisting of the 6th, 7th, and 341st division isolated and attacked to secure the town and destroy the defending southern troops. Both sides employed aggressive ground reconnaissance, but the southerners made better use of their recon teams and of the home terrain. The commander of the 18th Division correctly forecast the likely PAVN avenues of approach based on previous actions and set a regimental-level trap with interlocking direct fire and preregistered artillery. After a brief but intensive corps-level artillery barrage, two northern divisions attacked directly into different parts of the defensive line with T-54 tanks and infantry assault teams.

Part of this initial attack fell straight into the trap set by the ARVN commander. Tanks from the 7th Division drove into minefields covered by direct fire, while infantry were hung up on barbed wire and man-made trenches intended to slow their advance. Organic and supporting artillery slammed into the attacking force as it slogged through the defensive perimeter, and A-37 and F5-E fighter-bombers joined in with bomb and gun runs. Rocket launchers added to the anti-tank fusillade, taking out several of the advancing T-54s. Troops in the first assault wave did penetrate into the town, but they found every house defended by South Vietnamese infantry dug in behind sandbags. The 341st Division made more progress on the west side of town but suffered casualties from tripod-mounted .50 M2 machineguns and low-level close-air support from a C-119 gunship. Over the next several days the two sides traded attack and counterattack, with the ARVN forces pushing their own infantry into the attackers' toeholds at the edge of the town in a futile effort to dislodge them.

Both sides kept up intensive artillery barrages, and several more tanks were destroyed in the urban terrain. Forced through the streets into close combat, infantry engaged in room-clearing fights and hand-to-hand combat with bayonets. South Vietnamese artillery teams did their best to disrupt northern artillery with counterbattery fires and airstrikes, and they did manage to destroy most of the attackers' light and medium guns. But the advantage in numbers and firepower remained with the PAVN despite a lopsided disparity in reported casualties—nearly 2,000 attackers killed to a few hundred defenders—through the first few days of combat.

Northern leaders shifted from frontal attacks to envelopment when it became clear they were beating their heads against a brick wall. Attacking units received full reinforcement and resupply while the ARVN defenses began to crumble under the weight of continuous assault and artillery fire. In the final assault, thousands of PAVN infantry infiltrated through the dense overgrowth and forced a withdrawal.

Observations and insights from Xuan Loc, Republic of Vietnam, 1975. Like the Pakistani counterattacks against the Indian attackers at Hilli, the ARVN local counterattacks transformed their fixed defensive positions into pivot points for a more even-handed combined-arms exchange. Accurate artillery and air strikes took their toll on both sides. There was continuous PAVN and ARVN need for supporting fires throughout the battle. As some artillery and air targets were destroyed, new targets appeared; a point of full destruction was never achieved. Some infantry positions that looked to be demolished by fires in fact survived and held the line against infantry assault.

Urban terrain restricted the defenders' fields of fire, but it also forced the attackers into bloody close-range fights where they could not effectively employ their heaviest supporting arms. In more open terrain, obstacles like minefields, barbed wire, and even simple trenches, all covered by direct and indirect fires, were enough to slow the attacking troops and armor and expose them to destruction. Ultimately, aggressive infantry penetration through the defensive lines, and ARVN infantry collapse, signaled the end of this fight.

Beqa'a Valley, Lebanon, 1982[19]

Location: Beqa'a Valley, Lebanon
Combatants: Israel versus the Syrian Arab Republic and PLO[20]
Dates: June 8–12, 1982

During the 1982 invasion of Lebanon, Israeli armored and infantry forces organized under the ad hoc Beqa'a Forces Group advanced through eastern Lebanon to destroy defending Syrian 1st Armored Division and any found elements of the Palestine Liberation Organization (PLO). Israeli units were arranged in combined armor and infantry task forces with both organic and supporting artillery including heavy 203mm cannons. While they were only indirectly relevant to ground combat, the pre-attack strikes against the Syrian air defenses in the valley on June 9 are an important historical marker in the military-technical revolution debate. Israeli Air Force units employed a large number of drones (referred to in one source as a "wave") to trick the Syrians into turning on their antiair radars, then destroyed most of the air-defense missile and electronic warfare sites.[21] These preparatory attacks freed up the Israeli air crews to provide close-air support to the ground forces that followed up the Beqa'a valley.

Israeli mechanized infantry moving primarily in M113 armored personnel carriers advanced in concert with their new Merkava tanks.[22] Syrian mechanized infantry of the 91st Armored Brigade dug in to earthen revetments, covering the broad open plains with interlocking heavy fires. Israeli forces flew continuous sorties of Scout and Mastiff reconnaissance drones, pinpointing Syrian defenses.[23] Ground station drone monitors passed enemy defensive locations to the Israeli armored forces, while Israeli fighter jets decimated Syrian combat aircraft. This gave nearly free rein to the Israeli AH-1 Cobra attack helicopters to strike Syrian front lines. Israeli tanks engaged Syrian T-72 tanks on flat open ground, using laser rangefinders to outgun the Syrian defenders and destroy them in their fighting positions.[24] However, Syrian Gazelle helicopters firing HOT guided anti-tank missiles had equal success against the Israelis, destroying several attacking tanks.[25] Artillery on both sides traded almost continuous fire, with the Israeli self-propelled 155mm guns keeping pace with the advancing mechanized infantry.

Once the attackers hit the towns and villages across the valley, infantry dismounted from their M113s and jeeps to clear through with close-quarters fighting. While the Israelis had a distinct technical advantage in the open terrain, both PLO and Syrian fighters made good use of RPG-variant rocket launchers to damage and destroy Israeli armor in closer terrain. In the more flat, open ground of the valley, Israelis repeatedly called in close-air support from fixed-wing and rotary-wing attack aircraft to facilitate their advances.

Israeli paratroopers dropped in from helicopters and, employing World War II-era jeeps mounted with machineguns and TOW anti-tank missiles, made some daring assaults onto the Syrian flanks and into high-ground defenses. In one night attack, Israeli mechanized forces with tanks in the lead stumbled straight into the Syrian front lines. A close-range armor and rocket fight ensued, and after losing two tanks the Israelis were forced to withdraw.[26] But ultimately, the Israelis pushed the Syrians and the PLO back far enough to allow for freedom of movement and operations further west. A ceasefire ended the major engagements in the Beqa'a Valley.[27]

Observations and insights from Beqa'a Valley, 1982. Aerial drones were used throughout the Vietnam War, so Israel's drone employment in the Beqa'a Valley was far from novel in the post-World War II era.[28] In fact, Israel had previously advanced the use of drones in ground combat in the 1973 Yom Kippur War.[29] But while the 1982 Lebanon War may or may not have marked the first widespread operational use of aerial drones in ground combat support roles, it is probably the most notable pre-1991 Gulf War example in Western literature.

Israeli air-launched Firebee and Chukar drones were probably used to trigger Syrian radars, while the Israelis employed both full-size operational drones and smaller drones to monitor the battlefield, spot targets, and report on enemy movement.[30] The Israeli Aircraft Industries Mastiff employed in the Beqa'a Valley in 1982 was later adopted by the U.S. military and employed against the Iraqis as the RQ-2 Pioneer in 1991 and in 2003.[31]

Anti-tank rockets and missiles continued to blunt the potential effectiveness of tanks operating even in wide-open terrain (generally called "tank country"). Helicopter gunships on both sides ranged out over the battlefield in tank-killing roles, while fixed-wing aircraft dropped increasingly accurate munitions on both armor and infantry. The continual advance-counter advance of air and counter-air technology could be clearly observed in the Beqa'a Valley in 1982. Despite the air threat, tanks were effective against each other and against opposing infantry, providing mobile protected firepower to both sides. Small but important technological advances like laser rangefinders and sloped armor on the Merkava lent an important edge to Israel's well-trained tank crews.

Al-Faw, Iraq, 1986[32]

Location: Al-Faw (Fao) Peninsula, Iraq[33]
Combatants: Islamic Republic of Iran versus the Iraqi Republic[34]
Dates: February 9–25, 1986

Six years into the 1980–1988 Iran-Iraq War, the Iranians made a bid to seize the al-Faw peninsula from defending Iraqi forces.[35] The Iraqis had dug in to well-engineered trenches, bunkers, and ditches along the flat and marshy ground west of the Shatt al-Arab waterway and had positioned the 26th Infantry Division—one of its weaker units—along with thousands of ill-disciplined Popular Army militiamen behind this linear defense. Iranian commanders employed an operational feint toward the vital Iraqi city of Basra to the north and a tactical probe toward the nearby town of al-Qurna in order to draw off the Iraqis' corps-level reinforcements. Then they executed their surprise attack with tens of thousands of troops across the Shatt al-Arab directly into the surprised Iraqi frontline units.

In order to get across the broad part of the wet gap without giving away the element of surprise, the Iranians employed special operations teams to clandestinely build a floatable causeway that could be raised just before the moment of attack. After a brief but intensive artillery and rocket bombardment, Iranian troops conducted a night amphibious assault in a dense rainstorm using small boats and landing craft.

Those Iraqis who could muster a defense used their emplaced armor, cannons, machineguns, and extensive artillery and mortar support to break up the northern prong of the attack, but the Iranians were able to establish a beachhead on the southern part of the peninsula. Iraqi Popular Army and regular troops from the 26th Infantry Division cracked in the face of the onrushing Iranian infantry. Thousands of Iraqis dropped their weapons and fled north in a panic in order to escape death or imprisonment.[36] This allowed the Iranians to set their own hasty defensive line and prepare for the inevitable Iraqi counterattack.

At this point in the war, the Iraqis tended to keep their better units (typically Republican Guard divisions) as corps reserve. Iraq's V Corps rushed its best armored and mechanized forces down the main roads of the peninsula; marshy terrain on both sides of the roads prevented sound tactical deployment. They covered their advance with artillery bombardments, airstrikes, roaming helicopter gunship attacks, and extensive use of chemical warfare agents. While the Iraqis were able to kill and wound thousands of Iranian infantrymen during their counterattack, they were stopped cold on the roadways by Iranian anti-armor teams, artillery, and airstrikes. Iraqi commanders led with their tanks and made poor use of infantry-armor teaming.[37] Fighting continued well into March, but by the end of the first counterattack the Iraqis had lost most of two divisions and the Iranians had at least temporarily captured the peninsula.

Observations and insights from al-Faw, Iraq, 1986. This was one of many instances of preplanned and in-stride wet-gap crossings in the Iran-Iraq War. Water obstacles have always been, and probably always will be, a routine challenge for ground combatants, so water-crossing operations are also necessarily routine. As in similar cases cited above, surprise, heavy supporting fires, good planning, and the cover of smoke or darkness can help give the crossing force the edge it needs to establish a toehold on the beach or far side bank. Terrain played at least two other significant roles in this fight: Marshland prevented good off-road tactical mechanized infantry and tank deployment, channelizing Iraqi armor on the hardball roads for the piecemeal destruction that followed; and lack of cover and concealment on the flat, open ground left the Iranian infantry vulnerable to Iraqi fires during the counterattack.

While chemical munitions were not frequently used by regular armies in ground combat after the 1980s, the al-Faw case was also a good example of the routine employment of chemical attack in the latter part of the Iran-Iraq War.

These kinds of weapons are generally considered immoral and unethical—I and many others find their use abhorrent—and they are subject to various conventions and bans. Nonetheless, at least for the Iraqis they often proved to be effective in ground combat when properly employed.[38] Chemical munitions like mustard and nerve agent incapacitated opposing troops and instilled fear that in at least some cases contributed to withdrawal or collapse.[39]

Cuito Cuanavale, Angola, 1987–1988[40]

Location: Cuito Cuanavale, Angola
Combatants: UNITA and South Africa versus Angola, Cuba, SWAPO, and ANC[41]
Dates: September 5, 1987–mid April 1988

With direct advisory and materiel support from the Soviet Union, the Angolan armed forces conducted a large, mechanized offensive to destroy the UNITA rebel forces operating from their bases southeast of the crossroads town of Cuito Cuanavale.[42] Mechanized infantry pushed over the marshy flatlands, crossed a series of small creeks and the Lomba River, and then ran headfirst into defending South African adviser forces. This first engagement was settled with artillery, small arms, and direct fire between the Angolans' BTR-60s and South African Ratel armored vehicles; the South African's 90mm guns won out over the BTRs' machineguns. Angolan forces continued forward with T-55 tanks supported by sweeping rocket barrages, but the lead tanks were destroyed by South African ZT3 laser-guided anti-tank missiles; lack of infantry support had left the T-55s dangerously exposed.[43]

This first phase of the battle settled into a series of heavy skirmishes. Angolan troops dug zigzag trenches, while the UNITA forces joined in with the South Africans. Attacks and counterattacks ensued with continual artillery shelling, airstrikes from Angolan MiGs and South African Mirage fighter-bombers, and sometimes intense infantry combat in the areas of dense vegetation on the front lines. In at least one case the South Africans conducted a daring light-armor assault directly across the Angolan trenches but defending T-55 tanks chased them away.[44]

While there were few significant exchanges of ground in the first months of fighting, the South Africans' advanced weaponry, electronic warfare technology, good leadership, excellent training, and tactical elan appeared to give them a routine tactical advantage. As the Angolans faltered, expert Cuban forces were mobilized and deployed en masse along with their heavy equipment—armor, artillery, rockets, attack helicopters, and fighter-bombers—to take the lead in the fight against the combined South African-UNITA forces.

South Africans also stepped up their operations with fresh battalions of troops, new equipment for their rebel allies, and the addition of Olifant tanks with 105mm main guns capable of taking on the Angolans' more numerous T-55s. Throughout the most intense phases of combat, from November 1987 through March 1988, the South Africans made extensive use of Seeker aerial drones fitted with both thermal and color electro-optical cameras to spot targets for their long-range G5 artillery and Valkiri 127mm multiple-launch rocket systems.[45] The Angolans employed SA-8 antiaircraft missiles and SA-7 shoulder-fired missiles to keep the Seekers off their backs, but their shoot-down rate was poor. Meanwhile, UNITA troops employed U.S.-supplied Stinger antiaircraft missiles against Angolan and Cuban MiGs.[46]

Angolan troops on the back foot dug in hard to the edges of Cuito Cuanavale with an even more extensive interlocking trench-and-bunker complex, complete with minefields and barbed wire covered by direct and indirect fires. South African and UNITA forces pushed north and engaged in a series of counteroffensives, but ultimately the Cubans tipped the balance. While the Angolans had applied Soviet doctrine ineptly, leaving their tanks exposed to anti-tank fires and their infantry walking in the open exposed to artillery, the Cubans were well trained, well led, and even more well equipped.

Extensive logistics planning allowed the Cubans to mass their heavy rocket and artillery assets in support of Angolan and supporting combined infantry forces, deterring and in some cases breaking South African attacks launched toward and around the town. Possibly tens of thousands of land mines were laid by both sides, slowing offensive movement, channelizing mechanized infantry and tank forces, and making the kinds of sweeping attacks common in the early months of the battle almost impossible. Over time, the expert Cuban support and the sheer mass of Angolan and combined infantry and armor wore down both South African and UNITA military capabilities and their will to sustain the fight. While the Angolan offensive in September 1987 may have been ill-advised, success at Cuito Cuanavale is generally attributed to the Cuban-Angolan side.

Observations and insights from Cuito Cuanavale, Angola, 1987–1988. Cuito Cuanavale, frequently referred to as the African Stalingrad, is rarely incorporated into the American historical narratives driving character-of-war descriptions and forecasts.[47] Probably most Westerners who have a loose familiarity with the Cold War conflicts in Africa do not imagine tens of thousands of troops engaged in full-scale combined-arms ground combat, complete with motorized-mechanized infantry and tank battles, networked trench systems, drones with thermal imagers, advanced electronic warfare, laser-guided anti-tank missiles, fixed-wing close-air support, long-range artillery and rocket duels, and attack helicopters darting over the treetops evading antiaircraft artillery and man-portable air-defense (MANPAD) missiles.

Yet all of these elements of modern ground combat were integrated at Cuito Cuanavale. Some key points seen in other cases recur: Wet gaps were unavoidable and had significant tactical impact on the flow of a battle; tanks operating without infantry support were vulnerable to an array of anti-armor weapons, but tanks also helped tip the balance in several tactical fights; attacking in column down open roadways is difficult and dangerous; magazine depth, or the amount of artillery and rocket munitions available to each side, mattered for sustaining combat power in this long-running battle; drones were useful for artillery spotting, and smaller drones were hard to shoot down with antiaircraft weapons designed to kill combat aircraft; and mortars were routinely useful. Both sides employed at least 60mm through 120mm mortar fire extensively throughout the battle.

Battle of the Tawakalna, Iraq, 1991[48]

Location: Southeastern Iraq
Combatants: U.S.-led Coalition (U.S. Army) versus Iraqi Republic
Dates: February 26–27, 1991

As part of the broader defensive effort to stave off the advancing U.S.-led coalition in the 1991 Gulf War, Iraq's 3rd Mechanized Tawakalna Republican Guard Division set into defensive lines in the Iraqi desert to the west of the Kuwaiti border.[49] Reinforced by tank battalions from the 10th and 12th Armored Divisions, the Iraqi commanders dug hasty emplacements and set bristling infantry-armor perimeters with RPG rocket teams, T-72 tanks, BMP-variant fighting vehicles, and heavy artillery, all protected by sand revetments. American A-10 attack aircraft had picked away at the defending Iraqi units prior to the direct ground combat engagement, but the Tawakalna and its regular force attachments stood their ground.

Elements of the American 1st Armored Division, 3rd Infantry Division, and 2nd Armored Cavalry Regiment (ACR) advanced across the desert and ran headfirst into the Iraqi defensive perimeter. Darkness of night, bad weather, and heavy black smoke from burning oilfields had prevented coalition intelligence assets from pinpointing the Iraqi positions in time to prepare the American units for a carefully planned assault. Several noteworthy engagements took place over the course of that night and the following day.

The best known of these engagements took place between three troops of American M1 tanks and Bradley infantry fighting vehicles of the 2nd ACR as they attacked defending Iraqi T-72s and BMPs.[50] A sandstorm degraded visibility to the point that the lead American scout units (Bradley M2A2s) ran right up on the Iraqi forward bunker line. Many of the Iraqi vehicle teams were sitting on the ground or in bunkers rather than waiting ready behind their guns to avoid being coffined by airstrikes, so when the Americans emerged out of the sandstorm they had to scramble to mount up, start their cold engines, and return fire. This gave the 25mm chaingun and TOW missile gunners in the Bradleys and the M1 tank gunners the first shots, and heavy fire superiority thereafter. Well-trained, aggressive American vehicle crews employing advanced thermal imagers, stabilized guns, and advanced missiles outpaced and outshot the Iraqis. Nonetheless, the Iraqis counterattacked with infantry and armor. They were decimated. Over the course of this engagement the three cavalry troops probably destroyed most of an Iraqi mechanized infantry brigade.

Other engagements did not play out so favorably for the coalition. As the American 7th Corps pushed east, a Bradley scout unit with the 7th Cavalry Regiment also ran headfirst into an entrenched Tawakalna mechanized and armor force. This time the Iraqis were ready. They picked apart the Bradleys with cannon fire from their BMPs, heavy machineguns, close-range rocket fire from dismounted infantry, and 125mm main gun rounds from their T-72 tanks. They poured in a mix of mortar and artillery fire to pin the Americans in place to amplify their direct close-range attacks. This American troop lost seven Bradleys destroyed or damaged and took 14 casualties before they could disengage and hand the fight over to follow-on echelons of M1 tanks.

In another sector, the 1st Infantry Division's 3rd Brigade advanced in tactical lines through the Iraqi 37th Armored Brigade. Lack of thermal signatures from the cold Iraqi tank engine blocks prevented the Americans from using their advanced technology to kill the defenders from a good distance. Chaos reigned as M1s and Bradleys mixed with Iraqi armor and RPG teams in close quarters.[51] While the Americans still dominated the tactical fight, in the confusion of these mixed lines they wound up destroying several of their own vehicles and killing six friendly soldiers. The American commander pulled back and smothered the Iraqi infantry with his organic artillery before resuming the advance.

Observations and insights from Battle of the Tawakalna, Iraq, 1991. As I noted previously, military-technical revolutionaries generally describe the Gulf War as a pivotal event. In their meta descriptions, high-technology American forces overwhelmed the relatively low-tech Iraqis who were employing limited-capability export versions of Soviet and Chinese weapons, equipment, and munitions. There is no denying the coalition's technical advantage and the value of technology during ground combat. Air superiority allowed strike aircraft to reduce Iraqi defenses before ground combat ensued. Satellite and drone imagery helped sketch out the defensive lines for attack planning. In many close-range fights, thermal imagers probably gave American gun crews a significant technical edge.

However, none of these technologies, including thermal imagers, satellites, drones, or anti-tank missiles, were novel in 1991. There is also no way to ascertain the causation of American and other coalition force success against the Iraqis in engagements like the one at 73 Easting. Was the outcome dictated by technology, or by differences in training, leadership, and professional ethos, or other human factors? It seems clear that it was a mix of causative factors, so any binary claims about Gulf War ground combat ("it was all about technology" or "it was all about leadership" or adaptability, etc.) are empirically indefensible. This case is indeed an essential reference point for the assessment of contemporary debate over the character and future of ground combat, though not necessarily in support of any one particular argument.

Shusha, Nagorno-Karabakh, 1992[52]

Location: Shusha, Nagorno-Karabakh
Combatants: Armenia and militias versus Azerbaijan
Dates: Late April–May 10, 1992

Shortly after the collapse of the Soviet Union, both Armenia and Azerbaijan remained heavily armed with Soviet-era weapons and equipment. They had concentrated most of their combat power in and around the disputed region of Nagorno-Karabakh. In May 1992 Armenia attacked to seize the city of Shusha and expel defending Azerbaijani forces.[53] Shusha sits on a hilltop in steep, mountainous terrain and can only be reached on a narrow and isolated road, or on foot over rough terrain. Buildings in the city were, and still are, constructed with heavy stone walls.

Defending Azerbaijani regular and militia troops made every effort to use the steep terrain and heavy walls to their advantage, ringing in their armor, infantry, and BM-21 122mm multiple-launch rocket systems. Armenian commanders believed they had to draw the defenders out from the walls and so attacked nearby towns with mechanized infantry forces. A significant skirmish was fought between infantry and armor forces for a nearby hill position, with Azerbaijani infantry unsuccessfully attacking uphill against Armenian troops. Eventually, the Armenians circled in on Shusha.

The Azerbaijanis were hard-pressed from the outset, having failed to put sufficient combat power into the defense. They had raised a series of ad hoc militia infantry forces to defend the walls and buildings of the city, and they had a platoon of T-72 tanks lined up to stop the Armenian advance up the main road. At first, these defenses held. A lone Armenian T-72 pushed forward without infantry support and engaged in a gunfight with at least one of the Azerbaijani tanks and was destroyed. At about the same time, Armenian infantry assaulted the cliff faces around the city and were repulsed by defending infantry. But steep firing angles effectively prevented the Azerbaijanis from bringing their handful of multiple-launch rocket systems to bear on the attackers below. More importantly, they had insufficient strength to counterattack. This let the Armenians safely reconsolidate for a follow-on assault.

While the Armenians were also disadvantaged by the terrain, they were able to employ their fire support to suppress the defenders and allow for a second, larger assault into the city. On the second day of the all-out attack, Armenian armor and infantry pushed into the edge of Shusha, penetrating the outer defenses. Infantry started to work street to street reinforced by firepower from tanks, BMP infantry fighting vehicles, and BTR armored personnel carriers. In short order they were able to knock out or capture the Azerbaijani rocket systems and tanks, stripping away the defenders' combined-arms capabilities. Poorly trained and unsteady militia that had mixed in with the Azerbaijani regular forces began to crack in the face of the heavier-armed and more aggressive Armenians. By the end of the second day the defenders had effectively broken. Armenian forces swept into Shusha on May 10 and captured the city.

Observations and insights from Shusha, Nagorno-Karabakh, 1992. High ground is generally considered advantageous, and the defenders certainly benefited from the narrow mountain approach and rough terrain. However, combat videos showing the exposed terrain revealed the ease with which Armenian attackers could observe, target, and strike elevated defensive positions with their artillery and longer-range direct-fire weapons, even without the explicitly recorded employment of drones or observation aircraft.[54] Lack of vegetation and other concealment all but obviated the benefit of the high ground in this fight.

Unable to counterattack, the Azerbaijanis put up an *inactive,* or static defense, ultimately reducing their survivability. While we cannot know the causative factors in the Azerbaijani collapse, the poor will to fight of the hastily assembled militia seemed to be relevant in the infantry withdrawal across and out of the city.

Cenepa Valley, Peru and Ecuador, 1995[55]

Location: Cenepa Valley border area between Ecuador and Peru
Combatants: Ecuador versus Peru
Dates: January 24–February 2, 1995

In an effort to establish control over the contested Cenepa River Valley, Peru sent heliborne and foot-mobile infantry into the mountainous terrain that was dominated by a string of Ecuadoran observation posts and patrol bases.[56] Fighting started on the footpaths along the edge of the Cenepa River, with small but intense infantry skirmishes igniting a wider battle. After engaging Peruvian foot patrols in the contested zone, Ecuadoran commanders sent out aerial drones with night-vision optics and discovered newly established Peruvian patrol bases with helipads.

Ecuadoran troops first targeted patrol base "Roosevelt." They helilifted in both 81mm and 120mm mortars and then conducted a combined-arms assault against the defending Peruvian troops.[57] Ecuadoran Super Puma helicopters executed pre-attack strafing and rocket runs, mortar shells splashed into the defenders' positions, and the infantry moved in firing machineguns, rifles, and M72 shoulder-fired rockets. The Peruvians who survived the attack withdrew, leaving Ecuador in control of the high ground and the helipad.

In response to this defeat, the Peruvians attacked an Ecuadoran outpost. They swarmed the defenders by converging several satellite patrols up through the steep, densely vegetated terrain and on to the objective.[58] Ecuadoran troops withdrew under fire but then pinned the Peruvians in place with 122mm multiple-launch rockets, tube artillery fire, and mortars. When the Peruvians pushed out into the mountainous jungle in pursuit of the withdrawing defenders, the Ecuadorans inflicted casualties with antipersonnel mines, punji pits, sniper fire, and more indirect fire.[59] Both sides then rushed to move in more troops by helicopter.

While the ground troops fought for control of the hilltop and mountaintop bases, fighting for control of the airspace intensified.[60] The Peruvians attempted a daring helicopter attack on Ecuadoran ground positions, but they were pushed back with losses inflicted by heavy antiaircraft artillery and missile fire. Fixed-wing fighter jets engaged in dogfights above the battlefield, and jets from both sides risked enemy ground fire to support infantry attacks with rockets, guns, and bombs. Peruvian commandos attacked another Ecuadoran position, Base Sur, charging into bunkers and moving through supporting artillery and helicopter gunship fire to clear the base in close combat.

The final phase of the battle took place at Tiwinza and Coangos. Tiwinza is a broad mountain plain that was held by Ecuadoran forces dug in with a full combined-arms defense, including RPG-7 rocket launchers, grenade launchers, machineguns, 122mm multiple-launch rockets and 105mm pack howitzers, fixed-wing and rotary-wing aviation, trench lines, and minefields covered by fires. The Peruvians helilifted in their own 105mm artillery and a joint infantry force to assault these prepared defenses, initiating a series of attacks with fixed-wing airstrikes from A-37 and Kfir fighter-bombers. They also launched special operations raids against supporting Ecuadoran positions at Coangos.

Peruvian infantry advanced behind artillery fire into the minefields and were hit by a firestorm of defensive combined-arms fire. When the Peruvian infantry stalled, the Ecuadorans kept them pinned under sustained fire for a full day, bombarding the Peruvian assembly area and attack positions with mortars, rockets, artillery, and airstrikes. Peruvian commandos tried to pick away at the Ecuadorans from the flanks, but the defenders held their ground. Eventually the Peruvians had to withdraw, suffering perhaps four times as many dead and wounded as their adversaries.[61]

Observations and insights from Cenepa Valley, Peru and Ecuador, 1995. While control of the skies did not dictate the ground combat outcomes, low-level and above-the-clouds air battles and antiair fires played an important role in shaping both fire support and logistics. Because the rough terrain and distances from support bases forced heavy dependence on heliborne lift, both sides were to varying extent dependent on the ability to fly support helicopters around the battlefield. Antiaircraft artillery, surface-to-air missile, and fixed-wing attack threats reduced helicopter mobility, forcing the foot-mobile infantry to take on greater risk and carry heavier supply loads on their backs. Ecuador was able to better control the lower-altitude fight, so the Peruvians suffered repeated rotary-wing attacks from Ecuadoran Super Pumas and lost some of their own rotary-wing aircraft.

Most of the cited sources give the Ecuadorans considerable credit for their effective employment of mines and booby traps to slow and wound Peruvian infantry. Both sides made good use of mortar and artillery fire, but the Ecuadorans combined their fires more effectively and were able to leverage their shorter logistics lines to sustain heavy indirect fires on attacking Peruvian troops. Grenade launchers played an important role at the lowest tactical level, providing both sides—but primarily the Ecuadorans—with pocket artillery in the dense terrain.

INTERVAL-PERIOD GROUND COMBAT AND THE CHARACTER OF WAR

Evidentiary requirements that applied to the World War II cases apply equally to the interval period: Capturing and holistically describing the more than fifty years of global ground combat between 1945 and 2002 would require an effort similar to the one I undertook for the 2003–2022 period. Researchers would have to find, categorize, and code all skirmishes and battles that fit the basic requirements I laid out in the introduction: any combined-arms ground fight between two platoons or more. Major long-running conflicts like the Korean War, the Vietnam War, the Mozambican war of independence, the Soviets' Afghanistan war, the Iran-Iraq War, and the Angolan civil war would each yield a high volume of cases.[62] Such an effort to characterize ground combat in the interval period would generate at least thousands of individual cases.[63] Therefore, the exemplary cases above and the characteristics described in the following chapter are necessarily subjective in terms of both their selection and description.

They are, however, useful to bridge the gap from the World War II baseline to the beginning of what I describe as the modern period of ground combat starting in 2003. Centuries-old technologies like shoulder-fired projectile weapons and artillery evolved beyond World War II to become increasingly effective, though not dramatically different in form or function. New technologies like satellites and aircraft stealth coatings emerged and proliferated, but their impact on ground combat was in different cases idiosyncratically important, negligible, or unclear.

In the years immediately following World War II, proponents of the helicopter suggested that aircraft like the American UH-1 Huey and Soviet Mil Mi-8 could make ground combat universally less linear and more dynamic.[64] The helicopter's performance in ground combat in this interim period was, however, uneven and in practice something less than revolutionary. Use of drones became commonplace in some militaries but not in others. Battlefield tactics and techniques remained relatively consistent with World War II-era precedents. The next chapter describes these evolutionary advances toward the beginning of what I have bounded as the modern era of ground combat.

NOTES

1. Here I refer back to the cited sources in chapter 1.
2. Several of these picks were important technical showcases (e.g., Ia Drang and helicopters), while others were necessary to build follow-on discussions in later chapters. For example, the Battle of Shusha 1992 is a good reference point for the Battle of Shusha in 2020, and the 1991 battle with the Iraqi Tawakalna Republican Guard Division is one of the lynchpin American cases in the debate over the military-technical revolution as it applies to ground combat.
3. Edwin H. Simmons, *Over the Seawall: U.S. Marines at Inchon* (Washington, DC: Marine Corps History Division, 2000); Lynn Montross, "The Inchon Landing—Victory over Time and Tide," in *U.S. Marine Corps: Our First Year in Korea*, ed. Lynn Montross (Washington, DC: U.S. Marine Corps Historical Branch, G-3, 1952); U.S. Army Center of Military History, *Korea 1950* (Washington, DC, 1989); Robert D. Heinl, "The Inchon Landing: A Case Study in Amphibious Planning," *Naval War College Review* 51, no. 2 (Spring 1998), 117–134; Joseph H. Alexander, *Battle of the Barricades: U.S. Marines in the Recapture of Seoul* (Washington, DC: U.S. Marine Corps History Division, 2000); and Lynn Montross and Nicholas A. Canona, *The Inchon-Seoul Operations* (Washington, DC: U.S. Marine Corps Historical Branch, 1955).
4. This is a midpoint reference between the two cities, not a specific center point.
5. DPRK = Democratic People's Republic of Korea, or North Korea.
6. See Montross and Canona, *Inchon-Seoul*. The full narrative with graphics is available on a single website, https://www.gutenberg.org.

7. See Montross and Canona, *Inchon-Seoul*, and also Simmons, *Over the Seawall*, for references to the Air-Naval Gunfire Liaison Company, or ANGLICO.
8. LVT = Landing Vehicle, Tracked. For more on the LVTs at Seoul, see Alexander, *Battle of the Barricades*, various pages.
9. Primarily, the 90mm cannon employing high-velocity ammunition could shoot straight through both sides of the T-34. See Steven J. Zaloga, *T-34-85 vs M26 Pershing, Korea 1950* (Oxford, UK: Osprey, 2010).
10. Including Harold G. Moore and Joseph L. Galloway, *We Were Soldiers Once . . . and Young: Ia Drang—The Battle That Changed the War in Vietnam* (New York: Random House, 1992); J. P. Harris and J. Kenneth Eward, *Ia Drang 1965: The Struggle for Vietnam's Pleiku Province* (Oxford, UK: Osprey, 2020); Steven M. Leonard, "Steel Curtain: The Guns on the Ia Drang," *Field Artillery* (July–August 1998), 17–20; Merle L. Pribbenow, "The Fog of War: The Vietnamese View of the Ia Drang Battle," *Military Review* 81, no. 1 (January–February 2001), 93–97; John A. Cash, "Fight at Ia Drang, 14–16 November 1965," in *Seven Firefights in Vietnam*, eds. John A. Cash, John Albright, and Allan W. Sandstrum (Washington, DC: U.S. Center of Military History, 1985); and Robert H. Edwards, "The Battle of LZ X-Ray: Personal Experience of a Company Commander," *Infantry* (October–December 2015), 24–33.
11. This section is drawn largely from Harris and Eward, *Ia Drang 1965*, and from Pribbenow, "The Fog of War." While *We Were Soldiers* is the definitive account of the battle, it is also personalized and relatively narrow in perspective. Pribbenow provides the PAVN perspective.
12. I touch on this point in several sections of *Iraqi Army Will to Fight*.
13. Including Anuraag Chhibber, "The Battle of Hilli: Tactical Lessons," *Scholar Warrior* (Spring 2016), 110–116; D. P. Ramachandran, "The Story of My Squadron in the Bangladesh War of Liberation 1971," *United Service Institution of India* (October 2021); Ranbir Singh, *War in the East: The Liberation of Bangladesh, 1971* (New Delhi: Sabre & Quill, 2021); S. N. Prasad and U. P. Thapliyal, eds., *The India-Pakistan War of 1971: A History* (New Delhi: Natraj, 2014); V. Ganapathy, "Battle of Bogra," *Scholar Warrior* (Spring 2015), 116–124; J. B. S. Yadava, "1971 War: Battle of Bogra," *Indian Defense Review* 33, no. 4 (October–December 2018); and U.S. Central Intelligence Agency, *South Asian Military Handbook* (Langley, VA: Directorate of Intelligence, August 1973).
14. Recoilless rifles can also be fired from the shoulder and often are (World War II, Korea, Syria, etc.), though when taken off their mounts they are unwieldy.
15. Chhibber, "Battle of Hilli," 113–116, quote on 115.
16. Including Cao Van Vien, *The Final Collapse* (Washington, DC: U.S. Army Center of Military History, 1985); U.S. Defense Attaché Office, *RVNAF Final Assessment Jan thru Apr FY75*, declassified intelligence report (Saigon, RVN, 1975); George J. Veith and Merle L. Pribbenow II, "'Fighting Is an Art': The Army of the Republic of Vietnam's Defense of Xuan Loc, 9–21 April 1975," *Journal of Military History* 68, no. 1 (January 2004), 163–213; James H. Willbanks, *Xuan Loc: The Final Battle, Vietnam 1975*, paper presented to the Popular Culture Association (New Orleans, 2000); Hua Yen Len, "The Line of Steel at Xuan Loc (Long Khanh): 12 Days and Nights of Ferocious Combat against the North Vietnamese Communists," memorandum (February 1998); "General Le Minh Dao (Commander of the 18th Division/ARVN)," archival newsreel, Institut national de l'audiovisuel, n.d., YouTube

video; "Let Them Fight—America Leaves the Last Battle of the Vietnam War—Xuân Lộc," documentary, Dark Docs, n.d., YouTube video; "Trận Xuân Lộc năm 1975," archival newsreel, hinhanhlichsu.org, 1975, YouTube video.

17. In Vietnamese, Xuân Lộc is approximately pronounced "so'on lop." This common transliteration (Xuan Loc) is therefore inaccurate because it transposes Vietnamese Latin letters for common modern English Latin script letters. Nonetheless, it is commonly employed by historians, and I have kept it as Xuan Loc here to avoid confusing references. In other cases throughout this book and in the database, I have tried to provide more faithful transliterations, particularly from Modern Standard Arabic to English.
18. This narrative is drawn primarily from Veith and Pribbenow II, "'Fighting Is an Art.'" This is probably the definitive all-points historical source on this battle, though Hua Yen Len's memorandum and Le Minh Dao's video discussion are both quite informative.
19. Including Richard A. Gabriel, *Operation Peace for Galilee: The Israel-PLO War in Lebanon* (New York: Hill and Wang, 1984); Samuel Katz and Lee E. Russell, *Armies in Lebanon 1982–1984* (Oxford, UK: Osprey, 1985); Emmanuel Wald, *The Wald Report: The Decline of Israeli National Security since 1967* (Tel Aviv: Schocken, 1992); Benjamin S. Lambeth, *Moscow's Lessons from the 1982 Lebanon Air War* (Santa Monica, CA: RAND Corporation, 1984); Trevor N. Dupuy and Paul Martell, *Flawed Victory: How Lebanon Became a Culture of War and Hate* (Hero Books, 1986), ebook; U.S. Central Intelligence Agency, *Military Lessons Learned by Israel and Syria from the War in Lebanon*, declassified intelligence report (Langley, VA: Directorate of Intelligence, 1984); "Lebanon War 1982 (First Lebanon War)—Real Combat Footage," archival newsreel, 1982, YouTube video; "Modern Warfare: Lebanon 1982," documentary, parts 1–3, n.d., YouTube videos.
20. PLO = Palestine Liberation Organization.
21. Lambeth, *Moscow's Lessons*, provides a good explanation of this attack.
22. They employed a mix of Merkavas and older variant tanks including M60s and British Centurion tanks.
23. See "Modern Warfare: Lebanon 1982," part 2, for good video of the drone employment and combat footage of these battles.
24. This narrative is drawn from all of the cited sources, but primarily from Dupuy and Martell, *Flawed Victory*, and Katz and Russell, *Armies in Lebanon*.
25. The HOT is a French-made antitank missile developed in the late 1970s. It has a shaped-charge warhead, and the early versions employed by the Syrians had a range of well over 2,000 meters. For more on these engagements, see George W. Gawrych, "Attack Helicopters in Lebanon," chapter in *Combined Arms in Battle since 1939*, ed. Roger J. Spiller (Fort Leavenworth, KS: U.S. Army Command and General Staff College Press, 1992), 35–42.
26. Depuy and Martell, *Flawed Victory*.
27. Skirmishes and airstrikes continued for several months. This was less of a ceasefire than a tactical pause that dribbled out over time.
28. See *Evolution of Drones* in chapter 5 for more information on interim period drones.
29. John F. Kreis, "Unmanned Aircraft in Israeli Air Operations," *Air Power History* 37, no. 4 (Winter 1990), 162–164.

30. Firebee and Chukar are both target drones used for aerial missile and gunnery practice. They were employed by the U.S. Air Force to trigger North Vietnamese radar systems, and for electronic warfare purposes, during the Vietnam War. For more on drone use during the Vietnam War, see David Axe, *Drone War Vietnam*.
31. For more on the Pioneer, see Laurence R. Newcome, *Unmanned Aviation: A Brief History of Unmanned Aerial Vehicles* (Reston, VA: American Institute of Aeronautics and Astronautics, 2004), 92–97; Richard Major, "RQ-2 Pioneer: The Flawed System That Redefined US Unmanned Aviation" (thesis, Air Command and Staff College, 2012).
32. Including Kevin M. Woods, Williamson Murray, Elizabeth A. Nathan, Laila, Sabara, and Ana M. Venegas, *Saddam's Generals: Perspectives of the Iran-Iraq War* (Alexandria, VA: Institute for Defense Analysis, 2011); Pesach Malovany, *Wars of Modern Babylon: A History of the Iraqi Army from 1921 to 2003* (Lexington: University Press of Kentucky, 2017); Kenneth M. Pollack, *Arabs at War: Military Effectiveness, 1948–1991* (Lincoln: University of Nebraska Press, 2002); Pierre Razoux, *The Iran-Iraq War* (Cambridge, MA: Belknap Press of Harvard University Press, 2015); Anthony H. Cordesman and Abraham R. Wagner, *The Lessons of Modern War, Volume II: The Iran-Iraq War* (Boulder, CO: Westview Press, 1990); "Iran Iraq war, Operation Dawn 8, Faw region عملیات والفجر هشت منطقه فاو جنگ عراق و ایران," archival newsreel, n.d., YouTube video; "Operation Valfajr 8 (Dawn 8) Iran-Iraq War Operation 8 عملیات والفجر," documentary, Gates of Glory, n.d., YouTube video.
33. This is a general location.
34. Haqqani is an Afghan tribal and family name.
35. This section is primarily derived from Malovany, *Wars of Modern Babylon*; Razoux, *Iran-Iraq War*; and from the research I conducted for *Iraqi Army Will to Fight*.
36. Razoux describes "groups of crazed soldiers in tattered uniforms attempting to escape their pursuers through the salt marshes." Razoux, *Iran-Iraq War*, 354.
37. The 1980–1988 Iraqi Army was an armor-centric force with generally weak infantry divisions. See Connable, *Iraqi Army Will to Fight*.
38. Iran also employed chemical munitions but in far lower quantities and with concomitantly lessened effect.
39. See Connable, *Iraqi Army Will to Fight*, 51–55.
40. Including Peter Polack, *The Last Hot Battle of the Cold War: Decision at Cuito Cuanavale and the Battle for Angola, 1987–1988*, Oxford, UK: Casemate, 2013; Helmoed-Romer Heitman, "Operations Moduler and Hooper (1987–1988)," *South African Defense Force Review* (1989, www.rhodesia.nl); Helmoed-Romer Heitman, *Modern African Wars (3) South-West Africa* (Oxford, UK: Osprey, 2011); "Battle of Cuito Cuanavale 1987/88 Angolan Civil War," documentary, n.d., YouTube video; "Born to War Episode 9. Part I: The Siege of Cuito Cuanavale," documentary, Born to War, n.d., YouTube video; "Batalla de Cuito Cuanavale, proeza de los cubanos en la ayuda internacionalista prestada a Angola," archival newsreel, n.d., YouTube video; "Manobras militar das FAPLA, Batalha de Cuíto Cuanavale na Guerra Civil Angolana ocorrido em 1987/88," archival newsreel, n.d., YouTube video.
41. UNITA = National Union for the Total Independence of Angola; SWAPO = South West African People's Organization; ANC = African National Congress
42. Most of this narrative is drawn from Polack, *Last Hot Battle*, since it provides the most detail on tactical combat.

43. For more on the Denel ZT3 Ingwe, see Leon Engelbrecht, "Fact File: Denel ZT3 Ingwe Precision Guided Missile," *Defence Web,* January 7, 2011, https://www.defenceweb.co.za.
44. Polack, *Last Hot Battle,* 103–105.
45. Polack, *Last Hot Battle,* 47. The Seeker drone is quite similar to the Israeli Aircraft Industries Scout and U.S. Marine Corps and Navy Pioneer drones. For more on the early-model Seeker, see http://www.saairforce.co.za.
46. Polack, *Last Hot Battle,* 138.
47. For example, see Isaac Saney, "African Stalingrad: The Cuban Revolution, Internationalism, and the End of Apartheid," *Latin American Perspectives* 33, no. 5 (September 2006), 81–117; and Trevor N. Dupuy, "Technology and the Human Factor in War," *International TNDM Newsletter,* August 1997.
48. I refer to this as the Battle of the Tawakalna and not a place name or Battle of 73 Easting, because it occurred in the open desert and it encompasses more than the 73 Easting battle. Including Stephen A. Bourque, "Correcting Myths about the Persian Gulf War: The Last Stand of the Tawakalna," *Middle East Journal* 51, no. 4 (1997), 556–683; H. R. McMaster, "Eagle Troop at the Battle of 73 Easting," *The Strategy Bridge,* February 26, 2016, https://thestrategybridge.org; U.S. News and World Report, *Triumph without Victory: The Unreported History of the Persian Gulf War* (New York: Random House, 1992); Tony Wunderlich, "Lucky Scouts Dodge 'Big Bullets' That Ripped Their Bradley," *Armor* (May–June 1991); Frank N. Schubert and Theresa L. Kraus, eds., *The Whirlwind War: The United States Army in Operations Desert Shield and Desert Storm* (Washington, DC: U.S. Army Center of Military History, 1995); U.S. Department of Defense, *Conduct of the Persian Gulf War: An Interim Report to Congress,* official report (Arlington, VA, 1991); Stephen Biddle, "Victory Misunderstood: What the Gulf War Tells Us about the Future of Conflict," *International Security* 21, no. 2 (1996), 139–179; and Mike Guardia, *The Fires of Babylon: Eagle Troop and the Battle of 73 Easting* (Oxford, UK: Casemate, 2015).
49. This narrative is drawn primarily from Bourque, "Correcting Myths"; Guardia, *Fires of Babylon;* and U.S. News and World Report, *Triumph without Victory.* Also see my summary of the PL Bullet engagement (and a good overhead sketch) in *Iraqi Army Will to Fight,* 79–81.
50. A total of 28 M1A1 tanks and 37 Bradley IFVs were employed in the fight, along with six 120mm mortars, 16 155mm artillery tubes, and a multiple-launch rocket system. The Iraqis had 55 T-72s, 33 BMPs, twelve tubes of 152mm towed artillery, seven 81mm mortars, two SA-13 air defense systems, and seven 23mm anti-aircraft guns, as well as a handful of T-55s and a BTR-70. The Iraqis also had dismounted machinegun and RPG infantry teams, with approximately one hundred soldiers in the field. See Jesse Orlansky and Jack Thorpe, eds., *73 Easting: Lessons Learned from Desert Storm via Advanced Distributed Simulation Technology* (Alexandria, VA: Institute for Defense Analyses, April 1992), 10–12.
51. This narrative is drawn from Bourque, "Correcting Myths."
52. Including Thomas de Waal, *Black Garden: Armenia and Azerbaijan through Peace and War* (New York: New York University Press, 2013); "Shushi, Lachin, Goris—March 1992 the Artsakh War," archival newsreel, 1992, YouTube video; "Հարսանիք լեռներում," Yerevan News, n.d., YouTube video; "Ermenistan'ın Şuşa'yı İşgali ve O Günlerde Yaşananlar—Karabağ'ın Sessiz Çığlığı—TRT Avaz," TRT

Avaz, n.d., YouTube video; John Thor-Dahlburg, "Armenians Attack Karabakh City: Ethnic Warfare: Fierce Street Battles Are Reported in Shusha, an Azerbaijani Stronghold. Meanwhile, a Cease-Fire Is Signed in Tehran," *Los Angeles Times*, May 9, 1992; "Storming Shushi/Operation "Wedding in the Mountains/1992," archival newsreel, 1992, YouTube video; "Şuşanı necə satdılar (Qarabağ—ANS, 1997)," documentary, ANS Press, 1997, YouTube video.

53. This case is derived primarily from de Waal, *Black Garden*, and from the aggregated videos.
54. For example, see "Shushi, Lachin, Goris—March 1992 The Artsakh War."
55. Including Cristián Faundes, *El Conflicto de la Cordillera del Cóndor: Los Actores del Enfrentamiento Bélico no Declarado entre Ecuador y Perú* (Santiago, Chile: Pontificia Universidad Catolica de Chile, April 2004); David Spencer, "Peru-Ecuador 1995: The Evolution of Military Tactics from the Conflict of 1981," *Small Wars & Insurgencies* 9, no. 3 (1998), 129–151; Tom Cooper, "Peru vs. Ecuador; Alto-Cenapa War, 1995," online forum (Penn State University, Air Combat Information Group, 2007), https://ghdx.healthdata.org; "Cenapa's War (English subtitles)," documentary, Frente Nacional de ex-Conscriptos, n.d., YouTube video; "Guerra del Cenepa War (1995) (82 photos, Best photos)," archival photographs, YouTube video; "Campaña Militar del Alto Cenapa 1995 Perú," archival newsreel, n.d., YouTube video.
56. Responsibility for initiation of this conflict is disputed. This battle narrative is drawn primarily from Faundes, *El Conflicto*, and Spencer, "Peru-Ecuador."
57. For example, see Amaru Tincopa, *Air Wars between Ecuador and Peru: Aerial Operations over the Condor Mountain Range, 1995* (Warwick, UK: Helion, 2021).
58. Satellite patrolling is a tactic generally attributed to the British Army in Northern Ireland, but it was also employed (at least) by the U.S. Marines during Evans Carlson's Long Patrol on Guadalcanal in World War II.
59. A punji pit is a hole filled with sharpened stakes made of bamboo or other material designed to cause mobility casualties.
60. For more on the air component of this battle, see Tincopa, 2021.
61. See Spencer, "Peru-Ecuador," 146, for commentary and estimates of casualties.
62. For the sake of comparison, consider that the 2011–2022 Syria case in the modern database yielded ninety-three cases, many of which could be broken out into tense of smaller cases. Even a brief perusal of just a handful of the many hundreds of month-by-month U.S. Marine Corps command chronologies from the Vietnam War at the Texas Tech University Virtual Vietnam Archive reveals reporting on more independent ground combat cases than exist in my modern database. I am aware of probably thousands more from the post-2001 Iraq and Afghanistan conflicts archived at the U.S. Army's Center of Military History in Washington, DC.
63. For an exemplary but necessarily incomplete list, see Shuhui Kitamura, *World Historical Battles Database Version 1.1*, research paper, n.d., https://osf.io/mdjzu/.
64. For example, see Joseph Bonanno, "The Helicopter in Combat," *Ordnance* 38, no. 203 (March–April 1954), 868–872; Harry A. Jacobs, "The Army's Flying Truck," *Ordnance* 39, no. 210 (May–June 1955), 882–890; and Douglas Morris, "The Development and Use of Helicopters," presentation to the Royal United Services Institute (London, November 23, 1966).

FIVE

Interval-Period Ground Combat Characteristics

Evolutionary changes in the varying characteristics of ground combat emerged unequally from 1945 through 2022. I start this chapter by discussing consistent and emerging trends in ground combat in mid-term (~ten to fifteen-year) time blocks. I then dig in to significant issues that carried forward to affect modern ground combat. Perhaps the most important of these is the global proliferation of Soviet weapons, equipment, and munitions over the course of nearly half a century. I wrap up the chapter by revisiting the key characteristics identified in chapter 3.

Researchers recorded hundreds of major and minor conflicts involving some type of ground combat occurring between the end of World War II and the end of 2002.[1] As I argued in the previous chapter, these conflicts have the potential to generate perhaps many thousands of distinct ground combat cases. For example, in 1950 the Chinese People's Liberation Army (PLA) 52nd Division advanced and engaged Tibetan ground forces on the Kham Plateau in order to seize control of Chamdo city and its environs.[2] PLA forces conducted an aggressive division-strength pincer movement against entrenched Tibetan dismounted infantry, horse cavalry, and militia, effectively wiping out Tibet's organized combat forces in their first major engagement.[3] At least in readily available English-language sources, no other major ground combat events were recorded from the Communist Chinese invasion of Tibet in the early 1950s.

In contrast, the 1960–1975 Vietnam War included probably thousands of recorded battles and skirmishes, with some ground units engaging in daily combined-arms fights for months on end.[4] Gaps in our collective, public understanding of historical combat are vast, but some observations still can be made.

GROUND COMBAT OBSERVATIONS AND INSIGHTS FROM LATE 1945 TO 1959

Global investments in conventional warfare capabilities plummeted in the immediate aftermath of World War II. At least through the onset of the Korean War in 1950, American ground forces were partially retooled for simple survivability on a nuclear battlefield.[5] Imagined nuclear conflict never emerged, but postwar disorder in Asia, Africa, and the Middle East set the conditions for the decades of land warfare that followed. Colonial controls were weakened or removed in some countries, allowing for the emergence of violent insurgencies in the first wave of postwar independence movements. China, Greece, and other countries were left fragmented, with large and often well-armed military forces standing ready to vie for territorial control. At least 46 conflicts continued through or erupted between the end of World War II and the beginning of the 1960s.[6] As the Cold War intensified, competing great powers fueled these fights by injecting weapons, equipment, training, advising, and sometimes direct intervention forces.

From the mid 1940s through the end of the decade, insurgents and civil war combatants generally fought with the tactics, leadership, weapons, and equipment they had at hand. For example, Viet Minh and other Vietnamese groups seeking independence from French colonial rule fought against the reoccupation of Indochina with a mix of Japanese, British, and old French weapons including some turn-of-the-century bolt-action rifles.[7] They relentlessly attacked British and French patrols and bases in a series of hit-and-run skirmishes through the late 1940s. These relatively low-risk operations allowed them time to recruit new troops and build the infantry mass necessary to conduct larger-scale operations. At the end of the decade the Chinese began to ship weapons and equipment to the Viet Minh and also trained Vietnamese cadre in hard-earned ground combat lessons and tactics from their own wars with Japan and the Kuomintang.[8]

This external Chinese support steadily accelerated, and by the early 1950s the Viet Minh were armed with tens of thousands of machineguns, thousands of mortars, hundreds of artillery pieces, anti-tank guns, antiaircraft artillery, and increasingly effective small arms. Chinese trucks gave them motorized mobility.[9] By the time they engaged the French Foreign Legion, colonial forces, and paratroopers at the Battle of Dien Bien Phu in 1954, the ostensibly irregular-force Viet Minh vanguard was a well-trained, well-armed, well-led, combat-tested, combined-arms force capable of operating in all types of difficult terrain.[10]

At Dien Bien Phu, Viet Minh infantry and civilian porters dragged artillery into the high ground above the ill-situated French entrenchments in the valley below. Then Viet Minh troops slowly ground the defenders down with fires, creeping entrenchments, and continual infantry assaults. French airpower was rendered ineffective by concentrated antiaircraft fire. The Viet Minh routed the French in what is widely described as one of the greatest Western military defeats of the second half of the twentieth century.

Dien Bien Phu was one of the first widely reported instances of ground combat in the post-WWII global proxy land wars.[11] By the mid 1950s, ground combat on even the most remote battlefields increasingly evinced unmistakable Soviet, Chinese, Warsaw Pact, American, French, Belgian, or British influences.[12] All of the Cold War competitors began to manufacture and license knockoff copies of their best equipment for free distribution or sale to allied proxy forces, or just to groups or states with sufficient cash on hand.

Global proliferation of ground combat arms and equipment skyrocketed, putting at least basic combined-arms capabilities in the hands of some combatants who had previously fought with breech-loading rifles and knives. Ground combat forces capable of organized combined-arms warfare started to adopt either Soviet or Western training standards and doctrine, and sometimes a mix of both.[13] At least in my reading of the historical record, this period of rapid global militarization into what was contemporaneously described as the "third world" increased the relevance of seemingly minor and peripheral ground combat cases to the holistic understanding of modern ground combat.

GROUND COMBAT OBSERVATIONS AND INSIGHTS FROM 1960 TO 1969

American involvement in the Vietnam War (~1960–1975) influenced global characterizations of ground combat through and well beyond the 1960s, and for good reason.[14] From at least the point at which conventional U.S. Marine Corps units landed at Da Nang in 1965, the United States applied its most advanced ground combat weapons and equipment, its increasingly effective close-air support capabilities, intelligence collection assets, tanks, rotary-wing aviation, artillery, tactical doctrine, and experienced military leadership in ground combat. Week after week, month after month, year after year, American Army and Marine Corps units, allied units, and Republic of Vietnam armed forces engaged in repeated combined-arms engagements with both PAVN and PLAF units ranging in size from platoons of twenty or thirty soldiers to regiments of well over 1,000 soldiers.

All of the conventional combat power the Americans and their allies might bring to bear against the Soviet Union in a prospective war in Europe was put to full use in Vietnam. Sometimes it worked, sometimes it didn't. Contrary to a popular cliché, the Americans did not win every battle they fought in Vietnam; effective defeat at LZ Albany described in the previous chapter is just one counterfactual case.[15]

Other cases of defeat or near-defeat arguably include the 7th Marine Regiment's near defeat and loss of 126 killed—with some bodies left behind—and 448 wounded during Operation Utah in 1966, and the 1967 Battle of Ong Thanh in which two companies of the U.S. Army's 2nd Battalion, 28th Infantry Regiment lost 56 killed, 75 wounded, and 2 missing with only 2 enemy soldiers confirmed killed.[16] In 1969 RAND analysts Melvin Gurtov and Konrad Kellen wrote: "In all, it would appear that the enemy, on purpose or not, has managed in the course of the Vietnam war to pulverize almost all of our military and strategic concepts."[17]

Instead of telling a lopsided story of military-technical dominance, the thousands of ground combat engagements in the Vietnam War—many of which are thoroughly documented—suggest a continuity of many characteristics from at least World War II.[18] Terrain and physical distance had a significant influence on the ability of all forces, regardless of technical advantage, to find and target the enemy, advance to contact, and concentrate fires.[19] Infantry troops took and held ground at places like Khe Sanh and Xuan Loc, and ground was ceded in their absence.[20] Infantry units supported by effective combined-arms fires generally were more survivable and successful than unsupported infantry, while fires alone generally were insufficient to defeat enemy units.

Throughout the Vietnam War, function generally mattered more than form in ground combat: North Vietnamese AK-variant rifles, 82mm mortars, D-20 152mm howitzers, and T-54/55 tanks, and the Americans' M-16 rifles, 81mm mortars, M114 155mm howitzers, and M48 tanks all served identical purposes; in most cases the ways in which they were applied mattered more than their barely differing forms. Advantages in target detection and airpower gave some Americans some advantages in some fights and in most cases precluded battlefield disaster.

Technology, however, failed to deliver consistent battlefield domination in the Vietnam War. In 1969 Westmoreland looked back wistfully at several years of intensive ground combat. Instead of these continuities and practical limitations, he saw the unrealized promise of American military technology and then forecast military-technical dominance.[21] Given the context of the ensuing five decades, this was a questionable perspective.

At least twenty other conflicts involving some type of ground combat occurred during the 1960s.[22] At the Battle of Mount Handren in 1966, thousands of Kurdish Peshmerga fighters supported by mortars and artillery reportedly annihilated an Iraqi Army brigade in combined-arms combat.[23] From 1962 through 1968, Yemeni republican forces armed with Soviet tanks, artillery, and jets suffered a series of battlefield defeats at the hands of British- and Saudi-backed royalists.[24] Biafran Armed Forces brigades stocked with a kaleidoscopic mix of weapons and equipment, including Czech-made rifles, British armored cars, riverboats with mounted howitzers, and B-25 bombers, fought the Nigerian Army almost to a standstill in nearly three years of brutal combat across jungle, forest, and low-density urban terrain.[25] None of these battles are central—or really even peripheral—to the Western military professional education canon.

Only the 1967 Arab-Israeli (Six-Day) War had and has as much influence as the Vietnam War on collective understanding of the character of ground combat in the 1960s.[26] Even this seminal case may be misused. Historian George W. Gawrych makes a compelling argument that the Israelis learned the wrong lessons from their 1967 victory: They took their remarkable technical and tactical overmatch of the Arabs as a predictor of future dominance, overvaluing technological supremacy and failing to allow for prospective adversary technical and tactical adaptation.[27] As a result of the Israelis' irrational self-confidence and Arab—primarily Egyptian—adaptability and effective antiair missile employment, Israeli ground forces suffered a number of humiliating and painful defeats in the early part of the 1973 Yom Kippur War.

GROUND COMBAT OBSERVATIONS AND INSIGHTS FROM 1970 TO 1979

Through the 1960s the Soviets and, to a lesser extent, the Communist Chinese had increased their proliferation of weapons and equipment to proxies and global buyers primarily across the Middle East, Asia, and Africa. Together they distributed tens of thousands of copies of T-54/55, T-62/64, and Type-59 and 69 tanks, the then-new BMP-variant infantry fighting vehicle and BTR-variant armored personnel carriers, 122mm and 130mm towed artillery pieces, BM-21 Grad multiple-launch rocket systems and 2K6 Luna rocket launchers, close-air support fighter-bombers, attack helicopters, antiaircraft artillery and missiles, and the more basic necessities of ground combat including millions of AK-variant (AKM, AK-47) and Chinese knockoff rifles, RPK and PKM machine-guns, mortars, anti-tank rocket launchers, and recoilless rifles. Western states distributed their own weapons and equipment, in many cases to the same countries and nonstate groups that were being supplied by the Soviets and Chinese. However, the Western states were outpaced. It would be fair to say that by the early 1970s, most ground combat forces in the world were primarily armed with Soviet or Soviet-knockoff gear.[28]

A good bit of this gear was put to use in at least hundreds of distinct global instances of ground combat through the 1970s. Approximately fifty conflicts erupted during, or carried through, this decade.[29] These include the ongoing Chadian civil war, the Ethiopian civil war, the war for Bangladeshi independence, the Lebanese civil war, the war for Oromo independence, the continuation and conclusion of the Vietnam War, the Western Saharan war, and the collapse of Portugal's colonial system in Africa that unleashed violence across the southern part of the African continent. At least in American military professional literature, the 1973 Yom Kippur War was and remains the standout ground combat event of the decade.[30]

On the western flank of the combined Arab offensive in 1973, Egyptian forces surprised the Israelis with a prepared wet-gap crossing and obviated Israeli air-to-ground dominance by employing a dense network of advanced Soviet surface-to-air missile systems.[31] With the Israeli Air Force effectively prevented from reenacting its 1967 air-to-ground attack role, the Egyptians could advance and employ their Soviet Malyutka anti-tank missile systems against Israel's vaunted armored corps. While the Malyutkas did not in fact end the relevance of tanks or even alter the course of the 1973 war—by far, most Israeli tank losses reportedly were caused by Egyptian tank cannons and anti-tank guns—Egypt's adaptations helped to rebalance the battlefield, forcing commanders on both sides to deal with the full range of common World War II-era ground combat characteristics.[32]

Major 1970s-era ground combat events like the Yom Kippur War, the 1972 Vietnam War Easter Offensive battles at Loc Ninh and An Loc, the 1975 battle at Xuan Loc, and the battle for Lang Son in the 1979 Sino-Vietnamese War overshadowed poorly reported—or in many cases, never reported—lowest-level combined-arms skirmishes fought in remote parts of Rhodesia, Namibia, Nicaragua, the Philippines, etc.[33] Most of these engagements are only hinted at in contemporaneous surface-level news reports, minor historical monographs, and a handful of books written for narrow readership. While these engagements may have been inadequately recorded and reported, they nonetheless constitute a significant portion of global ground combat. Here is a brief sample of some of the important minor engagements that were recorded:

> In 1973, 300 Dhofar insurgents armed with RPG-7s, rifles, machineguns, and mortars attacked a patrol base defended by a reinforced platoon of Omani troops and British advisors. The insurgents had, but then lost the element of surprise, allowing the advisors to call in three BAC 167 Strikemaster attack aircraft and train their own indirect fires on the attackers. The defenses held.[34]
>
> In 1975, an Indonesian special forces platoon attacked a platoon of defending Fretilin fighters at Balibo in East Timor. The attackers broke into two squads and advanced with AK-variant rifles and supporting 90mm recoilless rifle fire, but their rounds bounced off the stone walls of the defenders' position. Both sides traded mortar and rifle fire, and eventually the attackers gained the upper hand.[35]

> In 1979, a Tanzanian infantry unit of about 500 soldiers backed by three T-55 tanks attacked and seized the Ugandan town of Lukoya. As they advanced in line down a narrow causeway, Libyan intervention force troops attacked them with 122mm rockets and then advanced with their own tanks. They, too, were stopped by indirect fire and an aggressive counterattack; the Libyans broke and fled.[36]

Soviet artillery, rockets, tanks, and armored vehicles played important roles in many of the well-recorded and not-so-well-recorded battles and skirmishes of the 1970s. By the middle of the decade, the amphibious BMP-1 and BMP-2 infantry fighting vehicles were abundant across Eastern Europe, the Middle East, Africa, and parts of South and East Asia. Both versions were generally viewed as reliable, effective, and easy to maintain.[37] The BMP-2 was thinly armored, but it was fairly cheap, tracked, lightweight, could carry ten soldiers, and mounted a powerful 30mm cannon and a 7.62mm machinegun. A South African colonel with extensive experience in Angola and other regional conflicts war said: "As long as it is regularly greased and its water and oil kept topped up, the BMP-2 will accomplish everything that is expected of it, including lengthy safaris across the face of Africa."[38] Starting in the early 1960s, more than 40,000 BMPs were eventually built and distributed around the world.[39] They remained in production and in regular use on battlefields in Syria, Ukraine, Libya, Iraq, Yemen, Nagorno-Karabakh, Ethiopia, etc. through the early 2020s.

GROUND COMBAT OBSERVATIONS AND INSIGHTS FROM 1980 TO 1989

Well over 1,000,000 combatants were killed and wounded in the more than thirty conflicts centered on ground combat throughout the 1980s. Perhaps 1,000,000 were killed in the 1980–1988 Iraq War alone.[40] Intensive ground combat between the Soviets and their Afghan partner forces against the Mujahed-din in the 1980s probably resulted in more than 300,000 combatant casualties.[41] Fog of war, poor recordkeeping, lack of free-press access to battlefields, and lying by government officials and nonstate groups ensured that these figures will never be accurate. But it is possible to break down the battles and some of the skirmishes in each of these conflicts to get a general sense of what caused these casualties. Most fighters on all sides probably were killed while on foot or in land vehicles by artillery, mortars, rockets, anti-tank missiles, machineguns, rifles, tank cannons, and mostly unguided aerial bombs and rockets.[42]

Most recorded casualties in this decade occurred in ground combat along the Iran-Iraq border between 1980 and 1988.[43] Both sides engaged in continuous combined-arms combat with corps-level foot, motorized, and mechanized infantry divisions; armored divisions; massed rocket and tube artillery; surface-to-surface tactical missiles; and both fixed-wing and rotary-wing close-air support. Iranian and Iraqi troops dug elaborate trench and bunker networks, planted probably millions of land mines, employed hundreds of thousands of iron-sight rifles and machineguns, conducted amphibious assaults across lakes and rivers, and often engaged in multidivision battles across deserts and swamps. Starting in 1986 Iranian Revolutionary Guards employed Mohajer-1 and Ababil-1 surveillance drones to trace the Iraqi front lines, reportedly flying over 600 drone reconnaissance sorties through 1988.[44]

Both sides employed chemical munitions, and by the end of the war the Iraqis had fully integrated chemical agent shells, rockets, and aerial sprays into their supporting fires schemes. In the mountains of northern Iraq, the Iraqis were engaged in combat with both Iranian mountain troops and Kurdish insurgents. High-altitude infantry combat required laborious foot marches and dangerous heliborne assaults onto mountain redoubts. In these fights, altitude and steep terrain frequently stripped away even the remote possibility of applying massed supporting arms, leaving lightly armed infantry to engage mostly on their own merits.[45]

Some technologies remained static while others evolved during the Iran Iraq War and also in the two 1980s cases reviewed in chapter 4: Beqa'a Valley in Lebanon in 1982 and Cuito Cuanavale in Angola in 1987. Syrian forces defending the Beqa'a Valley entrenched their Soviet armor and artillery behind earthen revetments while Israeli armored and infantry forces pushed down main roads to engage the Syrians in World War II-style combined-arms fire. Meanwhile, Israeli drone operators spotted and marked Syrian positions for targeting, and Syrian pilots flying Gazelle attack helicopters destroyed Israeli tanks with French-supplied anti-tank missiles.

At Cuito Cuanavale, Angolan and Cuban forces dug into World War I-era trench lines backed by heavy artillery, rockets, and 1950s-era Soviet tanks, while UNITA and South African troops advanced in infantry-armor teams through rough terrain and minefields. Meanwhile, the South Africans were doing their best to gain advantage with their Seeker drones and laser-guided anti-tank missiles, and the Angolans and Cubans were firing their SA-7 and SA-8 antiaircraft missiles to fend off South African close-air and interdiction strikes.

Two other cases from the 1980s provide good insight into contemporaneous Western infantry and combined-arms ground combat tactics and technology: the Falkland Islands (Malvinas) War in 1982 and the U.S. invasion of Panama in 1989.[46] British recapture of the Falklands required amphibious landings, foot marches through snow over high mountain passes, and channelized frontal attacks into dug-in Argentinian infantry protected by impenetrable rock outcroppings. At the battle for Goose Green, British infantry received fire support from an FA2 Sea Harrier fighter-bomber but primarily relied on their own rifles, 2-inch and 81mm mortars, machineguns, and grenade launchers to advance against Argentinian troops employing their own mortars, 105mm artillery, a recoilless rifle, and antiaircraft cannons firing on flat trajectory.[47]

In the 1989 invasion of Panama, the United States brought to bear large portions of its conventional arsenal including F-117 stealth bombers, AH-64 attack helicopters, special operations units, Marine Corps and Army infantry, an airborne assault, and light armor including Vietnam War-era M551 Sheridan tanks.[48] But in terms of scale, the American ground combat operations in the 1980s—Lebanon from 1982 to 1983, Grenada in 1983, Panama in 1989, and several special operations skirmishes—paled in comparison to the 1991 Gulf War.

GROUND COMBAT OBSERVATIONS AND INSIGHTS FROM 1990 TO 2002

American-led coalition ground warfare against Saddam Hussein's armed forces in Kuwait and Iraq in 1990 and 1991 dominates the global ground combat narrative from the 1990s. This is unsurprising and probably warranted. Nearly 1,000,000 ground and air troops employing thousands of armored vehicles, anti-armor weapons, advanced combat aircraft, long-range rocket and missiles, advanced electronic and antiaircraft warfare, and other technology faced off in a short but intense series of battles including the engagement with the Tawakalna Division described in chapter 4.

Embedded Western military historians ensured that the coalition perspective of the Gulf War would be recorded in explicit detail and then shared with the general public. After the war, Iraqi officers provided their perspectives in hundreds of hours of recorded interviews. An official American examination of the war generated a detailed five-volume accounting of every aspect of the campaign from logistics to air power to command and control.[49] Hundreds of books and articles were written about the war from all perspectives.[50] What, then, was the character of ground combat in the Gulf War?

As someone who fought in the war, has studied it as a government-funded researcher, and has interviewed combatants, I do not think this question has been answered in a way that provides holistic historical understanding. Instead, all of the differing perspectives on Gulf War ground combat sit gathering dust like scattered pieces in a long-unfinished puzzle. From the perspective of some airpower proponents—and particularly U.S. Air Force military-technical revolution advocates—there was no ground combat worth examining.

For example, in 2001 Air Force General David A. Deptula argued that the use of air power in the Gulf War signaled a change in the very nature of war. He allowed that ground forces "helped to protect Saudi Arabia and reoccupied

Kuwait after the air campaign had paralyzed enemy systems" but were otherwise barely relevant. Deptula suggested there might be no need for ground forces in future wars.[51] In contrast, Iraqi generals I and other researchers have interviewed in the years since 1991 stated that they lost primarily because they had weak will to fight.[52] In their telling, coalition air power provided the nudge to encourage 120,000 already weak-willed Iraqis to surrender during the air campaign and another 80,000 to surrender during the most intensive part of the ground war.[53] Still, well over 100,000 Iraqis survived coalition air attacks and stood their ground. Thousands of them counterattacked with their outmatched Soviet and Chinese ground systems and killed coalition troops.[54]

Perspectives on ground combat also differed within the coalition. At the various headquarters in Saudi Arabia, Europe, and the United States, ground combat between infantry and tank units was not immediately observable, while videos of airstrikes and drone footage of surrendering Iraqis flowed continually. Leaders and staffs in these headquarters came away from the war with their own conclusions about its character. On the ground, soldiers in tank units had a specific view of combat through their thermal scopes, while infantrymen who dismounted and fought on the desert sand experienced their own kind of combat. Pilots of F-117 stealth aircraft experienced ultrahigh-tech air war, while pilots of AH-1 Cobra attack helicopters and OV-10 observer planes experienced a more visceral type of gun-barrel air war run from paper maps.

Flat and open desert terrain gave the coalition troops with longer-range weapons and optics an advantage, while storm clouds, blowing dust, and oil smoke leveled that advantage for the Iraqis in many close-in fights. Ultimately, ground combat in the Gulf War had diverse and simultaneously occurring characteristics that defy homogeneity: lethal precision airstrikes along with old-school seat-of-the-pants close-air support; high-performing M1 main battle tanks with thermal sights and also older M-60A1 tanks with mid-century coincidence rangefinders; M2 Bradley IFVs with TOW missiles; and foot infantry engaged in desert trench warfare with iron-sight weapons.[55]

As in previous decades, big canonical cases like the Gulf War overshadowed tens of other important land wars and possibly thousands of instances of ground combat.[56] The American debacle in Mogadishu, Somalia, in October 1993 and Russia's own debacle in Grozny, Chechnya, 1994–1995 are probably the other best known cases. In Mogadishu, lightly armed American special operators and infantry were trapped in close urban combat with perhaps thousands of Somali fighters armed primarily with iron-sight AK-variant rifles and RPGs; the Americans were forced to withdraw.[57]

In Grozny, the Russians attacked with their BTRs, BMPs, and tanks in column into the urban terrain and were decimated by Chechen fighters with iron-sight AK-variant rifles, RPGs, and improvised explosives; the Russians were forced to withdraw and then effectively destroy Grozny with artillery.[58] The combined American-Northern Alliance defeat of the Taliban in 2001 is commonly—and Biddle, I, and others argue, inaccurately—chalked up as a special operation rather than a conventional fight. It deserves elevation. In addition to the Tawakalna, Shusha, Cenapa Valley, and Grozny cases, I coded two other 1990s–2002 battles that are often overlooked: Kupres in Bosnia-Herzegovina in 1992 and Koshare (Košare) in Serbia in 1999. Both of these battles involved heavy combined-arms combat with armor, artillery, air support, and guided missiles, and at Koshare, drones and naval cruise missiles.

SIGNIFICANT DYNAMIC: SOVIET AND RUSSIAN MATERIEL AND DOCTRINAL PROLIFERATION

Perhaps no characteristic of 1945–2002 ground combat was more common than the appearance and employment of Soviet and then post-Soviet Russian military equipment, weapons, munitions, doctrine, and training. One or both combatants in twenty-two of the twenty-five cases I coded for this period used Soviet or Soviet knockoff gear.[59]

At the battle of Lang Son in 1979, Chinese and North Vietnamese soldiers killed each other with AK-47s or Type-56 knockoff rifles, RPG-7 or B-40 rockets, and nearly identical 122mm and 130mm artillery tubes.[60] At the Battle of Afabet in Eritrea in 1988, Ethiopians and Eritreans killed each other with Soviet AKM/-47s, RPGs, KPV 14.5mm heavy machineguns, and 82mm mortars.[61] Soviet, Chinese, Czech, post-Soviet Russian, and other factories turned out tens of thousands of BTRs and BMPs, T-54 through T-90 tanks, BM-21 multiple-launch rocket systems, SPG-9 recoilless rifles, MT-12 Rapira anti-tank guns, Mi-24 and Mi-35 attack helicopters, Su-25 Grach ground-attack planes, and everything else needed on a modern battlefield.[62] Proliferation, capture, recapture, and redistribution of these systems were effectively uncontrolled.

Soviet gear often came with advisers who provided Soviet technical and tactical training. Military officers from across Africa, the Middle East, and parts of Latin America and Asia also attended Soviet military academies where they absorbed Soviet ground combat doctrine. The philosophy behind the design of the Soviet arsenal was also transmitted to non-Soviet end users. This can be summed as: All military equipment and weapons are disposable tools intended to be used, and if necessary used up, at high volume to achieve military objectives.[63]

The people who ride in the vehicles, fire the rifles, and launch the mortar shells also are disposable; they generally are unskilled or low-skilled and therefore in the cold calculus of some political and military leaders, easily replaced. This means that the mechanical tools of war can be designed for easy and low-cost mass production. Soviet tanks including the more advanced T-90 variants are relatively cheap, small, lightweight, and also more cramped and thinly armored compared to Western tanks. Crew survivability is at best an afterthought, even with bolted-on explosive-reactive armor (ERA).[64] The purpose of the Soviet tank is to provide mobile firepower that happens to be somewhat protected, not mobile protected firepower. Any army employing Soviet tanks either embraces this design philosophy and therefore also high-risk acceptance for gear and people (e.g., Russia circa 2024) or it spends resources to make protective improvements (e.g., Ukraine circa 2014– and its protective modifications of its T-64BV tanks, etc.).

SIGNIFICANT DYNAMIC: CREEPING RISK AVERSION IN THE WEST

Soviet risk philosophy permeated most non-NATO ground combat forces around the world, and it remained generally consistent in the post-Soviet era. By contrast, Western ground combat forces—and particularly in the United States—had gradually slipped into a state of collective risk aversion by the end of 2002. Most observers attribute creeping risk aversion in the United States to defeat in the Vietnam War, reinforced by later failures in Lebanon and Somalia.[65] In the Vietnam War, American commanders threw troops into battle as they did in World War II; casualty acceptance was generally high. In approximately ten years in Vietnam, the United States suffered over 58,000 killed and well over 100,000 wounded.[66] Equipment loss acceptance also was high. For example, of the approximately 12,000 American helicopters employed in support of ground combat operations during the Vietnam War, possibly over 5,000 were destroyed and over 2,000 crew were killed.[67]

A range of factors coincided to translate these losses into rising risk aversion: the advent of televised combat, popular anti-war protests, lack of clear strategic objectives, lying by senior government officials, and so on.[68] America's traumatic departure from Vietnam in 1975, symbolized by a panicked and widely televised helicopter evacuation, compounded the shared sense of loss, waste, and failure.[69] Loss without purpose begs the question of risk, so risk aversion and loss aversion became recurring, tightly interwoven themes in post-Vietnam conflicts. After the Vietnam War, mass casualty events generally correlated with plummeting national will to fight. When 241 American troops were killed in the Beirut barracks bombing in October 1983, the United States withdrew.[70] When 18 Americans were killed in Mogadishu in the popularized Black Hawk Down incident in October 1993, the United States withdrew.[71]

Retired U.S. Army officer and research professor Richard A. Lacquement Jr. makes a compelling case that contemporary risk aversion in the American officer corps far exceeds public risk aversion.[72] But he also makes clear this disparity is irrelevant to the outcome: Military risk aversion has influenced the ways in which Americans and some Western allies design equipment, train their ground combat forces, and employ those forces in war.[73]

For example, since the Vietnam War, Western tank design has been weighted heavily toward crew survivability and therefore exquisite per-unit cost and careful husbanding in combat; I dig deeper on tank design and risk aversion in chapter 9. And it is difficult to imagine American commanders allowing 50 helicopters, let alone 5,000, to be lost in any post-Vietnam conflict. By the late 1990s, ground combat involving Western military forces, doctrine, and equipment reflected many characteristics of risk-averse thinking. The military-technical revolution theories described in chapter 1—the pursuit of technological solutions that would allow victory with minimal combat or even without combat—were tailored for risk avoidance and therefore well suited to emerging American ground combat technological design and tactical application.

SIGNIFICANT DYNAMIC: THE CONSISTENT IMPORTANCE OF FUNCTION OVER FORM

Through World War II and to the end of 2002, the functions of ground combat remained effectively consistent. Combatants applied a mix of direct and indirect fires from the ground, air, and water to support the maneuver of ground forces to degrade the other side's physical assets and people in order to annihilate them, force them to surrender, or to give up a piece of contested ground. Returning to Albert Manucy's basic observation about the constant function of artillery—a tube launches a projectile in an arc from one point on the ground to another in order to smash things and kill people—the functional characteristics of ground combat from World War II through 2002 generally remained the same: Humans in vehicles or on foot aimed tubes to fire projectiles designed to smash enemy equipment or kill enemy soldiers. These tubes, projectiles, and vehicles took on evolving forms: The British Lee-Enfield rifle evolved to the L1A1 SLR, then to the SA80 rifle; the Soviet T-34 tank evolved to the T-55, then to the T-90 tank; the American M1A1 Bazooka evolved to the M72 LAAW and then to the AT-4 anti-tank rocket. But, with given case-by-case idiosyncrasies, the basic functions, purposes, and employment of all of these systems effectively remained constant.

In many cases, form and function both remained constant. World War II-era ground combat systems remained in use through and beyond the Cold War, and some remain in use in the mid 2020s. Most Cold War-era systems remained in common use well through 2002 and then well into what I have defined as the modern era of ground combat. Evolution of form—changes in and improvements to rifles, rockets, tanks, attack aircraft, sights, and so on—therefore occurred in parallel with the continuing use of older forms (equipment and weapons), not in sequence. In other words, a new capability did not always replace an older capability.

Good examples of this parallel evolution and employment occurred in the 1991 Gulf War, with Iraqi units employing both T-55 and more advanced T-72 tanks, and American units employing both 1960s-era M72 LAAWs and late-1980s-era AT-4 rockets.[74] When advanced ground combat forces like the U.S. Army and the Soviet Army replaced weapons and equipment with newer models, they often transferred older models to allies and partners.[75] This ensured a fairly consistent global distribution of ground combat materiel and recurrent appearances of large quantities of decades-old gear in cases through at least 2024.

TACTICAL CONTINUITY AND CHANGE

For the most part, ground combat tactics also remained consistent from the end of World War II through the end of 2002. Commanders massed infantry, armor, and artillery, and brought in close-air support to facilitate fire and movement onto ground objectives. Defenders dug trenches, built bunkers, emplaced mines, and counterattacked when they had the forces available. Terrain influenced tactics, and terrain often punished forces that ignored the realities of physical channeling, relative altitude, concealment, cover, and mobility.

For example, in Afghanistan the Soviet Army continued to move vehicle columns on isolated one-lane mountain roads long after mujaheddin forces had perfected high-to-low-ground, combined-arms ambushes with mines, machineguns, mortars, and rockets.[76] Western doctrine like AirLand Battle and maneuver warfare increasingly emphasized dispersal and semi-independent operations in order to counter increasingly effective precision munitions, but at least in the cases reviewed for this book, there was little indication of substantive U.S. military organizational or tactical change from World War II.

EVOLUTION OF MOBILE FIREPOWER (WELL PROTECTED AND OTHER)

Arguably, the last evolutionary blip in tank design occurred in 1980 with the production of the M1 Abrams and comparable NATO tanks.[77] Compared to the M60 tank it was designed to replace, the M1 was more survivable and lethal. But while its form and performance had improved, its function remained consistent with the M60 and the mid-century M4 Sherman.[78] All tanks in 2002 looked and performed similarly to tanks produced at the end of World War II. They still operated on two tracks and (with few exceptions) had a rotating turret with a main gun and mounted machineguns, and they could still be destroyed by rockets, artillery, missiles, and mines.[79] Light armor, including tracked models like the Soviet BMP, Israeli Achzarit, and American M113 and Bradley, and a wide array of wheeled armored vehicles both proliferated and evolved for increasing mobility, speed, and firepower. Whether or not tanks were present, light armor would play an important role in most of the post-2002 ground combat cases.

EVOLUTION OF ANTI-ARMOR WEAPONS

Recall that all of the components for development of improved anti-tank rockets and anti-tank guided missiles were designed, tested, and employed by the end of World War II. Command-guided missile technology had already been used in combat. Design improvements continued at a steady pace after the war. While the RPG became ubiquitous on global battlefields, rocket design evolved from the reloadable bazooka-style—really, a recoilless rifle—to disposable tubes (M72, RPG-26, etc.) with ever more lethal warheads. Anti-tank warheads effectively kept pace with armor design; no tank was impenetrable at any point during the interval period.

Anti-tank missiles evolved from manual, to semiautomated, to fire-and-forget guidance. Swedish designers recognized the weak top armor of most tanks and built top-down attack systems, starting in the 1980s with the Swedish RBS 56 BILL and advancing into the early 2000s with the RB 57 NLAW.[80] The American fire-and-forget, top-attack FGM-148 Javelin also was designed in the late 1990s. By 2002, anti-tank missiles with basic designs dating back to the mid twentieth century were commonly mounted on trucks, tanks, light armor, helicopters, drones, and fixed-wing aircraft, and were commonly employed in ground combat by high-tech armies as well as insurgents.

EVOLUTION OF AIR SUPPORT

Fixed-wing support to ground forces remained fairly consistent in function, with uneven evolution in form. Successive generations of aircraft were more capable of delivering increasingly precise munitions onto ground targets. For example, the World War II-era American P-47 Thunderbolt propeller-driven attack aircraft mounting .50 caliber machineguns and unguided rockets evolved to the A-10 Thunderbolt II jet aircraft mounting a large electric gatling gun and laser-guided missiles.[81] Technology for close-air support targeting also improved, with both air and ground laser designators and Global Positioning System (GPS) navigation allowing for precision ground strikes with minimized risk to aircraft and crew. However, while GPS was made universally available, most of these improved capabilities were limited to advanced and well-funded militaries.

Air-to-ground tactics also evolved unevenly. Well-organized point-of-contact coordination between ground and air teams remained rare. Even with the addition of attack helicopters in the post-World War II period, close-air support for ground troops in contact—even for advanced forces—remained a generally dangerous undertaking that frequently required visual target recognition by human pilots. Globally, unguided bombs, rockets, and guns probably were employed in much higher volume than precision munitions, and close-air support coordination probably was more often rudimentary than orchestral.[82]

EVOLUTION OF DRONES

Drone support to ground combat forces evolved unevenly through the interim period due to a complex mix of bureaucratic, technical, and cultural challenges.[83] While the U.S. Air Force routinely employed aerial drones in the Vietnam War, flying thousands of sorties and losing over 200 unmanned aircraft in combat, the U.S. military remained focused on operational and strategic drone technology through the interval period.[84] Soviet and Chinese indigenous investment in drone technology was negligible through 2002.[85] This left a capability gap for smaller states engaged in high-intensity ground combat.

Driven by immediate need, Israel and South Africa invested in tactical drones specifically designed to support ground forces. Israel modified and employed American Firebee drones in the 1973 Yom Kippur War, built their own drone program, and employed drones in ground combat in 1982 and then in every conflict thereafter.[86] South Africa built and employed the Seeker drone in ground combat in the 1980s.[87] By the 1990s, the United States, United Kingdom, and other states had adopted Israeli designs for ground observation drones.[88] With Israeli help, the United States developed and employed the Predator drone for observation in the 1990s Bosnia conflict, setting the stage for the widespread use of armed Predator drones in the post-2002 period.[89] Global drone use was uneven through the interim period but (based on a nonempirical survey of cases) was becoming more commonplace through the 1990s. Ground drone design was, perhaps surprisingly, an afterthought through the interim period.

EVOLUTION OF THE RIFLE

Rifle technology, design, and employment barely evolved through 2002. Magazine-fed rifles employed toward the end of World War II like the German Gewehr 43 and Sturmgewehr 44 were no less technically effective than the Cold War-era AK-47, M-16, FN FAL, or Heckler & Koch G3. For example, the Gewehr 43 weighed approximately ten pounds and with its iron sights could be used to hit a human target at 500 meters. The American M-16A2 used by the Army and Marine Corps through the 1990s weighed approximately eight pounds and could also hit a point target at 500 meters. The M-16 had a large-capacity 30-round magazine, but the Gewehr 43 fired a large 7.92mm round that caused more damage than the M-16's relatively light 5.56mm round.

To some extent, all rifles were (and arguably are still) a zero-sum mechanism. Changes in rifle design throughout the interim period were affected less by major technological advancements—none really emerged—than by periodic rebalancing between weight, range, caliber, accuracy, reliability, and magazine size. Infrared scopes were really the only significant technical adaptation applied through 2002, and for the most part all scopes remained specialist tools and not issued to regular infantry.

OTHER ADVANCES: SATELLITES, GPS, HELICOPTER MOBILITY, THERMAL IMAGERS

Through at least the 1990s, satellites provided strategic and in some cases operational intelligence; they effectively had no immediate impact on ground combat. Improved digitization of satellite data in the 1990s allowed for two important advances for ground combat.[90] First, the implementation of GPS allowed for accurate and precise ground location and timing, which in turn allowed ground combat forces to constantly know their own locations and more effectively target enemy locations.[91] And by the early 2000s, miniaturization of satellite ground stations from large vans to backpack-sized devices allowed for more reliable and secure tactical communication for remote ground forces engaged in combat.

Helicopter lift gave ground commanders greater mobility in rough terrain and opened up new options for tactical maneuver. Thermal imagers mounted on tanks, aircraft, and missile sights allowed shooters to spot and kill targets through smoke and against cluttered backgrounds. However, as useful as these technological advances were, none triggered revolutionary change in the function of ground combat. All of these capabilities have practical limitations, and all were and still remain vulnerable to technical countermeasures including GPS jamming and spoofing, antiaircraft artillery and missiles, and advanced multispectral camouflage and basic signature management behaviors.[92]

INTO THE MODERN PERIOD, 2003–2022

The next two chapters describe modern ground combat cases from the dataset. As in chapters 2 and 4, selected cases are used to present a diverse and sometimes converging range of observed characteristics. The descriptive cases that follow are neither necessarily representative of all ground combat during the whole period nor of any single five-year period. They will, however, give a fairly clear picture of the commonalities and idiosyncrasies in the characteristics of ground warfare from the World War II baseline, and more specifically since 2003.

NOTES

1. This figure primarily refers to the Correlates of War Dataset (https://correlatesofwar.org) and the Uppsala Conflict Dataset (https://ucdp.uu.se). Correlates of War is more aggregated, listing 229 conflicts carrying forward from 1944 through 2002, while Uppsala lists over 1,730 conflicts. The vast majority of these—but not all—include ground combat. The major disparity between these two figures (229 and 1730) is due to the ways in which the researchers have bound and coded their cases. Uppsala data are built for dyadic pairing, an approach that perhaps artificially generates more case counts.
2. See Claud Arpi, "War of Liberation: The Battle of Chamdo (Tibet)," *United Service Institution of India* 146, no. 604 (April–June 2016), pages not listed in online version.
3. Arpi, "War of Liberation."
4. See Connable, *Embracing the Fog*, for a description of the various databases and citations to reference these data in archives.
5. I refer here to the Pentomic Division described in chapter 1. For more, see R. F. M. Williams, "The Rise and Fall of the Pentomic Army," *War on the Rocks*, November 25, 2022.
6. These include Chinese Civil War (1946–1950); Greek Civil War (1944–1949); Vietnamese War of Independence (1945–1954); Forest Brothers War (1945–1951); First Kashmir War (1947–1949); Arab-Israeli War (1948–1949); Malayan Rebellion (1948–1957); Sino-Tibetan War (1950); Korean War (1950–1953); Mau Mau War (1952–1956); Hungarian Revolution (1956); Cuban Revolution (1958–1959); First Lebanese War (1958); etc. See the Correlates of War chronological list of all wars for an example of a conflict case list.
7. For more on Viet Minh weapons and equipment, see Martin Windrow, *The French Foreign Légionnaire versus Viet Minh Insurgent* (Oxford, UK: Osprey, 2018); and J. J. Zasloff, *The Role of the Sanctuary in Insurgency: Communist China's Support to the Vietminh, 1946–1954* (Santa Monica, CA: RAND Corporation, 1967).
8. Zasloff, *Role of Sanctuary*. Also see "Viet Minh Continue to Receive Aid from Communist China," *Chung-kuo Jah-Pao* (November 26, 1952), translated in declassified U.S. Central Intelligence Agency (CIA) report of the same title (March, 1953).
9. Windrow, *French Foreign Légionnaire*. Also see U.S. Central Intelligence Agency, *Development of the Capabilities of the Viet Minh for Conventional Warfare*, declassified intelligence analysis (Langley, VA: CIA Directorate of Analysis, 1955).
10. See, for example, Martin Windrow, *Dien Bien Phu 1954: The French Defeat That Lured America into Vietnam* (Oxford, UK: Osprey, 2021); *Battle for Dien Bien Phu: Prelude to the Vietnam War*, directed by Peter Batty (2005); and "The Ten Thousand Day War Dien Bien Phu Full Documentary," YouTube.
11. The French were supported by the Americans, and the Viet Minh were supported by the Chinese. See U.S. Department of Defense, *United States—Vietnam*

Relations: 1945–1967, declassified historical document (Washington, DC: Office of the Secretary of Defense, n.d.); Zasloff, *Role of Sanctuary*; "Viet Minh Continue to Receive Aid from Communist China."

12. Other states contributed to global arms distribution, but based on my case reviews these had the greatest impact on ground combat.
13. See more on the AK-47 and the less expensive AKM stamped version in the "Evolution of the Rifle" section later in this chapter. See C. J. Chivers, *The Gun* (New York: Simon & Schuster, 2011). Also see Mikhail Kalashnikov with Elena Joly *The Gun That Changed the World*, trans. Andrew Brown (Polity, 2006).
14. American advisers entered Vietnam prior to 1960, and the United States had provided considerable support to the French during their war with the Viet Minh. The year 1960 marks the beginning of the collective effort to unify Vietnam under the leadership of the Democratic Republic of Vietnam and the beginning of a gradual, and later rapid, uptick in U.S. presence.
15. This refers to a possibly apocryphal quote from a conversation between a U.S. and North Vietnamese officer that reportedly took place after the end of the war. This erroneous belief of total ground combat domination in all "major battles" is repeated in official U.S. military publications and was repeated by the president of the United States in 2011. See Barack H. Obama, quoted in The White House, "Remarks by the President at 93rd Annual Conference of the American Legion" (Minneapolis, August 30, 2011).
16. The terms *victory* and *defeat* are, of course, subjective. For more on these two battles, see Jack Shulimson, *U.S. Marines in Vietnam: An Expanding War, 1966* (Washington, DC: History and Museums Division, 1982), chapter 7; and George L. MacGarrigle, *Taking the Offensive: October 1966 to October 1967* (Washington, DC: U.S. Army Center of Military History, 1988), 354–365.
17. Melvin Gurtov and Konrad Kellen, *Vietnam: Lessons Learned and Mislearned* (Santa Monica, CA: RAND Corporation, 1969), 18.
18. One easily accessible source for primary and secondary source information on the Vietnam War is the Texas Tech University Virtual Vietnam Archive, https://www.vietnam.ttu.edu.
19. Observations and insights in this section on the Vietnam War are drawn from my research for *Embracing the Fog of War*, research for *Warrior-Maverick Culture*, research for *Will to Fight*, and unpublished archival research on ground combat and will to fight in Binh Dinh and Phu Yen Provinces in Vietnam conducted with support from the U.S. Army's Center of Military History from 2016 through 2019.
20. For more on Khe Sanh, see Moyers S. Shore II, *The Battle for Khe Sanh* (Washington, DC: U.S. Marine Corps History and Museums Division, 1969); and Bernard C. Nalty, *Air Power and the Fight for Khe Sanh* (Washington, DC: U.S. Air Force Office of Air Force History, 1986).
21. See chapter 1 for more on Westmoreland's vision.
22. Correlates of War dataset lists over 30, but some of these may not have included ground combat between two units applying combined-arms methods. Therefore, "more than twenty" is reasonable in the absence of detailed examination of each case.
23. Sources on this battle are limited. See, for example, Malovany, *Wars of Modern Babylon*, 64; Pollack, *Arabs at War*, 163–164.
24. For example, see Dana Adams Schmidt, *Yemen: The Unknown War* (New York: Holt, Rinehart, and Winston, 1968); Asher Orkaby, *Beyond the Arab Cold War:*

The International History of the Yemen Civil War, 1962–68 (Oxford, UK: Oxford University Press, 2019); "The Siege of San'a," *Time*, December 15, 1967.

25. See Philip S. Jowett, *The Biafran Army 1967–1970: Build-Up and Downfall of the Secessionist Military* (West Midlands, UK: Helion, 2020); and Frederick Forsyth, *The Biafra Story: The Making of an African Legend* (New York: Penguin, 1977).
26. See, for example, Randolph S. Churchill and Winston S. Churchill, *The Six Day War* (New York: Houghton Mifflin, 1967); and Kenneth M. Pollack, "Air Power in the Six Day War," *Journal of Strategic Studies* 28, no. 3 (2005), 471–503.
27. George W. Gawrych, *The 1973 Arab-Israeli War: The Albatross of Decisive Victory* (Fort Leavenworth, KS: Combat Studies Institute, 1996); Robert S. Bolia, "Overreliance on Technology in Warfare: The Yom Kippur War as a Case Study," *Parameters* 34, no. 2 (Summer 2004), 46–56.
28. According to the Stockholm International Peace Research Institute (SIPRI), in the 1970s the Soviets, Chinese, and Czechoslovakians distributed approximately 20,000 tanks, IFVs, and APCs, while the United States, United Kingdom, and France distributed about 6,500 vehicles. This figure of 6,500 is skewed by the large UK contract for over 2,200 MBT Mk1 tanks to India with delivery extending through the 1980s.
29. This is also a conservative count drawn from the Correlates of War dataset.
30. This is evident in the extensive references to the Yom Kippur War by at least U.S. Army, Marine Corps, and Air Force general officers and doctrine writers through the 1970s and well into the 1980s. Both the Army's Active Defense and AirLand Battle doctrines were heavily influenced by the 1973 war.
31. See Pollack, *Arabs at War*, 104–131; Amiram Ezov, *Crossing: Suez, 1973* (ContentoNow, 2016), ebook; and Simon Dunstan, *The Yom Kippur War 1973 (2): The Sinai* (Oxford, UK: Osprey, 2003). For a technical analysis of weapons and equipment, see J.R. Transue, *Assessment of the Weapons and Tactics Used in the October 1973 Middle East War*, declassified intelligence analysis (Arlington, VA: Weapons Systems Evaluation Group, 1974).
32. A combined team of federally funded research and development center analysts working under the U.S. military's Weapons System Evaluation Group found that 70 percent to 90 percent of Israeli tank losses were caused by Egyptian anti-tank guns and tank main guns. Some losses were caused by infantry rockets, some probably by friendly fire, some possibly by air attack, so probably at most the Malyutkas accounted for about a quarter of, and possibly only 5 percent or so, of all Israeli tank losses. Transue, *Assessment of Weapons*, 6.
33. For more on the Easter Offensive battles, see Ngo Quang Truong, *The Easter Offensive of 1972* (Washington, DC: U.S. Army Center of Military History, 1980); and James H. Willbanks, *Thiet Giap! The Battle of An Loc, April 1972* (Fort Leavenworth, KS: Combat Studies Institute, 1993). For more on the 1979 war, see for example, Christopher M. Gin, *How China Wins: A Case Study of the 1979 Sino-Vietnamese War* (Fort Leavenworth, KS: U.S. Army Command and General Staff College Press, 2016).
34. Ian Gardiner, *In the Service of the Sultan: A First Hand Account of the Dhofar Insurgency*, (South Yorkshire, UK: Pen & Sword Military, 2006), Kindle, locations 1383–1436.
35. Ken Conboy, *Kopassus: Inside Indonesia's Special Forces* (Singapore: Equinox, 2003), Kindle, locations 3826–3845. Fretilin, capitalized first letter only, is a

commonly used term for members of the Revolutionary Front for an Independent East Timor, or in Portuguese, Frente Revolucionária de Timor-Leste Independente (FReTiLIn).

36. Tom Cooper and Adrien Fontanellaz, *War and Insurgencies of Uganda, 1971–1994* (West Midlands, UK: Helion, 2015), 133–138, ebook.
37. Another version, the BMP-3, was designed and entered production in the mid to late 1980s; there is a BMP-4; and the so-called "Terminator" BMP variant was in use by the Russians in Ukraine as of early 2023.
38. Henni Blaauw, quoted in Al J. Ventner, *Battle for Angola: The End of the Cold War in Africa c1975–1989* (West Midlands, UK: Helion, 2016), 120, ebook.
39. For more on the BMP-series IFV and production and distribution data, see the SIPRI database and the U.S. Army's ODIN database, https://odin.tradoc.army.mil.
40. This is a rough estimate in the absence of detailed documentation available from either side. This figure is suggested in Cordesman and Wagner, *Lessons of Modern War*, 261, 268. Other sources range from 600,000 to one million dead. Also see Bethany Lacina and Nils Petter Gleditsch, "Monitoring Trends in Global Combat: A New Dataset of Battle Deaths," *European Journal of Population*, no. 21 (2005), 145–166.
41. Various estimates appear in Philip Taubman, "Soviet Lists Afghan War Toll: 13,310 Dead, 35,478 Wounded," *New York Times*, May 26, 1988; Lacina and Gleditsch, "Monitoring Trends"; Antonio Guistozzi, *War, Politics, and Society in Afghanistan* (Washington, DC: Georgetown University Press, 2000).
42. This review of 1980s battles is drawn from my extensive research on the Iran-Iraq War for *Iraqi Army Will to Fight*, on analysis of the Soviet war in Afghanistan for other RAND Corporation research projects, and from the case studies conducted for this project, as well as a review of additional sources listed herein.
43. This section is drawn primarily from Cordesman and Wager, *Lessons of Modern War*, and refers to cited battle studies in *Iraqi Army Will to Fight*.
44. I drew from Michael Rubin, "A Short History of the Iranian Drone Program," online article, *American Enterprise Institute*, 2020; and "نگاهی به نقش ناشناخته "تلاش" و "مهاجر" در کربلای 5 و الفجر 8," (Google Translate: "Mashreq's Report on the Power of Iranian Drones: A Look at the Unknown Role of [drone names] in Karbala 5 and Wal-Fajr 8"), *Mashregh News*, n.d., https://www.mashregnews.ir.
45. In the late 2010s I interviewed an Iraqi infantry commander who had led several of these operations. He described isolated infantry engagements conducted in often freezing conditions with minimal support.
46. The United Kingdom refers to these islands as the Falklands, and the Argentinians refer to them as the Malvinas. As of early 2023, they are officially registered by the United Nations as the Non-Self-Governing Territory of the Falkland Islands (Malvinas).
47. British paratroopers also used French Milan anti-tank missiles to destroy machine-gun positions as they advanced under fire. I coded Goose Green for this study. For more on the Falklands War and Goose Green, see Mark Adkin, *Goose Green: A Battle Is Fought and Won* (London: Leo Cooper, 1992); Martin Middlebrook, *The Falklands War* (South Yorkshire, UK: Pen & Sword Military, 2012); and Leonardo Arcadio Zarza, *Malvinas: The Argentine Perspective of the Falklands Conflict* (Fort Leavenworth, KS: U.S. Army Command and General Staff College, 2010). I have found the best resource to be the three-part UK series on the war available on

YouTube, including "Falklands: The Land Battle," documentary in three parts, BBC and ITN, n.d., YouTube video.

48. See U.S. Joint Chief of Staff: Ronald H. Cole, *Operation Just Cause Panama* (Washington, DC: Joint History Office of the Office of the Chairman of the Joint Chiefs of Staff, 1995).
49. Kearney and Cohen, *Air Power Survey.*
50. Connable, *Iraqi Army Will to Fight,* appendixes.
51. David A. Deptula, *Effects-Based Operations: Change in the Nature of Warfare* (Arlington, VA: Aerospace Education Foundation, 2001), 24; Mary C. FitzGerald, *The Impact of the Military-Technical Revolution on Russian Military Affairs: Volume I* (Washington, DC: Hudson Institute, August 20, 1993).
52. Connable, *Iraqi Army Will to Fight,* chapter 4. Also see, for example, Kevin M. Woods, Williamson Murray, and Thomas Holaday, *Saddam's War: An Iraqi Military Perspective of the Iran-Iraq War* (Washington, DC: National Defense University Institute for Strategic Studies, March 2009); Kevin M. Woods et al., *Saddam's Generals: Perspectives of the Iran-Iraq War* (Alexandria, VA: Institute for Defense Analysis, 2011); and Kevin M. Woods, David D. Palkki, and Mark E. Stout, *The Saddam Tapes: The Inner Workings of a Tyrant's Regime, 1978–2001* (New York: Cambridge University Press, 2011).
53. Connable, *Iraqi Army Will to Fight,* 74–89.
54. For examples of other Iraqi Army defensive operations and counterattacks in the Gulf War, see Charles J. Quilter II, *U.S. Marines in the Persian Gulf, 1990–1991: With the I Marine Expeditionary Force in Desert Shield and Desert Storm* (Washington, DC: History and Museums Division, Headquarters, U.S. Marine Corps, 1993); Dennis P. Mroczkowski, *With the 2d Marine Division in Desert Shield and Desert Storm: U.S. Marines in the Persian Gulf, 1990–1991* (Washington, DC: History and Museums Division, Headquarters, U.S. Marine Corps, 1993); and Robert H. Scales Jr., *Certain Victory: United States Army in the Gulf War* (Washington, DC: U.S. Government Printing Office, 1993).
55. A coincidence rangefinder uses overlap of two images to determine range to a distant target. See U.S. Army, *M60A1, M60A1 Rise, and M60A1 RISE (Passive) Series Tanks Combat Full-Tracked 105-mm Gun Update System Assessment* (Warren, MI: Logistic Management Division, PMO M60 Tanks, May 1980).
56. Correlates of War lists 49 cases in this period.
57. I did not code the Mogadishu case. For more on this case, see Roger N. Sangvic, "Battle of Mogadishu: Anatomy of a Failure" (thesis, School of Advanced Military Studies, 1999); and United States Forces, Somalia, *United States Forces, Somalia after Action Report and Historical Overview: The United States Army in Somalia, 1992–1994* (Washington, DC: U.S. Army Center of Military History, 2003).
58. I coded the Grozny case. For more on the Grozny battle, see Olga Oliker, *Russia's Chechen Wars 1994–2000* (Santa Monica, CA: RAND Corporation, 2001); Timothy L. Thomas, "Russian Tactical Lessons Learned Fighting Chechen Separatists," *Journal of Slavic Military Studies* 18, no. 4 (2005), 731–766; Adam Geibel, "Caucasus Nightmare, Red Dawn in Chechnya: A Campaign Chronicle," *Armor,* March–April 1995, 10–15; Lester W. Grau, "Russian-Manufactured Armored Vehicle Vulnerability in Urban Combat: The Chechnya Experience" (Fort Leavenworth, KS: Foreign Military Studies Office, January 1997); and Rustem Klupov,

"Грозный. Новогодний штурм от первого лица," *Novaya Gazeta*, December 31, 2021, https://novayagazeta.eu.

59. Exceptions were Paquisha Ecuador-Peru 1981, Goose Green Falklands (Malvinas) 1982, and Cenapa Valley Peru-Ecuador 1995.
60. For more on Lang Son, see Edward C. O'Dowd, *Chinese Military Strategy in the Third Indochina War: The Last Maoist War* (New York: Routledge, 2007); Xiaoming Zhang, *Deng Xiaoping's Long War: The Military Conflict between China and Vietnam, 1979–1991* (Chapel Hill: University of North Carolina Press, 2015); Christopher M. Gin, *How China Wins: A Case Study of the 1979 Sino-Vietnamese War* (Fort Leavenworth, KS: U.S. Army Command and General Staff College Press, 2016); and Jason H. Rosenstrauch, "Operational Art in the Sino-Vietnamese War" (thesis, U.S. Army Command and General Staff College, 2014).
61. Sources on this case are less detailed than other cases in this time period. For example, see Adrien Fontanellez and Tom Cooper, *Ethiopian-Eritrean Wars: Volume I, Eritrean War of Independence, 1961–1988* (West Midlands, UK: Helion, 2018); Vincenzo Meleca, "Afabet, March 1988: The Decisive Battle for Eritrean Independence," online article, February 20, 2019, https://www.ilcornodafrica.it; "ERi-TV Documentaries: ክንፈ መጸወድያ—ኣብ ሕምብርቲ ጸላኢ ብምእታው ዝተፈጸመ ስርሒት ስትራተጂካዊ ስልቲ," documentary, Eri-TV Eritrea, n.d., YouTube video; "Eritrea, Afabet ca 1988 part clip.wmv," archival newsreel, 1988, YouTube video.
62. I list these out here because all are still in use in Ukraine in 2023. I return to these systems in the following chapters and conclusion.
63. For example, see Arthur J. Alexander, *Armor Development in the Soviet Union and the United States* (Santa Monica, CA: RAND Corporation, September 1976); Sarah Ashbridge and Emily Ferris, "Why Mass Casualty Acceptance Is Part of Russian Warfare," *RUSI*, December 2, 2022; Andrew Monaghan, "Kennan Cable No. 75: Victory, Defeat, and Russian Ways in War," *Wilson Center*, March 2022, https://wilsoncenter.org.
64. Explosive-reactive armor (ERA) is a set of externally mounted blocks consisting of explosives designed to activate shaped-charge warheads before they reach the vehicle's armor, diverting the blast and protecting both the vehicle and crew.
65. For example, Richard A. Lacquement Jr., "The Casualty-Aversion Myth," *Naval War College Review* 57, no. 1 (Winter 2004); Trent Lythgoe, "Our Risk Averse Army: How We Got Here and How to Overcome It," *Modern War Institute*, May 9, 2019, https://mwi.westpoint.edu; Robert F. Wendel, "Casualty Aversion in the Post-Cold War Era: Defined and Analyzed through the Logic of Clausewitz" (thesis, U.S. Marine Corps Command and Staff College, 2001); U.S. Army Chief of Staff Mark A. Milley in Sydney J. Freedberg Jr., "Let Leaders Off the Electronic Leash: CSA Milley," *Breaking Defense*, May 5, 2017; Charles J. Dunlap Jr., "Kosovo, Casualty Aversion, and the American Military Ethos: A Perspective," *Journal of Legal Studies* (2000), 95–107.
66. "Vietnam War U.S. Military Fatal Casualty Statistics," electronic record report, U.S. National Archives, https://www.archives.gov.
67. This information was compiled by the Vietnam Helicopter Pilots Association and should be considered secondary source without better attribution to original, official data. See Gary Roush, "Helicopter Losses during the Vietnam War," *VHPA*, n.d., https://www.vhpa.org.

68. Add to this list the dishonest and illogical operations assessment process. See Connable, *Embracing the Fog of War*.
69. See Daniel L. Haulman, "Vietnam Evacuation: Operation Frequent Wind," U.S. Department of Defense press release, 2012.
70. This deployment and the bombing incident are described in Benis M. Frank, *U.S. Marines in Lebanon 1982–1984* (Washington, DC: History and Museums Division, Headquarters, U.S. Marine Corps, 1987).
71. See U.S. Army, *The United States Army in Somalia 1992–1994* (Washington, DC: U.S. Army Center of Military History, n.d.).
72. Lacquement Jr., "Casualty-Aversion Myth."
73. Also see insights on civilian perspectives in: Christopher Gelpi, Peter D. Feaver, and Jason Reifler, *The Human Costs of War: American Public Opinion and Casualties in Military Conflicts* (Princeton, NJ: Princeton University Press, 2009); Edward N. Luttwak, "Toward Post-Heroic Warfare," *Foreign Affairs* 74, no. 3 (May–June 1995), 109–122.
74. For example, my Gulf War heavy machinegun scout vehicle carried both M72s and AT-4s.
75. They also moved thousands of vehicles into cold storage for later use and distribution.
76. For more on these tactics, see for example, Ali Ahmad Jalali and Lester W. Grau, *The Other Side of the Mountain: Mujahideen Tactics in the Soviet-Afghan War* (Fort Leavenworth, KS: Foreign Military Studies Office, 1999).
77. Parallel design of the similar British Challenger, French Leclerc, and German Leopard II tanks is equally important and, to some extent, closely related as part of a combined allied design effort.
78. As of 2024, variants of the M60 tank are still in service and saw recent combat in northern Syria, Sudan, and in Yemen. See Michael Tong, "M60 Patton: 'Stopgap' Tank Clocks Up a Half-Century in Service," *International Institute for Strategic Studies*, July 22, 2019, https://www.iiss.org; Brent M. Eastwood, "A Main Battle Tank the US Hasn't Used in 30 Years Is Still Fighting Wars across the Middle East," *Business Insider*, December 17, 2021, https://www.businesinsider.com.
79. World War II assault gun designs (e.g., StuG) influenced some postwar designs even for what are typically referred to as main battle tanks. The Swedish Stridsvagn 103, or "S-tank," was a turretless tank designed for defensive operations. With the gun mounted directly in the chassis, the tank had a low profile that made it difficult to detect and target. See Kyle Mizokami, "Sweden's 'S-Tank' Had a Super Strange—But Not Stupid—Design," *Popular Mechanics*, April 4, 2016, https://www.popularmechanics.com.
80. The BILL probably was the first top-down anti-tank guided missile. It was designed in the late 1980s and entered production in the early 1990s. The NLAW did not see wide distribution until the 2010s and then probably no extensive combat employment until the 2022 phase of the Ukraine War.
81. For more information on these aircraft, see the official U.S. Air Force website.
82. Given the lack of available comparative detail on all close-air support missions flown in all global cases of ground combat from 1945 to 2001, this is reasonable supposition and not provable fact.
83. These include but are not limited to design cost; parts and assembly cost; operating cost; innovation risk factors; international treaty issues; opposition from manned

aircraft pilots; parallel evolution of manned aircraft capabilities; and acquisition opportunity costs. See Thomas P. Ehrhard, *Air Force UAVs: The Secret History* (Arlington, VA: Mitchell Institute Press, July 2010).

84. Ehrhard, *UAVs*, 28. Also see Axe, *Drone War Vietnam.*
85. See Yefim Gordon, *Soviet/Russian Unmanned Aerial Vehicles* (Midland, 2005); Elsa Kania, *The PLA's Unmanned Aerial Systems: New Capabilities for a 'New Era' of Chinese Military Power* (Montgomery, AL: China Aerospace Studies Institute, 2018).
86. Kreis, "Unmanned Aircraft," 46.
87. See the Cuito Cuanavale case in chapter 5.
88. For example, the Israeli-designed RQ-2 Pioneer drone was employed in the 1991 Gulf War. See Norman Polmar, "Historic Aircraft—The Pioneering Pioneer," *Naval History Magazine* 27, no. 5 (September 2013); U.S. Government Accountability Office, Unmanned Aerial Vehicles: DoD's Acquisition Efforts, congressional testimony (April 9, 1997).
89. See Richard Whittle, *Predator: The Secret Origins of the Drone Revolution* (New York: Henry Holt, 2014). Also see Frank Strickland, "The Early Evolution of the Predator Drone," *Studies in Intelligence* 57, no. 1 (March 2013).
90. See Donald H. Martin, *Communication Satellites: 1958–1992* (El Segundo, CA: Aerospace Corporation, December 31, 1991).
91. See Adam Goetsch, "The Evolution of GPS," *Illumin Magazine*, May 2, 2005, https://illumin.usc.edu. For more on GPS timing, see National Air and Space Administration, "The Role of GPS in Precise Time and Frequency Dissemination," information bulletin, n.d., https://ilrs.gsfc.nasa.gov.
92. See Deidre Moon, "746th Test Squadron Develops High Power Jammer System for Continuous Tracking," press release, U.S. Air Force Material Command, July 14, 2022; Kyle Rempfer, "More than Meets the Eye: Army Selects Next-Gen Camouflage System," *Army Times*, November 7, 2018; and the U.S. Army ODIN website for more on global antiair systems.

SIX

Modern Ground Combat from 2003 through 2012

This chapter and chapter 7 present a chronological survey drawn from the 423 nonrepresentative ground combat cases from the 2003–2022 period. Together, these two chapters set a descriptive basis for the data-focused analysis of the modern cases presented in chapter 8. I have broken down this twenty-year period into five-year increments starting in January 2003 and ending in December 2022.

Since we have no comprehensive accounting of all ground combat that occurred during this modern period (or, arguably, for any period in history), these 423 cases are necessarily nonrepresentative. No single battle or set of battles even within this bound set can possibly reflect the many complexities and disparities of the whole. With this known gap, I describe each five-year period and offer up what I intend to be a purposefully diverse sampling of brief battle descriptions from around the world.

Similarly to the 1945–2002 interim period, the modern period from 2003 to 2022 is best described through a double-helix narrative of evolutionary technical change and a nearly static continuity of function. Despite clear evidence of accelerating drone use in places like Ukraine, some battles fought in 2022 differed little from battles in 2003, or even from battles fought toward the end of World War II. One could scramble the chronological order of the 423 modern battles through 2022, strip out place names, and it would be quite difficult to determine if they had occurred nearer the beginning or end of the twenty-year span. Table 6.1 depicts the breakdown of total coded cases by frequency as they did occur across each five-year period:

I selected several cases per time period to highlight similarities and differences in ground combat characteristics. Each case highlighted in this chapter includes up to eight cited references, a general engagement location, combatants, inclusive dates drawn from the referenced sources, and a *confidence* rating.[1]

Table 6.1. Case Frequency by Period

Period	Count	~% of total
2003–2007	70	16%
2008–2012	89	21%
2013–2017	151	36%
2018–2022	113	27%

Given the disparity in available information and the quality of evidence from case to case, I applied a confidence rating of 1–3 to each case in the dataset. A rating of 1 indicates high confidence in the detail and reliability of the sources, 2 indicates gaps in detail or confidence, and 3 indicates a low-confidence case. I include some level-2 and -3 cases in these chapters to avoid reinforcing an endemic problem with the Western canon: Poor recording and reporting does not render a case unimportant. In fact, the existence of so many unknowns might make these cases relatively more important for the purposes of understanding global ground combat.[2]

This chapter and chapter 7 each present two of the four database time periods (ten years each). Along with the selected release of the database, further case descriptions will be posted online or in an annex to this book. Each case description is necessarily shorter than those in chapters 2 and 4 due to the inconsistent availability of detail from case to case.

2003–2007

Ground combat in Iraq from the initial coalition invasion in 2003 through the ongoing counterinsurgency campaign at the end of 2007 dominates the land-warfare narrative in this time period, overshadowing the often high-intensity combined-arms battles that took place across the Jaffna Peninsula in Sri Lanka, battalion-level operations in Afghanistan, and mountain warfare in Pakistan involving tens of thousands of soldiers. Table 6.2 aggregates the 2003–2007 cases by country from most to least.

Primarily American and British ground forces invaded Iraq in 2003, supported by Australians, Poles, and Kurdish Iraqis. American ground forces fielded the kind of hodgepodge of dated and cutting-edge equipment, weapons, and technology still found in every global army through 2024. Soldiers and Marines in the initial invasion were armed primarily with 1980s-era rifles, while a few lucky riflemen were given new turn-of-the-millennium scopes. Marines mounted up in 1960s-era amphibious tractors and then dismounted to fire

Table 6.2. Cases by Country, 2003–2007

Country	Count	Percent
Iraq	31	44%
Sri Lanka	9	13%
Somalia	8	11%
Afghanistan	7	10%
Lebanon	4	6%
DRC	3	4%
Pakistan	2	3%
Nepal	2	3%
Bhutan	1	1%
Liberia	1	1%
Chad	1	1%
Yemen	1	1%

modern Javelin missiles at Iraqi tanks. Hyper-advanced stealth aircraft flew overhead to drop advanced precision munitions on defensive positions, while 1960s-era AC-130 gunships provided pinpoint fires to soldiers on the ground. Opposing Iraqi units fielded mostly Soviet-era gear including ubiquitous AK-variant rifles, T-55 and T-72 tanks, multiple-launch rockets, and a grab bag of anti-tank and surface-to-surface missiles. Even as they made good use of their respective technologies, both sides employed tactics—forced-entry amphibious assault, tactical column ground attack up main hardball roads, block-by-block urban clearing operations, entrenched defense covered by fires—almost identical to those employed in World War II.

I recorded fourteen cases from the 2003 invasion of Iraq, including the battles at Debecka Pass, al-Kut, al-Zubayr, Haditha Dam, al-Nasiriyah, and Baghdad International Airport. In the opening hours of the invasion, a combined coalition force attacked division-level Iraqi defensive positions on the al-Faw peninsula.

Al-Faw, Iraq, 2003: Level 1 Case[3]

Location: Al-Faw peninsula, Iraq
Combatants: UK (U.S.-led coalition) versus Iraq
Dates: March 20–April 5, 2003

A joint and combined force of UK Royal Marine Commandos and U.S. Navy SEALs conducted a heliborne assault to establish a foothold on the al-Faw Peninsula. Iraqi naval infantry put up limited resistance with small arms, while other Iraqi troops abandoned intact bunkers, artillery positions, and armor. Coalition Predator and Phoenix drones, fixed-wing aircraft including AC-130 gunships, and attack helicopters conducted aerial surveillance and close-air support, while naval vessels provided gunfire support. With a foothold on the peninsula secured, Commando and other UK forces pushed out reconnaissance units in light Scimitar reconnaissance vehicles and Land Rover trucks respectively armed with cannons and guided missiles.

An Iraqi mechanized infantry unit counterattacked down the peninsula with a battalion of T-55 tanks supported by artillery and mortar fire. Coalition aircraft dropped laser-guided bombs and destroyed a number of the tanks with air-delivered missiles, while recon units destroyed more tanks with Milan missiles. A squadron of Challenger tanks then joined the coalition force and pushed toward the town of Abu al-Khasib, which was defended by another Iraqi mechanized infantry unit. A close-range tank battle ensued, with T-55s losing out to the far more advanced and better-crewed Challengers. Iraqi infantry tried to swarm the tanks but were killed by coaxial machinegun fire. Commandos then advanced on foot into Abu al-Khasib with tank, helicopter, drone, and fixed-wing support. They engaged aggressive Saddam Fedayeen light infantry at close range and destroyed the Iraqis' remaining T-55 tanks and a number of thin-skinned MT-LB armored personnel carriers.

Observations and insights from al-Faw, Iraq, 2003. No coalition troops were killed in the entire al-Faw operation. However, brief preinvasion fires did almost nothing to clear away Iraqi ground combat capabilities. Possibly two full battalions of T-55 tanks were left intact. Bad weather impeded aerial observation and strike during one period of the battle. Close-range fights by infantry-armor teams with near-constant air support were required to defeat these low-tier Iraqi defenders and militia.

Following the initial invasion of Iraq, coalition forces were dragged into a growing counterinsurgency battle against a diverse array of armed groups. Understandable Western fixation on the Iraq War pushed equally intensive—and in some cases, far more intensive—battles in Nepal, the DRC, and Pakistan into the shadows. Major 2004 battles at al-Fallujah, al-Ramadi, al-Najaf, Mosul, and others occurred generally in parallel with division-level combined-arms operations in the Wana area of Pakistan and light division-level infantry assault by Maoist rebels against an isolated Nepali Army mountain base at Beni.

Beni, Nepal, 2004: Level 2 Case[4]

Location: Beni, Myagdi District, Nepal
Combatants: Communist Party of Nepal People's Liberation Army versus Nepal
Dates: March 20–21, 2004

Four brigades of People's Liberation Army (PLA) infantry massed at the village of Lukum to prepare for a ground assault on the Nepalese Army positions at the Myagdi District headquarters at Beni. Approximately 3,400 Maoist troops and over 1,500 logistics porters were reorganized under what was effectively a division-level command. A full week was spent at Beni rehearsing the attack with sand-table walk-throughs, video intelligence, and field exercises. This task-organized light infantry division then conducted a weeklong foot march over mountainous terrain carrying their 2-inch and 81mm mortars, RPGs, AK-variant rifles, and both light and heavy machineguns. They crept in and established support-by-fire positions on the steep hills surrounding the ~450-man government force and then infiltrated teams of infantry into the perimeter in a daring night attack.

When the defending police and Army soldiers responded, the supporting fire positions lit up the town with heavy machinegun, rocket, and mortar fire. Infantry then poured in behind a wall of suppressive fire and closed on the defending troops. Teams of ten Maoists—about a squad—would fight intensively until they ran low on ammunition or suffered casualties, then a fresh squad would jump in to sustain momentum. They managed to surround the garrison, but Army helicopters (probably old Soviet Mi-8s) flew in, dropped much needed ammunition, and then bombed the Maoist troops in and around the town. Sensing a shift in momentum, the PLA division commander withdrew his forces under fire.

Observations and insights from Beni, Nepal, 2004. Both sides fought with equivalent basic infantry weapons, and the government troops might have been overrun if not for the intervention of the supporting helicopters. Attack aviation brought a new combined-arms component and a new attack angle—top-down—into the ground combat mix, effectively reducing the Maoists' comparative ~3-to-1 numerical advantage in foot soldiers. Government helicopters all but eliminated the Maoists' high-ground advantage.

Accelerating violence in Iraq through 2006, including major battles at Tala'afar, Turki, and al-Ramadi, continued to dominate Western headlines and the attention of military analysts. Meanwhile, heavy ground combat action continued across northeastern Sri Lanka. Rise of the Islamic Courts Union in

Somalia and an Ethiopian-led intervention sparked monthslong ground combat battles and skirmishes in Mogadishu, Jowhar, Heliashid, Bay, and Galkayo. Taliban elements in Afghanistan recuperated from their 2001–2002 defeat and had to be destroyed en masse by Canadian-led forces in Panjwaii, foreshadowing heavier fighting to follow.

In the same period, ground combat flared and ebbed across the DRC, Nepal, Chad, Yemen, and elsewhere. Israel's ill-fated invasion of Lebanon in 2006, and their engagements at Maroun al-Ras, A'aita al-Shab, Wadi al-Hujair (Wadi al-Saluki), and Bint Jbeil, offered an opportunity to compare their new maneuver-warfare army to the 1982 battle at Beqa'a Valley. The Mogadishu and Bint Jbeil cases follow.

Mogadishu, Somalia, 2006: Level 2 Case[5]

Location: Mogadishu, Somalia
Combatants: Islamic Courts Union (ICU) versus ARPC[6]
Dates: May–July 2006

In an ongoing struggle for control of Mogadishu, and for all of Somalia, the al-Qa'ida-affiliated ICU fought against the warlord network organized under the ARPC. Both groups were conglomerations of various militias, each with separate command and control but all well-armed with AK-variant rifles, a range of light and medium machineguns, RPG rockets, 60mm and 82mm mortars, pickup trucks with mounted heavy machineguns and antiaircraft artillery cannons, and in some cases indirect-fire rocket launchers and 122mm artillery. A chaotic swirl of skirmishes unfolded over the course of nearly three months, with intensive fighting in the urban core in Mogadishu and in the surrounding countryside.

Combatant units defended sections of the city by throwing together barricades made out of cars, tires, earth, and debris to prevent fast-moving pickup-truck assaults by opposing forces. Mortar, artillery, and rocket fires were probably employed in loose coordination with advancing and defending infantry and not with the kind of precise communication and timing practiced by professional ground combat forces. In many cases, stray indirect-fire rounds hit civilian areas. Despite almost running out of ammunition during the long-running battle, the ICU was able to force the warlords out of Mogadishu by July 2006.

Observations and insights from Mogadishu, Somalia, 2006. This is a level-2 case, which means that the publicly available details of the battle are limited and incomplete. Order of battle—units, equipment, weapons, organization—for both sides was not well recorded, and it was difficult to track the location and actions of specific groups through and around Mogadishu during the course of the battle. Instead, public records allow for a general understanding of the ebb and flow of ground combat, with some explicit incidents (in this case, fighting around a hotel and barracks) standing out.

Bint Jbeil, Lebanon, 2006: Level 1 Case[7]

Location: Bint Jbeil, Nabatia, Lebanon
Combatants: Israel versus Lebanese Hezb'allah
Dates: July 23–August 11, 2006

A mixed force of Israeli mechanized infantry centered on the 51st Reserve Brigade and the 35th Paratroop Brigade attacked to clear the town of Bint Jbeil of defending Hezb'allah forces. Forecasting the assault, Hezb'allah reinforced its troops in the town with special forces and additional cadre, massing about 250 troops with mortars, rockets, machineguns, mines and improvised explosive devices (IEDs), and Soviet-era anti-tank missiles. Israeli troops attacked upward into the high ground in Achzarit and M113 APCs backed by Merkava tanks from two brigades and supported by 155mm artillery, attack helicopters, and observation drones. Paratroopers were helilifted onto the high ground on the flanks of the advancing infantry.

As the 51st and attached units moved forward, they ran headfirst into Hezb'allah defenders and engaged in a close-range fight. Anti-tank missiles streaked out from the hillside and destroyed at least two Merkavas while the Hezb'allah screening force withdrew into better-prepared defenses. Dismounted Israeli troops pressed ahead but were met with intensive fire within hand grenade range. The battle devolved into a close-quarters rifle, machinegun, and grenade battle, with Hezb'allah mortars and rockets landing among the Israeli infantry. At the same time, Israeli artillery and helicopter attacks took their toll on the defenders. Another Merkava was lost to a large IED, stalling the tank advance. Paratroopers moved in to support the 51st and helped to beat back a Hezb'allah counterattack, allowing the Israelis to gather up their dead and wounded and evacuate by helicopter and APC. Several skirmishes at Bint Jbeil over the following days resulted in no ground changing hands. Hezb'allah held the town.

Observations and insights from Bint Jbeil, Lebanon, 2006. Prepared defenses on the high ground manned by aggressive and well-trained troops with combined-arms capabilities can be taken, but usually only at high cost. Israeli tanks were forced to push forward in the open, making them vulnerable to anti-tank missile and rocket fire. Civilians in the town prevented the Israelis from massing fires to disrupt the anti-tank teams, so the infantry had to move in with limited direct-fire support. In my analysis of this case, infantry then won or lost based on their most fundamental capabilities, presence of mind, and will.

As 2006 bled into 2007, thinly spread coalition forces in Afghanistan found themselves on the defensive in Helmand and Kandahar Provinces. Violence in Sri Lanka peaked with relentless combined-arms engagements back and forth across the Muhamalai Defensive Line and amphibious assaults along the Jaffna coast. Coalition forces in Iraq took advantage of their surge in forces to engage insurgents in al-Basra, Ba'aquba, Baghdad, and al-Najaf. Skirmishes and major battles between light and heavy forces continued across Somalia.

Quietly, with limited outside observation, combined-arms fighting flared in the Sa'ada Governorate of Yemen. In sub-Saharan Africa, government and militia forces fought for control of the Masisi Highlands in the DRC. These following three cases—Sa'ada Yemen; Chora, Afghanistan; and Thoppigala-Narakamulla, Sri Lanka—are nonrepresentative but indicative of the perhaps surprising scale and intensity of combat in conflicts commonly described as insurgencies or civil wars.

Sa'ada, Yemen, 2007: Level 3 Case[8]

Location: Sa'ada Governorate, Yemen
Combatants: Yemen versus Ansar Allah (Houthis)
Dates: January–June 2007

From early to mid-2007, the Yemeni Army attempted to suppress and destroy the burgeoning Houthi resistance across the Sa'ada Governorate. Army commanders deployed probably brigade-level combined-arms units fielding Soviet infantry weapons and T-55 and T-62 tanks, BMP-1 infantry fighting vehicles, BTR-variant armored personnel carriers, at least 122mm and 130mm artillery, 122mm multiple-launch rocket systems, and both fixed-wing and rotary-wing air support including Mi-8 helicopters with mounted rocket pods. Houthi fighters defended with their own Soviet infantry weapons including AK-variant rifles, machineguns, RPGs and mortars, antiaircraft guns mounted on trucks, and probably also T-55 tanks, artillery, and rockets.

Army units engaged Houthi elements with indirect fires and then moved in their armor-heavy units to try to pin and destroy the more mobile Houthi forces. Houthi units probably tried to maintain control of the terrain from the high ground, shooting down into advancing Army units from ridgelines. Yemeni Mig-29 fighter-bombers and probably Su-25 attack aircraft conducted mostly unguided bombing runs against Houthi positions throughout the battle. Negotiations temporarily halted the fighting in mid-2007.

Observations and insights from Sa'ada, Yemen, 2007. In the Sa'ada level-3 case, video evidence and news reporting provided enough information to show that the Army fielded mechanized forces, artillery, and aircraft against more lightly armed Houthi units, and these sources provided some insight into the course of events. But even the Arabic-language news sources from Yemen provide almost no explicit details of this large-scale, long-running battle. It looks like tens of thousands of soldiers employing tanks, artillery, rockets, and close-air support engaged in heavy combat for months on end across Sa'ada, but more and better evidence is needed.

Chora, Afghanistan, 2007: Level 1 Case[9]

Location: Chora, Afghanistan
Combatants: The Netherlands (U.S.-led coalition) and Afghanistan versus the Taliban
Dates: June 16–19, 2007

Through May and into early June 2007, Taliban forces massed in Uruzgan Province, Afghanistan, with the probable intent of overrunning the coalition combined force at Chora. This Dutch-led contingent included adviser teams, organic intelligence and surveillance assets, special operations forces, Afghan National Army troops with unarmored Ranger trucks, and a Dutch battlegroup centered on the 42 Armoured Infantry Battalion employing YPR-variant fighting vehicles (an up-gunned M113 APC), other light armor, and backed by Panzerhaubitze 2000 (PzH2000) 155mm self-propelled artillery, drones, and a full range of available coalition strike aircraft. Through mid-June, Taliban platoon and company-level elements of up to, or over, one hundred troops conducted combined-arms attacks with AK-variant rifles, machineguns, recoilless rifles, mortars, and 107mm indirect fire rockets.

On June 16, a reinforced company of about 200 Taliban—and perhaps up to 1,000 Taliban—conducted a massed attack on Chora, engaging the defenders with combined mortar, rocket, and direct fires while infantry advanced closer to checkpoints and defensive positions. Dutch troops dug in to the defense and on June 17 fired back with 155mm artillery and called in nearly thirty airstrikes with precision munitions. Undeterred, on June 18, the Taliban pressed their attack and maneuvered on foot and with pickup trucks to circle in on the now reinforced defenders. Heavy fighting continued for several hours but tapered off in the evening. On June 19, the Dutch pushed out of their defensive positions, took the high ground, and pressed their combined infantry forward. The Taliban retreated.

Observations and insights from Chora, Afghanistan, 2007. High ground played an important role for both sides, with the Taliban attempting to seize the high ground and deny it to the defenders, and the Dutch employing high-ground positions to make best use of their longer-range weapons including electro-optical and thermal-sight-targeted armored vehicle cannons and heavy machineguns. Precision-fire support guided by drone and ground observation helped to break up Taliban attacks, killing perhaps fifty of the attackers in the process. However, the Taliban continued to fight until they culminated, probably as ammunition ran low and as Dutch reinforcements increased the volume of defensive fires.

Thoppigala-Narakamulla, Sri Lanka, 2007: Level 2 Case[10]

Location: Thoppigala-Narakamulla, Sri Lanka
Combatants: Sri Lanka versus Liberation Tamil Tigers of Eelam (LTTE)
Dates: June 22–July 11, 2007

Tamil Tiger units had long maintained a well-entrenched network of basecamps across the jungle in an area anchored by a prominent mountain called the Baron's Cap. Army mechanized infantry advanced to clear this relatively flat jungle terrain in BMP-1s and BTRs, supported by (probably both) Type-69 and T-55AM2 tanks, artillery, rockets, and both fixed-wing and rotary-wing close-air support. Tiger defenses were well established, with log and metal-beam bunkers, fixed machineguns, and some antiaircraft artillery cannons overlooking minefields. Defending Tiger units also sustained foot mobility across their interior lines, quickly responding to Army advances in differing sectors and executing some local counterattacks.

Videos show Army infantry advancing on foot and in armored vehicles while tank gunners provided covering fire with machineguns and cannons. Army artillery, rockets, and mortars were used extensively to soften up the Tamil defenses and reduce infantry casualties. As they did in other offensive operations from 2006 onward, the Army probably employed commando teams for infiltration and assault operations, limiting the kinds of costly frontal assaults by regular infantry that had marked earlier operations. Tiger infantry fought aggressively from their bunkers and from interlocking trenches, in many cases dying in place. Army units pressed through and eventually cleared the Tigers' Beirut Camp at Thoppigala, ending the battle.

Observations and insights from Thoppigala-Narakamulla, Sri Lanka, 2007. At least in the cited sources there was no reported drone or ATGM use during this operation. But the Sri Lankan Air Force probably routinely flew drones for observation in 2007. So, this is one of many cases in which drone use may have gone unreported. Still, even the low-level jungle canopy provided good concealment of the Tamil defenses, probably requiring extensive foot-mobile reconnaissance. Bunkers reinforced with overhead cover, and particularly those with metal beams, survived pre-assault artillery and rocket barrages and had to be cleared out by infantry. Improvised explosives and mines probably limited and channelized Army movement to some extent. Flat terrain worked to the advantage of the attackers, allowing armor to move forward despite dense vegetation.

OBSERVATIONS AND INSIGHTS FROM 2003 TO 2007

With only seventy cases, this period had the fewest well-recorded, distinct ground combat events of any period through 2022. However, there were daily engagements between the U.S.-led coalitions and insurgents in Iraq and Afghanistan, effectively constant back and forth between the Sri Lankan Army and the Tamil Tigers, and probably hundreds, if not thousands, of unrecorded cases of ground combat in Yemen, Somalia, Chad, and other parts of the world. Most of these events went unreported in the public domain or are anchored by fewer than four basically reliable and independent sources of information (my floor for case coding). In this period and in all of the remaining periods in the database, often intensive combat in sub-Saharan Africa was poorly recorded, frequently to the point that cases could not be included. Even those African cases included in the database drew from limited public evidence.

For example, in 2004 a major battle was fought between the DRC armed forces and the Rally for Congolese Democracy (RDC) for control over the city of Bukavu.[11] RDC forces conducted what amounted to an amphibious assault in small boats across the Rusizi River and Lake Kivu and engaged in basic combined-arms combat—direct fire, mortars, and rockets—until they were pushed out of the city. This case may offer important insights into modern ground combat, but Bukavu DRC 2004 and similar cases in the DRC receive thin public coverage in all relevant languages.

2008–2012

I coded a total of eighty-nine cases of ground combat from the beginning of 2008 through the end of 2012. The volume of publicly available evidence on ground combat cases grew unevenly but significantly from the end of

2007 as social media use increased the volume and retention of some data. However, reporting volume did not translate directly into increased detail or more reliable evidence. A great many of the social media links remaining from this time period are now dead, and—at least in my reading of the case evidence—as the volume of information increased, reporting detail and reliability decreased.

Incidents of circular reporting exploded from 2008 onward: A single source of information would be repeated tens or in some cases hundreds of times on multiple websites and social media platforms, giving the false impression that a high volume of reliable evidence existed below the surface of the hyperlink deluge. While the proliferation of available information during this period was to some extent smoke and mirrors, the actual volume of global ground combat almost certainly did increase.[12] The Arab Spring in 2011 resulted in a spike in ground combat events from Syria, Libya, Yemen, and other Middle Eastern and North African countries.

Table 6.3 lists the number of battles by country and the relative combatant type. What would go on to become a raging land war in Syria was just heating up; even the dominant nineteen Syria ground combat cases in this time period pale in comparison to the sixty-six Syria cases in the 2013–2017 period. Next in frequency, the American-led surge of forces and renewed focus on defeating the Taliban generated an upswing of combined-arms warfare in Afghanistan. In third place, rebellion in Libya threw together tens of thousands of loosely organized troops armed from the state's vast stockpiles of Soviet-Russian hardware, while NATO piled on with airstrikes and naval gun and missile fire. By comparison, the remaining coded cases in this table (in Myanmar, Ivory Coast, etc.) appear almost as afterthoughts.

These apparently lesser cases might in fact be the tip of an iceberg of unrecorded or poorly recorded cases from this period. At least twenty-three other ground combat battles—and probably many more—took place around the world from 2008 to 2012.[13] Barely observed violence raged on across Africa and South Asia, with many cases that might be unearthed by further research. The details of some of these battles probably are lost to history. We know that ground forces fought each other at Rwindi in the Democratic Republic of the Congo; at Massaguet and Tamassi in Chad; at Kidal and Idelimane in Mali; Orakzai-Karram and Shangla in Pakistan; and Pangwa in Myanmar, but we don't know much about each case or adjacent battles. These poorly recorded and hidden cases should be kept in mind as we work to better understand modern warfare.

Ground combat in Iraq ebbed at the tail end of the American troop surge, though the Iraqi Army undertook a major operation against Jaysh al-Mahdi

Table 6.3. Cases by Country, 2008–2012

Country	Count	Percent
Syria	19	21%
Afghanistan	16	18%
Libya	10	11%
Somalia	7	8%
Mali	6	7%
Sri Lanka	5	6%
Pakistan	5	6%
Iraq	3	3%
Yemen	3	3%
DRC	3	3%
Chad	2	2%
Sudan	2	2%
Palestinian Authority	1	1%
Abkhazia	1	1%
South Ossetia	1	1%
Comoros	1	1%
Myanmar	1	1%
Libya-Tunisia	1	1%
Thailand-Cambodia	1	1%
Ivory Coast	1	1%

fighters in Basra in 2008. Israel launched a division-level ground assault into Gaza; heavy urban combat there left more than 1,000 dead. Preceding and immediately following the American surge in Afghanistan, violence in that country accelerated with major battles at Wanat, Ala'Saye, Kamdesh, Marjah, Sangin, Ganjgal, Jelawur, Zhari, Derapet, and others.

Heavy fighting raged across the Northern Province of Sri Lanka as the national army pressed home its final offensive against the Tamil Tigers. Battles at Vidattaltivu, Mannar, Muhammalai, and Puthukkudiyirippu-Ananthapuram set the stage for the end of the Sri Lankan civil war. Of particular interest to Ukraine War watchers, Russia and its Abkhazian proxies conducted a limited combined-arms offensive in the Upper Kodori Valley and at Tskhinvali-Gori in South Ossetia.

Tskhinvali-Gori, South Ossetia, 2008: Level 1 Case[14]

Location: Tskhinvali-Gori, South Ossetia
Combatants: Georgia versus Russia
Dates: August 8–12, 2008

Georgian mechanized infantry forces advanced into South Ossetia to establish control over claimed territory, while Russian and South Ossetian separatists pushed back to cement their own claims. A reinforced, tank-heavy Russian mechanized infantry division with special operations forces attacked in column through a tunnel pass to engage a thinly spread Georgian division that had pushed out from the edge of Tskhinvali city into hilly forest terrain. At first, Georgian troops were able to spot and target Russian columns with drones, precision-guided munitions, and artillery fires including cluster munitions launched from BM-21 MLRS. Russian commanders continued to press forward down hardball roads in column without deploying to the flanks, exposing their columns to Georgian ambushes. Lack of effective global positioning technology rendered the Russians' own precision munitions ineffective.

But in short order the Russians imposed their will on the Georgians by massing artillery, rocket, air, and naval missile fires, and by sustaining their forward momentum despite taking what should have been sobering losses in the first day of combat. Georgian armor and infantry teams employed more advanced technology than the Russians—night vision, thermal imaging, explosive-reactive armor, and so on, all lacking in the Russian inventory in 2008—but the Georgian troops gave up their relative technical and tactical advantages as they lost their will to fight. After the first day of the war, Georgian leaders grounded their own small air force to prevent its destruction, ceding the air to Russian attack helicopters and Su-25 ground-attack planes. Facing a much larger combined-arms force, under heavy fire, and with dwindling support, many Georgians abandoned their equipment and fled.

Observations and insights from Tskhinvali-Gori, Georgia, 2008. Russian commanders blindly followed their own doctrine, exposing their armor and infantry to probably unnecessary risk. If the Georgians had been better able to mass fires on the roadways, they might have stopped the Russians cold, or at least given their own infantry a chance to set in more effective defenses. Russian commanders also (arguably) employed South Ossetian militia as cannon fodder to help locate and target the Georgian front lines.

Pakistan undertook several major operations to root out Tehrik-e-Taliban Pakistani (TTP) and other militant groups from South Waziristan. Up to corps-level Army units backed by the Pakistani Air Force engaged militants at Inayat Qilla, Bai Cheena, Mamund, Khazai Sar, Damadola, and across the Swat Valley from mid- to late 2009.

Swat Valley, Pakistan, 2009: Level 1 Case[15]

Location: Swat Valley, South Waziristan, Pakistan
Combatants: Pakistan versus Tehrik-e-Taliban Pakistan
Dates: June–December 2009

In Operation Rah-e-Nijat the Pakistani Army conducted a corps-level combined-arms operation to clear the Swat Valley of Taliban fighters and to gain control of the civilian population. Ground combat operations proceeded along three axes spearheaded by the 7th, 9th, and 14th Divisions. Each division attacked from different directions in order to pin, surround, and destroy defending Taliban forces. Pakistani Air Force fighter-bombers preceded the ground movement, striking targets that had been identified through drone and other aerial reconnaissance. Each division then advanced from village to village along the lowland corridors, attacking down roads and through farmland with infantry-armor teams led by (probably Type-69 and T-55) tanks. Mechanized infantry moved in M113 armored-personnel carriers, while Army fire support teams provided multiple-launch rocket, heavy mortar, 122mm, 130mm, and probably 152mm artillery fire.

Taliban forces defended from prepared compound defenses in the lowlands and also from elevated redoubts that had to be cleared by Pakistani heliborne infantry. Cobra attack helicopters provided infantry commanders with close-air support during the advances. Some of the higher-elevation fights still required uphill infantry assaults. Taliban positioned 12.7mm heavy machineguns on elevated terrain to kill the Pakistani helicopters, but the Air Force successfully bombed most of these positions to free up the lower-level airspace. Operations culminated with the seizure of most towns in the valley and the temporary dissolution of the TTP forces.

Observation and insights from Swat Valley, Pakistan, 2009. At least based on Pakistani sources it appeared that the infantry commanders were able to smoothly coordinate close-air support, but it is not possible to tell the degree to which the Air Force F-16s and AH-1 attack helicopters were responsive to local, tactical ground control. The Pakistanis might have been closely coordinating aerial fires like the Marines at Inchon, or they might have received loosely coordinated support like the Soviets at Mutanchiang.

Civil war in Myanmar erupted in the late 2000s and accelerated through the early 2010s. This has been and remains through 2024 a dispersed, localized conflict driven by a wide array of ethnic, socioeconomic, and political grievances. Rugged jungle, forest, and mountain terrain complicates movement, logistics, and fire support for both sides. Anti-junta militant groups in the early 2010s were lightly armed but well organized. As they captured weapons from junta forces through the mid-2010s, they became increasingly powerful and effective. The battle at Myawaddy-Three Pagodas pass is illustrative of some of the earlier fighting.

Myawaddy to Three Pagodas Pass, Myanmar, 2010: Level 2 Case[16]

Location: Myawaddy to Three Pagodas Pass, Myanmar
Combatants: Democratic Karen Buddhist Army (DKBA) versus Tatmadaw
Dates: November 8–28, 2010

Karen rebels of the Democratic Karen Buddhist Army (DKBA) 906 Battalion and possibly other rebel groups attacked and seized Myanmar junta military positions in and around the town of Myawaddy and in the Three Pagodas Pass. Myawaddy is a small city, with surrounding farms giving way to dense vegetation and steep hills of the Three Pagodas Pass to the west. Karen fighters organized in probably platoon-sized elements with mortar support. They both attacked and defended with light Soviet-Russian and American-built arms including a mix of AK-variant and M-16-variant rifles, 60mm and 81/82mm mortar, and RPG-variant rockets.

Tatmadaw soldiers counterattacked in force against what appeared to be fairly dispersed DKBA elements, pushing into Myawaddy with light infantry armed with a mix of rifles and RPG-7s and backed by light artillery and probably 122mm rockets. After clearing Myawaddy of the Karen small units, junta forces pushed up into the more difficult terrain of the hilly (mountainous) Three Pagodas Pass. Karen fighters defended this terrain with infantry and mortars, but the attacking junta forces were reportedly able to advance into the high ground and seize a major DKBA base, bringing the organized fighting to a temporary halt.

Observations and insights from Myawaddy to Three Pagodas Pass, Myanmar, 2010. Based on limited video evidence, street fighting in Myawaddy resembled similar engagements in other cases: Infantry with rifles, machineguns, and rockets spotted and attacked each other block by block. Jungle combat had to have taken place at fairly close range given the density of vegetation and steep, uneven terrain. Junta airpower (possibly including drones) might have played a role in this fight, but there was no clear record of air support in the cited sources.

Global incidents of ground combat increased through 2011 as the Arab Spring unleashed chaos and, in many cases, well-coordinated combined-arms violence across parts of the Middle East and North Africa. Malian and French forces battled an array of militant groups at Tessalit, Ménaka, Aguelhok, Kidal, and Gao, and others. Engagements continued on and off in Chad, Somalia, and also in Iraq where brigade-level Iranian and Kurdish forces clashed in the mountains at Qandil. Yemen's civil war thrust tens of thousands of combatants into almost continuous ground combat and drew in high-order technology and fire support from Iran and Gulf Arab states.

NATO directly supported the rebellion against the Libyan regime in 2011. I coded battles in the initial uprising at Bin Jawad, al-Breeq'e, Ajdabiya, Misrata, Kikla, al-Qawalish, Tripoli, al-Zawiya, and Sirt.

Sirt, Libya, 2011: Level 1 Case[17]

Location: Sirt, Sirt Region, Libya
Combatants: National Transitional Council and NATO versus Libya
Dates: September–October 2011

Late in the 2011 war, the Libyan rebels, organized under the National Transition Council (NTC), massed considerable armaments and irregular infantry, then pressed in to destroy the last elements of loyalist resistance. Three major rebel fronts with probably thousands of troops advanced on the dense urban terrain of Sirt, moving over low-rolling desert and into the urban ring with T-55 (and possibly T-62) tanks, BMP-1 infantry fighting vehicles, heavy mortars, a wide array of multiple-launch rocket systems, technical pickup trucks with antiaircraft guns, artillery, and a full complement of Soviet-Russian small arms: AK-variant rifles, RPG-7s, machineguns, 60mm mortars, and so on. Rebel troops improvised from government arms warehouses, fixing aerial rocket pods and even what looked like an 85mm artillery piece on light trucks.

Despite long odds of success and incessant NATO airstrikes, loyalist troops put up a tenacious defense of Sirt, employing the same weapons and equipment as the rebels. At one point they may have fired an R-11 Zemlya (SCUD) surface-to-surface missile at rebel troops.[18] Neither of the opposing ground forces were terribly well organized, so the battle for the city devolved into a running series of skirmishes with rocket, mortar, and machinegun exchanges accompanying rapid light infantry advances down wide avenues and alleyways. Tanks and BMPs provided heavy direct firepower for the attacking rebels as they reduced loyalist defensive positions on the ground and in tall buildings. NATO fixed-wing reconnaissance aircraft and drones spotted and helped strike loyalist targets throughout the battle and the siege that preceded the final assault. The battle ended with the death of Libyan leader Ma'amr al-Qadthafi.

Observations and insights from Sirt, Libya, 2011. The impact of interdiction strikes and aerial reconnaissance on this battle is difficult to assess through unclassified sources. NATO had continually attacked loyalist targets in and around Sirt since March 2011, degrading defenses well before the final assault began in September.[19] Drones played an active role in targeting, but so did fixed-wing observation aircraft like the CP-140 Aurora maritime patrol aircraft and fighter-bombers. In turn, the loyalists also flew limited air sorties before most of their planes were destroyed, and a large number of their pilots defected to the rebels.

Well-publicized engagements in Mali in 2012 overshadowed significant battles on the Arabian Peninsula (e.g., Zinjibar and Ja'ar, Yemen), the Horn of Africa (e.g., Wabho, Mogadishu, and Garabaharey, Somalia), and sub-Saharan Africa. South Sudan and Sudan battled for control of Hejlij-Pandthau in the spring of 2012, while DRC military units fought with up to brigade-sized elements of the March 23 Movement and (possibly) Rwanda at Kubumba, Goma, Sake, and other locations in North Kivu Province. The Hejlij-Pandthau and Goma battles highlight some of the 2012 combined-arms ground combat events that were at best peripheral to Western awareness.

Hejlij-Pandthau, Sudan, 2012: Level 2 Case[20]

Location: Hejlij-Pandthau, Sudan[21]
Combatants: South Sudan and Justice and Equality Movement militias versus Sudan
Dates: March–April 2012

Ground combat elements of the South Sudanese defense forces attacked and seized the town of Hejlij and its oil facilities in a disputed area along the Sudan-South Sudan border. South Sudanese T-55 and T-72 tanks fixed with explosive-reactive armor tiles led the advance, with light motorized infantry taking the ground with Soviet-Russian infantry equipment, 107mm multiple-launch rocket systems, and technical pickup trucks. Sudanese soldiers reportedly fled their entrenched positions without putting up significant resistance. They left behind trenches and bunkers lined with heavy machineguns, recoilless rifles, and other equipment.

Southern forces held Hejlij for about a week while the Sudanese armed forces mobilized a counterattack force spearheaded by their own T-55 tanks and supported by cannon artillery and multiple-launch rocket systems. Sudanese fixed-wing fighter-bombers attacked the South Sudanese forces consolidated in and around Hejlij, destroying some of their armor and armed pickup trucks as the

Sudanese ground forces advanced from bases in the north of the country. South Sudanese troops advanced to meet the counterattack force north of Hejlij, and a series of battles ensued between armored columns and the motorized infantry forces. Sudanese Mig-29s conducted a number of unguided bombing attacks against South Sudanese positions, and the counterattack force expanded the front around Hejlij in what might have been an effort to encircle the defenders. The South Sudanese troops withdrew, leaving the town and the oil facilities in Sudanese hands.

Observations and insights from Hejlij-Panthau, Sudan, 2012. Limited training, uneven officer qualifications, poor tactical communications equipment, and the integration of unreliable mobilized and militia troops into regular formations appeared to constrain the tactical flexibility of commanders on both sides. Lack of aerial reconnaissance or effective ground reconnaissance further limited tactical options. Decent generalship allowed for basic flank attacks.

Goma, Democratic Republic of the Congo, 2012: Level 2 Case[22]

Location: Goma, North Kivu Province, DRC

Combatants: M23 and (probably) Rwanda versus Democratic Republic of the Congo

Dates: November 16–19, 2012

Thousands of motorized and possibly mechanized (BMP-1) infantry of the March 23 (M23) movement, in all likelihood reinforced by nonuniformed soldiers from the Rwandan armed forces, attacked through the province of North Kivu to seize the city of Goma from defending soldiers of the Armed Forces of the Democratic Republic of the Congo (FARDC, or Army). Attacking infantry were equipped with night-vision equipment, rockets, AK-variant rifles, RPG-7 rockets, machineguns, and mortars up to 120mm, and possibly some cannon and rocket artillery. Army forces attempted to stave off the impending attack on the regional capital, Goma, and were rolled flat by the advancing M23 ground force. Some United Nations observer attack helicopters may have attempted to provide fire support for the Army in this outskirts battle, but by the time M23 made it into Goma, the UN had removed itself from the fighting. This left lightly equipped and probably demoralized Army troops to hold back the surging attack force.

The M23 commanders reportedly sent in columns of ground reconnaissance teams to expose defensive positions and help plan the final assault. Heavy fighting between infantry units ensued on the streets of Goma, with troops employing direct-fire weapons and engaging in artillery and rocket exchanges.

Indirect fire impacted civilian areas, indicating poor accuracy by troops on both sides of the battle. Army troops tried to hold on, but by the time the M23 main body forced its way into Goma, the fight was over. The Army withdrew, ceding the city.

Observations and insights from Goma, Democratic Republic of the Congo, 2012. Like all other DRC cases, only narrow perspectives, quick snippets of video, and unconfirmed field reports are available for analysis of the Goma battle. One thing was clear: The M23 force was better equipped and appeared to have stronger will to fight than the defending Army elements. Night-vision goggles gave them the ability to effectively conduct low-light operations, a major comparative advantage over Army forces that almost certainly lacked the same capability.

Syria's civil war dominated the 2011–2012 period by volume of cases and, probably, also by relative intensity, force size, and variation in terrain type, combined-arms combinations, and tactical methods. It is impossible in these few pages to do justice to these variations or to convey the enormous volume of combat that took place in Syria just in this narrow time frame.

From 2011 to 2012, Syria, the Free Syrian Army, al-Nusra Front, and other well-armed and organized military forces engaged at al-Rastan, Ma'arat al-Na'aman, Wadi al-Dhaif, Harem, Aa'azaz, al-Haffa, Saraqib, al-Qusayr, Douma, various neighborhoods across Aleppo, Idlib, al-Zabadani, A'andan, Khirbit al-Jouz, and so on. Particularly focused engagements occurred as rebel and militant forces attempted to capture various military bases across western Syria. These battles are typically referred to by the unit designator, or number, of the defending Syrian government unit (e.g., Base 80 for the base of the 80th Brigade). While the Base 46 battle is not representative of all these engagements, it does help convey the remarkably regular nature of this purportedly irregular war.

Base 46, Syria, 2012: Level 1 Case[23]

Location: Aleppo Governorate, Syria
Combatants: Free Syrian Army (FSA) versus Syria
Dates: Mid-September–November 18, 2012

In September 2012, probably over 1,000 rebel fighters organized under the Free Syrian Army attacked to seize the base of the Syrian Arab Army 46th Special Forces Regiment, commonly referred to as Base 46. Well-armed rebel forces attempted to encircle and close on the base perimeter with T-55 (and probably some T-62) tanks, BMP-1 infantry fighting vehicles, 122mm artillery, multiple-launch rockets, recoilless rifles, mortars, and ubiquitous AK-variant rifles, RPG-7s, and machineguns. They also employed well-organized antiaircraft artillery up to 57mm mounted on trucks and massed these to help fend off repeated Syrian Air Force fixed-wing and rotary-wing attacks.

In the first weeks of the assault, Syrian forces positioned in a nearby town were able to coordinate fires with the base defenders to pin and kill rebel troops attempting to cross the mostly flat, open terrain around the base. But in turn Syrian armored relief forces driving down exposed roads were decimated. Both sides traded machinegun, antiaircraft, rocket, and tank fire as small teams of rebel troops attempted to infiltrate the chain-link-fence perimeter. In late October the rebels were reinforced and the base defenders were (probably) running low on some types of ammunition. Effective rebel antiaircraft fire—probably including SA-7 missiles—destroyed at least one fixed-wing jet, and rebel anti-tank teams were able to destroy some of the defenders' T-62, BMP, and MTLB armored vehicles with recoilless rifles and (probably) missiles. By mid-November, the rebels were in a much better position to push home their attack. They moved T-55 tanks, antiaircraft cannons, mortars, and rockets into support-by-fire positions and pushed infantry squads into the base. Remaining Syrian Army troops either died, fled, or surrendered.

Observations and insights from Base 46, Syria, 2012. Effective antiaircraft artillery fires, particularly when integrated with missiles, can go a long way toward offsetting adversary combat airpower advantage. Even advanced military forces often place their aircraft at higher altitudes to avoid low-level fires, reducing the aircrew or drone operators' ability to spot and target ground forces. In most of the recorded Middle East cases, one or both sides in the battle also employed their antiaircraft cannons in direct-fire mode against infantry and armor.

OBSERVATIONS AND INSIGHTS FROM 2008 TO 2012

This period was indelibly marked by the sudden and explosive surge in ground combat across the Middle East and North Africa. Tired third-order government armies in Syria, Libya, and (in an escalation of long-running conflict) Yemen found themselves engaged in brutal combined-arms battles with well-organized resistance groups. In each of these countries, rebel forces raided government warehouses and barracks, seizing full complements of Soviet-Russian weapons and equipment, thereby putting themselves on relatively equal materiel footing with the defending state units on the ground. In Libya and Yemen, interventions by regional and international militaries fueled the intensity and tempo of ground combat, adding advanced aircraft, drones, missiles, and a steady stream of ammunition and newer weaponry to the fight.

Many ground battles and skirmishes ensued. The descriptive cases in this chapter give a decent impression of the scope and scale of violence that erupted and was sustained just in Syria, Libya, and Yemen. As was the case in the 2003–2007 period, some of these engagements were clearly recorded by reporters, by *sousveillance*—organic digital video and photographic recordings by at least hundreds of combatants and civilian observers in the heat of combat—and by aerial footage collected and often disseminated by intervention forces (e.g., NATO airstrike videos). Others were poorly recorded and only hinted at in the public record. We may never have a good appreciation for what happened in the battle of Dofas, Yemen, or at the battle at Bin Jawad, Libya in August 2011, months after Libyan rebels and loyalist forces engaged in a better-publicized battle there in March 2011.

Even the relatively well-recorded 2008–2012 wars include many poorly recorded or unrecorded battles and skirmishes. For the purposes of characterizing ground combat from 2008 to 2012, these gaps in closely observed wars—generally, the ones in which major powers intervened—conceal what may be even more serious gaps in the historical ground combat record in places like Somalia, Pakistan, Sri Lanka, Sudan and South Sudan, Chad, Myanmar, and others.

Observed 2008–2012 cases in the database show parallel continuity and evolutionary change. Functional purposes of arms and equipment remained consistent. The Soviet-Russian mortars, recoilless rifles, AK-variant rifles, tank and artillery cannons, rockets, helicopters, armored vehicles, and aerial bombs used by combatants on both sides of most of the recorded conflicts had purposes, functions, and generally consistent forms with weapons and equipment from the World War II era. A good percentage of the tools of ground combat were in fact identical in form dating back to the period between the late 1940s and the mid-1960s. It would be practicably impossible to date all of the Soviet-Russian weapons and equipment used in the eighty-nine cases from this period, but in all likelihood most were manufactured in the mid- to late twentieth century.

At the same time, both purpose-built military drones and off-the-shelf commercial drones, night-vision equipment, cheap and reliable handheld communication devices, thermal imagers, GPS locators and mapping tools, and other increasingly sophisticated technology also proliferated and—albeit unevenly and with inconclusive causative impact in each case—gradually and unevenly began to alter some of the ways in which ground combat was practiced in some battles. Drones were used extensively in combat around the world, and particularly in Iraq and Afghanistan, throughout the 2003–2012 period.

Improved technology appeared to convey at least two general advantages: (1) better observation and targeting, and (2) better tactical coordination. Military forces employing drones were able to increase aerial reconnaissance loitering time and more effectively transmit combat information—enemy locations, movements, and so on—to commanders, and to cannon, rocket, and aerial attack teams. Longer dwell over battlefields, increasingly high-fidelity digital transmission, and fairly inexpensive and intuitive ground receivers signified an evolutionary improvement over observation aircraft pilots sending data by voice or digital images through legacy data-sharing systems like Link 16.[24] Global positioning satellites allowed for improved targeting and, when systems worked and were not jammed, for ground commanders to continuously monitor their own locations and the locations of other friendly units. Cheap handheld radios and cellphones gave even the least well equipped irregular forces the ability to rapidly share tactical information and more effectively coordinate attacks.

Even with these technical improvements, tactical functions and actions remained mostly consistent with all previous periods dating back to World War II. Ground units received reconnaissance information on the location of the enemy or just moved forward blindly until they made contact. Drones were not yet prolific enough to provide even advanced Western military ground combat forces with consistent and reliable real-time tactical information, so soldiers continued to look for each other primarily with the naked eye or through scopes and enhanced ground optics. Particularly irregular forces facing drone-equipped units adjusted their movements and concealment practices, often making good use of urban terrain to offset enemy observation and targeting.

Tactical aircraft played important roles when they were available, but I only coded manned aircraft as "decisive" in two of the eighty-eight cases from 2008 to 2012.[25] Commanders directed fires onto enemy positions to soften them up for infantry advances that were supported by armor when it was available. Terrain continued to have unavoidable impact on concealment, spotting, cover, and engagement ranges. Relative physical altitude of combatants continued to correlate with relative advantage; generally, the higher the better.

NOTES

1. See the appendix, "Methodology," for more on case sourcing and the annotated bibliography.
2. All source websites and additional online materials are available in full in the Excel database.
3. Including Mike Rossiter, *Target Basra*, (Transworld Digital, 2008), ebook; Tim Ripley, *Operation Telic: The British Campaign in Iraq 2003–2009* (Lancaster, UK: Telic-Herrick Publications, 2016); "Operation Telic January-April 2003," archival combat video, UK Royal Marines, 2003, YouTube video; "GWT: WRAP Battle for Peninsula Continue," *Associated Press*, March 23, 2003, YouTube video; Sara Beck and Malcolm Downing, *The Battle for Iraq: BBC News Correspondents on the War against Saddam* (Baltimore: Johns Hopkins University Press, 2003); David Sharrock, "Commandos Secure Foothold," *Guardian*, March 20, 2003, https://www.theguardian.com; Arnoud Franken, Chris Paton, and Simon Rogers, "Web Exclusive: How the UK's Royal Marines Plan in the Face of Uncertainty," *Harvard*

Business Review, March 20, 2003, https://hbr.org; "HMS Marlborough's Account of the Iraq War, March 2003," *Naval Historical Society of Australia*, September 2003, https:///navyhistory.au.

4. Including Aditya Adhikari, *The Bullet and the Ballot Box: The Story of Nepal's Maoist Revolution* (London: Verso, 2014); Prashant Jha, *Battles of the New Republic: A Contemporary History of Nepal* (London: C. Hurst, 2014); Kishore Thomas Bell, "Bad Blood in Beni," *Nepali Times*, March 26, 2004, https://nepalitimes.com; Amrit Baskune, "Thirteen Years of Beni Attack: System Changed Pain Remained," *INSEC Online*, n.d., https://inseconline.org; Kiyoko Ogura, "Realities and Images of Nepal's Maoists after the Attack on Beni," *European Bulletin of Himalayan Research*, no. 27 (2004), 67–125; "Beni Bidhanta 2060 sal. Nepali Army Nepali Police Vs Maobadi.," archival newsreel, 2004, YouTube video; "माओवादी जनयुद्ध भिडन्त भाग ३," archival newsreel, 2004, YouTube video.
5. Including "Fighting Intensifies in Somalia," *New York Times*, May 25, 2006; "Somalia: Mogadishu Tense after Weekend Violence," *Reliefweb*, May 29, 2006, https://www.reliefweb.org; Arthur Bright, "Despite Ceasefire Call, Fighting Continues in Mogadishu," *Christian Science Monitor*, May 10, 2006, https://www.csmonitor.com; Marc Lacey, "Alliance of Somali Warlords Battles Islamists in Capital," *New York Times*, May 13, 2006; "A Somali Technical Belonging to the Isla," photograph, Mogadishu, Somalia, https://www.gettyimages.com; "Somalia Islamists Seize Rival Base," *BBC News*, May 31, 2006, https://www.bbc.com; Tom Maliti, "Militia Fighting Intensifies in Mogadishu," *Washington Post*, May 26, 2006; "Bloody Street Battles in Mogadishu," *CNN*, May 13, 2006, https://www.cnn.com.
6. ARPC = Alliance for the Restoration of Peace and Counterterrorism, or the Somali Warlord Alliance (in Somali: Isbaheysiga Ladagaalanka Argagaxisadda).
7. Including Amos Harel and Avi Issacharoff, *34 Days: Israel, Hezbollah, and the War in Lebanon* (New York: St. Martin's Griffin, 2009); "מלחמת לבנון השניה—קרב הגבורה בבינת ג'בל," archival newsreel, 2006, YouTube video; William M. Arkin, *Divining Victory: Airpower in the 2006 Israel-Hezbollah War* (Maxwell Air Force Base, AL: Air University Press, 2007); Ali as-Sagheer, "Bint Jbeil Battle Outlines Divine Triumph: 'Spider-Web' Plot Foiled," *Al Ahed News*, n.d., https://alahednews.com; "Israeli Infantry Reservists Fight Their Way into a Hezbollah Held Village in Lebanon," documentary, 2006, Reddit video; "109[NO comment] Hit in Merkava 4_IDF Troops_CAT D9_31.07.06 MON," archival newsreel, YouTube video.
8. Including "بطلب من الرئيس ..الشيخ الأحمر يدخل معركة صعدة بداعي القبيلة," *Marba Press*, May 9, 2007, https://www.marba.org; "الحوثيون كانوا يستخدمون الريالات والهواتف النقالة السعودية تأتيهم من رجال دي سعوديين," *Al Watan*, June 30, 2007, https://www.elwatannews.com; "Yemen War 2007," *Al Jazeera Arabic*, 2007, YouTube video; "حرب صعدة," *Al Jazeera Arabic*, 2007, YouTube video; Mohamed Bin Sallam, "Sa'ada Fighting Fiercer as Mediation Is at an Impasse," *Yemen Times*, February 26, 2007, https://yementimes.com; Mohamed Bin Sallam, "15 Troops Killed, 32 Others Injured in Sa'ada Clashes," *Yemen Times*, February 1, 2007; Mohamed Bin Sallam, "Air Strikes Continue in Sa'ada with Hundreds of Victims," *Yemen Times*, February 22, 2007. Note: Two additional primary video sources for this battle were removed from YouTube during the editing process for this book and cannot be cited.
9. Including Ivor Wiltenburg and Lysanne Leeuwenburg, *The Battle of Chora: A Military Operational Analysis of the 2007 Defense of the Chora District Centre in*

Uruzgan Province, Afghanistan (The Netherlands Ministry of Defense, n.d.); Robert Beeres, Jan van der Meulen, Joseph Soeters, and Ad Vogelaar, *Mission Uruzgan: Collaborating in Multiple Coalitions for Afghanistan* (Radmoud University Nijmegen: Pallas Publications, n.d.); "Task Force Uruzgan—The Dutch Approach 2006–2010," documentary, *Dutch Docu Channel*, 2010,YouTube video; "10 Jaar Na Dood Timo in Uruzgan: Uitzending 15 Juni 2007," *RTL Nieuws*, June 15, 2007, YouTube video; "Dutch Soldiers in Battle of Chora Pt 1 2," archival newsreel, 2007, YouTube video; "The Battle of Chora/Pay Back Srebrenica 'We Can Fight,'" archival newsreel, YouTube video. Note: Two additional primary video sources for this battle were removed from YouTube during the editing process for this book and cannot be cited.

10. Including "Battle for Thoppigala—2007—Eelam War IV," *LRRP*, July 8, 2007, https://lrrp.wordpress.com; "COMBAT FOOTAGE: Sri Lankan Commandos Attack/ Live Footage/Thoppigala Operation 2007," archival combat video, 2007, "Sri Lanka Security Forces closing in to LTTE's Beiruit [sic] camp," archival newsreel, Sri Lankan Ministry of Defense, 2007, YouTube video; "කමාන්ඩෝ රෙජිමේන්තුව තොප්පිගල මුදාගත් අයුරු ||thoppigala mission commando regiment," archival newsreel, 2007, YouTube video; "Thoppigala Operation—27 Feb 2007 to 11 July 2007," official online article (Sri Lankan Army, Security Forces Headquarters [East], December 26, 2017), https://alt.army.lk. Note: Two additional primary video sources for this battle were removed from YouTube during the editing process for this book and cannot be cited.
11. For more on this case, see Francesco Fontemaggi, "La chute de Bukavu menace la fragile pax congolaise," *Liberation*, June 3, 2004, https://www.liberation.fr, 46; "The Fire Rekindles," *Economist* 371, no. 8378 (2004); Amnesty International Annual Index, July 2005, https://www.amnesty.org; "Dans Bukavu en guerre," *RFI*, June 2, 2004, http://www1.rfl.fr; "Quelques reflexions sur les affrontements armes de Bukavu du 26 mai au 9 juin 2004 et leur incidence humanitaire," diplomatic summary of humanitarian incidents and negotiations, June 10, 2004, https://repositories.lib.utexas.edu; "Notes sur la troisieme guerre d'agression contre la R.DC," *Umoya*, June 8, 2004, https://umoya.org; Stephanie Wolters, *Continuing Instability in the Kivus: Testing the DRC Transition to the Limit* (Pretoria, South Africa: Institute for Security Studies, October 2004); Jason Stearns, *North Kivu: The Background to Conflict in North Kivu Province of Eastern Congo* (Nairobi, Kenya: Rift Valley Institute, 2012).
12. I write "almost certainly" here because we cannot know the volume of unreported cases in the preceding period.
13. I recorded 23 cases not coded during this period out of a total of 125 cases not coded in the database.
14. Including "Dramatic Firefight on Bridge, Damage, Military Dead, Civilians," archival newsreel, Associated Press, 2008, YouTube video; Alexander Nicoll and Sarah Johnstone, eds., "Russia's Rapid Reaction: But Short War Shows Lack of Modern Systems," *International Institute for Strategic Studies* 14, no. 7 (September 2008), special issue; "Россия пришла на помощь. Южная Осетия 2008," archival newsreel, 2008, YouTube video; "რუსეთ-საქართველოს ომის დაწყებიდან 13 წელი გავიდა . . . ," *Georgian News Agency*, August 28, 2021, https://eng.ghn.ge; Ariel Cohen and Robert E. Hamilton, *The Russian Military and the Georgia War: Lessons and Implications* (Carlisle Barracks, PA: Strategic Studies Institute,

June 2011); Peter Finn, "A Two-Sided Descent into Full-Scale War," *Washington Post*, August 17, 2008; "Chronology of Events in South Ossetia 7–11 August 2008," *Государственное информационное агентство*, October 13, 2008, https://cominf.org. Note: One additional primary video source for this battle was removed from YouTube during the editing process for this book and cannot be cited.

15. Including "Pakistan Army 'Taking Back' Swat Valley—03 Jul 09," *Al Jazeera English*, July 3, 2009, YouTube video; "Operation Rah e Nijat report on Sararogha By Laiq Ur Rehman," ARY News, 2009, YouTube video; "Samaa TV: Ejaz Haider Operation Rah-e-Nijat (1/4)," four-part news report, *Samaa TV*, n.d., YouTube video series; "Pakistan's Swat Valley Devastated by Fighting—04 Jul 09," *Al Jazeera English*, July 4, 2009, YouTube video; "Waziristan Operation New Footage Street Battles," archival newsreel, Pakistani Army, *PakArmyChannel*, n.d., YouTube video; Frederick W. Kagan, Charlie Szrom, and Reza Jan, "The War in Waziristan: Operation Rah-e-Nijat—Phase 1 Analysis," *Critical Threats*, November 18, 2009, https://www.criticalthreats.org; Zahid Ali Khan, *Military Operations in FATA and PATA: Implications for Pakistan* (Islamabad, Pakistan: Institute for Strategic Studies Islamabad, n.d.).
16. Including Naw Noreen, "Burmese Army Takes DKBA Stronghold," *Democratic Voice of Burma*, November 11, 2010, https://english.dvb.no; "myawaddy 7 8 Nov 2010," archival combat video, 2010, YouTube video; "[Myanmar Karen] Mortar in Karen State," archival combat video, 2010, YouTube video; Kyaw Kha, "Karen Villagers Escape Fresh Clashes," *Mizzima*, November 29, 2010; Kyaw Kha and Thea Forbes, "Clashes Carry On between DKBA and Junta Troops," *Mizzima*, November 12, 2010, https://www.mizzima.tv; "200 Ethnic Group Flee to Thailand after Fresh Fighting Erupts in Myanmar," *Bernama.com*, November 15, 2010, https://www.bernama.com; "Artillery Fire Continues at Three Pagodas Pass," Irrawaddy, November 11, 2010, https://www.irrawaddy.com.
17. Including "Fierce Fighting Rages in Sirte [24-09-2011]," Al Jazeera English, September 24, 2011, YouTube video; "Fighting Continues onto Flooded Streets of Sirte—No Comment," *Euronews*, October 12, 2011, YouTube video; "Libya: 'Hand to Hand Fighting' in Sirte," *BBC News*, October 18, 2011; "Libya: Sirte 'Pummeled into Submission,'" *BBC News*, October 12, 2011; "Gaddafi Fighters Filmed Firing Scud Missile in Battle for Sirte," *The Telegraph*, October 8, 2011, YouTube video; "Libya Fighters Battle Pro-Kadhafi Snipers in Sirte," *AFP News Agency*, October 17, 2011, YouTube video; "Heavy Fighting on Sirte FRONTLINE—NO COMMENT," *Euronews*, October 7, 2011, YouTube video; "Gaddafi Loyalists Continue to Fight," *Al Jazeera English*, October 7, 2011, YouTube video.
18. See "Gaddafi Fighters Filmed Firing Scud Missile in Battle for Sirte."
19. One of the better resources for these operations is Karl P. Meuller, ed., *Precision and Purpose: Airpower in the Libyan Civil War* (Santa Monica, CA: RAND Corporation, 2015).
20. Including "South Sudanese Troops 'Advance' on Heglig," *Al Jazeera English*, April 25, 2011, YouTube video; "Sudan Army Advances on Disputed Oil Town," *Al Jazeera English*, April 13, 2012, YouTube video; "Sudán retomó control de campos petroleros de Heglig," TeleSur, April 23, 2012, YouTube video; "South Sudan Victory in Panthou Heglig Front Line. Long Live SPLA," archival combat video, 2012, YouTube video; "القوات السودانية على مشارف بلدة هجليج," *Al Jazeera Arabic*, April 13, 2012, YouTube video; "وزير الدفاع السوداني يعلن تحرير هجليج," Al Arabiya, April 20,

2012, YouTube video; "السودان يقصف بنتيو في جنوب السودان," Al Arabiya, April 12, 2012, YouTube video; "الجيش السوداني يستعيد سيطرته على هجليج ويتوعد بالتمرد," *Sudan Tribune*, April 21, 2012, https://sudantribune.com.

21. Sudanese refer to this area in Arabic as Hejlij/Hejleej, soft "j" (هجليج) or Heglig/Hegleeg hard "g" in dialect transliteration, and South Sudanese refer to it in Dinka/Jieng as Panthau, or Pand'Thau.
22. Including Jonny Hogg and Louis Charbonneau, "Well-Equipped Rebels Advance in Eastern Congo—U.N.," *Reuters*, November 17, 2012, https://www.reuters.com; Enough Project, *Field Dispatch: Civilians Under Siege in Goma*, November 2012, https://enoughproject.org; Alan Taylor, "Rebel Attacks in Eastern Congo," *Atlantic*, November 27, 2012; Pete Jones, "DR Congo Fighters Jubilant after Taking Goma," *Al Jazeera*, November 22, 2022, https://www.aljazeera.com; "DR Congo Rebels Seize Military Airport," *Al Jazeera English*, November 20, 2012, YouTube video; "RDC: Les rebelles du M23 aux portes de Goma," Euronews, November 18, 2012, YouTube video; Phil Moore, "M23 Fighters Capture Goma in the DR Congo," *Al Jazeera*, November 23, 2012; Jason K. Stearns, *The War That Doesn't Say Its Name: The Unending Conflict in the Congo* (Princeton, NJ: Princeton University Press, 2021).
23. Including "Syria Rebels Capture Large Military Base," Al Jazeera English, November 19, 2012, YouTube video; "تقرير المركز الاعلام الحصري لعملية الفوج 46 في حلب 24 9 2012," Al Arabiya, September 27, 2012, YouTube video; "أروع تفجير دبابة في الفوج 46," archival combat video, YouTube video; "ريف حلب الغربي—الفوج 46 ::(مقطع طويل للتحرير 18-11-2012م)," archival combat video, YouTube video; Ben Hubbard, "Syrian Rebels Seize Base, Arms Trove," *Times of Israel*, November 21, 2012, https://www.timesofisrael.com; "سيطرة الجيش السوري الحر على الفوج رقم 46," Al Jazeera Arabic, November 18, 2012, YouTube video.
24. See Rebecca Van Syoc, "Link 16: Keeping Aircraft Connected," official press article, U.S. Air Force, September 27, 2017; Daniel Gonzales, Daniel Norton, and Myron Hura, *Multifunctional Information Distribution System (MIDS) Program Case Study* (Santa Monica, CA: RAND Corporation, 2000).
25. These two cases are (1) FOB Salerno Afghanistan 2010; and (2) Do Ab Afghanistan 2011. See "TF Red Bulls Soldiers Fight Their Largest Battle since WWII," official article, U.S. Defense Visual Information Distribution Service (DVIDS), May 25, 2011; Ryan Matson, "JTACs Guide Air Strikes, Turn Tide during Major Battle," official article, U.S. Air Force Public Affairs, July 5, 2011; "Do Ab, Nuristan Province," archival combat video, U.S. Washington National Guard, May 25, 2011, YouTube video.

SEVEN

Modern Ground Combat from 2013 through 2022

This chapter presents descriptive case examples from the 264 coded cases of ground combat between 2013 and 2022. I recorded a nearly 70 percent increase in case volume from the 2008–2012 period into the following five-year period and then a modest decline in recorded cases in the final period (from 151 down to 113). This last case chapter is followed in chapter 8 by analysis of the entire dataset with illustrative charts and recorded insights.

2013–2017

Of the 151 total cases for this five-year period, 66 (~44%) took place in Syria as part of the ongoing, multifaceted land war fought between the Syrian government, pro-government militias, Islamists, Kurdish groups, the United States, Russia, Iran, anti-regime forces, and others. Syrian ground combat in this time period was a showcase for nearly all Soviet-Russian and a good deal of American hardware and technology, as well as competing Soviet doctrine, irregular-force tactics, and Western military tactics. Given the intensity, frequency, longevity, and scale of ground combat in Syria through this period, it is remarkable that the Syrian Civil War is barely recognized in discussions of the character of modern ground combat cited in this book.

This period also covers the combined Iraqi, American-led coalition, Iranian, and Kurdish war against the Islamic State in Iraq; battles in Mali and the Democratic Republic of the Congo; and major ground combat actions in the Philippines at Zamboanga, Butig, and Marawi. As in all other time periods, many cases—including in Syria—were poorly recorded or went unrecorded, and the prominence of land war in the Middle East pushed other important cases into the shadows.

Onset of the Russia-Ukraine War in 2014 generated nineteen observable cases in this five-year period, most of which were fought with a full spectrum

Table 7.1. Cases by Country, 2013–2017

Country	Count	Percent
Syria	66	44%
Iraq	19	13%
Ukraine	19	13%
Libya	8	5%
South Sudan	6	4%
Yemen	6	4%
Mali	5	3%
Afghanistan	5	3%
Myanmar	3	2%
Philippines	3	2%
DRC	3	2%
Nigeria	3	2%
Pakistan	1	1%
Gaza	1	1%
Egypt	1	1%
Nagorno-Karabakh	1	1%
Somalia	1	1%

of Soviet-Russian equipment, weapons, and advanced technology. These early Ukraine War cases provide an excellent comparative baseline for contemporaneous battles and for the 2022-onward phase of Russia's extended invasion. Table 7.1 depicts the country case count for the 2013–2017 period.

Several 2013 battles, including at Zamboanga City, the Philippines; Juba and Bor, South Sudan; Mutaho and Kibati, DRC; and the Tirah Valley, Pakistan; were overshadowed by the Arab Spring. Fighting across Syria accelerated into this five-year period with a total of 13 recorded cases in 2013 alone. Syrian Arab Army tank and mechanized infantry forces attacked en masse into the city of al-Qaboun, while other government units struggled to hold onto or recapture Menagh Airbase, Base 17, Base 80, Ma'aloula, al-Qusayr, Sadad-Mahin, and others.

Emergence of the Islamic State as a major ground combat force in primarily central and northeast Syria led to battles at Al-Ya'arubiyah-Til Koçer, preceding the much heavier fighting that followed. France deployed a large task force to Mali and, with a coalition of Malian and Chadian troops, took the offensive against various Islamist militant groups at Diabaly, Konna, Tibeggatine Valley, and Adrar des Ifoghas-Ametettai.

Adrar des Ifoghas to Ametettai, Mali, 2013: Level 2 Case[1]

Location: Adrar des Ifoghas, Kidal Region, Mali
Combatants: France, Mali, and Chad versus Islamist militants
Dates: February 22–March 3, 2013

French military intervention in Mali forced the coalition of Islamist militias that had threatened to overwhelm the Malian Army out of the populated zones and up into the inhospitable rocky hills of the Ametettai Valley. Militant groups intimately familiar with the terrain had already established a network of caves and weapons caches in and around the valley. Fighters laid improvised explosives along the likely routes of advance, set in ambush positions, and camouflaged their technical pickup trucks to avoid French airstrikes. A combined motorized and foot-mobile French, Malian, and Chadian task force attacked to clear the valley and surrounding desert. French and Malian troops organized under *Groupement Tactique Interarmes (GTIA) 4* dismounted and pushed into the hills carrying rifles, machineguns, Milan anti-tank missiles, mortar tubes, and disassembled heavy machineguns, backed by light armored vehicles.

Temperatures of over 120 degrees Fahrenheit (49 Celsius) required continual helicopter flights supplying water and other necessities. In another part of the valley a Chadian force of several hundred troops attacked to clear out a militant cave complex and were met with a suicide vest attack and concentrated direct fires. As the Chadians worked through the aftermath of a mass casualty event from the suicide bombing, the French continued their advance in the valley. Islamists ambushed the French troops with combined rocket, machinegun, rifle, mortar, and (probably) 122mm artillery fire. French troops fought back with their organic infantry weapons and called in 155mm artillery, close-air support from fixed-wing fighter bombers, and helicopter attack support from Eurocopter Tigers firing rockets and guns. Over several days of infantry combat they pushed the militants back through their own cave complexes, where they were killed or forced to flee.

Observations and insights from Adrar des Ifoghas to Ametettai, Mali, 2013. Solid French logistics planning was essential in keeping their infantry in the fight in the withering desert heat. Lack of adequate water provision in desert and tropical terrain has debilitated infantry in many historical cases (e.g., Peleliu 1944). Combined militant groups probably fielded just under 1,000 troops in this battle, but they either did not plan for or were unable to mass for a counterattack.

French fixed-wing reconnaissance planes and Harfang drones were able to spot, track, and help target militant positions in the bare desert and rocky terrain.

Arab Spring-related conflicts in Syria, Libya, and Yemen continued through 2014 and into 2015; I recorded forty-three battles in these three conflicts throughout this two-year period. Three new conflicts broke out toward the end of 2013 and into 2014: the Islamic State offensive into Iraq, Israel's ground offensive into Gaza, and the initial Russian invasion of Ukraine. I cover the battle for Ramadi, Iraq, further below in this section. The Israeli attack into Gaza serves as a good comparative anchor point for its late-2023 invasion, and the battle for Donetsk Airport serves the same comparative purpose for the 2022 Ukraine War.

Gaza, 2014: Level 1 Case[2]

Location: Gaza
Combatants: Israel versus Hamas and Palestinian Islamic Jihad and other militants
Dates: July 8–August 26, 2014

Israel conducted a multidivision combined-arms attack—arguably, a large raid—to temporarily seize territory in Gaza and destroy tunnels that had been used by Hamas and other militants to enter Israeli territory. The Israeli Army assembled task-organized infantry-armor teams centered on the 36th Armored, 162nd Infantry, and 643rd Gaza Territorial Divisions backed by 155mm artillery, observation and strike drones, and both fixed-wing and rotary-wing attack aircraft. Special operations forces were attached out to mechanized infantry units to conduct low-profile dismounted infiltration missions. Israeli naval forces closed in to the shoreline on the opposite direction of the ground attack to seal off defensive movement and add in their own observation and fires. Gaza is a narrow, mostly urban strip of land isolated on all sides and continuously monitored by advanced aerial and ground intelligence systems. Defending militants had become adept at using the concealment and cover provided by urban terrain and underground facilities and tunnels to cache weapons and conduct tactical movements.

Israeli armed forces started the assault with a week of targeted airstrikes and artillery fires—approximately 190 airstrikes per day—to destroy observable heavy weapons and then attacked in infantry-armor teams. Attacking tank units employed Merkava MkIV tanks, some of which were fitted with active protection systems capable of destroying incoming missiles and rockets. Still, militants firing RPGs, anti-tank guided missiles, and employing improvised explosives managed to destroy some vehicles and kill Israeli soldiers, including an entire squad boxed up inside an M113 armored personnel carrier. The battle ended in a mutual ceasefire.

Observations and insights from Gaza, 2014. Active protection systems employ radars to detect and rapidly target incoming projectiles with a shotgun blast of explosively formed penetrator munitions. Rafael Trophy active protection systems (APS) fitted to the Israeli Merkavas gave the tank teams confidence to push more aggressively into urban terrain that was well suited to anti-armor ambush. Possibly 15 Kornet ATGM missiles were destroyed by Trophy systems.[3] However, even APS did not fully mitigate the antitank threat from low-technology weapons like improvised explosive devices and mines.

Donetsk Airport, Ukraine, 2014–2015: Level 1 Case[4]

Location: Donetsk Airport, Donetsk Oblast, Ukraine
Combatants: Russia and Donetsk separatists versus Ukraine
Dates: September 2014–January 2015

In May 2014, separatist militiamen attempted to take control of the Donetsk Airport, temporarily defeating light security forces before being overrun by responding Ukrainian Special Forces. This attack prompted the Ukrainians to establish structured defenses and more robust quick-reaction forces around the airport in case of a subsequent attack. In September, separatists and Russian artillerymen began firing on the Ukrainian defenders, damaging the airport but signaling their intent to attack. A mix of Ukrainian units from the 93rd and 95th Brigades, paratroopers, and other units moved in and out of the defensive lines in an effort to fend off a combined separatist-Russian ground assault spearheaded by T-72 tanks and BMP-2 infantry fighting vehicles and backed by nearly all available calibers of cannon and rocket artillery including 203mm Pion, thermobaric rockets, and probably 2S4 Tyulpan 240mm mortars.

Separatists—probably with some Russian crews in separatist uniforms—gradually squeezed into the perimeter of the airfield, using indirect fire to suppress the defenders and tank and BMP cannons to reduce their point defenses at close range. Ukrainian troops fought back with their own Soviet-Russian equipment, including 122mm-152mm artillery, BM-21 MLRS, refitted T-64BV tanks, (probably Kornet or Metis) anti-tank guided missiles, SPG-9 recoilless rifles, and Mi-24 attack helicopters. Defensive anti-tank teams were able to destroy at least six T-72 tanks and at least five BMPs, some of which appeared to have made solo attack runs across the flat ground of the airport and even pushed directly into the hangars. Separatist infantry still made progress, and by the winter the two sides were almost continuously engaged in very-close-range combat within the airport terminal buildings. As ammunition ran low and supply became impossible, the Ukrainians withdrew.

Observations and insights from Donetsk Airport, September 2014–January 2015. Both sides employed drones in this battle, probably Orlan-10s on the Russian side and commercial drones on the Ukrainian side. However, drones did not appear to have a significant impact on this early-war battle in Ukraine. This was a fairly large scale (~brigade level) combined-arms fight in which probably most Russian combat equipment was employed by both sides against each other.

While there were many poorly reported conflicts in the 2010s, I was able to find some decent sources describing many aspects of the war against Boko Haram in Nigeria, Niger, and Chad. I recorded five total cases in Nigeria across the twenty-year modern period. Some of these battles occurred in open plains, others in dense jungle or in packed cities, and some in both jungle and urban areas. Boko Haram's attack on Maiduguri describes some of the urban fighting that took place in northeastern Nigeria in the 2010s.

Maiduguri, Nigeria, 2015: Level 2 Case[5]

Location: Maiduguri, Borno State, Nigeria
Combatants: Boko Haram versus Nigeria
Dates: February 2015

Boko Haram conducted a surprise attack to seize control of Maiduguri, the capital of Borno State. One unit of militants conducted a surreptitious entry through a military checkpoint on board tourist buses, unleashing a torrent of direct fire on unsuspecting security forces when they were discovered. They then offloaded and moved into the city to overrun military facilities. In concert a second column of Boko Haram fighters with some armored cars, heavy machineguns, mortars, and (probably 122mm) artillery captured from the Nigerian Army compound at Baga smashed through the outer security ring and took control of another part of the city. Nigerian Army troops and quickly organized militia fighters armed with Soviet-Russian weapons rushed to fix the attackers in place while Army commanders called in airstrikes. Militants continued to fire probably both mortars and artillery into the city as the Army organized a counterattack.

Other Boko Haram units circled around the city looking for ingress points. Army units from outside of Maiduguri counterattacked with infantry and light armor including probably Piranha armored reconnaissance vehicles. Mortar and artillery fire were traded back and forth as the Army and local militia fighters compressed the perimeter on the militants, killing many and forcing the remaining units to retreat back into the surrounding rural areas.

Observations and insights from Maiduguri, Nigeria, 2015. As with most level-2 cases, it is possible to describe many of the characteristics of fighting at Maiduguri—there was an assault with infantry, light armor, artillery, and mortars, airstrikes, and close-range urban combat—but it is difficult to pin down the force structure on both sides, the movement of units, precise and accurate timeline of events, and geometry of combatants on the battlefield. Boko Haram fighters and the Army units combined their fires in a loose approximation of what Western military professionals would describe as combined-arms fires.

Combined Iraqi and coalition efforts to expel the Islamic State from Iraq and northeastern Syria probably will be described to future generations as *irregular warfare.* While Islamic State units did often resemble irregular forces—they sometimes had mismatched uniforms or fought in civilian attire—the ground combat that took place across western and northern Iraq from 2014 through 2017 looked to me like traditional combined-arms ground combat.

Both sides in the Islamic State-Iraq war employed large infantry formations, main battle tanks, light armor, anti-tank guided missiles, all caliber of mortars and artillery, multiple-launch rocket systems, electronic warfare, and aerial strikes from fixed-wing and drone assets (coalition, Iraq) or just drones (Islamic State). Both sides used heavy engineering to dig trenches and berms. American ground forces delivered possibly tens of thousands of rounds of supporting high-explosive and obscurant-smoke rocket, mortar, and artillery fires to allow Iraqi security forces to attack into Mosul and other cities. The 2015–2016 battle for Ramadi, Iraq, is a useful reference point since it can be compared to the 2004–2007 and the 2014 battles for Ramadi.

Al-Ramadi, Iraq, 2015–2016: Level 1 Case[6]

Location: Ramadi, al-Anbar Province, Iraq

Combatants: Iraq, Popular Mobilization Force, and U.S.-led coalition versus Islamic State

Dates: May 2015–February 2016

At the tail end of the siege of Ramadi from 2014 (database case: Ramadi Iraq 2014–2015), Islamic State forces executed a well-coordinated combined-arms assault to take the city. Iraqi security forces fled, requiring an entirely new ground combat operation to reclaim this important provincial capital. Iraqi Counter-Terrorism Service (CTS) led the counteroffensive through Anbar Province with supporting Iraqi Army units and Popular Mobilization Force units. Iraqi ground forces moved primarily in column along roadways to gradually encircle Ramadi with motorized and mechanized infantry, clearing surrounding farmland and villages along the way.

This gradual advance allowed the Islamic State defenders to string improvised explosives along the approach routes into the city, build fortifications, dig tunnels, and cut hidden movement routes through buildings to avoid detection from the air. Simultaneously, coalition drones and fixed-wing aircraft flew continuously over Ramadi, spotting and picking away at heavy equipment including artillery, mortars, armored vehicles, and rocket launchers. In late November 2015 the joint Iraqi ground force attacked with an ad hoc mix of M1A1M and Russian tanks, armored cars, and infantry fighting vehicles through the Ta'mim district of the city, clearing up to the al-Warrar overflow channel (basically, a small river). Islamic State leaders blew the dam from the Euphrates River to the al-Warrar, flooding the area in front of the advancing forces and channelizing their movement to a single bridge.

Despite relentless coalition and Iraqi airstrikes, Islamic State fighters continued to defend the city in depth using both direct- and indirect-fire Soviet-Russian weapons and improvised explosives. Iraqi forces renewed their assault along three avenues of approach and after about three months of continual fighting, destroyed remaining defenses and scattered the last holdouts.

Observations and insights from Ramadi, Iraq, 2015–2016. Coalition and Iraqi air forces had effective superiority over the skies in Ramadi, allowing for degradation of visible ground systems and fighting positions (and probably a number of known leaders). Air superiority and dominant intelligence, surveillance, and fires probably made the outcome all but inevitable as long as the Iraqi ground forces stayed in the fight, but the militant defensive units adjusted to constant surveillance in the urban terrain by making effective use of interior building movement, tunnels, and (abhorrently) human shields.

Most of the previously recorded land wars—Iraq, Ukraine, Yemen, Syria, Afghanistan, South Sudan, Sudan, Libya, Myanmar, the Philippines—continued through 2016. Combined land and amphibious operations were employed by Houthi and pro-government coalition forces in a fight over Port Midi, Yemen. Afghan and U.S.-led coalition troops battled Islamic State forces for control of Achin District near the Pakistani border with Afghanistan. Another coalition force fought to displace the Islamic State from Sirt, Libya. Elements of two Tatmadaw divisions attacked to seize a Kachin Independence Army mountaintop fortress at Gidon, Myanmar. Ukraine fought off a combined Russian and separatist armor-infantry attack at Svitlodarsk. Iraq and its supporting coalition undertook a multidivisional offensive operation to clear the city of Mosul. Fighting in

Syria continued unabated. The battle for al-Mellah Farms and the Castello Road shows the sustained intensity of the Syrian land war in its fifth year.

Al-Mellah Farms and Castello Road, Syria, 2016: Level 1 Case[7]

Location: North-central Aleppo Governorate, Syria

Combatants: Syria, Hezb'allah, and Russia versus al-Nusra Front and Free Syrian Army

Dates: January–August 2016

During the broader battle to control Aleppo, a coalition of Syrian Arab Army, Lebanese Hezb'allah, and Kata'ib al-Hezb'allah units backed by Russian drones and fixed-wing aircraft conducted a ground offensive to control key terrain north of the city. An opposing coalition of al-Nusra Front and Free Syrian Army units defended the area around al-Mellah Farms and the tactically important Castello Road. Al-Nusra and FSA defenders dug in to the area around the sprawling farm complex, digging zigzag trenches and establishing strongpoints with sand-filled tires, Soviet-Russian heavy machineguns, T-55 tanks, recoilless rifles, and anti-tank missiles backed by well-coordinated mortar, 122mm artillery, and multiple-launch rocket teams.

Attacking units advanced into the edge of the farm and subjected the defenders in the villages along the Castello Road to cannon artillery, 122mm multiple-launch rocket fire, and drone-directed airstrikes. Long-range engagements over the flat and sparsely vegetated terrain led to a slow grind between the fairly equally matched ground forces, with neither side able to gain significant advantage. In the first part of the battle the attackers managed to push infantry-armor teams onto the farms and cut part of Castello Road, but al-Nusra Front and the FSA counterattacked and reset the status quo. Infantry assaults over flat, open ground were costly; in one attack possibly up to 50 al-Nusra/FSA fighters were killed. Al-Nusra Front elements conducted two effective suicide vehicle attacks, and the FSA units made good use of U.S.-supplied TOW anti-tank missiles, destroying a number of Syrian T-72s.

Observations and insights from al-Mellah Farms and Castello Road, Syria, 2016. Drones spotted and directed fires for both sides. However, the SAA-Russian coalition probably had the better-coordinated and -equipped drone targeting and strike capability. Artillery, recoilless rifles, RPGs, TOW missiles, and various Soviet-Russian anti-tank missiles destroyed Syrian and FSA tanks and light armor, while T-55s, T-62s, and T-72s provided mobile cannon and machinegun firepower for both infantry advances and defensive operations.

Armor generally worked with infantry support, but some videos showed SAA coalition armor suffering for lack of infantry observation and suppression.

Given Western fixation on Azerbaijan's use of drones in the 2020 war, all ground combat cases in Nagorno-Karabakh from the 1990s through the early 2020s are directly relevant to the contemporary debate over the character of modern land war. Azerbaijan's 2016 attack toward Talish and the Lalatepe Heights serves as an important pivot case between the early 1990s war and the 2020 war covered in the following section (2018–2022). It describes some of the technologies and tactics carried forward from 1992 and their evolutionary employment. It also lends some historical perspective to the 2020 battles.

Talish-Lalatepe Heights, Nagorno-Karabakh, 2016: Level 1 Case[8]

Location: Talish-Lalatepe, Nagorno-Karabakh
Combatants: Azerbaijan versus Armenia and Republic of Artsakh
Dates: April 2–5, 2016

Early in the morning of April 2, 2016, Azerbaijani forces executed a broad offensive across the line of contact with Armenia and the Republic of Artsakh in Nagorno-Karabakh in order to take control of disputed villages and territory. Employing a broad array of Soviet-Russian equipment and weapons, including T-72 tanks, mortars, 122mm-152mm artillery, 122mm and 220mm TOS-1 multiple-launch rockets, Buk M1–2 antiair missiles, and fixed-wing aircraft, Azerbaijani forces took the Armenian coalition frontline positions under intensive indirect fires. Since the last major engagement with the Azerbaijanis in the 1990s, the Armenian coalition had built an extensive trench and bunker network along the rolling, generally open terrain and covered their positions with Soviet-Russian 122mm-152mm artillery, multiple-launch rockets, and their own antiair missile systems, T-72 tanks, and infantry weapons including anti-tank guided missiles.

Azerbaijani special operation reconnaissance teams inserted by helicopter to seize the village of Talish, while armor units backed by infantry moved to seize the Lalatepe Heights to gain dominant elevated ground for probable follow-on operations. Both sides employed an array of commercial and military drones to spot ground targets, and the Azerbaijanis employed Israeli Aerospace Industries loitering Harop suicide drones to destroy Armenian armor and artillery. Armenian antiair defenses shot down several Azeri helicopters and drones and were able to stop the ground offensive with anti-tank missiles, artillery, and static infantry emplacements. In all likelihood, heliborne Azerbaijani units were unable to hold Talish in the face of an Armenian counterattack and withdrew. The battle ended in negotiated ceasefire.

Observations and insights from Talish-Lalatepe Heights, Nagorno-Karabakh, 2016. Along with the Shusha Nagorno-Karabakh 1992 and Shusha Nagorno-Karabakh 2020 cases (and other Nagorno-Karabakh cases in the database), this battle shows both the statis and evolution of ground combat in a single geographic location between two of the same opposing forces employing over time a gradually changing arsenal of primarily Soviet-Russian weapons and equipment. Tactics appeared to be generally consistent from 1992 through at least 2016. Armor on both sides operated semi-independently against dug-in troops, and neither side made good use of camouflage or obscurant smoke. Broad, open terrain was well suited to drone-artillery fires.

Iraq's campaign against the Islamic State culminated in 2017 with residual fighting in Mosul and battles at Tila'afar, al-A'ayadhiya, al-Hawija, al-Qa'im, al-Qairawan, and al-Ba'aj. In parallel, coalition-backed ground forces and Russian-backed Syrian ground units defeated remaining Islamic State holdouts at Raqqa, al-Tubqa, al-Sukhna, al-Mayadeen, and Palmyra, while anti-government Syrian militias continued to struggle for control of their remaining bastions. Other 2017 ground combat battles took place in Afghanistan, Ukraine (Avdiivka-Butivka Mine), the DRC, Somalia, South Sudan and Ethiopia, Libya, and the Philippines. Philippines armed forces engaged in an intensive urban battle for the city of Marawi.

Marawi, Philippines, 2017: Level 1 Case[9]

Location: Marawi City, Mindanao, Philippines
Combatants: Republic of the Philippines versus Islamic State Maute Group
Dates: May 23–late October 2017

Fighting broke out between a large contingent of perhaps over 1,000 Islamic State Maute Group militants and the Filipino armed forces during an anti-terror raid into Marawi City. An initial skirmish triggered what might have been a planned militant assault to seize the city: Irregular fighters armed with a mix of iron-sight rifles, machineguns, rockets, and mortars spread out into the streets, broke more fighters out of jail, and seized security force weapons. In response, Army forces moved to establish a ground cordon around the city and to clear militants out of surrounding villages, while naval patrol boats moved in to block coastal reinforcement.

Over the course of several weeks the armed forces formed a joint Army, Marine, Navy, Air Force, and special operations command and began to clear

Marawi City block by block. Militants put up stiff resistance and did not cede ground, forcing intensive close-range urban combat. Both sides traded indirect fire, with the Army and Marine units firing 105mm artillery, 60mm and 81mm mortars, and calling in naval gunfire and both fixed-wing and rotary-wing fire support to level insurgent defensive positions in houses and commercial buildings.

Army and Marine infantry advanced under fire and suffered over 1,000 casualties during the course of the battle from gunfire, shrapnel, improvised explosive devices, and rocket strikes on V-150 and M113 armored vehicles. Militants used civilians as human shields, complicating government fire support. At least two airstrikes mistakenly hit friendly positions. After several months of combat, the Filipino joint force, with extensive support from international partners, broke the last organized resistance.

Observations and insights from Marawi, Philippines, 2017. Marawi 2017 is similar to the Fallujah 2004 cases and many of the Syria and Libya urban cases: Buildings provide concealment from observation and physical cover from fires that reduce, and in some cases obviate, the advantages of superior military forces. Willingness to die in place and to use unethical tactics like shielding behind civilians allows militant groups like the Islamic State to force government militaries into an inescapable dilemma: Destroy the city and kill civilians to avoid military casualties, or limit fires and fight building-to-building, taking heavier casualties while still risking some civilian lives and damaging some infrastructure.

OBSERVATIONS AND INSIGHTS FROM 2013 TO 2017

Themes of continuity and evolutionary change remained consistent through the 2013–2017 battles: Infantry fought infantry with mostly 1960s–1970s-era Soviet-Russian weapons and equipment; tanks were more or less effective depending on tactical employment, anti-tank technology, terrain, and other factors; reported drone use gradually proliferated, and improved persistent observation contributed to battlefield advantage; precision-guided munitions continued to be effective tools, particularly to soften up urban defenses and to allow relatively smaller ground combat forces to engage larger forces on equal or superior footing.

In Libya, coalition precision attacks played a significant role in rebel battlefield success. However, it would still be almost impossible to prove—or even reasonably argue—that technical advantage was definitely causative in the recorded battlefield victories from this period. Inversely, it would be farcical to suggest that gradual improvements in military technology from the mid twentieth century had no demonstrable influence on the outcome of these 154 battles.

Battles of the Syrian Civil War from 2013 to 2017 can help unravel some of the complex intersections between continuous ground combat function and unevenly changing technical form. Particularly after the American, Russian, and Turkish interventions (2014–2015), Syria's battlefields evolved into live testbeds for Cold War-era and contemporary doctrine, tactics, weapons, equipment, and technology. Over sixty battles took place in Syria from 2013 through 2017, with tens of thousands of troops engaging each other across deserts, over rolling hills, in sparse forests, and in all types of urban terrain.

Together, Russia, Syria, Turkey, the United States, and other countries (e.g., United Kingdom) flew probably tens of thousands of drone, rotary-wing, and fixed-wing observation and strike sorties and fired hundreds of thousands of artillery and rocket rounds in support of their own modern ground forces, but mostly in support of the Cold War-era Syrian Arab Army and various irregular militias. Irregular forces like the Islamic State and Free Syrian Army acquired and adapted commercial drones, handheld electronic devices, and other technologies to support their otherwise low-tech ground units. In terms of scale, scope, intensity, frequency, and volume of violence, Syria offers probably the best resource for modern ground combat studies.

Syria also demonstrates many of the challenges inherent in studying modern ground combat cases described in previous chapters. Battle often was continuous and fluid, making it difficult to separate distinct events. I found the effort to bound and name battles in the Syrian war to be far more a process of subjective interpretation than of unearthing concrete historical facts. Formal English-language studies of tactical ground combat in Syria were wildly inconsistent, mostly shallow, and for many battles, effectively nonexistent.

This was part of an observable downhill trend in combat reporting over time from the middle of the 20th century: I had little trouble finding in-depth historical analysis of World War II battles, more difficulty finding detailed accounts of 1945–2002 cases, increasing difficulty finding any detail on non-Western ground combat from 2003 to 2012, and then found little of substance for some of the largest ground combat events of the 2013–2017 period. Describing and coding these cases required dredging through uneven primary and secondary source material on the Internet, some of which disappeared even during the research phase of this project (see the section "Oops! Cette Page ne Peut pas Être Trouvé" in the appendix).

There were also nineteen fairly well-recorded cases of ground combat in Ukraine from this period including the cases described above and the battles at the Karlivka border area, the Luhansk Airport, along the Kramatorsk-Sloviansk line, at Svitodarsk, and elsewhere. The Donetsk Airport 2015–2016 was not necessarily representative of all of the recorded cases. Some Ukraine battles were fought with integrated combined arms, while others included just a few mortars or light artillery pieces. Drones reportedly were employed in many Ukraine cases but not in all cases.

The character and quality of forces in the Ukraine War was also uneven, with poorly trained or untrained militia, basically competent separatist forces, paramilitary police, and professional soldiers often mixed together. However, there was a range of consistencies including the types of weapons and equipment employed (Soviet-Russian, almost without exception) and the routine use of trenches, bunkers, and urban terrain by both sides.

2018–2022

I coded 113 total cases of ground combat occurring from the beginning of 2018 through the end of 2022. This period included the first part of the newest phase of the land war in Ukraine; the Nagorno-Karabakh War between Armenia and Azerbaijan; the war between Ethiopia and the Tigrayan People's Liberation Force (TPLF) and other separatist groups; the civil war in Myanmar; the end of the U.S.-led coalition war in Afghanistan; and ongoing conflicts in Somalia, Syria, Libya, Yemen, Mozambique, and across the Lake Chad Basin.

At the time this book was written, the Ethiopia land war counted as one of the largest conflicts of the twenty-first century. Possibly hundreds of thousands of Ethiopian National Defense Force, Tigrayan People's Liberation Force, Eritrean, and other subnational and tribal armies engaged in fifty or more significant ground combat events between 2020 and 2022. However, readers will find only one case from the Ethiopia war in this chapter. This case (Tembien–Agbe–Abiy Addy Ethiopia, June 2021) is one of only seven coded Ethiopia cases out of thirty-eight possible cases I was able to identify from public sources. It is also the only case I rated level 2 rather than "low confidence," or level 3; I coded none of the Ethiopia cases as level 1.

In other words, for the purposes of building a public-facing, holistic, global understanding of modern ground combat, one of the largest and most recent land wars is effectively a null historical event. See "Observations and Insights from 2018 to 2022" at the end of this chapter and the appendix for more on this gap and similar issues with the Myanmar and Nagorno-Karabakh wars. Table 7.2 lists the cases from this period by country.

Yemen's civil war, ongoing through 2024, has generated at least tens of thousands of battlefield casualties and led to the destruction of perhaps thousands of armored vehicles and artillery systems. While most of the fighting in Yemen probably has been undertaken by lightly armed fighters and old Soviet-era tanks, fighting vehicles, and cannons, Saudi Arabia, the United Arab Emirates, and Iran have directly used or delivered to proxies some of their most advanced weapons and equipment. That includes Mohajer-6, Reaper, Puma, ScanEagle,

Table 7.2. Cases by Country, 2018–2022

Country	Count	Percent
Ukraine	42	37%
Yemen	13	12%
Libya	9	8%
Syria	8	7%
Afghanistan	7	6%
Ethiopia	7	6%
Myanmar	7	6%
Somalia	4	4%
Niger	3	3%
Nagorno-Karabakh	3	3%
Somaliland-Puntland	2	2%
Nigeria	2	2%
DRC	2	2%
Mozambique	2	2%
Kenya	1	1%
Chad	1	1%

and Wing Loong drones; M1A2 and AMX-56 Leclerc tanks; BMP-3 infantry fighting vehicles; loitering munitions; long-range surface-to-surface missiles; F-15S, F-16, Typhoon, Tornado, and Mig-29 fighter-bombers; AH-64 Apache and Mi-24 and probably Mi-35 attack helicopters; advanced naval gun and missile systems; anti-tank missiles; and antiaircraft missiles. There are a total of 23 Yemen ground combat cases in the database. As with other individual cases, the battle at al-Hudaydah City is informative but not representative of the whole body of Yemen cases.

Al-Hudaydah City, Yemen, 2018: Level 1 Case[10]

Location: Al-Hudaydah Governorate, Yemen
Combatants: Yemen and coalition forces versus Houthis and Iran
Dates: June–November 2018

Following a breakdown in negotiations between the Supreme Political Council (the Houthis) and the international coalition supporting Yemen's government, a force of several thousand tribal militiamen, soldiers, and advisers from the United Arab Emirates attacked to capture the port city of al-Hudaydah. Long columns of infantry mounted in mine-resistant trucks and pickups with antiaircraft cannons, machineguns, and recoilless rifles advanced down the hardball roads through the desert behind Emirati AH-64 attack helicopters, fighter-bombers, and (probably) 155mm artillery support.

Columns split as they reached the city and fanned out, disgorging infantry to attack on foot over flat desert terrain with mortar and machinegun support. Houthi forces were well prepared for the attack, having dug in behind antivehicle trenches and positioned their own mortars and machineguns to cover the most likely avenues of approach into the urban area. Houthi armor teams brought up some T-55 tanks to assist with the linear defense on the eastern and southern edges of the city, but these probably were destroyed by Emirati aircraft and drone strikes. Offshore, Saudi Arabian and Emirati ships prevented the Houthis from reinforcing by sea. These ships probably contributed gun and missile fires to the battle.

While the front lines solidified from late June to early November, fighting spread out across the desert in a series of skirmishes. By early November the Yemenis had brought up thousands of reinforcements, allowing them to make a renewed push that triggered another round of talks. Lower-intensity combat continued through the end of the year and intermittently thereafter.

Observations and insights from Al-Hudaydah City, Yemen, 2018. Urban terrain probably allowed the Houthis to survive what otherwise might have been a more lopsided battle. They probably managed to shoot down at least one Emirati drone and generally were able to use buildings to mask their infantry and provide some cover from even precision drone-directed fires. Pro-government infantry were forced to push in on foot, shifting the advantage to the urban defenders.

During this same period other battles in Yemen took place at A'aden, al-Hudaydah, al-Masini Valley, Damt and al-Qa'atabah, Wadi Jabara and al-Fra'a, Ataq, and at al-Dhala'a. Somaliland and Puntland fought over the Tukaraq border crossing. Islamic State forces struck the Nigerien base at Inates with over 200 troops employing combined arms—including a suicide explosive vehicle integrated into the ground assault—and killing possibly more than 80 defending soldiers.

From 2018 through 2019, fighting in Syria continued with battles at Homs and Hama, A'afrin, Khisham, al-Baghuz Fawqani, Ras al-A'ayn, Marees and al-Qa'atabah, and elsewhere. Fighting in Libya between the Government of National Accord, various regional protection forces, and the Libyan National Army flared at Derna, Ras Lanuf, al-Sidra, Sadada Castle, Tamanhint Airbase, Traghan, Sebha, and Tripoli.

Tripoli, Libya, 2019: Level 1 Case[11]

Location: Tripolitania Region, Libya
Combatants: Government of National Accord versus Libyan National Army
Dates: April–June 2019 (with continued fighting thereafter)

After a breakdown in negotiations between the competing GNA and LNA, General Khalifa Haftar's LNA launched an offensive to seize Tripoli, its ports, and surrounding towns from the GNA defenders. Spearheaded by MiG-variant fighter-bombers guided by drones provided by the United Arab Emirates, LNA ground forces advanced through the suburbs into the edges of Tripoli and on to the al-Watiyah Airport. Motorized infantry in armed pickup trucks dismounted and pressed into the urban area with T-55 tanks, while jets, artillery, mortars, and multiple-launch rockets pummeled the GNA defenders. Initially on the back foot, the GNA tried to stave off the attack with their own 1970s-era Czech L-39 Albatros light ground-attack jets and Bayraktar TB-2 strike drones.

Both sides were so heavily stacked with antiaircraft artillery, machineguns, and cheap shoulder-fired antiaircraft missiles that low-flying aircraft had to advance into a hailstorm of fire; both sides lost manned aircraft and drones during the battle. Some GNA ground units reportedly buckled, but others were more resilient. At least one GNA unit counterattacked toward al-Watiyah but was repulsed by heavily armed LNA ground units. Reinforcements were called up, increasing the intensity of the ground fight and adding volume to the indirect artillery, mortar, and rocket fire pouring back and forth over the front-line berms. Thousands of infantrymen were committed across the city and into suburbs as the GNA launched a counteroffensive, engaging with AK-variant rifles, light machineguns, ATGMs, rockets, and recoilless rifles. Fighting tapered out in June but continued on and off through at least 2020.

Observations and insights from Tripoli, Libya, 2019. Drones played an important role in this battle and in the general offensive and counteroffensive by both the LNA and GNA. A mix of advanced Chinese and Turkish drones, including Bayraktar TB-2s, Orbiter-3s, and Wing Loong IIs, flew regular combat sorties in support of ground forces and for interdiction strikes.[12] There were unconfirmed reports that over twenty large drones like the Bayraktar TB-2 were shot down over Libya, some probably during the Tripoli battle. In 2021 (so well after this battle) Russian Pantsir S1 antiaircraft vehicles—the same vehicles that appear to have performed poorly in Ukraine in 2022–2023—may have been far more successful against drones in Libya.[13]

In 2020 the DRC and United Nations Force Intervention Brigade fought off a militant attack on a remote base at Ngite in North Kivu Province. Niger engaged

Islamic State forces at Ghinagodrar, fighting in Libya continued, U.S. and Kenyan troops beat back an attack on the Manda Bay Air Base, and the first round of combat in the Ethiopia-Tigray war took place at Mek'ele (and elsewhere). I referred to the 2020 Nagorno-Karabakh War in the previous section and return to it at the end of this chapter. Here is a description of some of the hottest fighting at Mataghis, Sugovushan, and Talish.

Mataghis-Sugovushan-Talish, Nagorno-Karabakh, 2020: Level 2 Case[14]

Location: Nagorno-Karabakh
Combatants: Armenia and Artsakh militia versus Azerbaijan
Dates: Late September to early October 2020

During the broad Azerbaijani offensive into Artsakh-controlled parts of Nagorno-Karabakh, a probably brigade-level Azerbaijani combined-arms ground unit attacked to seize the towns of Mataghis (later renamed Sugovushan) and Talish, and the dam retaining the reservoir near the two towns. Both sides fought with primarily Soviet-Russian arms and munitions, employing BMP-2 infantry fighting vehicles and T-72 tanks, Konkurs and Kornet anti-tank guided missiles, 85mm to 152mm cannon artillery, light and heavy antiaircraft artillery and missiles, and probably 122mm-300mm multiple-launch rocket systems. Both sides also brought drones to bear in order to spot enemy targets; Azerbaijan may have also used Spike Firefly loitering munitions to strike Artsakh and Armenian positions.

Initial engagements took place at fairly long range over the rolling hills, with artillery-targeting infantry both sitting in trenches and moving on foot in the open with devastating effect. Anti-tank missiles and artillery degraded armor on both sides. As the two forces closed in the forest, an Artsakh unit ambushed an Azerbaijani company in a quick but brutal fight that left at least a full platoon of the ambushed unit dead. Despite some limited defensive success, the combined Artsakh and Armenian units were overwhelmed and forced to withdraw under fire as the Azerbaijani ground forces swept in to secure the towns, dam, and reservoir.

Observations and insights from Mataghis-Sugovushan-Talish, Nagorno-Karabakh, 2020. Terrain and range seemed to dictate the characteristics of the fight in this case. In the heavy clashes across the hillsides, with almost total absence of natural concealment and excellent long-range observation from both the ground and the air, competing artillery and anti-tank missile crews had a field day. Artillery appeared to have been particularly effective against both infantry and T-72 tanks, with at least one tank destroyed by (probably) a 152mm shell. The close-range company-level ambush highlighted the disparity of characteristics within a single battle and the unforgiving realities of infantry combat on a high-tech battlefield: Probably over sixty men were killed by rifle, grenade, and machinegun fire in just three to five minutes.

From 2020 through 2021, fighting against Boko Haram continued in the Lake Chad Basin, and the Taliban mounted their final assault against the Afghan government. In rapid succession Taliban forces seized control of Herat, Lashkar Gah, Baghlan, Kunduz, Mazar-e-Sharif, Kandahar, a range of smaller towns and cities, and then Kabul. Most of these battles were poorly recorded. Fighting continued in Somalia, while the rise of Islamic militants in southern Tanzania and northern Cabo Delgado Province led to a series of large-scale attacks against poorly defended Mozambican cities. In March 2021 Islamic militants temporarily seized Palma.

Palma, Mozambique, 2021: Level 2 Case[15]

Location: Cabo Delgado Province, Mozambique
Combatants: Ansar al-Sunna, Islamic State, al-Shabaab versus Mozambique
Dates: March 24–April 04, 2021

A mixed force of Islamic militants from various groups conducted a surprise attack to seize the town of Palma and the nearby Total Oil facility and airfield. Probably over one hundred fighters made a clandestine movement through dense vegetation up to the edge of the town and facilities before attacking, catching local security forces off guard. An Army unit of several hundred soldiers may have holed up at the oil facility to avoid fighting. As the militants pushed into Palma with AK-variant rifles, RPG rockets, machineguns, and mortars, they overran small paramilitary police units and pushed in around a hotel filled with foreign national guests. This triggered the involvement of the South African Dyck Advisory Group private military company (PMC), which flew helicopters in to conduct a rescue operation. Both Dyck and, later, Mozambican Mi-24 attack helicopters became caught up in the ground fight, firing down into militant troops as the Army organized its counterattack.

Militant forces consolidated in Palma and began committing atrocities, while Army units drove and were moved by sea and Mi-8 helicopter up the coast. Light government forces with effectively identical infantry equipment to the insurgents, and backed by some light armored cars, attacked into Palma.

The insurgents put up stiff resistance, firing at both ground and sea forces with machineguns, rockets, and mortars, and conducting some local counterattacks. Government units gradually consolidated combat power in the town and off the coast, eventually pushing the militants out of Palma and back into the jungle of Cabo Delgado province.

Observations and insights from Palma, Mozambique, 2021. Mercenaries have been a fixture on battlefields for well over a millennium, and they were employed in a number of the 2003–2022 cases (e.g., Najaf Iraq 2004, Khisham Syria 2018, Wadi Jabara-Al-Fra'a Valley Yemen 2019, Bakhmut 2022).[16] At Palma, mercenaries probably provided all of the air support to the Mozambican Army: Dyck crews fired machineguns from their private aircraft, and Ukrainian crews manned the government Mi-24s.

At the beginning of this chapter I described the large scale of the 2020–2021 war in Ethiopia and also the dearth of reliable evidence on this important conflict. One of my researchers engaged some of the top Western and Ethiopian experts on the war to gather details on the ground battles. It turned out that most of these experts had been kept in the dark due to lack of press or other external observer access to the battlefields. There is some good video evidence on the battles at Tembien, Agbe, and Abiy Addy that allowed me to record the case and code it with level-2 confidence.

Tembien-Agbe-Abiy Addy, Ethiopia, 2021: Level 2 Case[17]

Location: Tigray Region, Ethiopia
Combatants: Tigray People's Liberation Front versus Ethiopia
Dates: Mid June–mid July 2021

As the broad Ethiopian National Defense Force (ENDF) offensive into the northern reaches of the Tigray region slowly ground to a halt, the Tigray People's Liberation Front (TPLF) prepared for a major counteroffensive under Operation Alula Abanega. Troops unearthed buried arms caches and established positions on the high ground overlooking the broad plains around Kola Tembien. They set up mortars and heavy machineguns around open kill zones, preparing a hasty defense while assembling troops for their own advance.

A large column of at least hundreds and perhaps thousands of ENDF troops packed into buses and transport trucks (probably) attempted to push its way north, perhaps unaware of the thousands of Tigrayan infantry preparing to advance in the opposite direction. Ethiopian forces moving through the low ground were taken under concentrated direct and indirect fires from several mountaintops and hillsides. Tigrayan fires broke the advancing ENDF units, sending at least hundreds of troops fleeing back south under heavy fire. Tigrayan infantry poured down into the lower ground, moving mostly on foot across the broken desert terrain and overrunning the now badly exposed ENDF fire support elements.

This rapid reversal allowed the Tigrayans to capture the Ethiopians' Soviet-Russian 122mm artillery, truck-mounted antiaircraft guns, 120mm mortars, and (probably) T-55 and some T-62 tanks. Tigrayan antiaircraft teams also shot down an ENDF C-130 aircraft right over the central battlefield, giving their troops another jolt of positive energy. With their new armaments and vehicles, the Tigrayan counteroffensive gained momentum. TPLF forces pushed southeast toward Abiy Addy and Agbe, cracking open one and perhaps up to three ENDF divisions in the process.

Observations and insights from Tembien-Agbe-Abiy Addy, Ethiopia, 2021. This is the only Ethiopia-Tigray War case coded with as high as level-2 confidence and one of only seven cases with sufficient public evidence for any kind of coding out of thirty-eight total Ethiopia-Tigray cases. Even in the case of the Tembien-to-Agbe battles, evidence is almost entirely one-sided (mostly from Tigrayan sources) and at least partly unprovable.

War in Ukraine dominated Western discourse during my research period, but, as I wrote in the preface, I did not allow Ukraine to anchor my research. There are sixty-one total Ukraine cases in the database, forty-two of those occurring after Russia's accelerated invasion in February 2022. Putting aside intangibles like will to fight (see the introduction), most of the early 2022 battles pitted Soviet-era equipment against Soviet-era equipment, with a sprinkling of Western munitions and hardware giving Ukrainian troops a technical edge in some instances. As Western equipment began to flow into Ukraine in late 2022, these battles became virtual showcases for mostly old Cold War arsenals. Drones—and particularly commercial off-the-shelf micro-drones—proliferated on both sides.

Video from the battlefield has been transmitted in a deluge, overwhelming analysts and allowing for some interesting perceptual manipulation. These videos give plenty of ammunition to anyone ready to cherry-pick Ukraine battles to ram through their favored argument on the character of war. In order to help counter sousveillance-driven analysis, I co-led primary-source research on what my team refers to as the Battle of Irpin River. It is listed here as the Irpin River Crossing-Moshchun-Horenka battle, followed by the late-2022 battle at Pavlivka-Vuhledar to provide some chronological variance.

Irpin River Crossing (Moshchun and Horenka), Ukraine, 2022: Level 1 Case[18]

Location: Kyiv Oblast, Ukraine
Combatants: Russia versus Ukraine
Dates: February 24–mid March 2022

Part of Russia's northwestern advance toward the Ukrainian capital, Kyiv, depended on establishing a crossing point over the Irpin River and control over the east-bank town of Moshchun to allow for the successful follow-on movement of Russian armored ground forces from the air assault bridgehead at Antonov (Hostomel) Airport. Ukrainian troops dropped the bridges across the narrow, shallow Iprin and punched a hole in an upstream dam. But even as the air assault foundered at Antonov Airport, a joint force of Russian 106th Airborne Division and the 155th Naval Infantry Brigade operating light BMD-variant infantry combat vehicles began to cross the river. Russian infantry backed by massed heavy artillery support pushed their way into the western edge of Moshchun, taking Ukrainian troops of the defending 72nd Brigade—which included a number of recent volunteers and troops from other units—under fire from drone-directed cannon and rocket artillery.

Ukrainians fired back with their own drone-directed artillery and mortars and put up a stiff close-range defense in Moshchun and nearby Horenka. Infantry fought block to block with mostly iron-sight AK-variant rifles, machineguns, RPGs, and (for the Ukrainians) some Western NLAW anti-tank rockets as continual indirect fires rained down on both sides. Russian and Ukrainian soldiers dug trenches and fighting holes to protect themselves from indirect fire and advanced against each other on foot with minimal integrated armor support; BMP-1s and -2s for the Ukrainians and mostly BMDs and a few tanks for the Russians. As Russian ground forces massed on the western bank of the Irpin for a major push across pontoon bridges, the Ukrainians blew open the dam. This daring act effectively stopped the assault.

Observations and insights from Irpin River Crossing (Moschun and Horenka), Ukraine, 2022. Water played an important but not necessarily decisive role in the battle for the Moshchun-area crossing. Even without flooding, the tiny Irpin River—in some places just a deep stream—presented a major obstacle to the advancing Russian forces. Armored vehicles cannot be willed across inconvenient but unavoidable micro-terrain. By blowing the bridges across the river, the Ukrainians channelized the Russian advance onto a handful of pontoon bridges, slowing their advance into Moshchun and Horenka and giving the defenders time to organize defenses and counterattack.

Pavlivka and Vuhledar, Ukraine, 2022: Level 1 Case[19]

Location: Donetsk Oblast, Ukraine
Combatants: Russia versus Ukraine
Dates: March 2022 through the end of 2022

Russia's 155th and elements of the 40th Naval Infantry Brigades and separatist forces attacked to seize the towns of Pavlivka and Vuhledar from the defending Ukrainian 72nd Separate Brigade and teams of Ukrainian international legion troops. Several thousand Russian marines employing T-72 and T-80-variant tanks, BMP-2s and -3s, BTRs, all types of Soviet-Russian artillery and rocket systems, loitering drone munitions, air defenses, and combat aircraft conducted a long, continual series of mechanized infantry assaults into the prepared trenches and bunkers in the fields, windbreaks, and low-density urban terrain around these two towns.

In most recorded cases, Russian tactics were blunt: They shelled the Ukrainians relentlessly and then advanced in armored columns in broad daylight directly toward the defensive front lines. Thick roadside mud and belts of deadly TM-62 anti-tank mines encouraged these channelized advances. In order to push through the mines, Russian units generally led with counter-mine vehicles. But the Ukrainians also used artillery to drop remote anti-armor mines (RAAM) in behind the advancing units, cutting off their reinforcements and escape routes. On several occasions, Ukrainian drones spotted advancing armor and cued up artillery units that waited for the first tank to hit a mine.

Once the column stalled, artillery piled on, catching infantry dismounting into tree lines and light armor in the open. The 155th Brigade suffered so many casualties in these assaults that some Russian marines issued a plea for help on social media. Still, they were able to wear the Ukrainians down over time. Ukrainian counterattacks were not much more successful, and aggressive Russian infantry pushed into the trenches and eventually held Pavlivka for some period of time. The fight for Vuhledar extended well into 2024.

Observations and insights from Pavlivka and Vuhledar, Ukraine, 2022. Drones flew probably almost continuously on both sides throughout this battle. Russians flew Orlan-10s and ZALA Lancet loitering versions, while the Ukrainians used high volumes of DJI commercial drones to drop munitions and spot advancing enemy units. Drones allowed for more accurate artillery fire and caused casualties, but perhaps their biggest impact was to reduce opportunities for either side to achieve the element of surprise on a large, flat battlefield almost devoid of concealing vegetation. Absent drones, the Russian marines might have been able to punch through the Ukrainian defenses at Pavlivka much more quickly, or perhaps the Ukrainians could have mustered a successful counterattack.

OBSERVATIONS AND INSIGHTS FROM 2018 TO 2022

Just prior to the accelerated Russian invasion of Ukraine in February 2022, the war in Nagorno-Karabakh (and to a lesser extent, the war in Ethiopia) had been front and center in the public discourse on the nature and character of war. Given its impact on the debate over the character of modern warfare, it is worth revisiting some of the breathy and also the more measured interpretations of the 2020 war between Armenia and Azerbaijan in Nagorno-Karabakh.

Immediately after this brief but intense forty-four-day conflict, Azerbaijan's successful use of attack drones—and particularly the Turkish Bayraktar TB2 and Israeli loitering strike munitions—was offered up as tangible proof that the character of modern war had changed and that what is often described as "traditional" ground combat power (tanks, artillery, infantry) had been rendered nearly obsolete. Dramatic video montages of drone strikes and scorekeeping websites like Oryx helped actively and passively sell the drone narrative with raw and seemingly irrefutable evidence.[20] A singular causative explanation for Azerbaijani victory took root in Western defense establishments: Drones won the war.

Less than a month after the war ended, then-British Defence Secretary Ben Wallace spoke in awe of Turkish technical innovation. He stated that drones like the TB2 had been responsible for "the destruction of hundreds of armored vehicles and even air defense systems."[21] In 2021 the U.S. Marine Corps published an update to its *Force Design 2030* concept in which it argued without citation that "the victor [Azerbaijan] imposed their will primarily through the use of unmanned systems and loitering munitions."[22] In December 2021, another official Marine Corps report claimed that "almost all battle damage was inflicted by unmanned systems" in the Nagorno-Karabakh War, citing a single article in the *Small Wars Journal*.[23] These claims were used to underwrite the Marine Corps' force redesign and its premier, high-technology Stand-in Force concept.

But neither of the Marine Corps' claims about the Nagorno-Karabakh War—that drones were the dominant factor in Azerbaijani victory and that drones caused nearly all battle damage in the war—stand up to retrospective scrutiny.[24] Nor do they fairly represent contemporaneous interpretations by military experts.[25] Expert analyses were fairly consistent: Drones clearly played an important role in the war. But these analyses also found, or implied that Azerbaijan was able to destroy or capture a significant amount of Armenian and Artsakh military hardware primarily because of a broader imbalance in the quality and effectiveness of the opponents.

At the outset of the Nagorno-Karabakh War, the Armenian side fielded badly outdated, poorly coordinated, and generally inadequate air defenses. Their static ground defenses were situated in wide-open terrain with no concealment and almost no overhead cover and were therefore easily targeted. Armenian and Artsakh soldiers had inadequate military professionalism, poor adaptability, poor signature management, nonexistent counter-drone technology, and (at least in some units) low will to fight. By contrast, the Azerbaijanis were directly supported by NATO member Turkey, had solid doctrine and excellent organization, and executed their ground combat plan with professional expertise, integrated all-arms fire support, aggressive electronic warfare attacks, and ingenious deception measures.[26]

Even if one were to discount these collective factors, there remains a data problem underlying the official Western military interpretations of the Nagorno-Karabakh War. Widely cited drone kill statistics appear to have been inflated and perhaps even doubled or tripled in some cases. Many vehicles that looked to have been destroyed by drones probably had fallen victim to mines, artillery, or anti-tank guided missiles. Eado Hecht of the Israeli Defense Forces Tactical Command College revealed gross exaggerations by the Azerbaijani government and misinterpretations of publicly available video evidence.[27]

I did not set out to prove or disprove causation between means and outcomes in any ground combat battle. However, my review of the public evidence for the engagements at Mataghis, Sugovushan, Talish, Lachin, Qubadli, and Shusha in 2020 did not suggest any clear or defensible case for causation. All of these battles shared many characteristics with the Nagorno-Karabakh battles of 1992 and 2016. I found a roughly 70 percent commonality in characteristics between all five of the Nagorno-Karabakh cases in the dataset, 1992–2020.[28] Drones were far more prominent and almost certainly more effective in the 2020 war, but infantry, cannon artillery, manned aircraft, rocket artillery, rifles, machineguns, anti-tank missiles and rockets, and Soviet-era tanks also played varying and apparently important roles in 2020.

We cannot know with any certainty why Western military leaders were so inclined to bite on the hyperbolic, technophilic, and (at least given publicly available evidence) empirically indefensible drone narrative from the Nagorno-Karabakh War. It is clear that this narrative both correlated with and reinforced the near lockstep arguments about the changing character of modern warfare put forth by Work, Milley, Berger, and other American defense leaders. This was a characterization of war the way senior defense leaders wanted it to be, not necessarily as it was in late 2020. Bayraktar fever carried forward into the first months of the Ukraine War in 2022 but had broken by December of that year as many—and perhaps most or even nearly all—of the Turkish drones in the Ukrainian inventory fell victim to adaptive Russian air defenses.[29]

Beyond my analysis of the 2020 Nagorno-Karabakh War, examination of the Ethiopia-Tigray War, the Myanmar civil war, the Ukraine War, and the other wars from 2018 to 2022 suggests that at least in the public record our collective understanding of ground combat from this period is based on wildly uneven and often inadequate evidence. While a total of forty-two 2022 Ukraine cases are coded in the dataset, only thirteen of those (about one-third) are coded with a high degree of confidence based on publicly available sources in Ukrainian, Russian, and English. Putting aside all cases hidden from public view, I recorded as *not coded* at least sixty-seven other ground combat events in this last five-year period. These include most of the known battles in the Ethiopia-Tigray War; individual battles in Syria, Morocco, Afghanistan, Iraq, the Philippines, Yemen, and Burkina Faso; thirteen possible battles in Myanmar; and even eight prospective battles in Ukraine.

Therefore, while my research culminated during a period in which the Ukraine battlefield became increasingly visible and seemingly transparent, holistic understanding of global ground combat may actually have somewhat worsened. It may be that the more we see, the less we actually seek to understand and collectively examine ground combat and war writ large. There is a real possibility that policymakers and some members of the broad community of experts on modern warfare have come to accept that the volume of raw public information on battle constitutes latent historical knowledge. I return to this possibility in the appendix. In the next chapter I summarize the results of this analysis of 423 cases of modern ground combat and draw conclusions about its character.

NOTES

1. Including Joshua Hammer, "Mali: The Battle of Ametettai Valley," Pulitzer Center, October 9, 2014, https://pulitzercenter.org; Jean-Christophe Notin, *La Guerre de la France au Mali* (Paris: Tallandier, 2014); Bernard Barrera, *Opération Serval: Notes de Guerre, Mali 2013* (Nord Campo, 2015); "Serval: A Brigade in Combat," documentary, Délégation à l'information et à la communication de la défense, n.d., YouTube video; "FATIM dans l'Adrar des Ifoghas," *Al Nassr TV*, n.d., YouTube video. Note that this battle is commonly referred to as the Battle of Ifoghas, which includes a fight in the Tibeggatine Valley. I have broken out the Tibeggatine Valley fight as a separate case in the database of ground combat (Tibeggatine Valley Mali 2013).
2. Including Raphael S. Cohen, David E. Johnson, David E. Thaler, Brenna Allen, Elizabeth M. Bartels, James Cahill, and Shira Efron, *From Cast Lead to Protective Edge: Lessons from Israel's Wars in Gaza* (Santa Monica, CA: RAND Corporation, 2017); "قراءة في العمليات العسكرية بقطاع غزة 22/07/2014," *Al Jazeera Arabic*, July 22, 2014, YouTube video; "Operation Protective Edge: Israel Under Fire, IDF Responds," official web posting (Israeli Ministry of Foreign Affairs, August 8, 2014), https://www.gov.il; "Israeli Merkava Mk4 MBTs Rafael Trophy Active Protection System Successfully Deploys to Protect the Tank and Its Crew, Gaza Strip, July 2014," archival combat video, n.d., Reddit video; "al Qassam Brigades Targetting an Israeli

Merkava with a Fagot ATGM to the East of Juhor al Deak, Gaza 28/2/2014" [sic], archival combat video, n.d., Reddit video; "Hebrew Language Clips of Israel Special Forces Operating in Gaza during Operation Protective Edge, 2014," copy of Israeli combat documentary, no source, n.d., Reddit video; "Gaza War 2014: A Draw after an Unequal Confrontation," *Palquest.org*, n.d., https://www.palquest.org; "תיעוד נדיר של מצלמת גו-פרו על קסדה של חיילים בעזה," archival combat video, n.d., YouTube video.

3. See Cohen et al., *From Cast Lead*, 169–170.
4. Including "Battle of Donetsk Airport—Intense Combat Footage and Heavy Clashes Fighting War in Ukraine," archival combat video, n.d., YouTube video; "The Battle of Donetsk Airport: The War in Ukraine," documentary, no source, n.d., YouTube video; "'5 Cyborgs': Watch the Inside Story of the Battle for Donetsk Airport on Ukraine Today," documentary, *Ukraine Today*, n.d., YouTube video; "Stronger than Concrete: Ukrainian 'Cyborgs' and the Siege of Donetsk Airport," UATV English, n.d., YouTube video; "93: The Battle for Ukraine—First Days of the War. The Story of the 93rd Brigade Kholodny Yar," documentary, Ukrainian Cultural Foundation, n.d., YouTube video; "Ополченцы Гиви Абхаз и Моторолла в аэропорту Донецк Часть 1," *Trollka TV 2*, 2014, YouTube video. Note: One additional primary video source for this battle was removed from YouTube during the editing process for this book and cannot be cited.
5. Including: "News@10: Security Threat: Boko Haram Attack Maiduguri 01/02/15 Part 1," *Channels Television*, February 1, 2015, YouTube video; "New Boko Haram Video Shows Assaults on Military Positions in #Maiduguri—Several #IS References," Tweet, February 21, 2015, https://twitter.com; Alexis Okeowo, "The People vs. Boko Haram," *New York Times*, January 28, 2015; "Boko Haram, Nigerian Troops Battle for Control of Maiduguri," *France 24*, February 1, 2015, https://www.france24.com; "Nigeria Army 'Repels' New Boko Haram Attack on Maiduguri," *BBC News*, February 1, 2015; "Nigerian Troops Repel Boko Haram Attack on Maiduguri," *DW*, February 1, 2015, https://www.dw.com; Aminu Abubakar and Faith Karimi, "Boko Haram Attacks Nigerian City in Second Takeover Attempt," *CNN*, February 2, 2015. Note: One additional primary video source for this battle was removed from YouTube during the editing process for this book and cannot be cited.
6. Including "Retaking Ramadi from the Islamic State: The Battle for Iraq (Dispatch 11)," *VICE News*, 2015, YouTube video; "Behind the Iraqi Military's Fight to Retake Ramadi," documentary, *The Wall Street Journal*, 2015, YouTube video; "The Fall of Ramadi: How ISIS Seized a Key Iraqi City," documentary, *The Wall Street Journal*, 2015, YouTube video; "Iraq Forces Push into City Held by ISIS," *CNN*, 2015, YouTube video; "إصدار مرئي لتنظيم الدولة يظهر وقائع معركة الرمادي," *Al Jazeera Arabic*, December 31, 2015, YouTube video; "الرمادي معركة دون حسم," *Al Jazeera Arabic*, December 13, 2015, YouTube video; "تداعيات معركة الرمادي," *Al Arabiya*, December 22, 2015, YouTube video; "مؤشرات تؤكد قرب حسم معركة تحرير الرمادي," *Al Mada Group*, December 24, 2015, YouTube video.
7. Including "9/7/2016 بدء معركة كسر الحصاروتنفيذ عمليتان استشهاديتان في منطقة الملاح شمالي حلب," archival combat video, 2016, YouTube video; "معارك الملاح—شاهد كيف تم سحق إرهابيي النصر ة بالصواريخ المباركة أثناء محاولة تقدمهم," archival combat video, 2016; "الجيش العربي السوري يحكم السيطرة بالكامل على مزارع الملاح الجنوبية," *Al Akhbaria Channel*, 2016, YouTube video. Note: Three additional primary video sources for this battle

were removed from YouTube during the editing process for this book and cannot be cited.

8. Including "Nagorno Karabakh Four Days of War, 2017 Армения Нагорный Карабах Азербайджан, 4 дня," documentary, no source cited, 2017, YouTube video; "Թալիշի ուղղությամբ ոչնչացված Ադրբեջանի հատուկ ջոկատայինները," archival combat video, 2016, YouTube video; "ԱՊՐԻԼՅԱՆ ՔԱՌՕՐՅԱ ՊԱՏԵՐԱԶՄ // ԲԱՑԱՌԻԿ ԿԱԴՐԵՐ // 02. 04. 2016 //3-ՐԴ ՏԱՐԵԼԻՑ," archival combat video, 2016, YouTube video; "5 Aprel—Dağlıq Qarabağda Daha 3 Erməni Tankı Partladıldı," archival combat video, 2016, YouTube video; Tural Hesenqarayev, "4 Günlük Müharibə (Aprel Döyüşləri)," *Top Chubashov Center*, May 4, 2022; "Ապրիլյան պատերազմի ժամանակագրությունը," *Razm.info*, April 2, 2017; "Международные новости RTVi. 10 апреля 2016 года.," *RTVI News*, 2016, YouTube video.
9. Including "The Battle of Marawi, Every Day," documentary timeline mapping, Lyria Mapping, 2017, YouTube video; "Rebellion in Marawi," *CAN News*, 2017, YouTube video; "Battle of Marawi|AFP (Armed Forces of the Philippines) Run This Town," archival combat video, 2017, YouTube video; "Battle of Marawi The Bloodiest Battle of Philippines," documentary, *Vishnu*, n.d., YouTube video; Edwin Enriquez Amadar and Robert W. Tuttle, "The Emergence of ISIS in the Philippines" (thesis, Naval Postgraduate School, 2018); "[Dead Bodies] Longer Version of a Video Showing an IS-Linked Militant Disabling a Filipino V-150 and Killing Its Crew and Looting It of Its Weapons during the Early Stages of the Battle. Battle of Marawi, 2017, Philippines," archival combat video, 2017, Reddit video; Charles Knight and Katja Theodorakis, "The Marawi Crisis-Urban Conflict and Information Operations," *Australian Strategic Policy Institute*, July 31, 2019; "Philippines Special Forces Are on the Hunt for ISIS Militants (HBO)," documentary, *VICE News*, 2017, YouTube video.
10. I coded a separate case for the battle at the airport, Al-Hudaydah Airport Yemen 2018. Including Bethan McKernan, "Battle Rages in Yemen's Vital Port as Showdown Looms," *Guardian*, November 7, 2018; "Yemen War: Fighting Rages over Vital Port of Hudaydah," *BBC News*, June 14, 2018; "اليمن ..المقاومة تواصل معارك تحرير محافظة الحديدة," *Sky News Arabia*, 2018, YouTube video; "مستجدات تحرير مدينة الحديدة," *Al Arabiya*, 2018, YouTube video; "المقاومة الوطنية تداهم وكرا للمليشيات الحوثية داخل مدينة الحديدة," *Al-Yemen Al-Yom*, 2018, YouTube video; "مستجدات تحرير مدينة الحديدة," *Al Arabiya*, 2018, YouTube video; "مشاهد جديدة لمعارك تطهير مدينة الحديدة خلال الأيام الماضية," The National Brotherhood, 2018, YouTube video. Note: One additional primary video source for this battle was removed from YouTube during the editing process for this book and cannot be cited.
11. Including "Libya on the Brink: Battle for Capital Tripoli Reaches a Deadlock," *TRT World*, June 2019, YouTube video; "الجيش الوطني الليبي يتقدم نحو مركز طرابلس," *Al Arabiya*, 2019, June 2019, YouTube video; "غرفة الأخبار | عملية الكرامة ..5 أعوام من مكافحة الإرهاب في ليبيا," *eXtra news*, June 2019, YouTube video; "On the Front Line in Libya," *Sky News*, April 14, 2019, YouTube video; "Libya The Fight for Tripoli Explained from the Front Line—BBC News," *BBC News*, May 5, 2019, YouTube video; Wolfram Lacher, *Who Is Fighting Whom in Tripoli?* (Security Assessment in North Africa and Small Arms Survey, August 2019); Patrick Wintour, "Tripoli Hit by Airstrikes as Haftar Steps Up Assault on Libyan Capital," *Guardian*, April 21, 2019; "LNA Forces Assaulting the Khallet al-Furjan Neighborhood in Tripoli [April 8, 2019],"

archival combat video, n.d., Reddit video; Oded Berkowitz, "#Libya—Video from #LNA's Tariq bin Ziyad Bn. Showing Their AT Team Engaging #GNA Targets with 9M133 Kornet/AT-14 Spriggan on Several Occasions South of #Tripoli," April 26, 2019, Twitter video.

12. There are many conflicting reports on drone use in the Libya war. On the cited points, see for example, "Libya's Deadly Game of Drones," *Times Aerospace*, n.d., http://timesaerospace.com; Abdullah Bozkurt, "UN Experts Found Turkish Bayraktar Drones in Libya Were Easily Destroyed," *Nordic Monitor*, February 21, 2022, https://nordicmonitor.com; Alex Gatapoulos, "'Largest Drone War in the World': How Airpower Saved Tripoli," *Al Jazeera*, May 28, 2020; Franz-Stefan Gady, "Useful, but not Decisive: UAVs in Libya's Civil War," *International Institute of Strategic Studies*, November 22, 2019.
13. This is an aggregated analysis in need of additional vetting, but it provides useful information: Chris Cole and Jonathan Cole, "Libyan War Sees Record Number of Drones Brought Down to Earth," *Dronewars.net*, January 7, 2020, https://dronewars.net.
14. Including "Արցախի հյուսիսային սահմանագծին/The Northern Frontline of Artsakh," *BARS Media Film*, 2020, YouTube video; "Կիրակնօրյա "մատաղ" Մատաղիսի ձորում. նոր տեսանյութ," *Live24 AM*, 2020, YouTube video; "Azerbaijani Forces Recapture Strategic Dam in Nagorno-Karabakh," *Euronews*, October 27, 2020, https://www.euronews.com; "Azerbaijani MoD: Advantageous High Grounds around Talysh Village Cleared of Enemy—Video," *Azerbaijani Vision*, September 28, 2020, http://www.visions.az; "Intense Fighting Continued during the All Night—Video," [sic] Ministry of Defense of the Republic of Azerbaijan, September 29, 2020, https://mod.gov.az; Nvard Hovhannisyan and Nailia Bagirova, "Fiercest Clashes since 1990s Rage in Azerbaijan's Ethnic Armenian Enclave," *Reuters*, September 28, 2020; "Azerbaijan Army Takes Talish Village amid Conflict," *Reuters*, October 5, 2020; "Մատաղիսի դիրքերը," YouTube video.
15. Including "Cabo Ligado Weekly: 22–28 March," *Cabo Ligado*, March 30, 2021, https://www.caboligado.com; Tim Lister, "The March 2021 Palma Attack and the Evolving Jihadi Terror Threat to Mozambique," *CTC Sentinel*, April–May 2021, https://ctc.westpoint.edu, 19–27; "How Mozambique Failed a Town Attacked by Militants|Visual Investigations," *The New York Times*, 2021, YouTube video; "Cabo Ligado Weekly: 29 March-4 April," *Cabo Ligado*, April 6, 2021; "Mozambique Survivor Recalls Horrific Ambush," *Sky News*, 2021, YouTube video; Andrew Meldrum, "Rebels Leave Beheaded Bodies in the Streets of Mozambique Town," *Washington Post*, March 29, 2021; "On the Ground with Troops in Mozambique's Palma," *Reuters*, 2021, YouTube video.
16. For more on the history of the use of mercenaries in war, see George H. Dodenhoff, "A Historical Perspective of Mercenaries," *Naval War College Review* 21, no. 7 (1969), 91–109; and Will Mackie, "Soldiers of Fortune: Why U.S. Mercenaries Should Not Be Legal," *War On the Rocks* (August 26, 2021).
17. "#Short Film Prepared by Tigray Forces #Army-4," documentary, Tigray armed forces, n.d., YouTube video; "Tigray Defence Forces in Tembien Operation General Alula 2021#eritrea #ethiopia #tigray #ትግራይ," archival combat video, n.d., YouTube video; "Footage: TDF Routing Out ENDF from Tigray during the Operation Alula," *TNews*, 2021, YouTube video; "Video of C-130 Hercules When It Was Shot Down by TDF in Tigray," archival combat video, 2021, YouTube video;

"ወፍሪ ኣሉላ ኣበነጋ ቀዳማይ ክፍሊ Operation Alula—Part 1," *Tigrai Media House*, n.d., YouTube video; "Tigray: Breaking News from the Central Command of Tigray Army," *Eritrea Hub*, June 29, 2021, https://eritreahub.org.

18. Including James Sladden, Liam Collins, and Ben Connable, *The Battle of Irpin River*, British Army Review special edition (London: Centre for Historical Analysis and Conflict Research, February 2024); "Video of Fighting at Moshchun, a Northern Suburb of Kyiv," archival combat video, March 11, 2022, YouTube video; "Rare Footage from the Frontline as Ukrainian Troops Battle with Russian Troops near Kyiv," *The Sun*, March 15, 2022, YouTube video; "Russian Artillery D-30 Firing at Ukrainian Position in Moshchun, Ukraine," archival combat video, March 2021, YouTube video; "Destroyed & Abandoned Russian Vehicles, Moshchun [Russia Ukraine War] Day 41," [sic], archival combat video, April 2022, YouTube video; "300 Spartans 2.0: 80 Soldiers of the 72nd OMBR Restrained Thousands of Russian Moving toward Kyiv," documentary interviews, no source listed, April 2022, YouTube video; "Українські Герої #2. "Чорні Запорожці" і пекло Мощуна|LB live," *LB Live*, 2022, YouTube video.
19. Including Anna Pavlova, "'I Used to Condemn Desertion but Now It's the Only Way to Stay Alive.' A Marine Fighting in Pavlivka Describes the Morale of Russian Troops and the Command's indifference," *Mediazona*, November 23, 2022, https://en.zona.media; "South of Pavlivka, in the Donetsk Region of East Ukraine, Ukrainian Forces Used Drones to Drop Anti-Tank Grenades on Vehicles and Antipersonnel Grenades on Opposition Soldiers," archival combat video, n.d., Reddit video; "Graphic! Russian Soldiers VS Ukrainian Units in Pavlovka Ukraine," archival combat video, n.d., YouTube video; Luke Mogelson, "Trapped in the Trenches in Ukraine," *New Yorker*, December 26, 2022; Dmitry Plotnikov and Mikhail Kirillov, ""Недооценивать врага—преступление"Морпехи 155-й бригады—о боях за Павловку, танковых дуэлях и отношении к противнику," *Lenta.ru*, November 28, 2022, https://lenta.ru. Note: Three additional primary video sources for this battle were removed from YouTube during the editing process for this book and cannot be cited.
20. "The Fight for Nagorno-Karabakh: Documenting Losses on the Sides of Armenia and Azerbaijan," Oryx, September 27, 2020, https://www.oryxspioenkop.
21. Ben Wallace, quoted in Dan Sabbagh, "UK Wants New Drones in Wake of Azerbaijan Military Success," *Guardian*, December 29, 2020.
22. U.S. Marine Corps, *Force Design Annual Update*, 2.
23. U.S. Marine Corps, *A Concept for Stand-in Forces* (Washington, DC: Headquarters, U.S. Marine Corps, December 2021), 3. The article cited is Nicole Thomas, Matt Jamison, Kendall Gomber, and Derek Walton, "What the United States Military Can Learn from the Nagorno-Karabakh War," *Small Wars Journal*, April 4, 2021, 8–9.
24. For example, see Uzi Rubin, "The Second Nagorno-Karabakh War: A Milestone in Military Affairs," The Begin-Sadat Center for Strategic Studies, December 16, 2020; and Samuel Bendett quoted in "The 'Magic Bullet' Drones behind Azerbaijan's Victory over Armenia," *Forbes*, November 10, 2020, https://www.forbes.com.
25. This includes Thomas et al., "What the Military Can Learn."
26. See Shaan Shaikh and Wes Rumbaugh, "The Air and Missile War in Nagorno-Karabakh: Lessons for the Future of Strike and Defense," Center for Strategic and International Studies, December 8, 2020; Alexander Stronell, "Learning the

Lessons of Nagorno-Karabakh the Russian Way," International Institute for Strategic Studies, March 10, 2021; Zhirayr Amierkhanyan, "A Failure to Innovate: The Second Nagorno-Karabakh War," *Parameters* 52, no. 1 (2022), 119–134; Andrius Bivainis, "Maneuver, Modernization, and the Second Nagorno-Karabakh War," *AUSA*, March 31, 2022; Robert Bateman, "No, Drones Haven't Made Tanks Obsolete," *Foreign Policy*, October 15, 2020, https://foreignpolicy.com; Jack Detsch, "The U.S. Army Goes to School on Nagorno-Karabakh Conflict," *Foreign Policy*, March 30, 2021; Ben Ho, "The Second Nagorno-Karabakh War: Takeaways for Singapore's Ground-Based Air Defense," *Journal of Indo-Pacific Affairs* 4, no. 5 (Fall 2021), 24–39; and others.

27. Eado Hecht, "Drones in the Nagorno-Karabakh War: Analyzing the Data," *Military Strategy Magazine* 7, no. 4 (Winter 2022), 31–37. Hecht's points about the unreliable nature of video evidence were echoed by a U.S. Army officer who served in the Asymmetric Warfare Group, an organization dedicated to studying advanced adversary tactics and technologies to support army innovation. He is quoted in Detsch, "U.S. Army Goes to School," 2021. For an example of exaggerated statistics, see "Müharibə xronikası: Ermənistan SQ-nin itkiləri," *Sputnik Azarbaycan*, October 23, 2020, https://az.sputniknews.ru.
28. Confidence ratings varied: Shusha 1992 = 1; Talish-Lalatepe Heights 2016 = 1; Mataghis-Sugovushan-Talish = 2; Lachin-Qubadli 2020 = 3; and Shusha 2020 = 1.
29. It is difficult to know how many Bayraktar TB2 drones Ukraine had in its inventory at any one time, how many it fielded, and how many it lost, but reports of TB2 activity in the cited sources dropped precipitously through the end of 2022. Still, Russian claims of successful drone kills are almost certainly exaggerated. See Sakshi Tiwari, "Russia 'Shot Down' over 100 Bayraktar TB2 Drones in the Ukraine War & Kicked Them Out of Action," *EurAsian Times*, April 11, 2023, https://www.eurasiantimes.com; "Украинские военные практически перестали применять БПЛА Bayraktar," *TopWar.ru*, December 2, 2022, https://topwar.ru. As of mid June 2023, Oryx listed 23 TB2 drones destroyed, three of which appear to have been destroyed on the ground. "List of Aircraft Losses during the 2022 Russian Invasion of Ukraine," Oryx (publication date March 20, 2022, data updated to June 2023).

EIGHT

Observed Characteristics of Modern Ground Combat

I argue in chapter 9 that we cannot effectively describe a collective character of modern ground combat in a singular form. We can, however, helpfully identify a range of *characteristics* of modern ground combat that appear to be more or less common across cases in a given time period and across decades. Examination of characteristics including equipment, tactics, and technology employed by ground forces and supporting air and naval units can return useful and interesting insights into warfare without resort to hand waving.

Of course, subjective decisions over theory and method, and subjectivity in the interpretation of data are baked into even the most quantitative hard-science research findings. As I wrote in the introduction, subjectivity is unavoidably present in my qualitative work. I have done my best to increase the objectivity of these results through transparency, citation, and inductive case selection and coding. But the reader should be well aware that the findings that follow represent my subject-matter expert analysis of the cited evidence.

Beyond analyst bias, all cited evidence contains its own prospective subjectivity and flaws. And while I was able to observe a handful of these conflicts at fairly close range, I most certainly was unable to observe the entirety of global ground combat through an unclassified computer. Coded results reflect only the evidence I have cited in the database (approximately 2,500 annotated sources and approximately 20,000 other reviewed and listed sources). These findings and the evidence and data they represent should be rigorously challenged and improved on going forward.

Return of findings in this chapter begins with a broad categorization of the 423 coded modern ground combat cases. I describe where battles took place, generally what type of forces were aligned against one another, and the terrain on and within which they fought. I then break out specific characteristics of ground combat by broad category: (1) infantry, (2) indirect ground fires, (3) mobile firepower and armored vehicles, (4) airpower not including drones, and (5) drones.[1]

I also present results and my insights from attempts to code characteristics of ground combat that were most difficult to observe, including the use of electronic warfare; information warfare; artificial intelligence; cyber warfare; satellites; stealth technology; chemical, radiological, and biological munitions; and so on.

CASE INCIDENCE BY LOCATION

By frequency and density, most of the observed 423 ground combat cases occurred in the Middle East, across North Africa, and on the Horn of Africa (HoA). A total of 61 percent (256 cases) occurred in the Middle East-North Africa (MENA) region, with the majority of these (42 percent of the overall total) occurring in Middle Eastern countries like Syria and Iraq. Eastern Europe, Asia, and sub-Saharan Africa experienced roughly equivalent incidents of ground combat (9–16 percent of the remaining whole). Figure 8.1 depicts the total case count by region, with the aggregated regions in the left-hand pie chart and the disaggregated regions in the right-hand bar chart. The bar chart on the right shows the total absence of observed cases of combined-arms ground combat in Western Europe, Central America, South America, and North America.[2]

A noticeable shift from the MENA region to Europe emerges across the five-year periods depicted in Figure 8.2, below. Rise in the Europe cases is almost entirely explained by the war in Ukraine, while the decline in the Middle East cases primarily resulted from the culmination of the counter-Islamic State campaign and the overall decline in organized warfare across Syria. Marked decline in Asia cases starting in 2013 primarily resulted from the end of the Sri Lankan civil war and the end of the American surge of forces in Afghanistan.

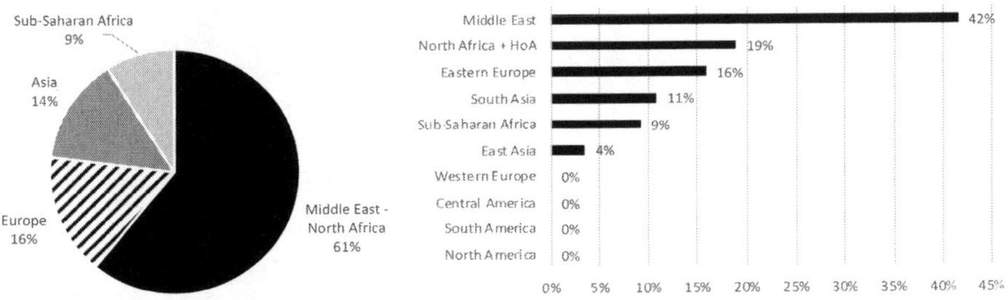

FIGURE 8.1. Total Ground Combat Case Count by Region, 2003–2022
Note: I placed each country in a region and subregion based on my experience with regional mapping for policy analysis. There are no hard-and-fast rules for regional bounding. All country-level data are available in the Excel dataset, a copy of which will be made available to researchers on request. Also see the map in Figure 9.3 for country-level frequency.

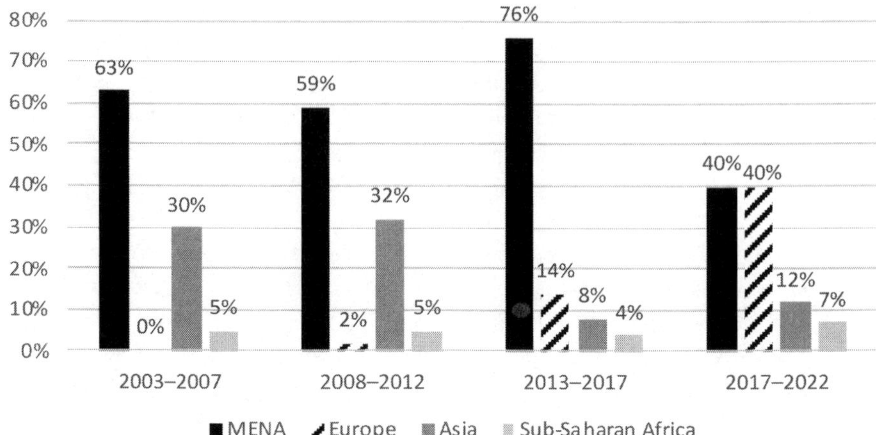

FIGURE 8.2. Total Case Count by Aggregated Region per Five-Year Period

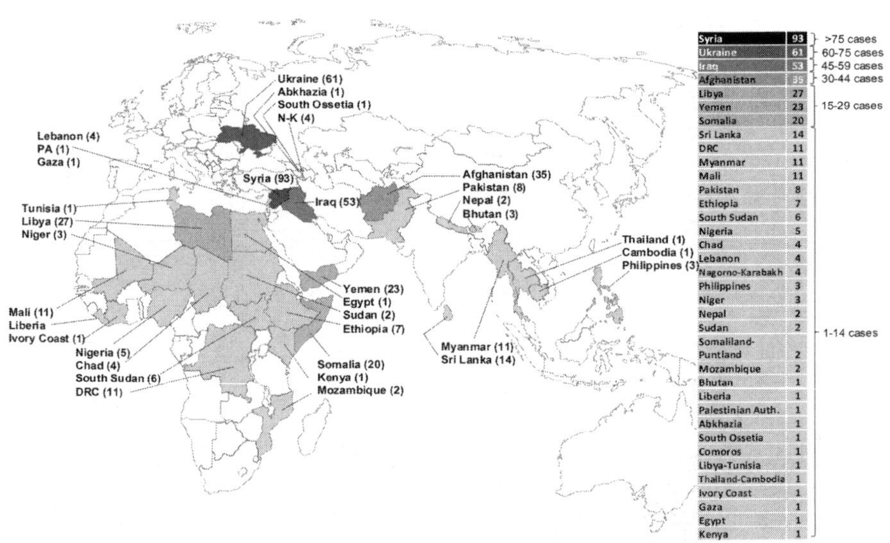

FIGURE 8.3. Total Ground Combat Case Count by Country, 2003–2022
Note: This map depicts only the 423 coded cases from the dataset 2003–2022. Cases with clear cross-border fighting—Libya-Tunisia and Thailand-Cambodia—show one incident per country; these should not be counted as additional cases. Darker fills indicate a higher density of cases, with black indicating more than 75 cases, darkest gray 60–75 cases, then progressively lighter gray for 45–59 cases, 30–44 cases, 15–29 cases, and 1–14 cases. Countries without cases have a white fill. There were no recorded cases in the Western Hemisphere. PA = Palestinian Authority; N-K = Nagorno-Karabakh

Recapping the lead case counts by country: Ground combat in Syria from 2011 through generally about 2018 constituted the majority of cases (ninety-three total, or 22 percent) in the database. Russia's initial invasion of Ukraine in 2014 and the broader war beginning in February 2022 generated sixty-one total cases (~14 percent), with forty-two of these occurring in the last year covered by this study. Wars in Iraq between the U.S.-led coalition and Saddam Hussein's government in 2003, between the coalition and insurgent groups through 2011, and then war with the Islamic State from 2014 through 2022 brought Iraq into third place with fifty-three cases (~13 percent), followed by the U.S.-led war in Afghanistan, post-Arab Spring wars in Libya and Yemen, chaos in Somalia, the Sri Lankan civil war, and then less well-represented conflicts in Asia and sub-Saharan Africa. The map in Figure 8.3 shows the highest incidence of cases by country throughout the twenty-year modern period.

LOCATION: OBSERVATIONS AND INSIGHTS

Governments around the world engaged in direct combat or supplied proxies to fight each other and a range of exceptionally well-equipped nongovernmental armies like the Islamic State, the Libyan National Accord, and Ansar Allah (Houthis).[3] Weapons, tactics, intelligence, and the highest and lowest forms of technology from across the world's armories and training halls were effectively globalized, but they were most concentrated and diversified in the Middle East and North Africa regions; Syria, Iraq, Libya, Yemen, Somalia, and so on. These MENA cases are therefore particularly relevant to future studies seeking to understand modern warfare, and particularly those focused on understanding war between great powers in the absence of any actual, modern great power wars; see the following section on competitor type.

CASE INCIDENCE BY COMPETITOR TYPE

Competitor type indicates in broad and subjective terms the relative power of the combatants in these ground combat cases. I assigned one of three ratings to the direct combatants and their proxy supporters: (1) low, (2) mid-minor, or (3) major. Low rating generally correlates with irregular, nongovernmental powers like the Somali al-Shabaab. Low-rated powers typically do not have air or naval forces, but they can have drones, robust indirect fire, and armor capabilities. Mid-minor rating correlates with governments or particularly strong nongovernmental powers that have large but generally low-technology armies, or in some cases small, higher-tech armies with limited military professionalism, leadership, and tactical capability. For example, Sri Lanka and the Tamil Tigers are both rated mid-minor because both had fairly robust but not high-technology

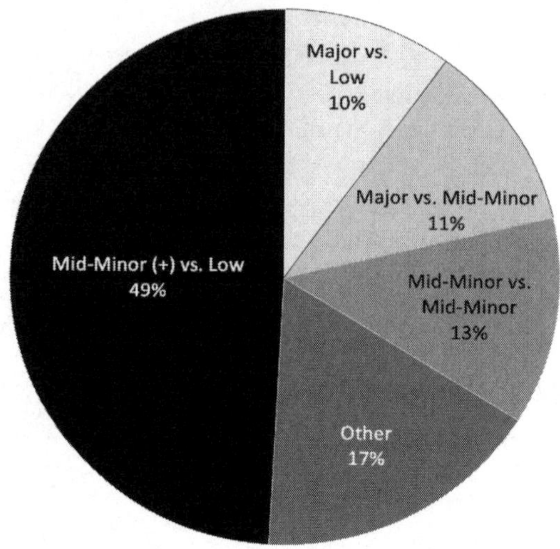

FIGURE 8.4. Competitor Types, Aggregated, 2003–2022

or otherwise advanced ground, air, and naval forces. Major powers include the United States, some other NATO countries, Russia, and China.

I started with nineteen possible combinations of competitor type including proxy teaming. For example, Harasta Syria 2018–2019 is coded as mid-minor + major versus low: Syria (mid-minor) was supported by Russia (major) in its fight against the Free Syrian Army (low). I only added supporting major powers when they were *directly* involved in combat with air support, naval fires, and/or ground forces.[4] For example, at Harasta, Russian aircraft attacked Free Syrian Army fighters with air-delivered munitions, so in that case Russia and Syria made up a major-mid team. Figure 8.4 shows the aggregated breakdown of competitor types:

By far the cases in which mid-minor powers like Myanmar fought low powers like the Kachin Independence Army were most prevalent. Out of these 208 total cases (49 percent of the overall cases), 55 included major power support to a mid-minor power. This included the Russian support to Syria at Harasta, U.S. support to Iraq in the al-Mosul Iraq 2016–2017 case, and the combined French-Afghan battle against the Taliban at Ala'Saye, Afghanistan in 2009.

COMPETITOR TYPE: OBSERVATIONS AND INSIGHTS

There were no incidents of major-versus-major-power (e.g., China versus the United States) direct ground combat in the dataset. Despite this rather significant gap in observable phenomenon, experts continue to make hedgehog-like claims about the character of such major-power wars in contemporary policy debates. I return to this point in chapter 9. A significant majority of all recorded engagements—about 90 percent of total—took place in the context of what generally are referred to as irregular wars.[5]

Given the apparent importance of these cases: What is meant by *irregular war* and how does it help us to understand modern ground combat? Clearly these battles are not irregular in terms of relative frequency. Are they therefore irregular in their characteristics when compared to what are generally referred to as regular, conventional, or traditional battles? That is less clear, particularly given the muddled meaning and bounding of these terms. Across Syria, Yemen, Sri Lanka, and other battlefields, so-called irregular forces fought what looked very much like regular conventional battles with infantry, heavy artillery, armor, and close-air support.

TERRAIN AND WEATHER

These 423 battles were fought over and within a variety of terrain and weather conditions. Most cases involved two or more types of terrain, like desert and urban in Umm Qasr Iraq 2003, or forest, jungle, and urban in Beni Nepal 2004. Of the nearly 300 cases that included fighting in some kind of urban terrain, over half (164) also included some other type of terrain like desert or swamp. Figure 8.5 shows the frequency of terrain occurrence across all cases. There was no significant deviation in terrain type over the five-year periods. It was not possible with the given evidence to record the impact of rainfall, excessive heat, or excessive cold, and so on. Snow was observed on the ground in approximately 2 percent of all recorded cases.

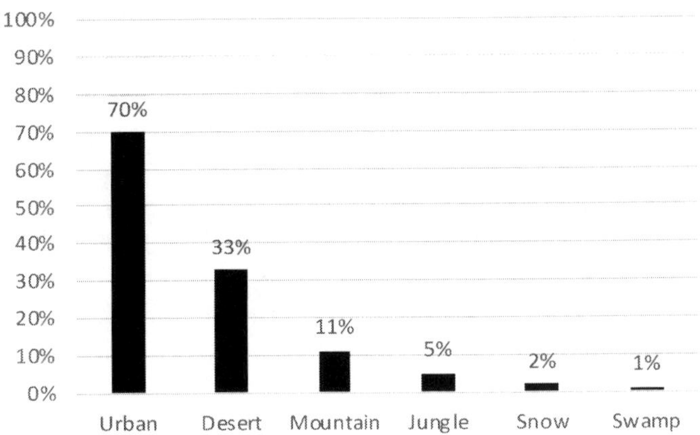

FIGURE 8.5. Terrain Frequency, 2003–2022

Coding for terrain requires subjective judgment. What constitutes a mountain for one observer might look like a large hill to another. I applied the broadest possible definition for *urban* terrain, including fighting in low-density, low-construction-height villages because no matter their construction, the presence and use of buildings changes engagement ranges, weapon effectiveness, and tactics. A tighter definition restricted to cities with high-rise buildings would return far fewer positive results.

TERRAIN: OBSERVATIONS AND INSIGHTS

Frequency of urban combat across the cases is observable and interesting, but I could not objectively code what I found to be the three most important terrain insights from the case research on (1) high ground, (2) micro-terrain, and (3) weapons employment. These are offered as subjective expert insights.

As it had in previous land wars in recorded history, high ground frequently gave tactical advantage to ground combat forces. Given that ground combat continued to center on direct-fire and surface-to-surface indirect-fire engagements—more on this below—high angle of fire, dominant visibility, and dominant positioning retained their historical relevance.

At Wadi al-Hujair Wadi al-Saluki, Lebanon, in 2006, advancing Israeli armored forces were pinned by Hezb'allah infantry and anti-tank teams firing from high to low ground. Israeli gunners were hard-pressed to fire up steep hillsides with any real effectiveness. In the battle for Haifah Street in Baghdad, Iraq, in 2007, both U.S. soldiers and Iraqi insurgents used high-rise buildings to rain fire down onto defending or advancing forces. At Inayat Qilla-Bai Cheena, Pakistan, in 2009, Tehrik-e-Taliban Pakistani fighters nearly dominated advancing Army columns with heavy fires funneled into the restrictive low ground of the valley floors.

Clausewitz described the influence of terrain "in the very smallest feature of the ground."[6] These small features are now referred to as micro-terrain. Micro-terrain is any ditch, hillock, rubble pile, rock outcrop, or even slight rise or drop in grade on the ground that provides concealment from enemy observation and/or cover protection from enemy fire.

Micro-terrain rarely shows up on maps and is hard to discern even through ultra-high-definition overhead drone feeds. Typically, it is discovered by vehicle crews and infantrymen as they advance or defend under fire. Despite its seeming innocuity, I observed in many of the cited cases that the right bit of micro-terrain could make a significant difference in the way in which battles were fought. This was true for the Germans defending broken ground along the steep slopes along Monte Altuzzo in 1944, for the Argentinians defending from rock outcrops on Mount Longdon in the Falkland Islands in 1982, and for U.S.

Marines taking cover in irrigation ditches as they advanced against the Taliban in Afghanistan in 2010.[7]

In every case I was able to confidently observe—all of the confidence level-1 and many of the level-2-rated cases from 2003 to 2022—terrain clearly had a significant influence on direct-fire engagement ranges and weapon types employable and employed. For example, throughout the expansive and long-running battle between the Syrian Arab Army and Free Syrian Army at Bureij, Aleppo, between 2014 and 2015, both sides engaged with armored vehicle main gun fire, heavy machineguns and antiaircraft cannons, and anti-tank missiles across the low-rolling hills outside the urban area. But as the two forces closed range to contest small built-up areas and military bases, emphasis shifted to AK-variant rifles, RPG-variant rockets, and hand grenades. Cannons and machineguns were still employed in built-up areas but much more cautiously. See the section on armor, below, for more on infantry-armor teaming.

INFANTRY CHARACTERISTICS

Infantry played a role in every one of the 423 modern ground combat cases. There is some risk of tautology with this finding given that the baseline requirement for a valid case required the presence of approximately a platoon of infantry on each side. However, throughout my inductive research process I found no modern ground combat cases, coded or other, in which infantry were completely absent on either side.

Three following charts break down the coded infantry results. In this first chart, Figure 8.6, I show the frequency of appearance of infantry-level weapons across all 423 cases. Rifles, machineguns, and with a few exceptions, direct-fire

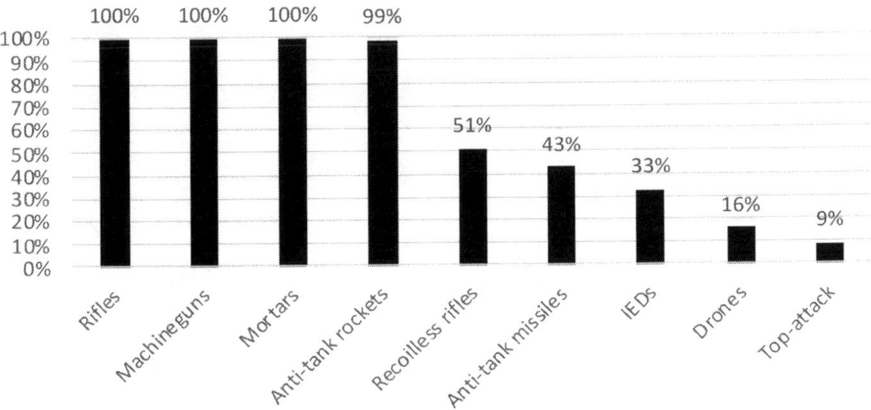

FIGURE 8.6. Infantry Weapons Frequency, 2003–2022

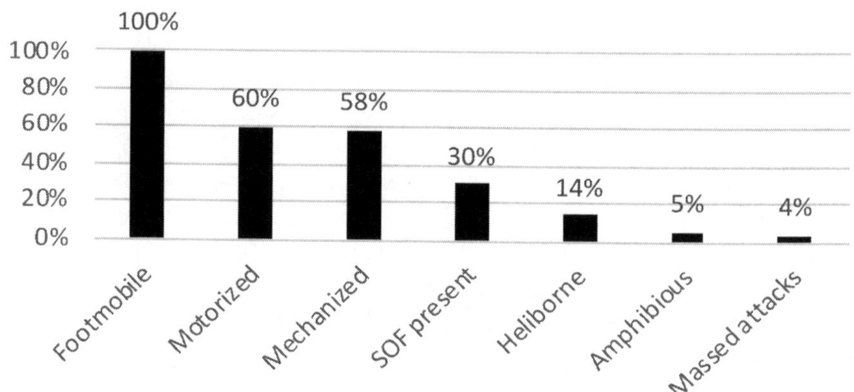

FIGURE 8.7. Infantry Movement, Tactics, Other, 2003–2022

rockets (e.g., RPG, M72 LAAW) were always present on one or both sides.[8] Recoilless rifles and anti-tank guided missiles were used in about half or two-fifths of all cases, improvised explosive devices in about one-third of all cases, and top-attack anti-tank missiles (e.g., Javelins) were used in just under one in ten cases. See below for more on infantry drones.

Foot-mobile infantry including all infantry fighting dismounted from vehicles were employed in every case, while motorized and/or mechanized infantry were employed in about 60 percent of all cases. Special operations forces like Afghan Commandos or Iraqi Counter-Terrorism Service (CTS) were observably employed by one or both sides in about one out of every three cases. I was able to record the heliborne landing of troops either to a location in close proximity of the battle or directly into the fight under fire in sixty-one cases (14 percent).

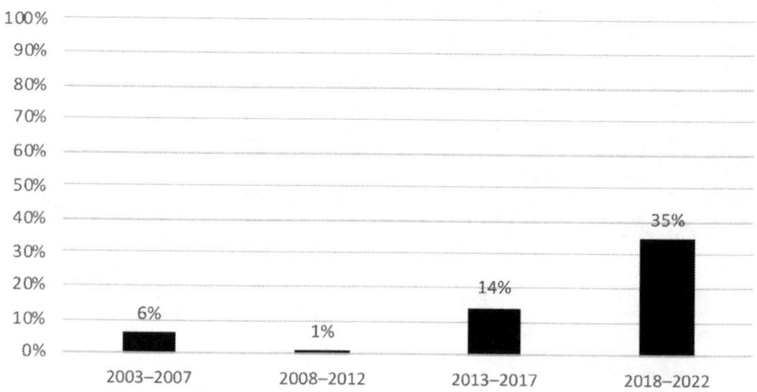

FIGURE 8.8. Observed Infantry Drone Use, 2003–2022

I also observed what I subjectively determined to be amphibious or smaller waterborne (e.g., riverine, major river crossing) operations in about 5 percent of all cases. These included the UK-led amphibious landings at the al-Faw Peninsula in Iraq in 2003, the Rally for Congolese Democracy (RDC) crossing of the Rusizi River and Lake Kivu into Bukavu, Democratic Republic of the Congo in 2004, and the Russian amphibious reconnaissance-in-force at Mariupol, Ukraine, in February 2022.[9] And I observed what I interpreted to be massed frontal infantry assaults in about 4 percent of all modern cases.[10] Figure 8.7 depicts these frequencies across all cases.

I coded separately for aerial drones employed by infantrymen and those flown by special nonorganic teams or national-level air forces. For example, an infantry platoon might fly a small commercial drone like the DJI Mavic 3 for close-range observation, while higher-level units might fly larger winged drones like the Russian Orlon-10, the Israeli Heron, or the American MQ-9 Reaper. See the section on drones, below, for more on overall drone use.

Clearly recorded, small-infantry-unit-level aerial drone use increased by approximately 600 percent from 2003 through 2022. In the most recent five-year period of observation, infantry on at least one side of the battle employed infantry drones in 35 percent of cases. American, Israeli, and other forces used ground drones in combat, but their observed use in the cited sources was negligible across all periods.[11] Figure 8.8 shows this change over time from 2003 to 2022.

INFANTRY: OBSERVATIONS AND INSIGHTS

Infantry units were the only type of unit represented on both sides of every modern case. Infantry weapons—rifles, machineguns, and mortars—were the only items of military equipment present and employed in every one of the 423 cases.[12] I observed no cases in which ground defensive positions or offensive objectives were held or taken without infantry engaging in at least direct-fire, and nearly always also indirect-fire, combat. There probably is no objective, evidence-driven method to judge the relative value of infantry compared to other combat arms in modern ground combat. It is, however, safe to say that infantry consistently played at least an important role, and in many cases a dominant role, in a significant majority of observed ground battles.

Almost without exception, infantry in various armed forces maintained consistent form and function across relative organizational structures, applying similar tactical methods, equipment, weapons, and technology from at least the mid twentieth century through the end of 2022. Evolutionary changes were evident but perhaps surprisingly limited given the passage of more than seventy-five years since the end of World War II. Given the U.S. Army's position as the world's premier large-scale global ground combat force, it provides a good basis for comparison over time.

Organization: At the end of World War II, a U.S. Army infantry battalion had three rifle companies with organic medium machineguns, 60mm mortars and anti-tank rockets, and a heavy weapons company with organic heavy machineguns, 81mm mortars, and anti-tank guns.[13] At least as of early 2024, a U.S. Army infantry battalion still had three rifle companies with organic medium machineguns, 60mm mortars and anti-tank rockets, and a heavy weapons company with organic heavy machineguns and both 81mm and 120mm mortars.[14] Triangular organization remained generally in place. Changes: Battalions were somewhat smaller with reduced support capabilities, anti-tank missiles were added to the infantry platoons and battalions, and the unit had some organic drone capability. Special drone units were on the drawing board.

Tactics: Late-war infantry tactics described in the 1944 War Department Field Manual 7–20, *Infantry Battalion*, are remarkably similar to those in the 2017 Army Techniques Publication 3–21.20, *Infantry Battalion*. Both manuals describe orderly movement of subordinate units in columns toward enemy objectives, ground reconnaissance to spot weak points in enemy defensive positions, coordination of supporting indirect and air fires onto the objective, violent infantry assault through the enemy positions, and consolidation into a defensive perimeter. Army units attacking into Iraq in 2003 (exemplary cases: Karbala Iraq 2003; al-Qa'id Bridge Iraq 2003, etc.) applied tactics that effectively mirrored those in the 1944 manual. Changes: Observable, substantive changes over time in doctrine, organization, and action are negligible.

Weapons and equipment: With four notable exceptions—rifle scopes, night vision goggles, anti-tank missiles, and drones—modern U.S. Army infantry kit is either a modest evolution of early to mid-twentieth-century equivalents (e.g., M1 carbine to the M4 carbine) or is nearly the exact replication of early to mid-twentieth-century weapons (M2 heavy machinegun). An individual infantryman in the early 2020s has better body armor, newer but not necessarily more effective rifles and machineguns, and effectively the same uniform and boots as a World War II-era infantryman. Changes: Wide dissemination of scopes for U.S. Army infantrymen has extended their ability to spot and target enemy infantry. Anti-tank missiles have significantly increased infantry capability to target and destroy enemy armor, but the Javelin is a nearly thirty-year-old system that represents a meaningful but (arguably) in many ways modest evolution from the 1970s-era M47 Dragon it replaced.[15] World War II-era night-vision devices have evolved to offer sometimes significant advantage for infantry fighting against other infantry who lack night vision, but the goggles are restrictive and can be blinded.

Table 8.1. U.S. Army Infantry Weapons and Drones from WWII to Early 2020s

	Decade item designed-fielded: 1910s through early 2020s											
Equipment	10s	20s	30s	40s	50s	60s	70s	80s	90s	00s	10s	20s
.30 / 7.62mm MG	M1919					M60			M240			
Hand grenade	M1-M67											
Heavy machinegun			M2 .50 caliber variants									
81mm mortar			M1		M29			M252				
60mm mortar			M2		M19	M224						
Semi-auto rifle				M1 Garand		M-14 and M-16 + M-4[1]						
Launched grenade				M11 +		M79 and M203				M320		
Rocket launcher				M1A1-M20			M72	AT4	Mk-153		M3 (1947)	
AGL						Mk19						
Anti-tank missile							M-47 Dragon		CCMS-M Javelin			
Infantry drones										RQ-11 Raven +		

Note: Consecutively lighter shading from left to right denotes newer equipment. There were too many versions of U.S. Army hand grenades to list here; all explosive grenades are similar. The .30 and 7.62mm rounds are equivalent machinegun (MG) calibers; AGL = automatic grenade launcher; "M" before a numeric designator stands for "model," with newer versions typically (but not always) labeled with sequentially higher numbers; the M4 rifle (carbine) is a modified version of the M-16-variant rifle based on the Vietnam War-era CAR-15 XM177 Commando; the 1950s-era M-14 rifle, Vietnam War-era M224 mortar, M79 grenade launcher, and M72 rocket remain in U.S. service in the early 2020s, as do the 1980s-era M252 mortar and AT-4 rocket, the 1990s-era M240 machinegun, Mk-153 rocket launcher and Javelin Close Combat Missile System-Medium (CCMS-M) ATGM, and the 2000s-era RQ-11 Raven. This table is relevant as of early July 2023, and does not include experimental systems or the Army's new M7 rifle and M250 automatic rifle.

[1]Not including the new Army rifle issued in 2023 alongside M-4s.

Table 8.1 depicts the evolution and sustained use of U.S. Army infantry weapons from World War II through the mid 2020s.[16] It shows the initial introduction of some weapons, including the M2 .50 heavy machinegun, in the interwar period. Infantry hand grenades, machineguns, and mortars have generally consistent design from World War II. Rifle design has evolved, but the M4 and M7 are not necessarily more effective against enemy soldiers than the mid-twentieth-century M1-variant rifles. Vietnam War-era rockets and grenade launchers remain in the U.S. inventory in the mid 2020s and are in wide use by the Ukrainian Armed Forces.

There has been no obvious revolution in infantry affairs since World War II. A mid 2020s-era U.S. Army infantry unit is organized, trained, and equipped to fight in ways that are remarkably similar to Army infantry units from the middle through the end of the twentieth century. Given that drones and night-vision devices were designed in the 1930s and anti-tank missiles were designed in the 1940s, the mainstay items of gear found in advanced, mid 2020s-era foot-mobile infantry units were at least conceptualized, designed, and tested approximately eighty years earlier. The newest item listed in Table 8.1—the RQ-11 Raven drone—was fielded in the mid 2000s.

Looking broadly across the whole case set through the end of 2022, this general consistency in organization, tactics, and gear applies to every other infantry force observed in ground combat. Russian Ground Force (RGF) infantry and probably most other uniformed and nongovernmental infantry (e.g., Islamic State, National Movement for the Liberation of Awzad, M23) around the world are armed with a mix of old and modern versions of the 1940s-era AK-47, the 1950s-era RPG-7, and mortars designed in the mid twentieth century.

Globally, observed infantry tactics in these 423 cases of ground combat remained consistent with World War II-era tactics. Terrain, weapons limitations, fog of war, restrictions to visibility, enemy actions, and other recurring factors continue to force infantry commanders into the same general decision patterns applied by their predecessors. See the section on drones, below, and the section on the Ukraine War in chapter 9 for insights into the changes brought about by drone observation and targeting.

GROUND INDIRECT FIRE CHARACTERISTICS

Infantry mortars and/or at least small indirect-fire rockets were used in 100 percent of all 423 cases; indirect fire use was of course a case prerequisite. Beyond infantry weapons, some type of tube artillery—a term I use here to include cannons, guns, and howitzers, as well as some large mortars above 120mm—or indirect-fire rocket artillery was employed in 82 percent (346 out of 423) of all cases.[17]

Tube artillery was more frequently employed (74 percent of cases), while rocket artillery was less frequently employed (59 percent of all cases). Caliber of cannon artillery pieces ranged from old World War II-era 75mm howitzers used in places like Somalia and Libya, and 85mm field guns used in Pakistan, Uganda, and Azerbaijan, to the Russian 203mm 2S7 Pion employed by both sides in the Ukraine War. Probably the most commonly used tube system around the world was the 1960s-era Soviet-Russian 122mm 2A18 (D-30) howitzer, followed by the Russian 130mm and 152mm systems, then Western 155mm systems.[18]

Indirect-fire rockets ranged from improvised light rockets fired like mortars by nongovernmental groups like the Free Syrian Army and the pre-2021 Taliban, to the ubiquitous Russian 107mm Type 63 and BM-21 122mm multiple-launch systems, to the American 227mm M142 and Russian 220mm BM-27 Urugan, and so on. There seemed to be no technical barrier to the employment of indirect-fire rockets. I routinely reviewed video footage of young men in flip-flops aiming launchers with old lensatic compasses and letting rip with salvoes of 107mm or 122mm rockets at their adversaries. Figure 8.9 shows the frequency of ground indirect fire used across all cases.

In some cases, one or both sides employed surface-to-surface missiles like the Russian R-17 Elbrus (Scud-B) and 9K720 Iskander, or the American MGM-140 ATACMS. However, at least through late 2022 the use of these missiles in ground combat was poorly annotated in the public record and was seemingly infrequent. In all observed cases, missiles were employed along with other indirect fires and were typically used for interdiction strikes rather than to support active ground combat.

While observed missile use was infrequent, throughout this twenty-year observation period most military forces—including a significant

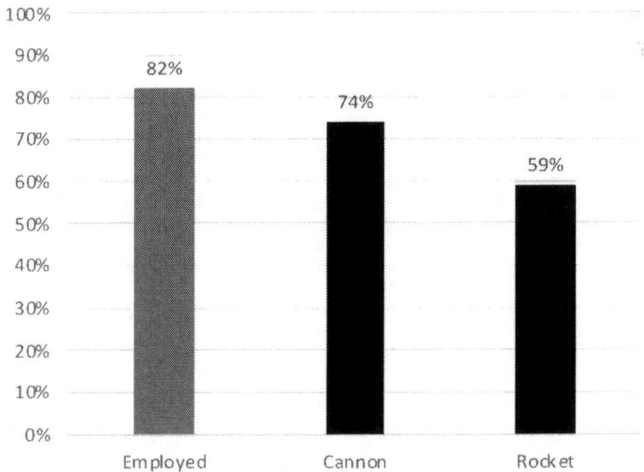

FIGURE 8.9. Ground Indirect-Fire Use Frequency Other than Infantry Mortars, 2003–2022

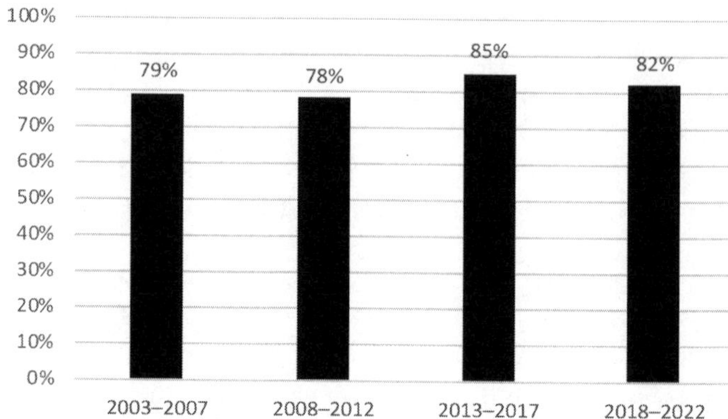

FIGURE 8.10. Ground Indirect-Fire Use Frequency over Time Other than Infantry Mortars

proportion of nongovernmental forces like al-Shabaab, Islamic State, LTTE, Ansar Allah, and so on—used some kind of tube-launched shell or rocket to soften up enemy defensive positions or fend off infantry and armor attacks. Figure 8.10 shows the consistent frequency of use of ground indirect fire over time.

Ground indirect fires destroyed both light armor and main battle tanks in a number of cases. Totaling these cases is difficult because causation is elusive even with clear video: Vehicles were destroyed by artillery, mines, missiles, rockets, machineguns, and other weaponry. Until the early 2020s, evidence was inadequate to draw reliable conclusions in most cases. Sometimes military units helpfully self-reported losses to artillery or offered up good ex post evidence of strikes against enemy armor (e.g., aerial surveillance footage). Video evidence from the Ukraine War made it possible to attribute causation with a fair degree of confidence in some cases. I attributed ground indirect fire kills to tanks in thirty-five cases from 2003 to 2022 and to light armor (including armed but unarmored trucks) in fifty cases. Actual incidents probably were more frequent across cases in which both ground fires and armor were present.

GROUND INDIRECT FIRE: OBSERVATIONS AND INSIGHTS

With few exceptions, the cannons, howitzers, and guns used by armies around the world were designed and fielded in the mid to late twentieth century. Some newer cannon artillery and rocket systems like the German Panzerhaubitze 2000,

American HIMARS, and the Russian 9A52–4 Tornado and S35–1 Koalitsiya-SV-KSh were fielded since 2000, but the old Soviet-Russian systems remain far more prolific and in regular use even through late 2022.[19] Some technological changes have significantly improved the accuracy and reliability of indirect fire since World War II, including GPS-assisted targeting, autoloading, and guided shells like the Western-manufactured Excalibur.[20]

However, the observation I made in chapter 5 about the consistency of function through 2002 also applies to the modern period: Modern ground indirect fire systems launch a shell or a rocket from one point on the ground to another, at which point they (typically) explode to kill and injure enemy soldiers, reduce enemy will to fight, and destroy enemy equipment. Gradually advancing technologies and improved designs continue to decrease time between rounds fired, increase range, increase accuracy, and in some cases increase lethality.

When good weather and lack of enemy countermeasures allowed, drone observation in some cases significantly improved the efficacy of tube and rocket fires. Spotting enemy positions was easier from the air and generally more effective and efficient from a loitering, high-definition camera than from a vulnerable balloon or fast-moving manned aircraft. However, drone spotting for ground indirect fires is not a new phenomenon.

Drones were used to help spot targets in the 1970s in the Yom Kippur War and the Vietnam War, and then more frequently in the 1980s in Lebanon, in Angola, and at least in the mid to late stages of the Iran-Iraq War. By the 1990s, drones were routinely used to help spot indirect fire targets in the Gulf War, in the Balkans, and in smaller engagements across the Middle East and sub-Saharan Africa. By the early 2000s, drones were commonplace across the skies in Iraq and Afghanistan and were considered essential and integral assets for Western indirect fire operations. In 2024 drones are ubiquitous but also remain vulnerable to countermeasures; see the section on drones, below.

This historical context suggests a continuing pattern of incremental improvement in ground indirect fires that generally extends a centuries-long trend from the first use of the Roman onager in the 4th century BCE. Despite all of these improvements and technical advances, unguided indirect fires still strike with circular errors of probability rather than absolute accuracy. Most artillery shells and rockets fired even in the 2022 Ukraine battles landed near, sometimes far, but not directly *on* the intended targets.[21] Even the approximately $100,000 USD guided Excalibur round—an early 1990s design intended to replace the 1970s-era laser-guided Copperhead guided round—has between an 88 and 92 percent success rate in testing and in combat, not perfect accuracy.[22]

All firing platforms, shells, and rockets are vulnerable to technical countermeasures including radar-guided counterbattery fire and interception by guns and lasers, and these countermeasures advance in parallel with improvements to the firing systems.[23] For example, reports from Ukraine through 2024 suggested that Russian counter-GPS jamming had sharply reduced the accuracy of Excalibur, HIMARS, and other Western precision ground-launched munitions, perhaps to the point of inefficacy.[24] One report suggests Russian jamming reduced Excalibur accuracy to just 10% in 2023, leading Ukrainian forces to rely on unguided rounds.[25]

Despite the proliferation of guided munitions, unguided indirect ground fires probably constitute at least a sizable plurality of all explosive fires on the modern battlefield.[26] There is a good possibility that they generate the majority of casualties and equipment destruction.[27] While no modern army has replicated the Soviet concentration of indirect fires at Seelow Heights in 1945—nearly 9,000 artillery and rocket systems launching about 1.2 million shells in a day—expenditure in Syria and Iraq in the 2010s alone would easily be counted in the high hundreds of thousands of rounds.[28] Shell expenditure by both sides combined in Ukraine in 2023 was measured in tens of thousands of rounds per day, and as of early 2023 the Ukrainian Ministry of Defense believed it needed over 350,000 artillery shells per month (apparently not including rockets) to sustain its general counteroffensive.[29]

In my subjective interpretation of the coded data, artillery remained in high demand and in frequent use across global battlefields due to its wide availability, relatively low cost compared to more complex systems, mechanical simplicity and reliability, tactical responsiveness at the lowest levels of command, and what is commonly referred to in Western military forces as *magazine depth.* This term describes the continuing availability of munitions over time.

An indirect-fire system that runs out of ammunition is not consistently reliable. Lack of indirect fire can slow the momentum of an offensive, leave defenders exposed to infantry assault, and undermine will to fight. For example, lack of sufficient artillery shells—particularly relatively cheap unguided rounds—reportedly contributed to the end of Ukraine's 2023 counteroffensive and rendered some of Ukraine's defensive positions tenuous through at least mid 2024.[30] Cheap unguided shells tend to be more readily available and therefore more responsive than more accurate and lethal precision-guided munitions. At least as of late 2022, precision munitions complemented but had not come close to replacing unguided ground-fired munitions in even the most advanced combat forces.

VEHICLE AND ARMOR CHARACTERISTICS

Ground vehicles were nearly ubiquitous with one or both sides employing at least armed-but-unarmored trucks (e.g., a technical pickup truck with an ad hoc, bed-mounted 23mm antiaircraft cannon) in 96 percent of all cases; I include these unarmored trucks in the diffuse category of "light armor" here. In all I coded for nine different types of armed vehicle including armored cars, wheeled scout vehicles, armored personnel carriers, and infantry fighting vehicles.

Stripping away the lightest vehicles, I coded heavy-hitting APCs like the BTR-82 and dedicated IFVs like the BMP-2 and M2 Bradley on one or both sides in 56 percent of all cases. Armed pickup trucks with machineguns and antiaircraft cannons probably were the most commonly used light vehicles on global battlefields, followed by a mix of Soviet-Russian BRDM-variant scout cars, BTR-variant troop carriers, and BMP-variant fighting vehicles.[31]

Ground combat units employed dedicated main battle tanks in approximately 69 percent of all cases (290 of 423). Soviet-Russian tanks by far made the most frequent appearances:[32] T-50-series tanks (T-54 and T-55) were present in 35 percent of all cases; T-60-series tanks (T-62 and T-64) were present in 34 percent of all cases; and T-72-series tanks were present in 30 percent of all cases. Several T-90 tanks were employed on Middle Eastern battlefields, and particularly in Syria, but T-80s did not make a significant well-recorded appearance until the 2022 phase of the Ukraine War.

American M1-series tanks fought in 9 percent of all cases, mostly in Iraq with American or Iraqi forces, while Leopard-variants appeared in four cases, all prior to the Leopard's employment in Ukraine. Israel continued to employ variants of its Merkava tank, Turkey rolled its updated American M60 tanks into Syria, Emirati forces at least presented (and may have employed) their new French AMX-56 tanks in Yemen, and one or more World War II-era Soviet T-34 tanks remained in service in the battles for Marees and al-Qa'atabah, Yemen, from 2019 to 2020. Figure 8.11 shows the frequency of all light armor including armed trucks, then tanks, and then heavy personnel carriers and dedicated IFVs across all cases from left to right.

While these results are not necessarily representative, and while the statistical significance of the change over time may be questionable, my coding showed about an 8 percent increase in tank employment and 7 percent increase in IFV employment from the first to last periods in the dataset. Armor-heavy operations in Syria, Iraq, and Ukraine accounted for the particularly frequent tank use in the 2013–2017 period. Tanks may or may not have played an increasingly important role in ground combat in the modern era, but they almost certainly were increasingly present. Figure 8.12 shows the coded change in light and heavy armor use over time.

Tank technology evolved but remained basically consistent from World War II onward. Like most of their mid-twentieth-century ancestors, modern tanks like the T-90, M1, and Chinese Type 99 have armored hulls mounted on two

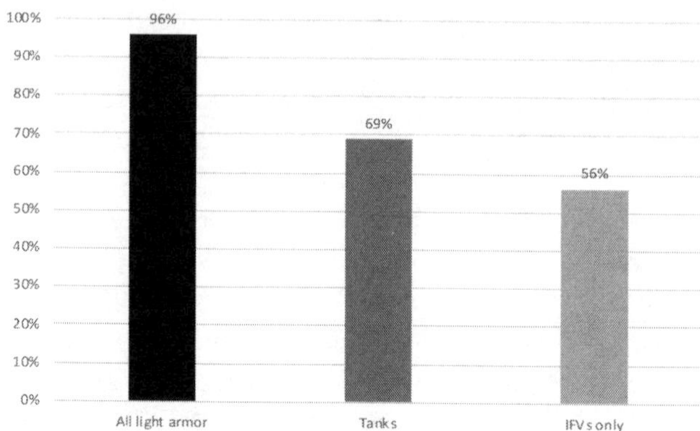

FIGURE 8.11. Light Armed and Armored Vehicles and Tank Frequency, 2003–2022

continuous wheel-and-track links with a rotating turret set into the top of the hull. All tanks mount a main gun that fires shells that are substantively identical to shells designed and employed in World War II, including high-velocity discarding sabot rounds and shaped-charge explosive warheads. Main guns can be accurately fired on the move using improved versions of World War II-era stabilization systems.[33]

Employing 1960s-era technology, some tanks can fire missiles from their main gun.[34] Tanks designed in the 1980s like the M1 usually have dense composite armor. As part of the continual, unending competition between advancing technology and countermeasure, many tanks have been fixed with external

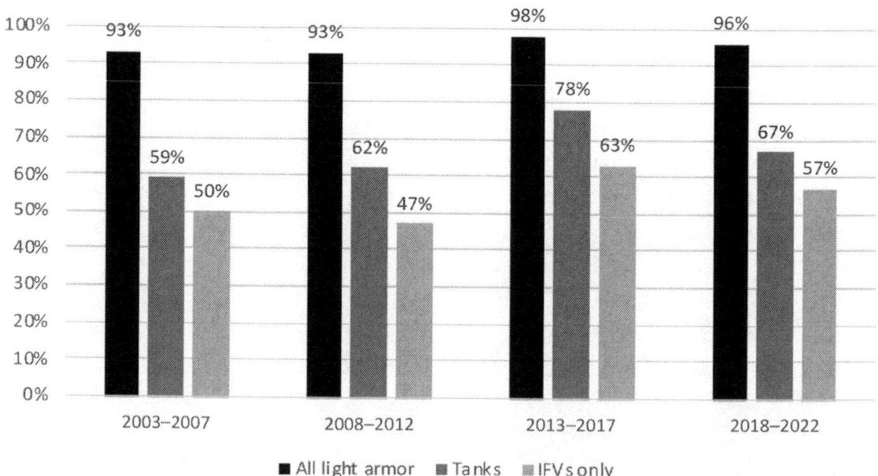

FIGURE 8.12. Light Armed and Armored Vehicles and Tank Frequency over Time

explosive-reactive armor like the Soviet-Russian Kontakt-5 to disrupt shaped-charge warheads.[35] Newer tank models sometimes are protected by active defense systems like Trophy, an Israeli technology that detects and blasts incoming missiles, rockets, and tank rounds with explosively formed projectiles. Israeli forces successfully employed Trophy in Gaza in 2014 and probably also in the 2023–2024 Gaza War.[36]

Vehicle and armor employment remained generally consistent from the interim (1945–2002) period into the modern period. Cheap, mass-produced, and globally available light trucks put motorized infantry movement into the hands of even the least technically capable and most poorly resourced military forces. The Soviet Union, then Russia, saturated the world's hotspots with inexpensive and generally reliable light armor and tanks, giving most of these low-tech, poorly resourced forces the ability to deploy infantry right up to defenders' trenches and to provide tank assault support. Western countries piled on with their own mass production. Possibly over 80,000 early 1960s-era American M113 armored personnel carriers were built, and tens of thousands were sent out to pro-Western ground combat forces. These cheap, aluminum-hulled, tracked boxes were commonly employed through 2024 in advanced Western militaries and frequently alongside Soviet-Russian vehicles on Middle Eastern battlefields.[37]

Terrain continued to restrict tank employment for all global forces regardless of relative sophistication: All military forces that employed tanks routinely drove them down hardball roads in column directly into enemy defenses. American military forces applied this ill-advised (but sometimes successful) tactic in the invasion of Iraq in 2003, the Syrians did it at al-Qaboun in 2013, and Russian military forces did the same thing in Ukraine in 2022.

In most of the observed cases in the modern period, tanks were employed solo, in pairs, or in platoons of three to four vehicles and rarely in large formations. Infantry-armor teaming continued to be a commonplace tactic and technique. Every observed ground force with armor used light vehicles to move troops to the point of contact and tanks to provide fire support, often side by side with infantry in street fights or along trench lines. Sometimes tanks also operated independently, usually in small numbers, and with what were at best mixed results.

ARMOR: OBSERVATIONS AND INSIGHTS

None of the tanks observed on modern battlefields from 2003 through the end of 2022 were invulnerable to anti-tank weapons. In most recorded cases in which tanks were used, some were rendered inoperable or suffered catastrophic kills from mines, rockets, missiles, artillery, airstrikes from manned aircraft, and drone strikes. In many cases, tanks simply became stuck in the mud, ran out of fuel, or suffered mechanical breakdowns. Many Russian and Ukrainian tanks had been lost on the battlefields of Ukraine through the end of my observation period. Oryx claimed to have documented approximately 2,130 tanks on both sides destroyed or seriously damaged from February 2022 through October 2023.[38]

This tank loss rate—2,130 over nearly twenty months of intensive ground combat—pales in comparison to the reported loss rate during the 1973 Yom Kippur War. A declassified CIA analysis lists approximately 2,000 Egyptian and Syrian tanks destroyed or significantly damaged, and possibly as many as 500 Israeli tanks also rendered inoperable, for a possible combined loss of 2,500 tanks over just two and a half weeks of ground combat. This equates to a loss rate of about 138 tanks per day.[39] In the air and ground phases of the 1991 Gulf War, the Iraqis and coalition combined lost approximately 3,100 tanks; and in the 44-day Nagorno-Karabakh War, both sides reportedly lost a combined 500 tanks destroyed or significantly damaged.[40]

In a rough comparison, the average daily tank loss rates in Ukraine is about thirty-four times lower than the loss rate in the 1973 war, nineteen times lower than the loss rate in the 1991 Gulf War, and three times lower than the 2020 war in Nagorno-Karabakh. See Table 8.2.

On the surface, this table suggests that daily tank losses in ongoing ground combat battles have plummeted through the modern era, not significantly increased as implied by some cited articles and official policy documents.

Table 8.2. Comparative Approximate Tank Losses across Four Historic Cases

War	Year	~Total Lost	Duration	~Lost/Day	~Daily Loss Multiples
Yom Kippur	1973	2,500	18 days	138	34x Ukraine War
Gulf	1991	3,100	42 days	74	19x Ukraine War
N-K	2020	500	44 days	11	3x Ukraine War
Ukraine	2022–23	2,130	583 days*	4	

Note: N-K = Nagorno-Karabakh. These numbers are estimates derived from multiple sources and not intended to reflect actual battlefield losses accurately or precisely. Some tanks identified in the source documents as damaged *may have been recovered and returned to combat. Actual reported, approximate loss rate per day in Nagorno-Karabakh is about 11.3 and Ukraine is about 3.65, both rounded off here. Actual tanks lost may significantly exceed or be significantly lower than reported figures in each case. Losses reflect tanks reported destroyed or significantly damaged, not abandoned and/or captured.*

**Indicates the Ukraine war is ongoing as of 2024; these estimated numbers only account for February 2022–October 2023.*

However, it does not therefore follow that tanks have become far more survivable than they were five decades earlier. Many idiosyncratic factors influenced all the results in Table 8.2 including the scale of the battles (size of forces directly engaged across varying lengths of front), operational tempo, overall number of tanks employed, relative use of airpower, terrain, will to fight, tactics, leadership, technology, training, drone observation impact on massing, and so on. In any event, no four cases are representative of all historical ground combat even in this fifty-year period.[41]

While no four cases are empirically representative, neither is any other handful of cases. Nor for that matter is any single battle or war. My point here is that the policy conclusions regarding the relative value of armor in warfare cited in chapter 1—and specifically those made by the U.S. Marine Corps citing the Nagorno-Karabakh War—are based on cherry-picked and nonrepresentative data. These deeply consequential conclusions look suspect in the face of even this cursory historical case comparison of tank losses. Tanks remain vulnerable to all types of anti-tank weapons, but we have no conclusive evidence that they are necessarily any more or less vulnerable or useful in ground combat than they were half a century ago, or even at the end of World War I. I return to the issue of armor in modern ground combat in chapter 9.

AIR AND ANTIAIR

One or both combatants employed manned aircraft in something approximating close-air support roles, or at least general ground support roles, in 82 percent of all cases. In 74 percent of all cases this meant jet aircraft of various types, ranging from old 1970s-era MiG-23s, Su-22s, and L-39s operating in the post-2011 Libya battles to advanced American fifth-generation fighter-bombers flying over Syria and Iraq. Rotary-wing aircraft (in the dataset this includes helicopters and vertical takeoff propeller aircraft like the V-22 Osprey) flew combat support missions in about 61 percent of all cases.[42]

Helicopter operations included British forces at al-Zubayr-al-Basra Iraq in 2003, French forces at Konna Mali in 2013, and Syrian pilots at Palmyra in 2016 all flying effectively the same Gazelle attack helicopters employed by the Syrians against the Israelis in 1982; Americans, Dutch, and Emiratis flying 1980s-era Apaches in Iraq, Afghanistan, and Yemen; and a wide array of forces employing 1970s-era Soviet-Russian Mi-24 attack helicopters and a variety of Mi-8 transport helicopters.[43]

For example, recall that Ukrainian pilots reportedly flew Mi-24s in support of Mozambican ground troops at Palma in 2021. I recorded some type of propeller-driven aircraft—American AC-130s, Philippine OV-10s, Afghan A-29s, and others—flying combat support missions in about 8 percent of all

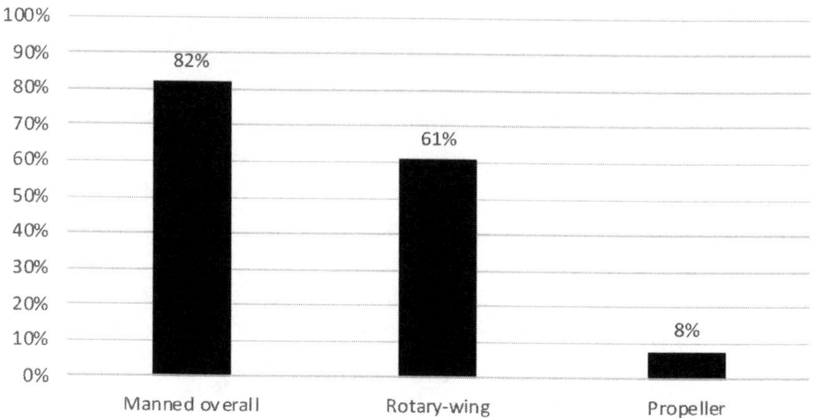

FIGURE 8.13. Manned Aircraft Frequency, 2003–2022

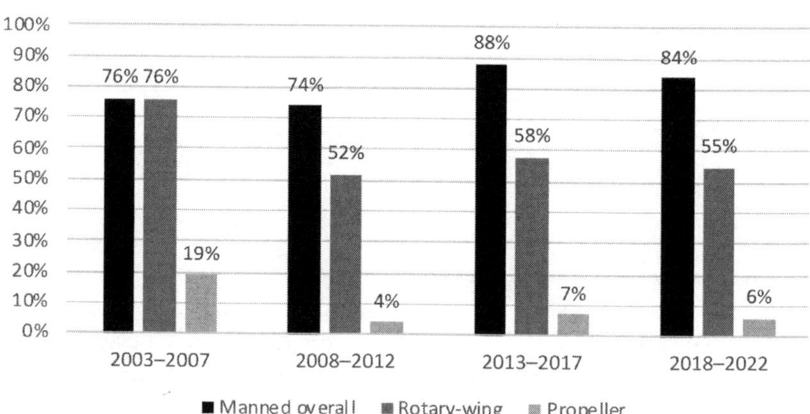

FIGURE 8.14. Manned Aircraft Frequency over Time

cases, though actual use probably was higher. Figure 8.13 depicts overall manned aircraft use across the 423 cases.

Manned air employment in ground support roles remained fairly consistent over the five-year periods within the modern era. High frequency of helicopter and propeller-driven aircraft employment in the 2003–2007 period reflected routine use of coalition AH-64s, UH-60 Blackhawks, CH-47 Chinooks, U.S. Marine Corps AH-1 Cobras, AC-130s, and a range of other attack and support aircraft in Iraq and Afghanistan. Figure 8.14 shows the recorded use of manned aircraft support in ground combat cases over time.

I coded some presence of antiair fires in nearly every case because I counted heavy machineguns as antiair weapons. For example, the M2 .50 machinegun and the DShK 12.7mm machinegun (roughly the same size round) are designed in part to be antiair weapons. I coded the use of man-portable air defense systems like the Russian 9K38 Igla or American FIM-92 Stinger in about 18 percent of all cases. However, because dedicated antiaircraft missiles—man portable and vehicle mounted—typically were kept behind the front lines, I have little confidence that I was able to record their presence with any consistency.

I was, however, able to spot the routine use of antiaircraft cannons ranging from 23mm through 57mm across global battlefields. Yemenis, Libyans, Iraqis, Nigerians, Ukrainians, and others used mostly Soviet-Russian antiaircraft cannons as flexible tools that could immediately shift between their antiair roles and ground fire roles. For example, probably thousands of old Soviet-Russian ZU-23-2s were mounted on pickup trucks, flatbeds, and on rooftop bunkers and used to pour a high volume of explosive shells directly into approaching aircraft and infantry or to support assaults. Antiaircraft cannons probably contributed a significant percentage of overall ground fires in most of the 423 cases.

AIR AND ANTIAIR: OBSERVATIONS AND INSIGHTS

Tying back to my chapter 3 comments on close-air support tactics and techniques in World War II, I observed across the 347 cases with clearly recorded manned airpower a generally loose approach to aerial ground combat support. Western military forces typically employed tightly coordinated strikes.[44] Well-trained controllers on the ground or in the air sometimes directed aerial fires onto targets within 100 meters of friendly forces. British, Canadian, Australian, Norwegian, American, and other Western commanders generally could count on responsive, accurate, and effective aerial fires that in many cases significantly amplified their combat power, allowing them to fight against larger infantry and armor units and, with notable exceptions, without real fear of being overpowered by ground fires. Non-Western ground forces typically had to rely on their organic fires.

Through late 2022, close-air support as it was applied by the U.S. Marine Corps in World War II was not available to most of the world's ground forces. Instead, I observed both fixed-wing and rotary-wing aircraft flying the same kind of loosely coordinated interdiction strikes the Soviets tended to fly with their Il-2 ground attack aircraft on the European battlefields in the early to mid 1940s.

There were some indications of tighter control by the Pakistanis and the Filipinos, who respectively called in F-16 jet and Cobra helicopter fires on TTP positions in the Swat Valley in 2009, and OV-10 propeller aircraft and MG-520 helicopter rocket fires against the Islamic State Maute Group at Marawi in 2017.

But across Syria, Libya, Myanmar, Ethiopia, Somalia, Nigeria, and the other battlefields in the dataset, control appeared to be loose at best.

While I could not directly observe control measures in most cases, many air forces appeared to operate semi-independently from ground forces. In some cases (e.g., Libya, Syria, Myanmar) air commands seemed to be working on their own interdiction agendas. I see no way to evenly apply the term *close-air support* across all of these cases of ground combat. Instead, aerial fires played varying roles, sometimes in close coordination and in many others with questionable control. Disparity in responsiveness, dependability, and relative accuracy could be generally assumed to give Western forces a significant advantage against non-Western forces with less integrated support.

Russia is an interesting case. With limited behind-the-curtain insight into ground-air coordination, I can only judge Russian techniques from external observation. In many hundreds of videos, articles, and other sources cited in the database, it appeared Russian aircraft flew a mix of preplanned interdiction strikes, roaming Il-2 type general support missions, and fewer of what Western forces would consider direct close-air support.[45] Across the 132 cases in which Russian forces either provided air support or engaged in direct combat, I saw no substantive evidence of a networked, fast-moving reconnaissance-strike complex.[46]

In Syria, Russian special operations forces sometimes called in airstrikes delivered with primarily unguided munitions; this is a World War II-era technique. A 2022 RAND investigation of the Russian air campaign in Syria brought recon-strike into question: "[Russia was reluctant] to invest in expensive precision-guided munitions [and had] underdeveloped targeting and penetrating ISR capabilities. . . . Most airstrikes [up to 95% estimated] used unguided munitions that were dropped on preplanned targets. Older Russian fixed-wing aircraft, such as those used in Syria, possess extremely limited capability to conduct precision strikes."[47]

Through late 2022 these same aircraft—mostly old 1970s-era Su-24s, Su-25s, some 1990s-era Su-34 jets and Ka-52 attack helicopters—also appeared to have flown most of the combat sorties in Ukraine. Jets frequently swooped in to drop what looked like iron bombs while the attack helicopters lofted unguided rockets from a distance or flew something closer to direct-support missions over the heads of Russian assault forces. In these rotary-wing missions, pilots and weapons operators appeared to use direct visual (eyeball, electro-optical, thermal-infrared) identification to spot their own targets. Loss rates appear to be fairly high, though it is not true that, as one pundit suggests, "all of Ukraine's airspace has been close to a no-go zone."[48]

Russia probably has continuously flown combat air support sorties over Ukrainian territory since early 2022, albeit at small scale, and with apparently scattershot planning and questionable results. Evidence of improved Russian airstrike effectiveness emerged in early 2024 with the aggressive use of heavy Soviet-era glide bombs.

DRONE CHARACTERISTICS

I was able to record some type of drone use, from infantry-level commercial quad copters to strategic-level aircraft like the American RQ-4 Global Hawk, in 53 percent of the 423 coded cases. However, drones are more survivable and often more effective when they are unseen, so by intent they are not always flown in view of ground troops or reporters on battlefields.

Therefore, overall drone use from 2003 to 2022 probably was higher—and perhaps was much higher—than coded. I also observed what I believed to be armed drone use in about 24 percent of all cases, and a few cases in which drones were used to drop grenades or fly munitions directly into ground targets. I confidently recorded only one drone swarm attack flown in direct support of ground units (Islamic State, Mosul, Iraq, 2016). Other swarm attacks probably occurred.[49] Figure 8.15 shows these counts.

Recorded overall drone use in these cases (inclusive of infantry drone use) increased over time, from 41 percent in the 2003–2007 period to 64 percent in the last period through the end of 2022. However, based on my subjective interpretation of the available evidence across this twenty-year period, I believe recorded incidents of drone use became increasingly observable over time at least in great part because videos and still photographs of drone use were posted with increasing frequency to YouTube, Reddit, and various social media sites.

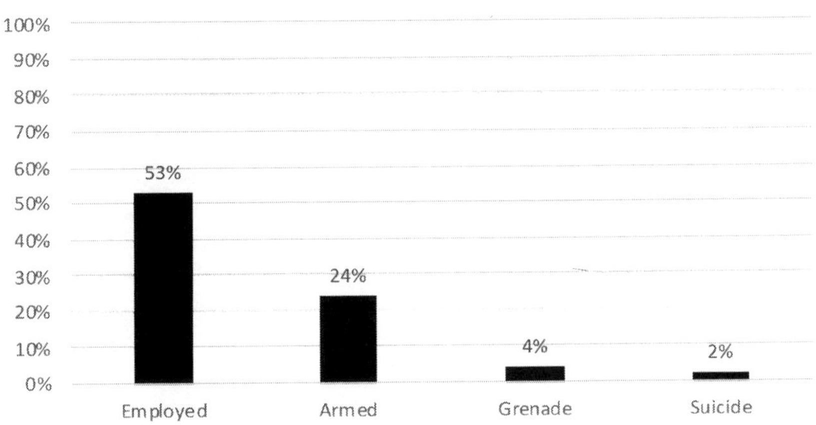

FIGURE 8.15. Drone Use Overall, 2003–2022

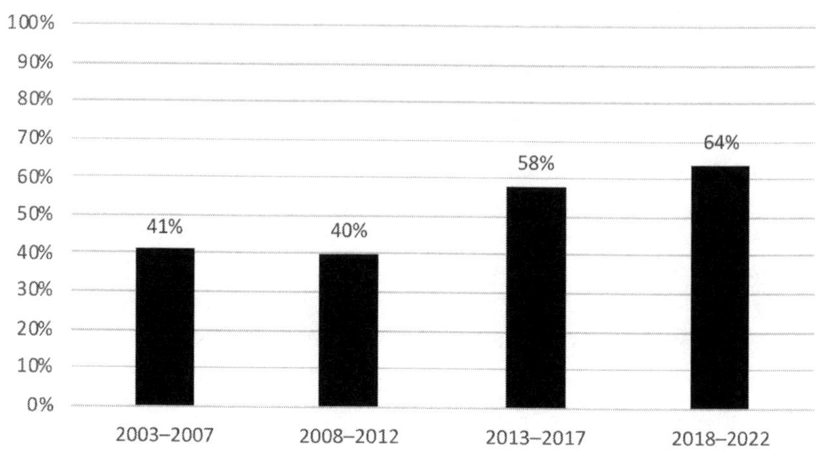

FIGURE 8.16. Drone Use over Time

YouTube did not exist from 2003 through early 2005, and it did not become a common repository for combat videos until probably about ten years later (~2015).[50] Video recording devices like mobile phone cameras that now proliferate across the world's battlefields were rare in the early to late 2000s. Since evidence of drone use is commonly recorded on video, I am not confident this change in drone use over time is accurate. See Figure 8.16.[51]

Other cited sources do show that drone *proliferation* did, however, clearly increase over time, with commercial off-the-shelf drones putting cheap, responsive, high-definition aerial surveillance in the hands of just about every ground combat force around the world. From 2001 through 2003, drones were used mostly by well-organized military forces.

For example, American forces flew Pointer, Pioneer, Global Hawk, Hunter, Shadow, and armed Predator drones in Iraq and Afghanistan.[52] By the end of the first five-year period in 2007, drones were in routine use by the Pakistani Air Force, both sides in the Sri Lankan civil war, and probably all mid-minor powers around the world. Low-level groups like the Taliban and Iraqi insurgents still did not have regular access to drones in the mid to late 2000s. This changed by the mid 2010s as commercial drones became more widely available. By the late 2010s, as forecast by T. X. Hammes and others, barriers to small drone use had effectively disappeared.[53]

Drone technology also improved throughout the twenty-year modern period.[54] The autonomy, processing speed, munitions capacity, imagery capture technology, and other technical facets of the most advanced military drones improved steadily but—arguably—not dramatically from early 2003. For example, the MQ-9 Reaper drone commonly employed by the United States is basically a larger, more effective version of the twentieth-century MQ-1 Predator, a copy of which has been displayed as a historical artifact in the Smithsonian National Air and Space Museum in Washington, DC.

Counter-drone technology appeared to lag far behind drone development and proliferation. There were few dedicated counter-drone programs or technologies even in experimental design in the early 2010s.[55] Revelatory though wholly ahistorical shock in reaction to reports of Islamic State drone use in Syria and Iraq, and by Russia in Ukraine, generated interest and funding for both dedicated military and commercial counter-drone technologies. Lasers, guns, radars, jammers, spoofers, high-powered microwaves, shotguns, drone-killing drones, net guns, and cyber systems were developed to blast, burn, confuse, ram, crash, capture, or control enemy drones.[56]

DRONES: OBSERVATIONS AND INSIGHTS

Based on a review of thousands of primary- and secondary-source videos and written reports across 423 cases, I gained little confidence in the ability to track even a preponderance of incidents of dedicated military drones flying observation and strike sorties, infantry unit drones flying local recon, commercial drones tracing enemy positions for an assault, suicide drones flying shaped-charge warheads into tanks, and so on. In a great many of the cases in which I coded for drones, I did so having glimpsed a drone in a random mobile phone video, unearthed a photograph of a downed drone buried in an obscure tweet, or referenced a government report that may or may not accurately reflect reality.

As a retired intelligence officer, I can state with some confidence that it is unlikely any intelligence agency in the world has a clear and comprehensive, or even broadly representative, accounting of drone use by adversary, allied, or partner forces. It is doubtful that even the highly bureaucratic U.S. military has an accurate tabulation of its own drone use in ground combat support roles. Videos by combatants like the Russian Ground Force, Syrian Arab Army, Islamic State, and Myanmar Tatmadaw posted online are carefully edited and are highly selective. Combatants almost always post drone footage that is favorable to their messaging and very rarely post footage of failed strikes or defeated friendly ground forces. Yet thousands—probably more like many hundreds of thousands—of hours of unfavorable footage certainly have been recorded and then either hidden or discarded.

In other words, we do not really know all of the ways, or just how frequently, drones have been used around the world, and therefore we cannot effectively understand their overall impact on ground combat as a global phenomenon. Any declarative statements about drone use or the relative value of drones in modern ground combat should be tempered by the limits of the data. Instead of confident declaration I offer my necessarily imperfect summation of drone use in global ground combat from the evidence reviewed:

Significant increase in overall use. There has almost certainly been a sharp increase in overall drone use since the beginning of 2003. It is highly likely that some type of drone was used by both sides in most, and perhaps nearly all, battles fought in 2022. Western military drone use accelerated in the early 2000s and then increased more gradually through 2022.

Often dominant view. In many cases, drones gave combatants a dominant, top-down or high-angle view of the battlefield. For example, a 2016 Tatmadaw ground assault on the Kachin Independence Army's 252nd Infantry Brigade mountaintop trenches and bunkers was filmed overhead and at close range by a light commercial drone.[57]

Rapid and effective targeting. Western military forces, and to a lesser extent Russia and the mid-minor powers (Nigeria, Philippines, Pakistan, and others), have proven able to rapidly transmit target locations from drone feeds to mortar, artillery, and rocket units. Ukrainian forces have demonstrated a particular talent for this kind of targeting.

Airspace penetration. At least while counter-drone technologies were coming online through the early 2020s, drone operators had almost free rein to position their aircraft over enemy positions, drop grenades on unsuspecting enemy troops, and attack with suicide drones. Broad freedom of movement has since decreased, perhaps sharply.

Increasing relative losses. As counter-drone technologies have started to catch up with proliferating drone use, it appears drones are being eliminated at higher rates relative to their frequency of overall use. One 2023 estimate put Ukrainian drone losses at 10,000 per month.[58] Counter-swarm technologies are being successfully tested and fielded. In mid 2024 the chief of staff of the French Army, General Pierre Schill, stated that 75 percent of drones employed in Ukraine by either side were lost.[59] Schill believed the drone advantage in Ukraine was "a moment in history" that might end in just a few years. He specifically noted that the Bayraktar TB-2, which he described as being "the king of war" in early 2022, was out of use due to countermeasures.

Unclear generalizable impact on ground combat. This study did not seek to attribute causation to success or failure in ground combat, so I cannot make any collective judgment about the general causal impact of drones. However, I observed uneven, frequently overstated, and ultimately inconclusive impacts on specific ground combat battles. I did not see clear evidence supporting a generalizable argument regarding the relative value of drones in ground combat.

Negligible ground drone use. Carrying forward a post-World War II trend I reported in chapter 5, ground drone development remained an afterthought through the modern period.[60] A number of combat ground drones were developed and deployed in at least Iraq and Afghanistan, but I recorded no clear evidence of ground drone combat uses, only use for noncombat tasks. It appeared that both sides were making increased use of ground drones in Ukraine in 2023, several months after the end of my period of research observation. See chapter 9 for more on the modern and future employment of drones.

These last sections briefly describe catchall, but possibly important, observations that did not fit neatly into the categories above.

NULL RETURNS ON HARD-TO-OBSERVE TECHNOLOGY

In the evidence I reviewed, use of electronic warfare, satellites, cyber attacks, stealth technology, and artificial intelligence *in direct support of ground combat* appeared to be negligible. By design, electronic warfare, cyber, and stealth technologies are intended to be used without observation. Electronic warfare was routinely used and in some cases described in interviews, but I cannot effectively describe its use based on publicly available evidence. Stealth aircraft were employed by some Western forces in a few cases, but not clearly for direct ground combat support. Artificial intelligence may have been used in many ways, but if so it did not have any observable trace or impact on combat in the cited sources.

INFORMATION OPERATIONS APPEARED TO BE HISTORICALLY CONSISTENT IN FUNCTION AND FORM

A good number of military forces employed some kind of psychological or information operation in support of their ground operations. Leaflets were dropped by aircraft and launched in artillery shells, loudspeakers blared out messages to soldiers and civilians, and propaganda material was disseminated online in often hotly contested battles for human will and nonmaterial support. Reporters often were present on battlefields, and in many cases they clearly were working with (and arguably for) one side. At ground level, these actions seemed fairly consistent from World War II: leaflets, loudspeakers, and friendly reporters. While I did not seek to identify causation between messaging and ground combat outcomes, I believe it would be quite hard if not impossible to do so with defensible accuracy.[61]

EQUIPMENT AND TECHNOLOGY FREQUENTLY CHANGED HANDS IN COMBAT

Military forces with little or no armor, few heavy weapons, and limited advanced technology at the outset of a ground battle were often able to shift the balance of power by capturing enemy equipment. Lightly armed Islamic State forces captured entire brigade-level mechanized infantry and armor stocks in Syria and Iraq in the early to mid 2010s, transforming them from a technical pickup truck army into a mechanized force with organic heavy artillery, T-72 and M1 Abrams tanks, anti-tank and antiair missiles, and so on.[62] Initial Tigrayan (TPLF) counteroffensive operations around Tembien in 2021 started mostly with old 1930s-era heavy machineguns and well-worn AK-variant rifles unearthed from emergency stores but ended with the capture of BMP-2s, artillery batteries, mortars, and missiles seized from parts of four Ethiopian divisions.[63] This recurring dynamic has implications for forecasting ground force military capabilities.

CIVILIANS WERE COMMONLY PRESENT IN GROUND COMBAT

Civilians were recorded present in two-thirds (281 cases, or 66 percent) of all cases in the dataset. In most of these cases, noncombatant civilians were caught up in the fighting, and in many they were killed or displaced by a mix of direct and indirect fires. Civilian presence complicated ground fights, mostly for military forces intent on minimizing civilian casualties. In many cases, civilians were simply steamrolled by advancing ground troops. They often were purposefully abused, and in some cases (e.g., Fallujah Iraq 2004, Zamboanga City Philippines 2013) civilians probably were used as human shields.[64] I recorded no clearly observable shifts in civilian presence on the battlefield over time from 2003 through 2022. While I cannot empirically extend my findings to the period before 2003, my review of the World War II and Interim Period cases suggests no clear, substantive change in the frequency of noncombatant presence in land war.

ENTRENCHMENT AND MINES WERE COMMONLY EMPLOYED

One or both combatants dug trenches, built earthworks like berms or street barricades, or prepared bunkers with overhead cover and firing ports in about 70 percent of all cases. Use of general combat engineering preparations did not shift considerably over time; this was a fairly constant practice. Coalition forces across Iraq and Afghanistan used HESCO barriers to fortify their operations bases, both Sri Lankan Army and Tamil Tiger ground units dug trench and bunker networks across the Muhamalai defensive line, Sudanese forces dug in at Heglig-Pandthau, and both sides in the Ukraine War have been digging in and fighting from trenches and bunkers since 2014. It was harder to accurately account for mine use other than improvised explosive devices (IEDs, 138 cases, 33 percent overall). Land mines often played an important role in slowing or stalling attacks in many cases including recently in Ukraine.[65]

OLD AND NEW WEAPONS WERE ALMOST ALWAYS EMPLOYED IN PARALLEL

In a few cases in Somalia, Yemen, and elsewhere, ground forces employed only older, mid-twentieth-century weapons and equipment. But in all observed cases in which more modern weapons and equipment were used, older gear was used in parallel. Canadian troops fighting in Panjwaii, Afghanistan, in 2006 fought with 1960s-era mortars, 1990s-era rifles, and LAV III vehicles while receiving air support from 2000s-era drones. Islamic State troops fighting in Syria and Iraq employed 1950s-era T-55 tanks alongside 1970s-era T-72s while employing 1990s- and 2000s-era U.S. equipment. The same trend identified in infantry equipment, above, applied across the board with armor, aircraft, indirect fire support, and even many drone systems. There were no observed cases in which a ground force had entirely, or probably even mostly, modernized its force with equipment fielded after the turn of the millennium.

CATCHALL: NAVAL FIRES, CHEMICAL ATTACKS, SUICIDE VEHICLES, TOTAL LOSS, FRIENDLY FIRE

Naval fires were recorded in about 6 percent (twenty-four total) of cases. This included NATO ship-fired missile support to ground forces along the Libyan coastline, Egyptian naval gunfire support to counter-Houthi fighters in A'aden in 2015, and Ukrainian gunboats providing riverine fires in support of the Kherson counteroffensive in 2022. Chemical attacks were made in support of ground combat operations in at least six cases, but most of these are disputed. I recorded no biological, radiological, or, thankfully, nuclear attacks in any ground combat case. Suicide-vehicle-borne improvised explosive devices (SVBIEDs) were used in about 18 percent of all cases, with most of these occurring in Syria and Iraq. I coded fifty-one cases (12 percent of total) in which one side appeared to suffer a total loss: disintegration, destruction, or capture. While I did not code for friendly fire incidents, they generally appeared to be commonplace, fairly consistent in frequency over time, and were committed by all force types, low to major.

FINAL CHARACTERISTIC: STEADY FUNCTION, EVOLUTIONARY FORM

Across the board, military tactics, weapons, equipment, and behaviors retained consistent function from 2003 through the end of 2022. Infantry forces were employed by both sides in 100 percent of the 423 coded cases. Combatants employed infantry indirect-fire weapons in 100 percent of all cases, and some kind of heavier artillery or indirect-fire rockets in 82 percent of the cases; armed or armored vehicles in 96 percent of these cases, with main battle tanks employed 69 percent of the time; and manned aircraft in 82 percent of the coded cases. Drones frequently were employed throughout this twenty-year period, though probably far more frequently by lesser powers through late 2022. Even as drone use increased, though, the other observed characteristics effectively remained constant across the large-*n* case set. Table 8.3 lists consistencies of major ground combat weapons and systems characteristics across the entire twenty-year period of modern ground combat.

While I cannot definitively characterize tactics applied by both sides in each of the modern ground combat cases, tactical applications of these consistently appearing capabilities are broadly observable even in the most modern cases through the end of 2022.

Table 8.3. Recurrence of Characteristics in Modern Cases over Time, 2003–2022

Characteristic	Consistency
Infantry employment by both combatants	100%
Indirect fire use by both combatants (at least infantry mortars, small rockets)	100%
Heavy indirect fire use by one or both combatants	82%
Armed and/or armored vehicle use by one or both combatants	96%
Manned aircraft use by one or both combatants	82%
Main battle tank use by one or both combatants	69%
Drone use by one or both combatants	53%*

Note: Both infantry and indirect fire use were prerequisite case characteristics, though all cases coded and not coded included reported infantry use by both sides.
**Drones are the only characteristic system that appeared in the cited evidence (see the database) in significantly greater frequency across the five-year case periods, beginning at 41 percent and rising unevenly to 64 percent. All other characteristics remained 100 percent consistent or varied in ways that either were not particularly significant or that were easily explained by conflicts generating idiosyncratically large case volume (e.g., Iraq, Syria, Ukraine).*

In large battles like the one around Chernihiv, Ukraine, in 2022, commanders maneuvered infantry troops on foot, in wheeled or tracked vehicles, or on board helicopters into attack positions. Some supporting units flew manned aircraft and drones overhead to trace enemy lines and mark targets, while others fired mortars, tube artillery, and rockets. Sometimes they dropped bombs, fired aerial cannons, and launched missiles to soften up the defenses. Infantry and sometimes armor then rolled forward to attack, take, and hold ground.

On the other side of the attack, defensive units dug trenches, piled up earth and debris, laid mines, and holed up in buildings while emplacing interlocking machinegun fires and setting kill zones with combined arms. Opposing infantry fired at each other with rifles, light machineguns, and explosive rockets, and as they closed range they threw grenades and sometimes stabbed each other with bayonets and knives.

In some cases two units clashed in an unexpected meeting engagement, one unit ambushed another, and sometimes two sides just fired at each other in a skirmish without exchanging ground. This description is consistent from the World War II cases in chapter 2 through all the interim cases in chapter 4 and to the end of 2022.

Both form and the frequency of use of weapons and equipment also remained fairly steady. Keeping in mind the evolutionary development of guided weapons from the early twentieth century, global precision-guided munition use appeared generally consistent from 2003 onward. By 2003, most Western forces had already fully integrated precision munitions into their arsenals and routinely used them in even the earliest days of the Iraq and Afghanistan wars. I observed in the recorded evidence I reviewed no significant increase in PGM use (either overall or relative to unguided weapons use) within Western forces over this twenty-year period, and no significant increase in use by Russia or any mid-minor power.

Observed Russian PGM employment in combat was lower than anticipated in the literature on the recon-strike complex I cited in chapter 1. Precision munitions did not widely proliferate to mid-low powers by the end of 2022. Drones were in routine use by Western forces throughout the 1990s in the Balkans, and then consistently in Iraq and Afghanistan and elsewhere, from the early 2000s onward, so the drone proliferation I observed in the mid to late 2010s reflected a catch-up by low-end forces rather than any kind of uniform leap. Whether or not increased drone proliferation in the past ten years constitutes a revolution in ground combat is a subject of discussion in chapter 9.

This chapter has primarily reported observed characteristics of ground combat in the modern era. I have done my best here to isolate more subjective judgements from plain observation of recorded evidence. In the last chapter I present my general conclusions and tie back to the issues I raised in previous chapters regarding the character and nature of modern ground combat, land warfare, and the forecasting of war writ large.

NOTES

1. See the appendix, "Methodology."
2. Regional breakdowns are subjective codes.
3. This does not constitute a forecast.
4. Therefore, I did not include military sales, financial aid, equipment donation, or even more active but indirect support like intelligence gathering and collaboration or advising outside of combat.
5. Nearly all the cases involving a major power fighting a mid-minor power (forty-eight total, or 11 percent) took place either in Iraq in 2003 or in Ukraine from 2014 onward.
6. Carl von Clausewitz, *On War* [*Vom Kriege*], trans. Michael Howard and Peter Paret (Princeton, NJ: Princeton University Press, 1984), 109.
7. See Alejandro L. Corbacho, *Reassessing the Fighting Performance of Conscript Soldiers during the Malivas/Falklands War (1982)(*)* (Buenos Aires: Universidad del CEMA, 2004); and David Aldea, "Mount Longdon: The Argentinian Story," February 20, 2012, https://web.archive.org.
8. Anti-tank rockets were commonly used for anti-personnel attacks, and several systems including the RPG-7 series have dedicated anti-personnel explosive rockets that can be loaded interchangeably into the launcher.
9. See Heather Mongilio and Sam LaGrone, "UPDATED: Russian Navy Launches Amphibious Assault on Ukraine; Naval Infantry 30 Miles West of Mariupol," *U.S. Naval Institute News*, February 25, 2022; and B. J. Armstrong, "The Russo-Ukrainian War at Sea: Retrospect and Prospect," *War on the Rocks*, April 21, 2022. This appears to have been a reconnaissance-in-force preceding a planned but then aborted large-scale amphibious assault.
10. This is a highly subjective finding given the difficulty associated with defining and observing a massed frontal assault.
11. Armed ground combat drones, often referred to as ground robots or unmanned ground systems, were employed in combat in both Iraq and Afghanistan, and probably in Gaza and the West Bank. See, for example, Noah Shachtman, "First Armed Robots on Patrol in Iraq (Updated)," *Wired*, August 2, 200, https://www.wired.com; Peter W. Singer, "Military Robots and the Laws of War," Brookings Institution, February 11, 2009; "The Inside Story of the SWORDS Armed Robot 'Pullout' in Iraq: Update," *Popular Mechanics*, September 30, 2009.
12. At least thirty-one of the cases reviewed but not coded lacked sufficient evidence of combined arms use by both sides (other cases evinced combined arms use but lacked sufficient evidence for coding altogether).
13. U.S. War Department, *Infantry Battalion*, field manual, FM 7–20 (Washington, DC: U.S. Government Printing Office, October 1, 1944).
14. U.S. Army, *Infantry Battalion*, technical publication, ATP 3–21.20 (Washington, DC: Headquarters, Department of the Army, December 2017). A new plan entitled *Army 2030* reorganizes the Army towards a more World War II-style structure centered on divisions rather than brigades. Infantry formations play a central role

in this proposed redesign. See Kevin Hadley, Savannah Spencer, and Justin Martens, *How the Army 2030 Divisions Fight*, white paper, version 3.5 (Fort Leavenworth, KA: U.S. Army Training and Doctrine Command, February 2, 2023).

15. The M47 Dragon was a direct replacement for the Army's World War II-era 90mm anti-tank gun. See Matt Fitzsimmons, "The M47 Dragon Antitank Guided Missile System," *On Point* 24, no. 1 (Summer 2018), 14–17; U.S. Department of Defense, *Acquisition of the Advanced Antitank Weapon System-Medium*, official audit, Report 92–023 (Washington, DC: Office of the Inspector General, December 17, 1991); U.S. Army, *Javelin—Close Combat Missile System, Medium*, technical manual, TC 3–22.37 (Washington, DC: Headquarters, Department of the Army, August 2013).
16. I have not included flamethrowers since their use generally was discontinued in the twentieth century.
17. I used this 120mm delimiter to differentiate between an infantry mortar and a mortar used in general or direct support by a larger unit like a brigade. There is inherent subjectivity in these judgments.
18. While I coded for tube caliber, I am not sufficiently confident in the reliability and consistency of sources, nor in my ability to differentiate various types of cannons, guns, and howitzers from often fleeting images or video clips, to report percentages of system appearance here.
19. For more on non-U.S. global artillery systems, see the U.S. Army's ODIN website referenced above. For U.S. systems, see updated summaries on the U.S. Army and U.S. Marine Corps official websites as well as Michael Green, *American Artillery from 1775 to the Present Day* (South Yorkshire, UK: Pen & Sword Military, 2021).
20. For more on the Excalibur round, see U.S. Department of Defense, *Excalibur Precision 155mm Projectiles (Excalibur)*, selected acquisition report (Picatinny Arsenal, NJ: Defense Acquisition Management Information Retrieval, March 21, 2016); Audra Calloway, "Picatinny's GPS-Guided Excalibur Artillery Round Deemed 'Amazingly Accurate' by Troop," press release (U.S. Army, September 11, 2008).
21. This is a subjective observation based on a review of hundreds of hours of Ukraine War combat video footage, some of which is cited in this book and in the database.
22. U.S. Department of Defense, *Excalibur Precision 155mm Projectiles*; and Calloway, "Picatinny's GPS." Copperhead was employed in combat in the 1991 Gulf War and reportedly remains in the U.S. inventory. "Copperhead and LRLAP: Smart Investments," promotional article (Lockheed-Martin, October 1, 2020); Jakub Palowski, "Copperhead vs. ISIS," *Defence 24*, November 29, 2021; Michael Peck, "New Precision-Guided Shells Are Giving Ukraine an Edge over Russia in Their Grinding Artillery Battle," *Business Insider*, October 3, 2022. See this declassified CIA report for more on the 1970s and 1980s-era assessments of Soviet guided munition technology: U.S. Central Intelligence Agency, *Soviet Artillery Precision-Guided Munitions: A Conventional Weapons Initiative*, declassified intelligence report (Langley, VA: Directorate of Intelligence, September 1986).
23. For example, the U.S. military reportedly has fielded in combat a Raytheon Corporation laser system that has successfully shot down incoming mortar rounds and drones. See Jen Judson, "Army Readies to Deliver First Set of Strykers with 50-Kilowatt Laser Weapons," *Defense News*, January 13, 2022; Devon L. Suits, "Army to Field Laser-Equipped Stryker Prototypes in FY 2022," *U.S. Army News Service*, August 24, 2021. The Raytheon claim of operational use and videos of

the system and testing can be found here: "Can Laser Weapons Stop Iran's Drone Attacks?," *Task & Purpose*, June 30, 2023, YouTube video.

24. For example: Joe Barnes, "Russia's Electronic Warfare Tactics Are Helping It Turn the Tide against Ukraine," *The Telegraph* (December 27, 2023); Isabelle Khurshudyan and Alex Horton, "Russian Jamming Leaves Some High-Tech U.S. Weapons Ineffective in Ukraine," *Washington Post* (May 24, 2024); Carlotta Gall and Vladyslav Golovin, "Some U.S. Weapons Stymied by Russian Jamming in Ukraine," *New York Times* (May 24, 2024).
25. Khurshudyan and Horton, "Russian Jamming."
26. If one includes explosive-shell antiaircraft artillery fire used against ground targets in this consideration, then the ratio shifts. See the section "Air and Antiair," below.
27. This is a subjective judgment based on the cited evidence in the dataset.
28. Just one relatively small U.S. Marine Corps unit in Syria fired over 35,000 artillery shells in five months in one sector of the battlefield. Shawn Snow, "These Marines in Syria Fired More Artillery than Any Battalion since Vietnam," *Marine Corps Times*, February 6, 2018. Together, Syrian Arab Army, Free Syrian Army, Islamic State, Turkish, Iranian, Russian, and other armed groups certainly fired many more rounds collectively over the course of approximately seven to ten years.
29. "FT: Ukraine Appeals to EU to Provide 250,000 Artillery Shells per Month," *Kyiv Independent*, March 4, 2023, https://kyivindependent.
30. Olena Harmash and Tom Balmforth, "Ukrainian Troops Face Artillery Shortages, Scale Back Some Operations—Commander," *Reuters*, December 18, 2023; Marc Santora, "'They Come in Waves': Ukraine Goes on Defense against a Relentless Foe," *New York Times*, February 4, 2024; and others.
31. This is a subjective judgment based on the cited evidence in the dataset.
32. There is a high likelihood that I incorrectly identified tank variants in a number of the coded cases, particularly those coded at the beginning of the research period. My rusty tank recognition skills improved over time.
33. See U.S. Army, *Gun Stabilization Systems (Vehicular)* (Aberdeen Proving Ground, MD: U.S. Army Test and Evaluation Command, 1983); Gold V. Sanders, "Why Our Tanks Can Score Hits on the Run," *Popular Science* 145, no. 3 (1944), 82–85.
34. This technology dates back to at least the mid 1960s with the MGM-51 Shillelagh ATGM designed to be fired from the main gun of the MBT-70, M551 Sheridan light tank, and the mostly experimental M60A2 tank. Several Soviet and Russian vehicles can fire missiles through their main guns, including the BMP-1 and T-72. For example, the T-72B can fire the 9M119 Svir (AT-11) from its main gun. See the U.S. Army's ODIN website for more on this round and the T-72B.
35. See John D. Pinder, *Reactive Armor Tiles for Army and Marine Corps Armored Vehicles: An Independent Report to the Department of Defense and the United States Congress* (Santa Monica, CA: RAND Corporation, 1999); "Reactive Armor of Armored Vehicles: Experience in Use in the Russian-Ukraine War," Ukraine Ministry of Defense, July 6, 2023; and others.
36. This video shows a Trophy system destroying an incoming rocket or missile: "Israeli Merkava MK4 MBTs Rafael Trophy Active Protection System Successfully Deploys to Protect the Tank and Its Crew. Gaza Strip, July 2014" [sic], archival combat video, July 2014, Reddit video.
37. As of early 2023, it appeared that M113s remained in service with the U.S. Army and possibly other U.S. military services. It is scheduled to be replaced by the

Armored Multi-Purpose Vehicle (AMPV). See "The Army's Armored Multi-Purpose Vehicle (AMPV)," *Congressional Research Service*, January 25, 2021.

38. Oryx publishes its results online (https://www.oryxspioenkop.com).
39. Transue, *Assessment of Weapons*, 5, 41–49. Arab tank losses are published with dates redacted, while Israeli losses were entirely redacted. However, on page 41 Transue reports that Israeli losses probably were about 2.5 times fewer than Arab losses. I subjectively reduced the possible 800 Israeli tank losses (800 × 2.5 = 2,000) to 500 to reflect a range of estimates from other sources and to acknowledge the lack of access to Transue's original, redacted data. Other sources cite Gawrych, 1996, who in turn cites secondary sources and does not refer to Transue's intelligence analysis. All of these data are estimates.
40. An official U.S. Army source suggests a total of 3,300 Iraqi tanks were destroyed or significantly damaged. This number is impossible to verify, and the author cites two secondary sources. I slightly reduced this to 3,100 (with negligible U.S. losses to enemy fire) to put it more in line with a variety of other widely referenced sources on the Gulf War. Stephen A. Bourque, *Jayhawk! The VII Corps in the Persian Gulf War* (Washington, DC: U.S. Army Center of Military History, 2001), 455. This number on the Nagorno-Karabakh War is drawn from the previously cited Oryx article.
41. It was not possible to ascribe the cause of tank losses with any degree of accuracy or precision across the 423 modern cases.
42. I coded for rotary-wing infantry or logistics lift as well as attack, but it was difficult to spot lift actions in some cases.
43. I include here the Mi-35, an updated version of the Mi-24.
44. I include under this broad umbrella Australia, New Zealand, Israel, and other countries that apply Western-standard military doctrine, training, and techniques.
45. By *general support* I mean that the aircrews flew near supported ground units and generally supported them with fires. This should not be confused with the American military use of the term *general support*, which implies tight control once aircraft are assigned from general to direct roles.
46. These are best summed up in Lester W. Grau and Charles K. Bartles, *The Russian Reconnaissance Fire Complex Comes of Age* (Oxford, UK: University of Oxford Changing Character of War Centre, May 2018). Also see Dmitry Adamsky, "Russian Lessons from the Syrian Operation and the Culture of Military Innovation" (Garmisch, Germany: George C. Marshall European Center for Security Studies, February 2020).
47. Michael P. Simpson et al., *Road to Damascus: The Russian Air Campaign in Syria, 2015–2018* (Santa Monica, Calif: RAND Corporation, 2022), 78–80, 85.
48. James Hasik, "Precision Weapons Revolution Changes Everything," Center for European Policy Analysis, February 17, 2023; Justin Bronk, *Russian Combat Air Strengths and Limitations: Lessons from Ukraine* (Arlington, VA: Center for Naval Analyses, April 2023); Rafael Ichaso, "Russian Air Force's Performance in Ukraine, Air Operations: The Fall of a Myth," *Journal of the Joint Air and Space Power Competence Centre* no. 35 (Winter 2022–2023), 14–25.
49. See U.S. Director of National Intelligence, *The Future of the Battlefield* (MacLean, VA: April 2021), 6; Thomas Gibbons-Neff, "ISIS Drones Are Attacking U.S. Troops and Disrupting Airstrikes in Raqqa, Officials Say," *Washington Post*, June 14, 2017; Ulf Laessing, "Islamic State Uses Drones to Attack Iraqi Army in Mosul: Military,"

Reuters, November 24, 2016; Kerry Chavez and Ori Swed, "Off the Shelf: The Violent Nonstate Actor Drone Threat," *Air & Space Power Journal* 34, no. 3 (Fall 2020), 29–43; and others.

50. This is a subjective assessment based on a review of several thousand YouTube combat videos showing battlefield events from 2003 through 2022. For example, an Associated Press video showing fighting in Jowhar, Somalia, in 2006 was posted to YouTube on July 23, 2015. "WRAP Fighting in Jowhar between Troops and Islamic Fighters, Looting in Capital," *Associated Press*, 2006, YouTube video.
51. Despite evidentiary challenges, my review of evidence in my transparently recorded database suggests global drone use increased over time.
52. Daniel L. Haulman, *U.S. Unmanned Aerial Vehicles in Combat, 1991–2003* (Air Force Historical Research Agency, Maxwell Air Force Base, AL, June 9, 2003).
53. T. X. Hammes, "The Democratization of Airpower: The Insurgent and the Drone," *War on the Rocks*, October 18, 2016.
54. For example, Peter Finn, "A Future for Drones: Automated Killing," *Washington Post*, September 19, 2011.
55. See Jonathan B. Bell, "Countering Swarms: Strategic Considerations and Opportunities in Drone Warfare," *Joint Forces Quarterly* no. 107 (October 2022), 4–14; U.S. Department of Defense, *Unmanned Aircraft Systems Roadmap 2005–2030* (Washington, DC: Office of the Secretary of Defense, August 2005); Austin B. Taylor, "Counter-Unmanned Aerial Vehicles Study: Shipboard Laser Weapon System Engagement Strategies for Countering Drone Swarm Threats in the Maritime Environment" (thesis (Naval Postgraduate School, December 2021); and others.
56. See Greg Hadley, "THOR Hammers Drone Swarm with High-Power Microwaves," *Air & Space Forces Magazine*, May 19, 2023, https://www.airanspaceforces.com; Inder Singh Bisht, "Ukraine Receives Drone Hunters to Neutralize Iranian Shaheds," *Defense Post*, February 9, 2023, https://www.thedefensepost.com; U.S. Department of Homeland Security, "Counter-Unmanned Aircraft Systems (C-UAS)," article and video (DHS Science and Technology, n.d.). Probably the best primer is Arthur Holland Michel, *Counter-Drone Systems*, 2nd ed. (Annandale-on-Hudson, NY: Center for the Study of the Drone at Bard College, December 2019).
57. "Amazing Drone Footage of the Battle between Myanmar Army (Tatmadaw) with Kachin Rebels," archival combat video, 2016, YouTube video. Fake audio effects probably were added to this video, but the terrain in the video coincides with terrain in open-source imagery.
58. Jack Watling and Nick Reynolds, *Meatgrinder: Russian Tactics in the Second Year of Its Invasion of Ukraine* (London: Royal United Services Institute, May 19, 2023).
59. Rudy Ruitenberg, "Small Drones Will Soon Lose Combat Advantage, French Army Chief Says," *DefenseNews* (June 19, 2024).
60. See U.S. Army, *U.S. Army Unmanned Aircraft Systems Roadmap 2010–2035* (Fort Rucker, AL: U.S. Army UAS Center of Excellence, 2010). For a brief overview of ground drone technology, see Sarah Grand-Clement and Theo Bajon, *Uncrewed Ground Systems: A Primer* (United Nations Institute for Disarmament Research, 2022).
61. For more on IO assessment, see Christopher Paul et al., *Assessing and Evaluating Department of Defense Efforts to Inform, Influence, and Persuade: Handbook for Practitioners* (Santa Monica, CA: RAND Corporation, 2015); and Miriam

Matthews et al., *Frameworks for Assessing USEUCOM Efforts to Inform, Influence, and Persuade* (Santa Monica, CA: RAND Corporation, 2020).

62. They routinely employed T-72s and T-55s, artillery, and missiles in combat, but their ability to employ captured Iraqi M1A1Ms for any extended period of time was questionable. See, for example, "How Islamic State Got Its Weapons," *Amnesty International*, January 12, 2018, https://www.amnesty.org; Sean D. Naylor, "The Islamic State's Best Weapon Was Born in the USA," *Foreign Policy*, June 4, 2015; Conflict Armament Research, *Weapons of the Islamic State* (London, December 2017); "Armour in the Islamic State—The Story of 'The Workshop,'" Oryx, August 31, 2017; "U.S.-Supplied Equipment Abandoned by Iraqi Troops in Ramadi," *CBS News*, May 19, 2015, https://www.cbsnews.com.
63. This information is drawn from interviews with Tigrayan general officers and from combat video footage. In a widely circulated video clip, a Tigrayan general describes the process of arming his soldiers with weapons and equipment captured on the battlefield. See citations in chapter 7.
64. This is a low-confidence assessment requiring mostly subjective judgment.
65. See Andrew E. Kramer, "Small, Hidden and Deadly: Mines Stymie Ukraine's Counteroffensive," *New York Times*, July 16, 2023.

NINE

Conclusions on Ground Combat and on War

This last chapter provides my broader conclusions on the character of war, forecasting, the revolution in military affairs, and innovative American defense programs like the Marine Corps' Force Design 2030. Some of these conclusions will be provocative and are directly intended to disaffirm claims cited in chapter 1. But purposeful disaffirmation is not wanton negativity. I seek to puncture these myths of modern war in order to inspire better policymaking and to improve the ground combat readiness and effectiveness of the United States, its allies, and its partners.

NO UNIVERSAL CHARACTER OF WAR, ONLY VARYING AND NONREPRESENTATIVE CHARACTERISTICS

As I wrote in the introduction to this book, the term *character of war* is ill-defined. With only one ineffective exception—see below—it appears to be undefined in official Western military literature. Coupled with a lack of more globally comprehensive and empirical historical evidence, this definitional vacuum grants a virtual license to analysts, military officers, and defense industry proponents to describe the character of war in ways that best suit their personalized or institutional agendas. Working from within this vacuum, they tend to make confident and unequivocal statements about war's character. In doing so they effectively claim the existence of an unimpeachable universality across this complex human condition. That inherent claim of universality is unsubstantiated by either evidence or logic.

At the surface level of military discourse, the idea that war has an unchanging nature and a constantly changing character is attributed to Clausewitz, a man whose work German historian Hans Rothfels described as "more quoted than actually read."[1] This oft-repeated Clausewitzean dualism between the nature and character of war appears to be built on a foundation of sand.

In his contemporary analysis of *On War*, Antulio J. Echevarria II wrote that "Clausewitz saw the nature of war, not just its character—its subjective characteristics—as dynamic."[2] Echevarria's assessment appears to be well supported. Even a basic search through various translations of *On War* for key terms like nature and character knocks this artificially dualistic phraseology off the rails.[3]

Clausewitz wrote that war must "conform to the spirit of the age and its general character," and in some parts of *On War* he describes what he believed to be enduring features of warfare—its ostensible nature—including chaos and violence.[4] But Echevarria, Beatrice Heuser, and other contemporary analysts walk us through his many written equivocations and self-contradictory musings on the nature of war.[5]

Clausewitz fixed broadly agreed-on strategic concepts about war as a contest of wills, but he described the nature of war *as it is practiced in ground combat* as inherently uncertain and effectively unfixed.[6] In other words, its inalienable nature at the point of violent contact is inherent uncertainty. War in practice is therefore not amenable to the kinds of rigid principles commonly attributed to Jomini.[7]

Extending into this gray area between the constant nature and constantly changing character of war: Clausewitz either purposefully or unintentionally avoided defining *the character of war*. He fell back instead on the term "characteristics" of war, emphasis added here: "In order to get a clear idea of the difficulties involved in formulating a theory of the conduct of war and so be able to deduce its *character*, we must look more closely at the major *characteristics* of military activity."[8]

He never did seem to clearly deduce its character. Instead, Clausewitz applied a dialectical approach to explore the many facets of warfare.[9] He made strong claims about specific characteristics, but a dialectic is a necessarily unresolved inquiry. I did not read *On War* in the original German, but I cannot see any substantive basis in its various cited translations to build a universal and enduring definition of the character of war.

I do not stand alone in my discomfort with this term. Oxford's Changing Character of War Centre avoids what would be an eponymous definition and focuses instead on identified "prevailing characteristics" of war in order to help circumscribe and flesh in a range of observable commonalities and discontinuities.[10] The U.S. Army's capstone field manual, *Operations*, describes "characteristics of warfare" but neither defines nor describes a universal character of war.[11] The U.S. Marine Corps' core philosophical treatise on warfare, *Warfighting*, also does not define the character of war. Instead, it describes war by breaking out what it suggests are its component *characteristics*.[12] A U.S. Joint Force definition comes as close as any other to pinning a rose on a definition.

The character of war in *Strategy* is defined as "what war looks like *at any point in time and space*; its face, shape, practice, dynamics, intensity and scope."[13] This description suggests there is no universal character of war and that all wars, battles, and skirmishes are idiosyncratic. This probably was not the authors' intent since it undercuts the idea that war can be characterized as a whole phenomenon or concept. That is also not my point here. I argue that there is a rational middle ground between incoherent idiosyncrasy and sweeping, unsubstantiated universality.

Returning to definitions, the 2017 British Army manual, *Land Operations*, equivocates a bit and then cuts right to the heart of the matter. It leaves the definition of the character of war in tautological limbo—it is the character of war—but then makes explicit what the American joint staff perhaps unintentionally implied: "Because each conflict is unique, a single description of the character of contemporary conflict is not possible."[14]

In other words, it is not possible to describe the character of all war in any given era because of the inherent discontinuities between and even within wars. The authors of *Land Operations* go on to argue that it is "important to understand the factors that influence character, and the general implications of those factors." Factors are characteristics. Disparate, uneven, and empirically nonrepresentative characteristics do not constitute a singular character.[15]

None of these referenced definitions, descriptions, or list of characteristics were transparently anchored in empirical evidence. While I was able to identify a number of commonly occurring characteristics in modern ground combat (chapter 8, table 8.16), my examination of this new body of evidence did not generate a clear definition or a description of the character of even this subset of war.

Given that ground combat constitutes a significant portion of land warfare, I believe I can safely extrapolate this argument about evidence and universality to all of land warfare. Even as a subset of war in its broadest interpretation, I found land warfare to be far too diverse an experience to be logically distilled into a single descriptive explanation. If anything, examination of the large-*n* dataset further undermined the idea that a universal character of land war exists.

Since land warfare probably constitutes most of the interactions in global warfare throughout human history, and if one accepts the conclusion that land warfare defies universal distillation into a common character now, then it follows that war in its grandest interpretation may never have had a global, collective, and definitive character.

Therefore, I argue there is no singular character of ground combat, of land war, or of war. My finding that war cannot be neatly characterized is shared explicitly in writing by the British Army—"a single description of the contemporary character of conflict is not possible"—and implicitly by the U.S. Army, U.S. Marine Corps, and NATO in their unwillingness to commit to a written definition or practical description.[16]

Until these conceptual barriers are effectively breached, the term "the character of war" remains undefined and is, in my opinion, undefinable for practical use. It is therefore, at least for now, a junk term employed as a placeholder primarily because it has yet to be debunked and replaced with more defensible terminology.

Common use of a junk term exposes military and policy decision-making to error and manipulation. As I wrote above, the term "character of war" has been unconsciously and in far too many cases consciously misused by experts and policymakers to further questionable military innovation and procurement agendas. Too many of these agendas have no sound basis in historical analysis or rational, methods-and-evidence-driven forecasting.

Lawrence Freedman describes the unanchored prognostication that occurs in the absence of deliberate method and evidence: "A variety of agendas [have] long informed writing on future war. The intent has rarely been deliberately predictive not only for the obvious reasons—prediction is difficult and likely to be wrong—but also because the concern was often to make the audience aware of lurking dangers or exciting prospects . . . [leading to] a blurred concept and a range of speculative possibilities."[17] In other words: Too often, policy hedgehogs have taken advantage of our collective uncertainty to bend professional opinion to their will.

This is an unacceptable state of affairs for rational policymaking. It is at least partly repairable. Acknowledging uncertainty is the first step toward improving knowledge. Military experts and people in positions of responsibility should jettison the term *character of war.* Collectively, we can instead observe and describe characteristics, leaving us with a perhaps dissatisfying but more rational explanation of warfare than we have now. From these characteristics we can begin to understand threads of the whole and gradually build a more complete tapestry with many irreducible and irreconcilable patterns. Some broad conclusions may still be made.

For instance: Evidence cited in this book suggests that characteristics common to most observed ground combat experiences—infantry assaults and defense, armored warfare, indirect fire, air support, the impact of terrain, the functions and form of weapons and equipment, and so on—have changed little and then mostly gradually and unevenly since 2003; probably not much more in relative terms since World War II; and perhaps never more rapidly or with greater impact at any point in history.

Following this chain of logic and given the relative importance of ground combat to all cases of warfare, there have been no provable military revolutions in recorded human history.

NO MILITARY REVOLUTIONS, JUST UNEVEN EVOLUTION

I started my examination of American perspectives on military revolutions with William Westmoreland's 1969 testimony to Congress. Westmoreland believed that with the right technical investments and doctrinal changes, by the end of the 1970s the United States would have the ability to see and kill everything on the battlefield with near impunity. I also noted that the Soviets had started to use terms like *military revolution* in the mid 1960s. Dimitry (Dima) Adamsky attributes at least the institutionalization of the concept to Soviet Marshal Nikolai Ogarkov and Andrew Marshall.[18] But neither the Soviets nor the Americans can lay claim to the idea of military revolutions. Williamson Murray suggests British historian Michael Roberts coined the idea in 1955.[19] Murray, too, may have brushed over a more gradual—perhaps even evolutionary—emergence of the concept of military revolutions, or revolutions in military affairs.

Roberts was preceded by a range of experts and futurists. In 1953, the fervent armor advocate J. F. C. Fuller described two "great revolutions which have radically changed the organization of armies," the horse and the tank.[20] These were questionable claims: It would have been news to horses that their almost certainly gradual introduction into war was revolutionary even in 4000 BCE. Relative impact of the tank on the practice of ground combat in World War I is at the very least debatable.[21]

In *The Future of War*, Lawrence Freedman traces the hypothesis of military revolution even further back in time to the end of the nineteenth century. In 1899, Polish economist I. S. Bloch kickstarted contemporary debate with *Is War Now Impossible?* Concepts of revolution took on more concrete form in Italian General Giulio Douhet's 1921 *The Command of the Air* and were then solidified by B. H. Liddell Hart in two treatises, *Paris—or—the Future of War* (1926) and *The Revolution in Warfare* (1947).

First, Bloch suggested that a combination of shifts in the global economy and population, coupled with technical advances like the mass-produced rifled firearm were so revolutionary that future wars had been rendered impossible.[22] No government could stomach the costs of modern war. Military units would be frozen in place by weapons that could reach out and kill them with impunity. Bloch's essentialist and binary forecasting is consistent with similar late-twentieth-century writing. His econometric proofs and military forecasts about the impossibility of war were of course shattered on the battlefields of Europe in the 1910s.

Bloch's binary overreach did not deter Douhet, who came out the other side of the First World War enthralled by the idea of military revolution. Douhet argued that with as few as twenty bombers with 6,000 horsepower engines armed with conventional aerial bombs, Italy could "break up the whole social structure of the enemy in less than a week, *no matter what his army and navy may do*."[23] Douhet was so confident that he demanded broad obeisance to his one-man analysis: "In face of this state of affairs [which had not in fact occurred], is it possible to deny that a revolution has taken place?" Douhet wrote that until the 1910s, all technological advances were evolutionary. But the kind of airpower demonstrated in World War I was:

> [A] new and different factor which brings its own peculiar characteristics and possibilities into the group of age-old factors which shape the forms and characteristics of war. From this point the graph line of the evolution of war loses its continuity from the effects of this new factor and veers sharply in a completely different direction. It is no longer a matter of evolution; it is revolution. Woe to him who keeps on following the old graph line during this period of transition . . . history of the basic ideas used up to this time in the art of war cannot teach us anything.[24]

With these eye-popping claims, Douhet may have established a permanent high-water mark for revolutionary hyperbole. His arguments energized airpower advocates for decades thereafter; see below.

Unlike Douhet, Liddell Hart leaned heavily on historical lessons.[25] He wrote that forecasts of future war must be evidence driven.[26] Yet his claims about the character of war in his present time and in his near future were just as grandiose as those of Bloch and Douhet. In *Paris* (1927) Liddell Hart made some thoughtful arguments about the speed of foot movement and logically suggested a need for mechanized infantry on future battlefields. Then his overconfidence got the best of him.

Also in *Paris,* Liddell Hart argued that infantry could never attack tanks because a tank could use its speed to avoid their fires. Nor could infantry ever hope to attack aircraft. He summed up with the observation that the vulnerability of infantry to tanks and aircraft made their offensive value in war "nil" in the absence of supporting arms.[27] Each of these statements was thoroughly disproven in World War II and in many conflicts thereafter. In *Revolution in Warfare,* Liddell Hart argued that flying bombs like the German V2 had shattered the illusion of war, forcing a realization that it was just a mechanical process of destruction rather than any kind of two-way fight.[28] "Automatic warfare" would henceforth cancel out human factors like courage, skill, and patriotism.[29]

After cherry-picking military history throughout *Revolution in Warfare,* he offered an epilogue on atomic warfare in which he suggested that atomic attacks had rendered history useless as a guide to future war. He wrote, "Warfare as we have known it in the last thirty years [World War I through World War II] is not compatible with the atomic age."[30] Any nation that did not possess atomic weapons could not fight a nation so armed. In this line of thinking, neither the North Koreans nor the Chinese could reasonably fight against the nuclear-armed United States, but they both did so with some success just a few years after *Revolution* went to print. Quite a few conflicts since 1947 have rendered null Liddell Hart's confident forecast about the revolutionary impact of nuclear arms on the conduct of war, and also about the so-called automatic-warfare revolution.

Douhet bluntly rejected the relevance of history, while Liddell Hart disingenuously claimed to embrace evidence-driven analysis. Liddell Hart's flights of fancy may have been burnished with historical narratives, but they were no more evidence driven and no more accurate than Douhet's. Looking back through other canonical military literature, similar personalized (but less hyperbolic) rhetorical style, claims, and counterclaims of revolutionary change are evident in a range of other oft-cited works in the Western canon.[31]

Looking forward from the mid twentieth century, the prophesizing and ahistoricism evident in Bloch, Douhet, and Liddell-Hart were echoed in William Owens's revolutionary writings and perhaps most clearly in U.S. Air Force Lieutenant General David Deptula's 2001 unbridled ode to airpower *Effects-Based Operations: Change in the Nature of Warfare.*[32]

Just as Douhet had built his argument from a single case (World War I), Deptula took one case—the 1991 Gulf War—and argued that modern airpower had changed the very nature of war. With traditional ground and naval power rendered obsolete by precision-guided air munitions, he suggested the entire American military might be reorganized around stealthy, precision airpower.[33] Deptula's arguments were generally more cogent but ultimately no less radical and ahistorical than Douhet's post-World War I fever dreams.

Given the existing reviews by Lawrence Freedman and others, and the evidence I have presented here, it seems that claims of military revolutions are at least over a century old, they are almost always deeply personalized and subjective, and they either reject historical lessons or use (arguably, abuse) one or a handful of historical cases to substantiate what might be read alone as vaporous hyperbole.

Still, bad argumentation does not belie the possibility that revolutions have occurred. In order to support my hypothesis that they have not, in fact, occurred, I must first clearly define a military revolution, or revolution in military affairs; then identify the characteristics of a revolution; then examine cited claims of revolution; and then prove evolutionary change where revolutionary change is purported to exist. If revolution cannot be defined or characterized, then it can be neither proven nor disproven.

Scholar of strategy Colin S. Gray found Krepinevich's definition in the Office of Net Assessment's *The Military Technical Revolution* to be fatally flawed. He offered up his own version that is similarly open-ended: A revolution would be "a radical change in the character or conduct of war" that generated a dramatic increase of *an order of magnitude* (~10x) or greater increase in combat potential and military effectiveness.[34] He left the character of war, conduct of war, combat potential, and military effectiveness undefined, and in his overt skepticism of the concept as a whole, Gray offered no observable and measurable thresholds. Other definitions tend to be even looser.[35]

Keeping in mind Gray's critique, Krepinevich's oblique but somewhat more thorough description arguably sets the standard without offering a precise definition:[36]

- Revolution requires convergence of four, and perhaps up to six loosely defined and open-ended factors including: (1) technological change, (2) military systems evolution, (3) operational innovation, (4) organizational adaptation, (5) shifts in the geopolitical environment, and (6) "the nature of military-technical competition."
- A revolution happens when the character and conduct of military operations and *the nature of war* have been fundamentally altered, rendering useless contemporary definitions and measurements of military effectiveness; the term "nature of war" is left undefined.
- There is no concrete evidentiary threshold for the existence of a revolution.[37]
- A revolution can occur over *any* timeframe and in hard-to-differentiate stages emerging at different *levels* (e.g., a technical level and a tactical level).
- Often, we will not know a revolution has occurred until after the fact, and then perhaps not with any clarity.

Definitions are intended to help narrow an understanding of a term. By leaving just about every requisite condition for revolution ill-defined and open-ended, by failing to provide a concrete evidentiary threshold, and by setting a limitless timeline, this apex definition of military revolution from the Office of Net Assessment commits the fallacy of intentional vagueness.

In *The Dynamics of Military Revolution, 1300–2050*, Knox and Murray offer no precise definitions or thresholds. They effectively suggest we apply the 1964 Justice Potter Stewart test for obscenity to spot a revolution: We will know one when we see one.[38] But to their credit, they take this position knowingly, transparently, and while acknowledging the problematic nature of the whole concept.[39]

Barring a better definition and standard of proof, occurrence of any military revolution cannot be proven. Absent a clear and disprovable standard, I cannot make an empirically defensible claim that no revolutions have ever occurred. This entire debate over military revolutions is, therefore, hypothetical (high concept) rather than practical. It should neither be blindly accepted nor in any way applied to real-world policy, and certainly not to the practice of modern ground combat.

Therefore: The existence or nonexistence of military revolutions boils down to personal opinion. Colin Gray has already established this point. Existence of military revolutions is "as much a matter of intellectual taste and political convenience as it is of historical evidence. . . . RMAs are intellectual constructs; they are the inventions of scholars and other thinkers."[40]

If the existence of revolutions is a matter of opinion rather than a defensible fact, it follows that any reasonable, evidence-informed opinion on the subject has prospective relevance to the debate over the character of modern ground combat. Since the concepts of the RMA continue to influence Western military policy and acquisitions related to ground combat, I offer my case-evidence-informed opinion here.

By even a loose interpretation of Krepinevich's pseudo-definition, I observed in my collected and coded evidence no revolution in military affairs in ground combat from 2003 through 2022. Change I recorded over this period was globally uneven, fit within my rational understanding of the term *evolutionary*, and did not appear in any way to fundamentally alter the ways in which ground combat forces were organized, equipped, trained, or operated.

While I formally examined only forty-five cases from World War II through 2002, I also observed only evolutionary change in ground combat during this period or from the end of World War II to the end of 2022. None of the declarative statements about the changing character of war or revolution from 1899 onward bore out: Bloch, Douhet, Liddell Hart, Westmoreland, Krepinevich, Watts, Work, and others either were proven wrong by subsequent events or their open-ended forecasts have at least not yet emerged by mid 2024.

Adaptation to the combat necessities of land warfare has periodically accelerated the speed of some innovation some of the time. Williamson Murray, Paddy Griffith, and many others have clearly documented the acceleration of various technical innovations during wars. But in all the cited evidence and literature, I observed no sudden, shocking discontinuities (revolutions) in the fundamental form of military ground combat from 1900 onward. Given the preponderance of ground combat and land war as a portion of war, writ large,

I believe I can safely extrapolate this observation to all war at least from 1900 onward.

If I am right that there were no revolutions from 1900 onward, then it is at best doubtful any provable revolutions in military affairs occurred prior to 1900. By process of elimination, without revolution the historical changes in warfare necessarily have been evolutionary—even if somewhat jaggedly so—through at least mid 2024.

DRONES HAD EVOLUTIONARY IMPACT ON GROUND COMBAT

Drones have been at the heart of the debate over the character of war and military revolution. From at least the late 2010s, drones have been referred to as game changing, as dramatically altering the character of ground war, and even been credited with reordering the essential but still undefined nature of war. For example, in a 2022 hagiography of the Turkish Bayraktar family, Stephen Witt described the TB-2 drone as having altered the very nature of war.[41] All this hyperbole is in keeping with the central arguments raised in chapter 1.

At least for ground combat in the modern era, the cited cases suggest these claims are indeed hyperbolic. I observed no evidence that drone use had substantively and universally altered the ways in which ground units generally engaged in battle; see a modestly counterintuitive and nonrevolutionary exception from the Ukraine War, below.

Nor did I see evidence that drone technology itself had changed in any dramatic way. Evolution of drone technology is widely observable from the 1910s through the early 2020s. The Bayraktar TB2 is clearly an evolutionary derivation of the 1990s MQ-1 Predator, which in turn evolved from the 1980s Israeli and South African designs, which had all evolved from the 1950s Ryan Firebee, which in turn had evolved from the TDR-1 and Kettering Bug, and so on.

Practical quadcopter technology is well over a century old. French engineers tested the Breguet-Richet Gyroplane (quadcopter) before 1910.[42] Breguet's initial design was incrementally improved on by engineers around the world, and by at least the late 1980s four-rotor flight technology had been successfully merged with drone technology. Quadcopter drones were in mass production by at least 1989, and quadcopter drones with cameras—the predecessors to the ubiquitous Chinese DJI Mavic 3—were commercially manufactured by at least 1999, a full twenty-three years before the accelerated phase of the Ukraine War.[43]

Throughout this gradual process of evolutionary design, testing, operational experience, and redesign, functions of drones remained consistent while their form shifted only gradually. Japanese toy quadcopters produced in 1989 look and function almost exactly like early versions of the Mavic 3, sans camera.

Drones are tools. They serve two broad functions: seeing and destroying. They are much better at seeing than was a soldier with a telescope perched in a balloon basket at the Battle of Fleurus in 1794. They are safer and much quicker to transfer field reports than a World War I Royal Air Force observer overflying German front lines in an R.E.8 propeller plane, or a U.S. Air Force pilot spotting ground formations from the seat of an OV-10 Bronco over Vietnam in the late 1960s, or a Philippines Air Force pilot flying an MD-500 helicopter over Zamboanga City in 2013.

Drones are responsive, and in Iraq, Afghanistan, Syria, Libya, Ukraine, and elsewhere, they have provided continual or even continuous near-real-time surveillance to commanders far from the line of contact. Drones can drop hand grenades directly on soldiers, fly explosive charges into tanks from miles away, and put at risk enemy soldiers far behind the front lines. Indirectly, they have in some cases greatly facilitated the use of legacy systems like cannon and rocket artillery.

But even the best drone observation directly above a trench in broad daylight, uninterrupted by electronic countermeasures and with immediate radio communication to the soldiers on the point of attack, cannot prevent the need for combat. Intensive combined-arms ground combat remained necessary in Ukraine despite the use of hundreds of thousands of drones. This is true for all other battles in which drones have been employed.

At least across the 225 cases in which I recorded drone use, drone operations—particularly when compared to actual or prospective manned-aircraft employment—could not be equated with reduced ground combat intensity or faster and cleaner tactical outcomes. For example, widespread and almost uncontested drone use has not been empirically proven to have reduced the need for ground combat or to have significantly reduced coalition casualties in instances of direct ground combat across Iraq and Afghanistan.

Counterintuitively, wide proliferation of drones over the battlefields in Ukraine—where they are employed over almost entirely flat, open terrain, and with a consistency and density that may be unachievable in most other contexts—may actually have slowed the tempo of some ground combat and contributed to a more grinding style of warfare than most analysts would have anticipated. In other words, drones may have partially regressed some battlefields to early-twentieth-century form instead of pushing them toward the revolutionary techno-purity envisioned by Westmoreland, Owens, Work, and others.

On battlefields saturated by high-density and near-continuous drone surveillance, massing ground forces for attacks and achieving local tactical surprise have become somewhat more difficult.[44] Decisive offensive action is hard to achieve without concentrated mass and surprise. Through mid 2023, both Ukrainian and Russian units frequently were forced to conduct attacks with two or even just one squad of eight to ten soldiers.[45] This is just enough to take a small trench but nowhere near enough to achieve an operational breakthrough.

Without the element of surprise, poor tactics resulted in high casualties (Pavlivka Ukraine 2022), and even the best tactics that put shock troops right up to the trench lines ended in grinding slugfests at least in part because defenders were forewarned. Breakthroughs that might have shortened the war may have been rendered at least somewhat less likely by drones. But even the most prolific use of drones in the history of warfare (Ukraine) did not stop or—in my reading of the cited evidence—consistently or radically alter the machine-on-machine, soldier-to-soldier fight taking place under their gaze.

Further, when both sides rely far more heavily on drones than on manned combat aircraft, overall aerial destructive power—specifically, munitions delivered from the air to the ground—may be sharply reduced compared to other cases. Suicide drones necessarily can hit only a single target. Handheld drones carry barely enough explosives to kill a single soldier or knock out a single armored vehicle. Even a tailor-made killing drone like the Turkish TB-2 or the American Reaper carries only a handful of precision missiles, or about 350 pounds of ordnance.[46]

By comparison, a single A-10 Thunderbolt II manned ground attack aircraft mounts a tank-killing 30mm cannon with 1,174 rounds and can carry another 16,000 pounds of bombs, precision missiles, and rockets. So even putting aside its center-mounted cannon, the A-10 delivers over forty-five times more lethal payload than a TB-2. Just a single 500-pound guided bomb dropped by a combat aircraft like the A-10 delivers approximately ten times as much explosive as a missile from a small drone and is capable of collapsing bunkers or an entire section of trench.[47]

While modern manned jet aircraft cost more than even most higher-end drones like the Reaper, and while aircrew lives are at stake any time a manned plane overflies a battlefield—see the next section on risk aversion—manned aircraft also are far more lethal by volume of payload and probably also by the raw number of targets they can attack over a given period of time.

As of late 2023, Russia had rediscovered the power of aerial bombing and was causing serious problems for Ukrainian infantry with its high-payload, 1950s-era FAB-500 general purpose bombs. It was using an even larger ~3,300-pound bomb to flatten entire apartment buildings.[48] And in less than two weeks during the March 2011 Odyssey Dawn bombing campaign in Libya, just six 1970s-era AV-8B Harrier jets destroyed over seventy ground vehicles including thirty-five T-72 tanks.[49] Other U.S. and NATO allied aircraft destroyed hundreds of other

Libyan targets in the same short time span. They were guided to target primarily by electronic intercepts and manned-aircraft technical observation, not drones. Western manned aircraft did not win the Libya war, but they made a significant difference on the ground.[50]

So there does not appear to be any defensible empirical proof that drones are on the whole more lethal than manned aircraft, though they are without argument highly effective in spotting and tracking ground targets when terrain, weather, and countermeasure conditions are favorable. Looking back to the comparative daily tank losses in ground combat from 1973 to 2023—a loose correlation with a comparative reduction in manned air sorties across the four cited wars—and at the quick, deadly results achieved primarily by manned aircraft in Libya in 2011 (and in other cited wars), big questions about the actual efficacy of drones in ground combat remain.

Drones are not proven game changers. They are at the very least useful tools that have, over about a century-long evolutionary period, gradually enhanced ground combat operations in various ways in many cases and had more impact in some instances than in others. This is true of every other tool on the modern battlefield including gradually improving models of artillery cannon, main battle tank, surface-to-surface missile, aerial cannon, tripod-mounted machineguns, radios, thermal imagers, anti-tank rockets, and the lowly rifle.

WESTERN RISK AVERSION + TECHNOPHILIA = LOWERED OVERALL COMBAT POWER

In chapter 5 I described creeping risk aversion in Western military theory, operational concepts, material design, and acquisitions. Owens, Work, and others believe risk aversion has inhibited adequate high-tech investment (aversion to innovation risk). I find that risk aversion actually has helped make acquisition of excessively complex and high-technology ground combat equipment far more enticing. Clean war concepts—and particularly military revolution theory—fed the acquisition of increasingly intricate and expensive ground combat and close-air support systems explicitly designed to protect vehicle and air crews and avoid equipment loss. I believe that while per-unit tank, helicopter, and cannon combat power increased, overall Western ground combat power may have declined.

Western armored vehicle design perhaps best reflects the interrelated influence of risk aversion and technophilia, particularly within the U.S. military. The failed early-2010s U.S. Army Ground Combat Vehicle (GCV) program is a compelling case in point. Need to replace the aging 1970s-era Bradley design carried

Table 9.1. U.S. Army Prioritized Criteria for Ground Combat Vehicle Design

Criteria	Priority Weighting
Total life cycle cost	0.25
Protection/survivability	***0.20***
Lethality	0.15
Mobility	0.10
Communications	0.10
Space, weight, power growth potential	0.10
Sustainment	0.05
Carrying capacity	0.05

Note: Emphasis added to row 3, Protection/survivability 0.20.

forward after the earlier failure of the Future Combat System (FCS) program. Army leaders set their initial criteria for the new vehicle.

Crew survivability was a priority (Tier 1) requirement, while mobility and lethality were secondary (Tier 2) requirements.[51] When asked to compare alternatives to the GCV, Army leaders weighted their requirements in order of importance. Table 9.1 shows these official weights. First priority was cost (0.25); followed closely by protection and survivability at 0.20; lethality came in third place; followed by mobility, communications, sustainment, and lastly, *carrying capacity*—the space to move soldiers to the fight—prioritized at 0.05 out of 1.0.[52]

Two manufacturers competed for the contract. Both design teams set out to build an air-transportable, lighter-weight version of the Bradley with better survivability and the capacity to hold a full squad of soldiers. Then they started adding on every possible layer of passive and active protection, including heavy underside anti-mine plating, radar-triggered active protection systems, and modular side armor that could max out vehicle weight at over eighty tons, about ten tons heavier than an M1 main battle tank.[53] At max weight this vehicle would have been all but immobilized on a European battlefield.

This ground vehicle program was canceled in 2014.[54] At least through that point it represented an apogee in American risk-averse armor design rooted in the 1960s-era MBT-70 project. Modern Western tanks operating in 2024—the American M1, the German Leopard II, the British Challenger 2, and the French Leclerc—all derived to some extent from the combined MBT-70 program and were fielded between the late 1970s and the early 1990s.[55] All of these tanks have similar safety features: big, fast engines; thick composite armor; and in newer models, active protection systems, laser warning systems, advanced fire control systems, other technical protection, and advanced gun systems allowing for safer long-range combat.

Protection comes at a cost. These big tanks guzzle fuel, have complex mechanical subsystems requiring hours of maintenance for every hour of operation, and are expensive. Compared to a less survivable ~$1.5m dollar T-72, the most advanced M1 and Challenger 2 can cost over $8.5 million, while a Leclerc can cost over $16 million per tank or about ten times the cost of a T-72.[56]

Still, better survivability should in theory translate to reduced demand to offset cost. If Western tanks were impervious to anti-armor weapons and maintained the lethal edge they demonstrated over Soviet-Russian tanks in the 1991 Gulf War, risk-averse design might make sense. As American tankers demonstrated at the Battle of 73 Easting in the 1991 Gulf War, a handful of well-crewed Abrams can decimate a larger unit equipped with older T-72s.

But risk-averse tank acquisition has serious implications for battlefield capability. It closes its eyes to the unending, continual, and evolutionary process of counter-design that led to top-attack missiles and shells that render excellent (but costly and heavy) composite front and side armor less relevant and that will ultimately outmatch even the best contemporary active protection system.[57]

High costs; exquisite and sensitive subsystems; large armored frames; and high fuel, maintenance, and spare parts demands mean fewer Western tanks can be purchased, fielded, and supported in combat. Partner forces like the Iraqis and Ukrainians that lack the industrial infrastructure of the United States have struggled to field and employ Western tanks. All this means fewer tanks at the point of contact, fewer tanks in reserve to counterattack or exploit offensive success, and fewer replacement tanks for prospective long wars like the one being fought against Russia in Ukraine in 2024.

With this continuing risk-averse design philosophy, any replacement for the American M1 tank would have to be able to survive any attack by any weapon at any angle of approach, keep the crew safe from chemical attacks, integrate ultra-high-end networked communications technology, kill any threat on the battlefield, and still fit in a C-17 transport plane.[58]

Separately, these are all desirable objectives. But much like rifles, tanks are self-contained systems with some inherent zero-sum trade-offs. Adding armor and subsystems adds weight, which reduces mobility; adding active protection and data networking increases complexity and cost; and so on. Frankenstein-like prototypes generated in the FCS and GCV programs showed the folly of institutionalized risk aversion coupled with technophilia.

Western forces have adopted similar risk-averse and technophilic approaches to helicopters, utility vehicles, and artillery system design. In the Vietnam War, helicopters effectively were flying trucks. They had little or no armor, barely any advanced technology, and were mass produced with the understanding that many would be lost in combat. In the modern ground combat era, helicopters like the MV-22 Osprey tiltrotor and the newest attack models are increasingly exquisite high-technology instruments. A failed 1997 design for the U.S. Army's Crusader self-propelled artillery system was expected to cost ~$14 million in 2024 dollars and weighed twice as much as the system it was intended to replace due primarily to its heavy composite armor.[59] Other examples abound.

As some vehicles and helicopters became more expensive and scarcer through the early 2000s, both the equipment and crews increasingly were treated as precious compared to the infantrymen who probably engaged in the highest relative volume of combat. There probably is no better tactical example of this dynamic than the risk-averse approach to helicopter operations in the battles for Ramadi, Iraq, from 2004 to 2007.

In Ramadi, infantrymen fought on foot or in mostly unarmored vehicles throughout the most dangerous parts of the city. Despite protestations from some risk-embracing analysts and aircrews, those same areas were often coded "black," or no-go for helicopters, due to fear of airframe loss and a redux of the 1993 disaster in Mogadishu, Somalia (Black Hawk Down).[60] Infantry combat power on the ground in the hot spots in Ramadi was reduced as aerial observation and fires from Marine Corps helicopters was periodically lost.[61]

Solutions to the design problem triggered by risk aversion and technophilia are fairly straightforward but require difficult cultural change. Western military officers will need to revisit the idea of loss acceptance. Without having to drift into a Soviet-era philosophy that bordered on cynical enthusiasm for casualties, and without having to give up lethality, Western leaders can demand less complex vehicles and helicopters. These will have somewhat reduced survivability but could be produced in far greater numbers and employed with greater tactical flexibility.

There are good early signs that at least in the United States minds may be opening to alternative acquisition strategies, though some troubling intent persists. Army leaders have purchased an initial run of the M-10 Booker mobile-protected firepower system (really, a light tank) mounted with an effective but forty-year-old 105mm gun and an effective but nearly century-old .50 M2 heavy machinegun.[62] The M-10 is fairly simple, lightweight, and may cost less than half as much as the lowest-model Abrams.[63]

At the same time, though, Army leaders are championing yet another Bradley armored fighting vehicle replacement, the XM30. It has an active protection system, a hybrid electric powertrain, the ability to launch loitering drone munitions, and "advanced third-generation software and intelligent control" designed to provide "leap-ahead advantages" described in the Army's ReARMM plan.[64] It seems likely to evolve into the kind of platform that U.S. Deputy Defense Secretary Kathleen Hicks called "large, exquisite, expensive, and few."[65]

If risk aversion and technophilia can be tamped down by taking an M-10 design approach instead of an exquisite XM30 approach, overall *combat power* and *combat effectiveness* can be increased. To assess the best approach, these two widely applied standards must first be explained.

COMBAT POWER AND EFFECTIVENESS ARE UNDEFINED AND HAVE NO COMMON STANDARD

As of the writing of this book, no Western military force has published a clear, universal definition or standard for combat power or combat effectiveness for ground combat, land war, or any other type of warfare.[66] American military descriptions and standards are, to be kind, vague. American doctrine defines combat power as "the total means of destructive and/or disruptive force that a military unit/formation can apply against the opponent at a given time."[67] No other explanation, definitive list of component elements of power, or method for assessing combat power is offered. Combat effectiveness is undefined and unexplained. Still, like *the character of war*, both of these undefined terms are still widely employed.

Absent clear definitions and at least a broadly agreed-on method to assess combat power and effectiveness (or other applicable and undefined terms), advancing the research presented in this book will be quite difficult. I have laid out generally how ground combat was fought in the modern era and identified most of the equipment and weapons applied across the world's battlefields. I have not provided any causative explanation for victory or defeat in any specific case. Nor have I fixed on any generalizable causal factors that increase or decrease the likelihood of victory. Holistic definitions and standards for combat power or effectiveness would establish an anchor point for comparative analysis—even improved net assessment—and better understanding of ground combat, land war, and of all other aspects of warfare.

In the introduction I wrote that Western capstone doctrine centralizes the human will, sustaining the Clausewitzean notion that war is a contest of opposing, independent, hostile wills and that any useful assessment of ground combat power or effectiveness must incorporate the will to fight. Yet the term *will to fight* is also officially undefined and unexplained in the American military lexicon.

In 2018 my team at RAND defined it as the "disposition and decision to fight, act, or persevere as needed." Will to fight is intrinsically interwoven with material capabilities like firepower and medical support, and it is affected by contextual factors like battlefield terrain, allied support, and enemy actions. It is not possible to measure will to fight in a way that produces quantitative certainty, but it is possible to assess will to fight to help narrow uncertainty and inform a broader understanding of combat power or combat effectiveness.

British Army doctrine settles on a decent overarching model that includes human dynamics and that might be more widely employed. It describes "fighting power" (effectively, combat power) in a Venn diagram connecting physical components like equipment and training; conceptual components like doctrine and education; and moral components including motivation, moral cohesion, and ethical foundation for behavior.[68]

Integrating tangible and nontangible military elements into a central understanding of power is a good start. This conceptual approach should be extrapolated to perhaps NATO-wide definitions, along with more detailed explanations and, ideally, a holistic assessment method that could be applied to any military force. With those standards we can undertake the more comprehensive (or perhaps holistic), empirically driven approach to understanding at least military ground combat power.

ESTIMATES OF CHINESE GROUND COMBAT POWER MAY BE HYPERBOLIC

None of the 548 modern cases I examined (423 coded and 125 noncoded) included China as either a direct combatant or a direct-force contributor (e.g., air-to-ground strike). There is no clear record of Chinese People's Liberation Army ground or special operations forces engaging in platoon-level or above combined-arms combat from 2003 through the end of 2022.[69] Probably the last well-recorded battle—referred to by some analysts as Lan Jian-B—took place along the Laoshan Mountain front just across the Chinese border in northern Vietnam in 1986.[70] If this is accurate, as of the mid 2020s there are at best a handful of old Chinese ground force senior officers with combat experience on active duty.

Some Chinese equipment and weapons were observed in a few of the modern ground combat cases. Pakistani Army forces employed older-model Chinese-manufactured tanks in the Swat Valley in 2009, Government of National Accord fighters used FN-6 missiles in Tripoli, Libya in 2019, and the Nigerian Army put newer model Chinese armor and artillery including SH5 self-propelled howitzers into the field at Gamboru Ngala-Marte-Dikwa in 2021.[71] A number of countries including the United Arab Emirates, Saudi Arabia, and Nigeria probably used Wing Loong variant drones in combat-support roles. However, there were no battles in the dataset in which Chinese ground combat equipment or weapons clearly played a central and important role.

Therefore, if (1) there is no definable character of war; (2) there is no clear definition of, or proven empirical method to assess, combat power; (3) China's modern ground forces have never been tested in combat; and (4) only some of China's ground combat weapons and equipment have been used in only a handful of cases, then there is no logical or empirical basis on which to claim that China's ground forces may in some way overmatch those of American and allied forces.[72]

A counter to this finding might argue that China's ground forces are least comparatively relevant, and that its combined naval, air, space, and cyber forces would be more than sufficient to defeat (for example) the United States in a prospective regional war in the Western Pacific. Indeed, many prominent war forecasts pay little or no attention to the PLA ground forces.[73] However, conditions (1) and (2), above, would apply and still render any such argument about China's overall power suspect.

China may or may not be as dangerous as the U.S. government makes it out to be.[74] Given the rather overstated assessments of Russian combat power made by American think tanks and government analysts prior to February 2022—and also the overstated estimates of Iraqi combat power in 1991—considerably more work needs to be done on the study of war before any defensible claims can be made about Chinese ground combat power relative to any Western nation's ground combat power.[75]

HIGH-CONCEPT WESTERN MILITARY REDESIGN—PARTICULARLY FD 2030—NEEDS REEVALUATION

If all these conditions stand—no character of war, no definition or method to assess combat power, no robust public evidence of Chinese military effectiveness, and also no revolution in military affairs—then Western force structure changes and acquisitions strategies anchored in countervailing assumptions need to be reevaluated.

There are implications here for UK and Canadian efforts to shrink and reorganize their ground forces, Germany's plans to grow its ground forces, and American plans to reorganize large portions of the U.S. Army and Marine Corps for a highest-order fight with China. Whether or not it remains in effect by the time this book is published, Force Design 2030 (relabeled simply as "Force Design" through 2024) remains an important and enduring case because it was put directly into action and because its structural trade-offs are so potentially stark.

I described the Marines' force redesign in chapter 1. Briefly: In response to a broad directive to prepare to face China (the "pacing threat") in combat, Commandant Berger reorganized a significant portion of the Marine Corps to secure advanced bases in the Pacific theater in order to help control sea lanes of communication with advanced reconnaissance and high-technology missiles.

To pay for this transformation and shift what it viewed as legacy ground combat responsibilities to the Army, the Marine Corps quickly divested all its tanks, three-fourths of its cannon artillery, half of its amphibious tractor units, and about one-fifth of its infantry. Force Design 2030 had broad support in Congress, but it also was publicly attacked by former Marine Corps generals including retired Commandant Charles C. Krulak and by Paul Van Riper, an original proponent of maneuver warfare and the critic who eviscerated the 2002 Millennium Challenge exercise.

At least three of the foundational assumptions behind Force Design 2030 are unproven and may be unprovable: (1) the character of war has undergone revolutionary change rendering "traditional" ground combat power less relevant and less useful, (2) China has harnessed these revolutionary changes to render existing Marine Corps amphibious capabilities irrelevant, and (3) advanced sensors and missiles can effectively replace and improve on "traditional" Marine Corps ground combat equipment and weapons.

My argument regarding the character of war stands. I addressed estimates of Chinese military power above. Berger's various arguments about amphibious warfare—a seaborne method of delivering ground combat forces to a fight and supporting them in battle ashore—were inherently contradictory and therefore difficult to analyze.[76] I focus here on the third assumption: that advanced technology sensors and munitions can effectively replace existing ground combat people and kit.

As I wrote in chapter 1, Berger's critics have often employed hyperbole and ad hominem attacks to pick apart his force redesign plans. We can ignore their tone and pull out a few substantive critiques. Opponents of the plan zeroed in on changes to Marine infantry battalions, tanks, and artillery. Infantry battalions have long been considered the most effective and indispensable elements of Marine Corps ground combat power, so changes to infantry design generally are significant.

Before FD 2030 each infantry battalion had approximately 900 troops and retained a World War I-era command structure (see chapter 3) with a weapons company and three rifle companies. Each weapons company had 81mm mortars, M2 machineguns, Mk19 automatic grenade launchers, and Javelin anti-tank missiles. Each rifle company had 60mm mortars, M240 machineguns, and anti-tank rockets.

A new Force Design infantry battalion will have about 811 troops and retain all its machineguns, rockets, and missiles.[77] Assets in the weapons company may be broken up and sent to the rifle companies. Plans to introduce advanced loitering missiles are still on the drawing board. At least as of mid 2024, I see no substantive change to combat power within the infantry battalion. A reduction of three battalions is in keeping with historical changes in Marine Corps manpower; battalions regularly furl and unfurl colors.

Divestiture of tanks and artillery are a different matter. With the elimination of its M1 tank fleet, the Marines have given up all mobile-protected firepower over 25mm, about the same caliber as a ZU-23-2 cannon that irregular forces frequently mounted on pickup trucks in Syria and Yemen.[78] Even after the new Amphibious Combat Vehicle (ACV) is fully fielded, the Marines probably will have only a 30mm cannon for firepower support.[79]

Absent tanks, Marine infantry units engaging in combined-arms combat in any environment, and particularly in urban terrain, will have the worst of three worlds available for direct-fire support: a thinly armored LAV-25 or ACV; that cannot effectively smash through walls or maneuver over broken ground like a tracked vehicle; sporting a light automatic cannon that will not significantly outmatch a modestly well-armed militia unit. Given the continuing reliance on mobile-protected firepower by nearly all ground combat forces in my dataset through the end of 2022—nearly 70 percent overall tank use, about 56 percent IFV use, and routine infantry-armor teaming by all force types low to major—loss of tanks can be broadly equated with lowered Marine Corps combined-arms capability.

In the initial redesign plan, the Corps planned to cut its cannon artillery to less than one-quarter of its standing strength and, over an uncertain period of time, to replace most of those cannons with HIMARS rocket launchers.[80] Marine artillery policy is in flux in 2024, but many of these cannon units have been cut. That leaves some infantry battalions with limited supporting fires until the new rocket units can be brought online. Even when those rocket units are fielded, issues of magazine depth and weapon suitability are likely to affect ground combat capabilities.

Each HIMARS guided missile costs over $100,000, weighs about 600 pounds, and is about thirteen feet long, while a basic 155mm artillery shell costs just over $300, weighs about 80 pounds, and can be hand carried by a single person.[81] Artillery rounds typically have about a tenth of the explosive power of these missiles (~23:200 pounds). Therefore, a Marine fires unit could carry ten HIMARS missiles and strike ten targets, or for the same cargo weight carry seventy-five artillery shells and strike 7.5 times as many targets, albeit with at least less range and a narrower lethal footprint. Given cost and logistics limitations, Marine units more reliant on missiles are more likely to run out of supporting fires during protracted conflicts due to relatively shallow magazine depth.

And while a HIMARS missile delivers far more lethal payload than a 155mm artillery round, and while these missiles have proven to be highly accurate and effective in Iraq, Syria, Afghanistan, and in the early phases of the Ukraine War, they are vulnerable to jamming. According to the reports I cited in chapter 8, they can be rendered all but useless with the right electronic countermeasures. And large missiles are not always the best tool for ground combat support.

Not every target beyond the range of organic mortars requires a guided-missile fix. Large warheads have large blast radii and have to be targeted far away from friendly troops. Cannons are more suitable for a wider variety of ground combat situations and with guided rounds are equally as accurate.[82] Therefore, any deficit in cannon artillery may also reduce Marine combined-arms ground combat capability.

Neither the tank nor the artillery gap may undermine combat capabilities if the Marine Corps never again engages in ground combat. At least in terms of large-scale land war, that outcome appears to have been Berger's intent. He and other champions of force redesign continually stated or suggested that the Marine Corps should not become the "second land army" of the United States.[83] But historical trends and current policies suggest the Marine Corps will indeed be called on to fight alongside the Army (or without the Army) in future large-scale ground combat operations.

History informs forecasting. By type, from its inception in 1775 most Marine Corps operations have centered on noncombatant actions like humanitarian assistance or demonstrations of force.[84] But from at least the beginning of the twentieth century the Corps has been routinely involved in major and minor combat operations involving some type of combined-arms engagement.

Marines have played a central role in every major ground combat operation since the early 1900s. They fought in World War I, World War II, the Korean War, the Vietnam War, the 1991 Gulf War, the 2001 Afghanistan invasion, and the 2003 Iraq invasion. Marines also routinely fought in often intensive combined-arms engagements in what commonly are called irregular wars, including in China, the Philippines, Panama, Nicaragua, Haiti, Lebanon, the Dominican Republic, Grenada, Panama, Somalia, and in the long-running, large-scale, and often high-intensity post 9/11 counterinsurgency operations in Afghanistan, Iraq, Syria, and elsewhere, through 2024.

In almost all of these operations, Marines fought alongside U.S. Army ground combat forces. Army units frequently worked for Marine commanders and vice versa; Army and Marine ground combat capabilities generally were viewed as interchangeable. Therefore, for well over one hundred years of its existence, the Marine Corps effectively has operated as America's second land army.

Given this historical demand and the continuing inclusion of Marine Corps combined-arms units in a range of global contingency and land war operational plans, a reasonable forecast would suggest the Marine Corps will be called on to engage in combined-arms ground combat and to serve as a second land army in any number of future conflicts.

Summing up: Berger's redesign plan rested on the belief that the character of war had dramatically changed due to a military-technical revolution; that Chinese technical capabilities have rendered traditional amphibious and combat power irrelevant; that drones and advanced missiles would offset reductions in organic indirect-fire capabilities; and that the Marine Corps will not again serve as the second American land army.

If there is no definable character of war, no proven revolution, no proven Chinese capability, no proof that drones or missiles have or can offset existing ground combat systems, and a high likelihood of future combined-arms ground combat that will, given my broader findings, demand long-proven capabilities like tanks and cannon artillery, then Force Design 2030 appears to have been built on shaky ground.

No matter what happens with his plan, Berger's will to innovate and his unimpeachable desire to improve the Marine Corps are laudable. He may yet be proven right. But his assessment of modern military history and forecasting of the near future were, at least in my reading of the public record, methodologically unsound. Lack of sound, evidence-informed method puts this innovation and others like it at risk. Other Western military forces applying similar assumptions and methods should take note.

FORECASTING WAR FOR POLICY REQUIRES EVENHANDED AND DETAILED HISTORICAL STUDIES

My critique of Berger's methods applies equally to his critics and champions. None of the public criticisms of Force Design 2030 I reviewed were derived from empirical analysis. Most relied on cherry-picked historical examples, and many were personalized and at least vaguely intemperate.[85] In my opinion these critiques also violated a long-standing Marine Corps cultural norm: Any Marine who points out a problem must offer up a viable and immediately practicable solution. In the most prominent articles by Van Riper and others I found some thinly veiled ad hominem attacks but no detailed alternatives to Force Design 2030.[86]

Champions of the plan like Robert Work have put forth equally personalized, cherry-picked, and ad hominem defenses. In a mid-2023 jab at the plan's critics, Work let rip the snark, implying three former Marine Corps generals wrote their anti-FD 2030 articles with the help of a chatbot.[87] Coming from retired generals and senior policymakers, these exchanges were surprisingly unhelpful and, at least for some Marines, embarrassing.[88]

My biggest concern with the back-and-forth over the Marine Corps redesign is its ahistorical nature. It is hard to read either the original plan or its criticisms and conclude that any of these authors applied a thorough and objective review of the historical record to guide their work. I see similar ahistoricism in some of the U.S. Army plans and forecasts cited in chapter 1, as well as in some arguments underlying UK and European defense reforms.

In the introduction to this book I argued that effective understanding of the present and forecasting requires a thorough, evenhanded, and longitudinal examination of relevant history. It bears repeating that history does not dictate the future, but it does clearly inform our collective understanding of evolutionary change. When properly recorded and studied, it establishes trend lines that should be used to inform forecasting.

This returns us to Michael Howard's early 1960s call to study military history in width, depth, and context, and also to the old Soviet forecasting model I described in chapter 1. Soviet writers were overly enthused with complex quantitative formulae. But they also were incisive and adept at conveying complex ideas in simple graphical conceptual models. Their explanation of the use of historical research to inform forecasting is sufficiently clear to guide what I believe should be an improved approach to ground combat studies and, more broadly, war studies. As a reminder, the Soviets described an *observation interval* (history), a *lead interval* (present to forecast time) and a *forecast time*, or the point at which a condition is expected to exist. Figure 9.1 resurfaces this conceptual model.

As a general concept this model is wholly unoriginal and, at least in theory, broadly accepted by Howard and probably most (perhaps all) other military historians: Study the past to better understand the present and future. But as Biddle, Knox, Murray, Strachan, Freedman, and others have argued, the problem lies not with the general concept of historical study; it lies instead with the generally inadequate coverage and thin detail found in the large-*n* case history data and analysis effort in the post-WWII period.

Our collective historical understanding of ground combat through the end of World War II is excellent. In comparison to the breadth and depth of

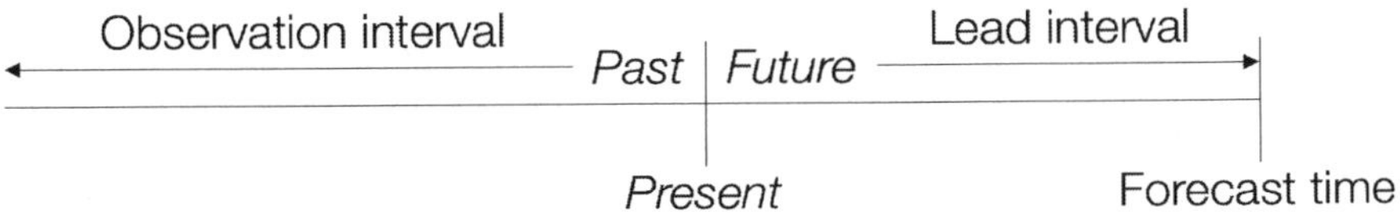

FIGURE 9.1. Observation Interval, Lead Interval, and Forecast Time

contemporary holistic global knowledge, it is brilliant. Since the end of World War II, many military historians have written empirically sound case studies and historiographies, but as a community of scholars they have not collectively achieved anything close to the scope, scale, and thoroughness of pre-Cold War knowledge. Work on the global collective history of ground combat in the post-2003 period has been particularly thin.

Political scientists and some military analysts work to address this gap by applying deductive selection and reasoning to help us learn from a few cases, or they build large databases like those listed in the introduction to distill collective lessons.[89] Certainly over the past few decades, they have significantly improved our understanding of historical context. But as I argued in the introduction, at least in the post-World War II period the few large-*n* studies that exist have failed to successfully capture the kind of global, tactical detail necessary to further the practical study of ground combat and, more broadly, of modern warfare. With these important shortfalls in relevant disciplines, the overall gap in knowledge occurs and persists.

Without the needed analyses to flesh out the observation interval, military officers and policymakers are left to interpret the collective history of ground combat on their own accord. Sometimes they do so thoughtfully and with conscious objectivity. But as I have shown, in far too many cases they founder or even take advantage of the lack of more comprehensive empirical knowledge to bend military innovation agendas to their subjective will. Until this gap in knowledge is filled, policy will remain vulnerable to shallow analysis and manipulation. The gap in the observation interval can be addressed at least in part—but not in whole—with inductive, thorough, large-*n* historical ground-combat case studies.

LOOKING FORWARD: WHAT ABOUT THE FUTURE OF GROUND COMBAT?

My study helps to fill gaps in the observation interval to support improved forecasting. It does not, by itself, constitute a forecasting methodology. A good method would include a range of analytic techniques, objective assumptions checks, and a thorough examination of alternative sources of information.[90] The following thoughts on the future of ground combat are therefore subjective opinions informed by the cited research.

Trend lines over at least the last twenty years suggest the phenomenon of ground combat will continue to be unevenly experienced by different military forces around the globe. Some core characteristics are likely to remain relevant for at least the next decade. Infantry almost certainly will continue to remain ubiquitous and necessary to hold and take ground. Supporting arms, including artillery and rocket units, tanks, aircraft, and drones, are likely to continue to shape the battlefield. Evolutionary advances in technology will be met by counter-advances that will in part nullify seemingly dramatic leaps forward; the advance-counter-advance cycle will almost certainly continue far into the future. Adaptability and survival are well practiced human behaviors. Historian Paddy Griffith's 1981 forecast of future land war ages well:

> There will be novel features in abundance—yet below the surface there will also be much that is conceptually familiar. Small groups of tanks will fight fleeting duels of maneuverer and rapier-thrust, in the knowledge that to halt for long in any one position will inevitably attract a thunderstorm of indirect fire. Command and communication will be intermittent, to say the least, and much will depend on individual qualities of leadership, training, and quick thinking at the lowest levels. Battles will be fought in a fog of tension, uncertainty, and confusion—just as they always have been, in fact.[91]

History also is replete with broken trend lines. As I also wrote in the introduction: No matter how compelling historical evidence of evolutionary change may be, assuming past to be a prologue to a certain or near-certain future is a logical fallacy. While I find possible revolutionary futures to be highly unlikely given the long-standing trend of evolutionary change, even skeptical experts and policymakers must remain open to the possibility that war as it is practiced in Ukraine or Gaza through 2024 might look nothing like war practiced on those or other battlefields in 2025 or beyond.

Some of the characteristics that appeared to have little or no impact on ground combat through the end of 2022 may have substantive roles in the coming decade. Though unlikely, artificial intelligence, quantum computing, or stealth technology might indeed create a shocking discontinuity in the thus-far consistently evolutionary changes in land war. Normative shifts in the willingness to employ chemical, biological, or nuclear weapons might reshape battlefields. Climate change might force thus-far unimagined deviations to military operations. A Rumsfeldian unknown "unknown" might rear its head, rendering some or all of my findings irrelevant.

All of these things are unlikely but at least remotely possible. Still, no amorphous fear of uncertain change should drive the ways in which Western nations shape their military forces. All possible eventualities should be considered, and thoughtful military innovation must continue to help the United States, its allies, and its partners sustain sufficient military force to accomplish their strategic goals. But again: Innovation is not an unalloyed mechanism for good. It can be harmful when impelled by a toxic cocktail of cherry-picked history, technophilia, technophobia, and wise-old-man bravado.

It will be possible to maintain a combat edge effectively and efficiently without the kind of fearmongering and hand-waving so prevalent in our current system. With a clear-eyed epistemology and working from a collective understanding of the past and present, we can address technological threats and opportunities through a more measured approach to innovation. Thoughtfully reducing uncertainty is the first step to abating what at least thus far have been unwarranted strategic fears.

I offer up this book and the accompanying database with the earnest hope that my work will support more thoughtful and objective Western policymaking. Or, as needed, I hope to arm thoughtful critics of ill-formed designs with transparent and empirically derived ammunition so they may engage in more cogent debate. My methods are no more novel than the Soviet conceptual model, above, but they are aggressive in their pursuit of transparent and informative detail. I also hope they inspire others to cast an even broader net in the same aggressive pursuit of an ever more objective and refined understanding of war.

NOTES

1. Tip of that hat here to Alan Beyerchen for resurfacing this quote in a 1993 article. See Hans Rothfels, "Clausewitz," in Edward Meade Earle, ed., *Makers of Modern Strategy* (New York: Atheneum Press, 1969), 93; Alan Beyerchen, "Clausewitz, Nonlinearity, and the Unpredictability of War," *International Security* 17, no. 3 (Winter 1992–1993), 59–90.
2. Echevarria II, *Clausewitz*, 76.
3. Hew Strachan provides a good critique of the Howard and Paret translation in Hew Strachan, "The Elusive Meaning and Enduring Relevance of Clausewitz," in Hal Brands, ed., *New Makers*. Also see Beatrice Heuser, *Reading Clausewitz* (London: Pimlico, 2002), ebook.
4. Clausewitz [Howard and Paret], *On War*, 33. We focus here on the nature of the *practice* of war as combat, not the Clausewitzean trinity describing the nature-of-war relationship between military leaders, the government, and the citizens of the nation-state.
5. Heuser, *Reading Clausewitz*.
6. See Christopher Bassford, "Clausewitz's Categories of War and the Supersession of 'Absolute War,'" working paper, version 12, December 2022, https://clausewitzstudies.org.
7. On page 85 of the Howard and Paret translation (Clausewitz [Howard and Paret], 1984) he writes: "If we now consider briefly the *subjective nature* of war," emphasis original. Howard and Paret provide an insightful comparison with Antoine Henri de Jomini on this subject throughout their foreword. They quote Jomini as stating "Methods change but principles are unchanging" (57). In other words, the idea that the nature of war is unchanging while the character of war changes frequently may stem from Jomini, not Clausewitz. At least in the G. H. Mendell and W. P. Craighill translation of Jomini's 1862 *The Art of War*, this quote is not found, the

nature of war is not clearly defined, the character of war is not defined, and even Jomini seems somewhat reluctant to nail down universally fixed rules. Antoine Henri de Jomini, *The Art of War*, with G. H. Mendell and trans. W. P. Craighill (West Point, NY: U.S. Military Academy, 1862).

8. Clausewitz [Howard and Paret], *On War*, 137. For further analysis of this interpretation, see Antulio J. Echevarria II, "War's Changing Character and Varying Nature: A Closer Look at Clausewitz's Trinity," *Infinity Journal* 5, no. 4 (Summer 2017), 15–20. Also see this excellent and accessible translation: Karl von Clausewitz, *On War*, trans. O. J. Matthijs Jolles (1943), in Caleb Carr, ed., *The Book of War: Sun-Tzu The Art of Warfare & Karl von Clausewitz On War* (New York: Random House, 2000), 358–361, 454, and other pages.
9. Strachan and Scheipers, eds., *Character of War*, 18–19.
10. "Research: The Changing Character of War—What Is War Today?," University of Oxford Changing Character of War Centre, n.d., https://www.ccw.ox.ac.uk.
11. U.S. Army, *Operations*, FM 3–0 (Washington, DC: Headquarters, Department of the Army, October 2022), 1–8. It is also undefined and not even mentioned in the higher-level ADP 3–0 (U.S. Army, ADP 3–0 *Operations*).
12. U.S. Marine Corps, *Warfighting*, 3, 15, 16, 38, and 46.
13. U.S. Joint Staff, *Strategy*, Joint Doctrine Note 1–18 (Washington, DC, April 25, 2018), 1–4, emphasis added.
14. UK Army, *Land Operations*, 1–1.
15. Returning to the OED, the probable best definition of *character* is II.8.a: "The aggregate of the distinctive features of something; essential peculiarity; distinctive nature, style, or quality; sort, kind, description."
16. See, for example, North Atlantic Treaty Organization, *NATO Warfighting Capstone Concept* (Norfolk, VA: Allied Transformation Command, n.d.).
17. Lawrence Freedman, *The Future of War: A History* (New York: Public Affairs, 2017), xvi and xxi.
18. Adamsky, "Two Marshals."
19. Also see Williamson Murray, "Thinking about Revolutions in Military Affairs," *Joint Forces Quarterly*, no. 16 (Summer 1997), 69–76, on 66; and Knox and Murray, *Dynamics of Military Revolution*. Clifton J. Rogers makes the same attribution and identifies an 1898 work contemporaneous with Bloch. See Clifford J. Rogers, "The Military Revolutions of the Hundred Years' War," *Journal of Military History* 57, no. 2 (April 1993), 241–278; C. W. C. Oman, *The Art of War in the Middle Ages*, with John H. Beeler, ed. (Ithaca, NY: Cornell University Press, 1898/1953).
20. J. F. C. Fuller, "Warfare and the Future," *Armor*, March–April 1953, 42–48, on 42.
21. Horses evolved approximately 55 million years ago, and, depending on the source, the first recorded use of horses in ground combat dated back to at least 2500 BCE and probably to 4000 BCE. Of course they may have been used in earlier, unrecorded ground combat events as well. For more on the impact of the tank in WWI, see for example, Tim Travers, *The Killing Ground* (South Yorkshire, UK: Pen & Sword Military, 1987/2009); J. P. Harris, *Men, Ideas, and Tanks: British Military Thought and Armoured Forces, 1903–1939* (Manchester, UK: Manchester University Press, 1995).
22. I. S. Bloch, *Is War Now Impossible? Being an Abridgement of "The War of the Future in Its Technical, Economic and Political Relations*, with ed., trans. W. T. Stead (London: Grant Richards, 1899).

23. Giulio Douhet, *The Command of the Air*, trans. Dino Ferrari (Maxwell Air Force Base, AL: Air University Press, 1921/2019), 128. He set the precondition for this dominating strategic air attack as conquering the air, or in modern parlance, achieving air supremacy (fully unchallenged airspace control and secure freedom of movement).
24. Douhet, *Command of the Air*, 128 and 227.
25. B. H. Liddell Hart, *The Revolution in Warfare* (London: Faber and Faber, 1947), 8.
26. Basil Henry Liddell Hart, *Paris—or—The Future of War* (New York: E. P. Dutton, 1926), 86.
27. Liddell Hart, *Paris*, 68–69, or 74 depending on which edition is referenced.
28. Liddell Hart, *Revolution*, 32.
29. Liddell Hart, *Revolution*, 32.
30. Liddell Hart, *Revolution*, 83.
31. Marshal Foch, *The Principles of War*, trans. Hilaire Belloc (New York: Henry Holt, 1920); Ardent du Picq, *Battle Studies: Ancient and Modern Battle*, trans. John N. Greely (New York: Macmillan, 1921).
32. Owens and Offley, *Lifting the Fog*; Deptula, *Effects-Based Operations*.
33. Deptula, *Effects-Based Operations*.
34. Colin S. Gray, *Strategy for Chaos: Revolutions in Military Affairs and the Evidence of History* (London: Frank Cass, 2002), 4. This "order of magnitude" figure probably was derived from a parenthetical statement by Marshal Ogarkov in the early 1980s. See U.S. Department of State, *A Reordering of Soviet Military Priorities*, memorandum from George P. Shultz to Caspar W. Weinberger, William J. Casey, and Robert C. McFarlane (July 2, 1984).
35. See Richard O. Hundley, *Past Revolutions, Future Transformations* (Santa Monica, CA: RAND Corporation, 1999), Summary; Elizabeth A. Stanley, *Evolutionary Technology in the Current Revolution in Military Affairs: The Army Tactical Command and Control System* (Carlisle Barracks, PA: Strategic Studies Institute, 1998), various; James R. Fitzsimonds and Jan M. van Tol, "Revolutions in Military Affairs," *Joint Forces Quarterly*, no. 4 (Spring 1994), 24–31; James R. Blaker, "Understanding the Revolution in Military Affairs," *Officer* 73, no. 5 (May 1997), 23–34. Also see Eliot Cohen's writings on the RMA: Eliot A. Cohen, "Change and Transformation in Military Affairs," *Journal of Strategic Studies* 27, no. 3 (2004), 395–407.
36. Krepinevich, *Military-Technical*, 3.
37. Krepinevich, *Military-Technical*, 3. "At some point the cumulative effects of technological advances and military innovation will invalidate former conceptual frameworks by bringing about a fundamental change in the nature of warfare and, thus, in our definitions and measurement of military effectiveness."
38. See Knox and Murray, *Dynamics of Military Revolution*, 12. In a 1964 ruling in *Jacobellis v. Ohio*, Supreme Court Justice Potter Stewart stated, "I know it when I see it" in reference to a judgment on the social value of hard-core pornography.
39. Knox and Murray, *Dynamics of Military Revolution*, 12.
40. Gray, *Strategy for Chaos*, 8.
41. Stephen Witt, "The Turkish Drone That Changed the Nature of Warfare," *New Yorker* (May 9, 2022).
42. Gordon J. Leishman, "The Breguet-Richet Quad-Rotor Helicopter of 1907," *Vertiflite* 47, no. 3 (2002), 58–60.

43. See Ed Darack, "A Brief History of Quadrotors," *Air & Space Magazine*, May 19, 2017; "The Story behind Draganfly [sic] Innovations," commercial brochure with timeline, December 12, 2016, https://investor.draganfly.com; "New Addition: Early Multi-Rotors," *National Model Aviation Museum Blog*, March 19, 2015, https://amablog.modelaircraft.org; "KEYENCE Gyrosaucer TVCM 1991," television commercial, Keyence TVCM, 1991, YouTube video.
44. This is a subjective expert judgment.
45. For example, Marc Santora, "A Brutal Path Forward, Village by Village," *New York Times*, September 2, 2023.
46. Ukraine has effectively employed larger, night-operations-capable Vampire agricultural quadcopter drones capable of carrying at least one air-dropped TM-62 mine with seventeen pounds of explosives, and perhaps heavier munitions.
47. A U.S. Mk82 500-pound bomb carries nearly 200 pounds of explosives, while a single AGM-114 Hellfire II variant missile carries approximately 18 pounds of explosives.
48. The FAB-500 is a 500-kilogram (~1,100-pound) bomb originally fielded in the mid 1950s. Russia also uses other guided bombs including the UPAB-1500, a massive 1,500-kilogram (~3,300-pound) device.
49. Fred H. Allison, "26th MEU at Operation Odyssey Dawn," *Marine Corps Gazette*, vol. 104, no. 5 (May 2020), 22–26.
50. Karl P. Mueller, "Victory through (Not by) Airpower," in *Precision and Purpose: Airpower in the Libyan Civil War*, ed., Karl P. Mueller (Santa Monica, CA: RAND Corporation, 2015), 373–392.
51. Bernard Kempinski and Christopher Murphy, *Technical Challenges of the U.S. Army's Ground Combat Vehicle Program* (Washington, DC: Congressional Budget Office, 2012), 13.
52. Kempinski and Murphy, *Technical Challenges*, 16; derived from U.S. Department of the Army, *Ground Combat Vehicle (GCV) Analysis of Alternatives*, December 17, 2010.
53. See Congressional Budget Office, "Cancel the Army's Ground Combat Vehicle Program," official report, November 13, 2013; Kempinski and Murphy, *Technical Challenges*.
54. Andrew Feickert, *The Army's Ground Combat Vehicle (GCV) Program: Background and Issues for Congress* (Washington, DC: Congressional Research Service, March 14, 2014).
55. See Steve E. Dietrich and Bruce R. Pimie, *Developing the Armored Force: Experiences and Visions* (Washington, DC: U.S. Army Center of Military History, December 1989). For more on the Leopard II development, see Michael Jerchel, *Leopard 2 Main Battle Tank 1979–98* (Oxford, UK: Osprey, 1998). For more on the Challenger II development, see Simon Dunstan and Tony Bryan, *Challenger 2 Main Battle Tank 1987–2006* (Oxford, UK: Osprey, 2006).
56. See, for example, Congressional Research Service, *The Army's M-1 Abrams, M-2/M-3 Bradley, and M-1126 Stryker: Background and Issues for Congress* (Washington, DC, April 5, 2016); "Cost of Battle Tanks Double Initial Estimate, O'Connor Reveals," *CBC*, May 18, 2007; "Germany to Buy 18 Leopard 2 Tanks to Replenish Stocks—Sources," *Reuters*, May 12, 2023; Sebastien Roblin, "Czech Super T-72M4 Tanks Seen Headed to Poland—Ukraine Border," *Forbes*, October 28, 2022; Sébastien Chènebeau, *Le Franc-Tireur Terre* (Paris: L'École de Guerre, Terre, 2022), 50.

57. For example, the Russian RPG-30 is specifically designed to simultaneously defeat active protection systems (APS) and explosive-reactive armor (ERA), employing a (probably inert) dummy rocket to prematurely trigger the APS and then a tandem warhead to defeat the ERA. See Andrew Feickert, *Army and Marine Corps Active Protection System (APS) Efforts* (Washington, DC: Congressional Research Service, August 30, 2016).
58. See U.S. Department of Defense, *Abrams M1A2 System Enhancement Packages (SEPs) Main Battle Tank (MBT) and Trophy Active Protection System* (Washington, DC: Office of Testing and Evaluation, 2020).
59. John M. Matsumura, Randall Steeb, and John Gordon IV, *The Army's Next Self-Propelled Howitzer and Resupply Vehicle* (Santa Monica, CA: RAND Corporation, 1998); U.S. General Accounting Office, *Army Armored Systems: Meeting Crusader Requirements Will Be a Technical Challenge* (Washington, DC: National Security and International Affairs Division, June 1997); Timothy Rider, "Extended Range Cannon Artillery system demonstrates rapid-fire precision and lethality during Project Convergence 2021," press release, U.S. Army, March 3, 2022.
60. This description of operations in Ramadi is based on direct observation by the author from January through July 2004 and December 2005 through June 2006 in Ramadi and Fallujah, Iraq, as well as from a review of evidence cited in the modern ground combat database.
61. This is a subjective opinion derived from direct observation and the cited sources.
62. "Army Names Its Newest Combat Vehicle after WWII and Operation Iraqi Freedom Soldiers," press release, U.S. Army Public Affairs, June 14, 2023; U.S. Department of Defense, *Mobile Protected Firepower (MPF)* (Washington, DC: Director, Operational Test and Evaluation, 2022).
63. Cost estimates on the Booker range from a few million to over $10 million per unit.
64. Stew Magnuson and Allyson Park, "JUST IN: GD Rheinmetall Win Optionally Manned Fighting Vehicle Contract," *National Defense*, June 26, 2023, https://www.nationaldefensemanagazine.org; U.S. Army, *Army Multi-Domain Transformation: Ready to Win in Competition and Conflict* (2021), 23.
65. Kathleen Hicks, quoted in Noah Robertson, "Pentagon Unveils 'Replicator' Drone Program to Compete with China," *DefenseNews*, August 28, 2023.
66. On this point, see Jason Lyall, *Divided Armies: Inequality & Battlefield Performance in Modern War* (Princeton, NJ: Princeton University Press, 2020), 8, and other pages.
67. U.S. Joint Chiefs of Staff, *Dictionary of Military and Associated Terms* (Washington, DC: Joint Staff, November 2021), 39.
68. UK Army, *Army Doctrine Primer* (Wiltshire, UK: Development, Concepts and Doctrine Centre, 2011), 1–4.
69. Chinese peacekeepers were engaged in limited ground combat with at least two armed factions in the battle for Juba, South Sudan (case: Juba South Sudan 2016). However, there were no indications they possessed or employed indirect-fire weapons in that battle. See a disputed account in Lauren Spink and Matt Wells, *Under Fire: The July 2016 Violence in Juba and UN Response* online report (Center for Civilians in Conflict, 2016).
70. For a fairly detailed account of this battle, see: "老山炼狱: 78名突击队员血洒高地的兰剑-B战斗," *Sohu.com,* May 30, 2017, https//www.sohu.com.

71. See the GCD-V1 for a full list of references. Several systems were observed in videos. For example, in this video from TVC News Nigeria on Operation Tura Takaibango, the Nigerian Army is seen putting its SH5 into the field: "Army Launches Operation Tura Takaibango in Yobe," *TVC News*, January 8, 2021, YouTube video.
72. For more on these forces, see U.S. Army, *People's Liberation Army "Ground Forces" Quick Reference Guide* (Fort Leavenworth, KS: Training and Doctrine Command, 2020).
73. See, for example, U.S. Defense Intelligence Agency, *China Military Power: Modernizing a Force to Fight and Win* (Anacostia, MD: Directorate of Analysis, 2019); U.S. Department of Defense, *Military and Security Developments Involving the People's Republic of China 2022* (Washington, DC: Office of the Secretary of Defense, 2022).
74. For example, see U.S. Department of Defense, *Summary of the 2018 National Defense Strategy of the United States of America* (Washington, DC: Office of the Secretary of Defense, 2018).
75. For example, see U.S. Defense Intelligence Agency, *Russia Military Power: Building a Military to Support Great Power Aspirations* (Anacostia, MD: Directorate of Intelligence, 2017); Ben Connable, *Iraqi Army Will to Fight.*
76. See Berger, *Commandant's Planning Guidance*, 5; David H. Berger, *Statement of General David H. Berger, Commandant of the Marine Corps, as Delivered to the House Appropriations Committee—Defense on the Posture of the United States Marine Corps*, congressional testimony (2021, https://www.cmc.marines.mil); Mallory Shelbourne, "Marine Corps Requirements Call for 9 Light Amphibious Ships per Regiment," *USNI News*, February 14, 2023, https://news.usni.org; U.S. Marine Corps, *Force Design 2030: Annual Update* (Washington, DC: Headquarters, U.S. Marine Corps, June 2023), 4.
77. See Caitlin M. Kenney, "Marines Will Restructure Infantry Battalions by September," *Defense One*, June 5, 2023.
78. See Andrew Feickert, *The Marine Corps' Amphibious Combat Vehicle (ACV)* (Washington, DC: Congressional Research Service, March 13, 2023).
79. See "Rocket versus Recoilless: A Brief History of the RPG," *Small Arms Review*, August 2, 2022, https://smalarmsreview.com.
80. Berger, *Force Design 2030*, 7.
81. See Paul E. Turner, *Precision Fires Rocket and Missile Systems: New and Evolving Armaments and Subsystems for Future Conflicts* (U.S. Army Precision Fires Rocket & Missile Systems Project Office, April 27, 2016).
82. See Mark Schauer, "Honing on the Range: Germans Fire Precision Artillery at U.S. Army Yuma Proving Ground," press release, U.S. Army, October 17, 2014; Christopher F. Foss, "Longer Range, Greater Accuracy," *Asian Military Review*, March 11, 2022, https://www.aisianmilitaryreview.com.
83. See David H. Berger in Paul McLeary, "Marine Commandant: Less a Second Army, More Light Amphib Ships," *Breaking Defense*, April 30, 2020.
84. Data are derived from Marine Corps historical documents including a long, unclassified chronology of operations from 1775 that is no longer available online as of July 2023.
85. For example, see Terrence R. Dake and Charles E. Wilhelm, "Reduce the Risk to national security: Abandon 'Force Design 2030,'" *The Hill*, December 21, 2022,

https://thehill.com; Paul K. Van Riper, "Jeopardizing National Security: What Is Happening to Our Marine Corps?," *Marine Corps Times*, March 21, 2022; Charles Krulak, Jack Sheehan, and Anthony Zinni, "War Is a Dirty Business. Will the Marine Corps Be Ready for the Next One?" *Washington Post*, April 22, 2022; John J. Sheehan and James Amos, "Former Marine Generals: 'Our Concerns with Force Design 2030,'" *National Interest*, December 12, 2022; Gary "GI" Wilson, William A. Woods, and Michael D. Wyly, "Send In the Marines? Reconsider Force Design 2030 beforehand," *Defense News*, August 4, 2022.

86. A thoughtful but still generally vague counterproposal by former commandant Charles Krulak and General Anthony Zinni has no clear empirical basis and almost no detail sufficient for execution: Charles Krulak and Anthony Zinni, "Vision 2035: Global Response in the Age of Precision Munitions," *National Interest* December 16, 2022.
87. Robert Work, "Marine Force Design: Changes Overdue Despite Critics' Claims," *Texas National Security Review* 6, no. 3 (Summer 2023).
88. This is an unquantifiable conclusion.
89. I refer here to political scientists, international relations scientists, social scientists, experts on conflict studies, and similar experts.
90. For an intelligence example, see U.S. Government, *A Tradecraft Primer: Structured Analytic Techniques for Improving Intelligence Analysis*, March 2009.
91. Griffith, *Forward into Battle*, 2. Also see David J. Betz, "Citadels and Marching Forts: How Non-Technological Drivers Are Pointing Future Warfare towards Techniques from the Past," *Scandinavian Journal of Military Studies* 2, no. 1 (2019), 30–41.

APPENDIX

Methodology and Source Insights

This appendix describes the approach and methodology I applied to conduct the study described in the preceding chapters. All analytic methods are imperfect and inadequate to achieve absolutely complete and accurate knowledge. They are instead relatively more or less conceptually sound, appropriate to the task, objective, empirical, and repeatable; and they produce results that are more or less precise, accurate, and provable. Qualitative analyses of a large number of cases of war—a complex, hard-to-observe, and at least partially idiosyncratic human phenomenon—are inherently subjective, hard to repeat, incomplete, generally less accurate than small-*n* studies, and at least conceptually unprovable. My selected method acknowledges and seeks to mitigate these inherent flaws to the greatest possible extent.

RATIONALE FOR A LARGE-*N* STUDY

As I noted in the introduction, I selected a large-*n* approach to this research for two primary reasons. First, I saw a gap in general knowledge. Many databases of global wars exist and are readily available online, along with newer databases of individual incidents of violence. Most war researchers have accessed the Uppsala Armed Conflict Dataset, the Fearon-Laitin dataset, and the Correlates of War Database at some point in their careers.[1] But I found only two efforts to record and analyze all global instances of modern tactical combat—military skirmishes and battles—in a single database or book.[2] The first of these is the Dupuy Institute's Land Warfare Data Base (also known as CDB90), and the second is Shuhei Kitamura's World Historical Battles Database.

The Dupuy Institute lists a number of tactical databases that capture some ground combat events down to small unit levels. Of these, only the Land Warfare set appears to be publicly available. It provides a good list of battles through the early 1970s.[3] It is coded with some useful detail and has been widely referenced and employed, including by Biddle in *Military Power*. There have even been some good efforts to translate the battle data into geospatial mapping tools. However, the Dupuy database only covers battles in major conflicts like World War I and the 1967 Arab-Israeli War, eschewing noncanonical battles from hundreds of other conflicts. Its end date also limits its utility for the study of twenty-first-century warfare.

Kitamura's database is a good aggregation of thousands of battles and a useful resource. Still, it primarily summarizes Wikipedia entries and does not examine the evidence behind each case. After I scratched the surface of exploratory cases, it became clear that many of these events were poorly recorded in their original sources. Biddle's prodding, gaps in both battle databases, and shortfalls in the underlying data further encouraged me to explore what looked like a yawning gap in at least the Western (or perhaps more fairly, English-language Western) understanding of modern global warfare. Studying tactical skirmishes and battles can provide a sound footing for broader analyses of land war and then war. So, I focused on tactical combat.

Second, smaller-batch case studies are inherently more subjective than larger-batch studies, and my goal is to help reduce subjectivity. When experts pick their cases for a smaller-batch study, they are making subjective and arguably, deductive, choices about which cases are most representative. For example, I took the small-batch approach in my 2022 study of the Iraqi Army's will to fight.[4] While the Iraqis had fought in a number of wars over the course of a century, I picked the Iran-Iraq War, the 1991 Gulf War, and the post-2003 counterinsurgency period for deeper study. In doing so I made value judgments as I discarded other cases including the 1967 Arab-Israeli War and the 1973 Yom Kippur War. My results were therefore informative but not necessarily representative. For my present work, a larger-batch, inductive study of tactical combat would help me to reduce subjectivity while producing a more representative body of evidence.

LIMITATIONS OF FINDINGS

My objective was to produce a database of all known and recorded modern ground combat battles available in the public domain.[5] Results could not be representative of all modern ground combat because the total number of actual cases, recorded and unrecorded, is unknown. I am aware of many hundreds of cases among what may be many thousand cases of combined-arms ground combat that took place between platoon-level or larger entities, employing combined arms, just in Iraq and Afghanistan between 2001 and 2021, and that are not available in the public domain. All my findings are therefore descriptive and representative only of the cited cases. They almost certainly are, however, relatively more representative than any small-*n* dataset built from deductive selection or other large-*n* datasets with fewer modern ground combat battle cases (e.g., CDB90 or World Historical Battles Database v1).

MITIGATION STRATEGY

Given the inherent limitations and flaws in large-*n* qualitative research on complex human phenomena, I designed my methods for data collection and analysis to be *inductive, transparent,* and *stratified* by both confidence and subjectivity ratings.

Inductive. I applied a broadly inductive method to case identification, code selection, and evidence acquisition. All cases identified from any source were included, and none were removed from the dataset; any case with insufficient evidence was retained as "not coded" for further prospective examination. I built some starting codes using a deductive approach (see below) but kept the coding fully open-ended, adding code categories as they appeared in the evidence. No relevant evidence was rejected out of hand.

Transparent. The database is fully transparent. I have included reference to all evidence cited and even those sources given just a cursory review for each case. A copy of the database will be made available to the general public on publication of this book.

Stratified. No two cases of warfare are ever observed with equal consistency, transparency, and detail. To reflect this reality, I assigned confidence ratings to each case (see below). Codes represent characteristics (e.g., use of tanks, type of terrain), all of which are more or less observable across most cases. I then assigned each code a confidence-subjectivity rating to help stratify characteristics by accuracy.

GENERAL APPROACH

In order to build the most complete and objective database possible with my given resources, I immediately scoped known modern cases (2003–2022) using a range of online sources including Wikipedia, historical anthologies, annotated bibliographies, and official military historical monographs. I initially found 269 modern cases. In parallel I created an Excel database within which to record the cases, codes, evidence, and findings; expanded the case set through additional research; researched and coded the World War II and interim cases; and engaged four research assistants to help gather evidence. I then proceeded to research and code the modern cases, expanding the modern database to 548 total cases coded and not coded, with a total of 593 cases including the World War II and interim cases. As I wrote the manuscript I refined the database and then completed the project.

CODING PROCESS

Qualitative coding is a method designed to isolate and organize phenomena within individual cases and then to compare and contrast (usually the frequency of) codes across cases. I began the coding process by building a deductive starting set of approximately 220 codes across nineteen categories, including a catch-all *other* category that ultimately included use of earthworks and SVBIEDs. I built this initial set based on my subject-matter expertise in the study of warfare.

Throughout the course of the research I expanded this list to include 432 codes (~100 percent increase). For example, I added a code for horse-mounted cavalry after examining the Battle of Changde, 1943; Polish cavalry operations in 1939 would also qualify. I later removed forty-one codes for various reasons. Most of these were cut after I decided to code only two sides per battle rather than up to four sides per battle. I made this decision after it became clear that isolating more than two actors was generally a highly subjective choice, and that in the vast majority of cases—approaching 100 percent—there clearly were only two sides engaged in combat, often with supporting actors.

Coding a characteristic was a fairly straightforward process. If I observed a ground combat characteristic (e.g., use of a type of mortar) in a video, read about it in a book or report, or heard it referred to in an interview, and so on, I included it as a code. I did not and could not verify the accuracy of all these sources, so inaccuracy, uncertainty, and subjectivity are built into the coding process at the first step. Source reliability did, however, feed directly into my case confidence rating. I coded by source, recording characteristics as they appeared, recorded the codes in the Excel database, added new codes as necessary, and then described the coded characteristics in a separate cell. This narrative description of the codes included identification of key equipment by side, an overview of tactics employed, and use of probabilistic language to help add stratification to the data (e.g., emphasis added: "the Islamic State fighters *probably* used *primarily* iron-sight AK-variant rifles").

Once the research was complete, I retroactively assigned confidence-subjectivity ratings of 1–4, green to red, to each of the remaining 391 (432–41) codes. These ratings were based on my experience with each characteristic, some of which were readily observable and typically binary (a cannon is or is not present), and some of which were hard to observe and/or required subjective interpretation. For example, the code *Infantry Side 1* was clearly observable and required minimal subjectivity, so it received a rating of 1 (green) for confidence and subjectivity. The code *Ground Changed Hands 3x*, indicating a swap of ground control on three occasions within a battle, was both difficult to observe and required subjective judgment regarding control. That code received a 4 (very low) rating for confidence and subjectivity.

After reviewing all the available evidence and both coding and describing the characteristics within each case, I assigned two additional codes. First, I gave the case one of nineteen possible *type* ratings that described the combatants in comparative terms (see chapter 8). Then I gave the case itself a *confidence* rating of 1–3, with a 1 denoting high confidence in the overall coding and findings, a 2 denoting middling confidence, and a 3 poor confidence. I based the confidence rating on the availability and perceived reliability of sources, and also on four criteria that I determined were essential to building case-specific knowledge:

1. Order of battle: Often referred to simply as OOB, this is a list and description of equipment, weapons, and troops on both sides of the battle.
2. Battlefield geometry: Geometry describes the positioning of units at various points in the battle and how forces were arrayed against one another.
3. Timeline: This can be a day-by-day or even an hour-by-hour accounting of combat events throughout the battle
4. Narrative: What happened, from start to finish? How did the fight play out? How did ground change hands, if at all? What tactics were used? And so on.

Few cases in the database had sufficient and sufficiently clear evidence to effectively describe all four of these criteria, or factors. I used subjective judgment to determine if the mostly uneven evidence was sufficient to describe the case with more or less confidence.

EVIDENCE GATHERING

Coding requires evidence. This was a desk research effort that, with the exception of the Moshchun Ukraine 2022 case and the 2021 Ethiopia-Tigray War, was conducted entirely through computer-assisted searches and with published hardcopy materials. I built and recorded evidence for each case and had three research assistants mirror my evidence gathering for the original 269 cases to help improve completeness and as a check against my efforts. I also engaged a Ukrainian researcher to build a parallel evidence set for all Ukraine cases from 2014 onward. Parallel evidence gathering was done in the blind for all cases. Research assistants had no role in coding the cases or writing the manuscript.

In order to gather evidence for a case, I first reviewed the best readily available evidence (books, online reports, etc.) and from those developed a set of search terms in English and in other relevant languages. I included a range of alternative spellings for each search term to help ensure completeness and added to this search term list as I reviewed each case. This was most often a snowball process: I started with a handful of sources and search terms and expanded everything as I went forward. I used a variety of channels to obtain evidence. A typical search included at least:

- Amazon, ABE Books, and Google Books search for published books
- Google Scholar search for scholarly journal articles and other publications
- Date-bound search engine queries for other online material
- ProQuest, JSTOR, and other firewall-restricted database searches for relevant articles
- Twitter, Telegram, Reddit, and so on searches for videos, maps, and photographs
- YouTube and Reddit Combat Forum and other searches for video evidence

Probably about half of the approximately 20,000 sources reviewed for this project were published in languages other than English. In these cases I used browser translators and Google Translate or, in cases of less common languages, other online machine translation programs to generate English-language material. No machine translation service is fully accurate, so this step added additional inaccuracies into the evidence review process. However, for the purposes of coding characteristics, a good gist of meaning or rough translation of a technical weapon name generally was sufficient.

For the Moshchun Ukraine 2022 case, I relied heavily on primary-source evidence generated through a parallel research effort funded by the Madison Policy Forum. Three colleagues, including the Ukrainian research assistant, conducted interviews with combatants in Ukraine. They also walked the battlefield and took photographs of the terrain, fighting positions, and so on. For the Ethiopia-Tigray War, the initial gap in evidence and large number of noncoded cases led me to task another research assistant with more active gathering. She reached out directly to both Western and Ethiopian-Tigrayan experts in the United States, Europe, and Ethiopia to identify better sources of information on the identified ground combat cases. That process returned few positive results and generally did not improve the database. It did, however, reinforce the finding that little is known about this land war in the public domain and even among the community of subject-matter experts.

After my initial test run with the World War II and interim cases, I settled on a baseline requirement of four independent and at least modestly reliable sources for each case; this was a subjective decision based on my initial case examinations. For each case that followed, I recorded at least four and up to eight sources in a brief annotated bibliography in the Excel database, and then added hyperlinks or bibliographic reference data for all other evidence reviewed in a separate cell. Each case had anywhere from about 10 to more than 150 additional recorded sources, some of which were circular (i.e., stemming from the same original source).

GENERATING THE DATA

Once all cases were coded, I reviewed and cleaned the data and then distilled results. I separated out what I believed to be overly detailed or less important codes (e.g., ground robots used for noncombat actions) and built a separate Excel sheet with fifty-eight characteristics. I then organized results for each characteristic across the five-year periods and summed them for the full twenty-year modern period. Charts presented in chapter 8 were built from these coded characteristics.

IMPROVING ON THIS METHODOLOGY

All research efforts are undertaken with limited resources and time. Ideally, this would have been a full team effort like the kind I typically led at the RAND Corporation. At least three researchers would have independently reviewed all the evidence and coded each case for inter-coder reliability. Accepting evidence without detailed investigation is far from ideal and builds fundamental flaws into the results. However, vetting sources would require a dedicated small-*n* case approach or even a detailed historical analysis of each case. With nearly 600 total cases, an effort of this scope and scale would require many researchers working perhaps for several years. Until this kind of investment is made, this database can be incrementally improved with better source vetting, inter-coder reliability, and perhaps with more detailed narrative case descriptions, maps, and so on.

A NOTE ON WIKIPEDIA

Any good high school teacher admonishes her students: Wikipedia is not a source! It is, of course, *a* source. The point here is that it is at best a secondary source and typically a tertiary source that should never be directly cited in student or professional research. However, as Jon Gertner of the *New York Times* accurately wrote in "Wikipedia's Moment of Truth" (July 18, 2023), it has become the most commonly referenced source for most subjects. When

I started this project I reluctantly turned to Wikipedia to build my initial case list.

Over the course of months I discovered that it was the single best resource for initial case identification. Editors generally have kept up to date with battlefield events in Ukraine, Syria, and across other major land wars. There are few other running lists as complete or useful, and most of those I was able to find typically referred back to Wikipedia (e.g., World Battle Database). In the absence of a good database of modern cases of ground combat, Wikipedia was a necessary and useful tool.

In many cases, the content within the battle-case pages was fairly good. The most detailed entries could reference a hundred or more sources, included maps that could not be found elsewhere, and provided what later bore out to be fairly accurate narratives. Selected sources often represented a mix of opinion and fact and generally were egalitarian.

However, for every good page there was another with some mix of thin sourcing, clear bias, and unsubstantiated narrative. For every battle listed as a "battle," there was another listed as a *siege*, or a *crisis*, or some other term that made aggregate searches more difficult. It is not clear who named the battles or decided when they started and stopped. Even in some of the better entries, battle narratives frequently were built on the thinnest of evidence. Unsubstantiated interpolation was commonplace. I found that after reviewing a case in full, the Wikipedia narrative did not hold up or added interesting but possibly fabricated detail into frustrating gaps in evidence. Given Wikipedia's near total reliance on Internet hyperlinks, the proliferation of dead links compounded all of these problems.

OOPS! CETTE PAGE NE PEUT PAS ÊTRE TROUVÉ

This is a subjective observation based on the cited research: A general consensus seems to have emerged in at least contemporary American culture that the Internet is passively yet safely recording and storing historical events for posterity. Following this line of thought, if primary source detail resides permanently online, then detailed books and lengthy reports about ground combat (or any other type of combat) are unneeded to accrue, safeguard, and pass along useful knowledge. Moreover, sousveillance, or pervasive electronic data collection through cellphones, drones, and so on, renders the process of actively collecting primary source information by walking battlegrounds, interviewing combatants, and gathering up official documents, unnecessary except for a few lonely historians looking to write a book.

Leaving aside the idea that the mere existence of disparate online sources can be equated with knowledge, the belief that the Internet is an eternally enduring cloud storage server is unfounded. Primary source evidence, and even most secondary source material, on modern ground combat is disappearing at an alarming rate. While I did not keep a running tabulation of dead links, I estimate that half of all links I checked throughout this yearlong research effort were dead. If there are about 20,000 links in the database that were live when annotated, that means I ran into roughly 20,000 dead links over the course of a year. My research assistants reported similar issues.

Some Wikipedia pages on modern battles were electronic cemeteries populated entirely by dead-end hyperlinks. Social media sites like Twitter and Facebook—relied on by many people to provide up-to-the-minute news—certainly cannot be relied on to store our collective history; they also are choked with dead links. Websites close or sweep out their archives. Reddit channels that once stored thousands of hours of combat video are shut and their material removed. Perhaps the biggest loss for the kind of detailed ground combat research I conducted took place on YouTube.

When I started this project, I assumed YouTube's terms of service would exclude the most useful ground-truth combat footage from even restricted posts. I quickly discovered that YouTube is a gold mine of primary source material, particularly when the right original language search terms are applied. Large parts of the entire Syrian Civil War are recorded on YouTube. Obscure footage of equally obscure ground combat that took place in the jungles of Myanmar, in remote deserts in Somalia, and elsewhere—often the only recorded source of information on a battle—can only be found on YouTube. Yet as the site periodically scrubs its accounts for inappropriate material, entire databases of videos are destroyed. Users violate terms of service, their accounts are removed, and the videos are destroyed. Essential historical data routinely falls victim to site-sweeping algorithms.

There are at least two prospective solutions to this problem. The first is costly but straightforward: A project to vacuum and organize these sources should be undertaken and sustained indefinitely. The links in my database provide a good starting point, though many of them will be long dead by the time this book is published. The second prospective solution requires a broad cultural shift, at least in the community of military experts (historians, political scientists, military leaders, etc.). Perceptions that military history resides safely online must be disabused. In any event, passive data collection does not substitute for the kind of primary-source historical research needed to inform military leaders and policymakers. Additional resources should be put toward collecting field information during and just after combat, and toward writing the detailed historical narratives necessary to preserve and transmit history for future generations.

NOTES

1. See online as of February 1, 2023: Correlates of War Project, the Peace Research Institute Oslo (PRIO) Conflict Recurrence Database (https://www.prio.org), and the Armed Conflict Location & Event Data Project (ACLED) (https://acleddata.com), as well as various RAND Corporation large-*n* projects on insurgency and terrorism. For more on these datasets, see James D. Fearon and David D. Laitin, "Ethnicity, Insurgency, and Civil War," *American Political Science Review* 97, no. 1 (February 2003), 75–90; and the PRIO list of replication data articles.
2. Such a database or book may of course exist. See Kitamura, *World Historical Battles*. Also see John Laffin, *Brassey's Dictionary of Battles: 3,500 Years of Conflict, Campaigns, and Wars* (New York: Barnes & Noble, 1986).
3. The original report on the database was published in six volumes for the U.S. government, starting with Trevor N. Dupuy et al., *Analysis of Factors That Have Influenced Outcomes of Battles and Wars: A Data Base of Battles and Engagements* (Dunn Loring, VA: Historical Evaluation and Research Organization, 1984).
4. Ben Connable, *Iraqi Army Will to Fight.*
5. A Microsoft Excel database of these coded cases (Ground Combat Database Version 1, or GCD-V1) is available at https://benconnable.com, https://groundcombat.org, and https://ground-combat.com.

SELECTED BIBLIOGRAPHY

This section lists references cited throughout the book except some of those used to describe individual case examples. A short list of key case references is provided in an endnote for each case. All YouTube videos referenced in the main body of this book can be found at https://www.youtube.com, and all referenced Reddit videos can be found at https://www.reddit.com/combatfootage. All sources used for each of the cited ground combat cases, including hyperlinks for all online videos, are available in the Microsoft Excel Ground Combat Database, Version 1 (GCD-V1) located at https://benconnable.com, https://groundcombat.org, and https://ground-combat.com.

10 U.S. Code § 8043—Commandant of the Marine Corps, U.S. law.

"AirLand Battle Future: The Other Side of the Coin." *Military Review* 71, no. 2 (1991): 13–34.

"The Armed Robots." *Naval Aviation News*, January 1973.

"Armour in the Islamic State—The Story of 'The Workshop.'" Oryx, August 31, 2017.

"The Army's Armored Multi-Purpose Vehicle (AMPV)." *Congressional Research Service*, January 25, 2021.

"GB-4 2000 Lb. Television Glide Bomb." Declassified program report, U.S. Army Air Corps, October 1, 1945.

"How Islamic State Got Its Weapons." *Amnesty International*. January 12, 2018.

"List of Aircraft Losses during the 2022 Russian Invasion of Ukraine." Oryx, March 20, 2022 (updated to June 2023).

"Reactive Armor of Armored Vehicles: Experience in Use in the Russian-Ukraine War." Ukraine Ministry of Defense, July 6, 2023.

"Rocket versus Recoilless: A Brief History of the RPG." *Small Arms Review*, August 2, 2022.

Adamsky, Dmitry. "Russian Lessons from the Syrian Operation and the Culture of Military Innovation." Garmisch, Germany: George C. Marshall European Center for Security Studies, February 2020.

Adamsky, Dmitry (Dima). "The Two Marshals: Nikolai Ogarkov, Andrew Marshall, and the Revolution in Military Affairs." In *The New Makers of Modern Strategy*. Princeton, NJ: Princeton University Press, 2023, 895–917.

Adkin, Mark. *The Western Front Companion*. London: Aurum Press, 2013. Kindle.

Alexander, Arthur J. *Armor Development in the Soviet Union and the United States*. Santa Monica, CA: RAND Corporation, September 1976.

Allison, Fred H. "26th MEU at Operation Odyssey Dawn." *Marine Corps Gazette* vol. 104, no. 5 (May 2020): 22–26.

Amierkhanyan, Zhirayr. "A Failure to Innovate: The Second Nagorno-Karabakh War." *Parameters* 52, no. 1 (2022): 119–134.

Andrade, Tonio. *The Gunpowder Age: China, Military Innovation, and the Rise of the West in World History*. Princeton, NJ: Princeton University Press, 2016.

Arpi, Claud. "War of Liberation: The Battle of Chamdo (Tibet)." *The United Service Institution of India* 146, no. 604 (April–June 2016), pages not listed in online version.

Arquilla, John, and David Ronfeldt. *In Athena's Camp: Preparing for Conflict in the Information Age*. Santa Monica, CA: RAND Corporation, 1997.

Ashbridge, Sarah, and Emily Ferris. "Why Mass Casualty Acceptance Is Part of Russian Warfare." *RUSI*, December 2, 2022.

Axe, David. *Drone War Vietnam*. Yorkshire, UK: Pen & Sword Military, 2021.

Ballarini, Phillippe. "Mistel." Translated by Mike Levelliard. Aerostories, n.d.

Ballendorf, Dirk Anthony. "Earl Hancock Ellis: A Marine in Micronesia." *Micronesian Journal of the Humanities and Social Sciences* 1, no. 1–2 (December 2002): 9–17.

Bassford, Christopher. *Clausewitz in English: The Reception of Clausewitz in Britain and America, 1815–1945*. Oxford, UK: Oxford University Press, 1994.

———. "Clausewitz's Categories of War and the Supersession of 'Absolute War.'" Online working paper, version 12, December 2022.

Beevor, Antony. *The Fall of Berlin 1945*. London: Penguin Books, 2020. https://www.amazon.com/Fall-Berlin-1945-Antony-Beevor-ebook/.

Bell, Jonathan B. "Countering Swarms: Strategic Considerations and Opportunities in Drone Warfare." *Joint Forces Quarterly*, no. 107 (October 2022): 4–14.

Benton, J. G. *Ordnance and Gunnery*. New York: D. Van Nostrand, 1862.

Berger, David H. *Commandant's Planning Guidance: 38th Commandant of the Marine Corps*. Washington, DC: Headquarters, U.S. Marine Corps, July 15, 2019.

———. *Force Design 2030*. Washington, DC: Headquarters, U.S. Marine Corps, March 2020.

———. In "Marine Commandant: Less A Second Army, More Light Amphib Ships," edited by Paul McLeary. *Breaking Defense*, April 30, 2020.

———. *Statement of General David H. Berger, Commandant of the Marine Corps, as Delivered to the House Appropriations Committee—Defense on the Posture of the United States Marine Corps*, congressional testimony, 2021.

Betz, David J. "Citadels and Marching Forts: How Non-Technological Drivers Are Pointing Future Warfare towards Techniques from the Past." *Scandinavian Journal of Military Studies* 2, no. 1 (2019): 30–41.

Beyerchen, Alan. "Clausewitz, Nonlinearity, and the Unpredictability of War." *International Security* 17, no. 3 (Winter 1992–1993): 59–90.

Biddle, Stephen. *Military Power: Explaining Victory and Defeat in Modern Battle*. Princeton, NJ: Princeton University Press, 2004.

Bivainis, Andrius. "Maneuver, Modernization, and the Second Nagorno-Karabakh War." *AUSA*, March 31, 2022.

Bivins, Harold A. *An Annotated Bibliography of Naval Gunfire Support*. Washington, DC: U.S. Marine Corps Historical Division, 1971.

Blaker, James R. *Transforming Military Force: The Legacy of Arthur Cebrowski and Network Centric Warfare*. Westport, CT: Praeger Security International, 2007.

———. "Understanding the Revolution in Military Affairs." *Officer* 73, no. 5 (May 1997): 23–34.

Bloch, I. S. *Is War Now Impossible? Being an Abridgement of "The War of the Future in Its Technical, Economic and Political Relations."* Translated and edited by W. T. Stead. London: Grant Richards, 1899.

Boggs, Charles W, Jr. *Marine Aviation in the Philippines*. Washington, DC: Headquarters U.S. Marine Corps Historical Division, 1951.

Bolia, Robert S. "Overreliance on Technology in Warfare: The Yom Kippur War as a Case Study." *Parameters* 34, no. 2 (Summer 2004): 46–56.

Bonanno, Joseph. "The Helicopter in Combat." *Ordnance* 38, no. 203 (March–April 1954): 868–872.

Bonds, Timothy M., Joel B. Predd, Timothy R. Heath, Michael S. Chase, Michael Johnson, Michael J. Lostumbo, James Bonomo, Muharrem Mane, and Paul S. Steinberg. *What Role Can Land-Based, Multi-Domain Anti-Access/Area Denial Forces Play in Deterring or Defeating Aggression?* Santa Monica, CA: RAND Corporation, 2017.

Bourque, Stephen A. *Jayhawk! The VII Corps in the Persian Gulf War*. Washington, DC: U.S. Army Center of Military History, 2001.

Brecher, Michael. "International Studies in the Twentieth Century and Beyond: Flawed Dichotomies, Synthesis, Cumulation: ISA Presidential Address." *International Studies Quarterly* 43, no. 2 (June 1999): 213–264.

Brisky, Larry A. "The Reconnaissance Destruction Complex: A Soviet Operational Response to Airland Battle." *Journal of Soviet Military Studies* 3, no. 2 (1992): 296–306.

Bronk, Justin. *Russian Combat Air Strengths and Limitations: Lessons from Ukraine*. Arlington, VA: Center for Naval Analyses, April 2023.

Brown, Michael L., and Tammy M. Furrow. *"Revolution in Military Affairs Conference": Report on the Conference Conducted at the Strategic Assessment Center, 12–13 November 1996*. McLean, VA: Science Applications International Corporation, 1997.

Burleson, Omar. "Special Subcommittee on the M-16 Rifle Program." Washington, DC: U.S. Government Printing Office, 1967.

Campbell, James B., "Origins of Aerial Photographic Interpretation, U.S. Army, 1916–1918." *Photogrammetric Engineering & Remote Sensing*, January 2008, 77–93.

Cancian, Mark F. "The Marine Corps' Radical Shift toward China." Center for Strategic and International Studies, March 25, 2020.

Carter, Ashton B., William J. Perry, and John D. Steinbruner. *A New Concept of Cooperative Security*. Washington, DC: Brookings Institution, 1992.

Cebrowski, Arthur K., and John H. Garstka. "Network-Centric Warfare—Its Origin and Future." *Proceedings* 124, no.1 (January 1998).

Chandler, Katherine Fehr. *Drone Flight and Failure: The United States' Secret Trials, Experiments and Operations in Unmanning, 1936–1973*. Thesis, University of California, Berkeley, 2014.

Chavez, Kerry, and Ori Swed. "Off the Shelf: The Violent Nonstate Actor Drone Threat." *Air & Space Power Journal* 34, no. 3 (Fall 2020): 29–43.

Chènebeau, Sébastien. *Le Franc-Tireur Terre*. Paris: L'École de Guerre, Terre, 2022.

Chivers, C. J. *The Gun*. New York: Simon & Schuster, 2011.

Churchill, Randolph S., and Winston S. Churchill. *The Six Day War*. New York: Houghton Mifflin, 1967.

Chuyev, Yuri V. and Yuri B. Mikhaylov. *Forecasting in Military Affairs: A Soviet View.* Translated by Canada Secretary of State Department. Moscow: 1975. Distributed by the U.S. Government Printing Office, Washington, DC.

Clary, David A. *Rocket Man: Robert H. Goddard and the Birth of the Space Age.* New York: Hachette Books, 2003.

Clay, Steven E. *U.S. Army Order of Battle, 1919–1941.* Fort Leavenworth, KS: Combat Studies Institute Press, 2010.

Clover, Kevin R. "Maneuver Warfare: Where Are We Now?" *Marine Corps Gazette* 72, no. 2 (1988), 59–99.

Cohen, Eliot A. "Beware the False Prophets of War." *Atlantic Online,* September 11, 2023.

———. "Change and Transformation in Military Affairs." *Journal of Strategic Studies* 27, no. 3 (2004): 395–407.

———. "Lifting the Fog of War by William A. Owens, Ed Offley." *Foreign Affairs* 79, no. 4 (July–August 2000): 154.

Cole, Ronald H. *Operation Just Cause Panama.* Washington, DC: Joint History Office of the Office of the Chairman of the Joint Chiefs of Staff, 1995.

Conboy, Ken. *Kopassus: Inside Indonesia's Special Forces.* Singapore: Equinox (Asia), 2003. Kindle.

Conflict Armament Research. *Weapons of the Islamic State.* London, December 2017.

Congressional Budget Office. "Cancel the Army's Ground Combat Vehicle Program." Official report, November 13, 2013.

———. *Technical Challenges of the U.S. Army's Ground Combat Vehicle Program.* 2012.

Congressional Research Service. *The Army's M-1 Abrams, M-2/M-3 Bradley, and M-1126 Stryker: Background and Issues for Congress.* Washington, DC, April 5, 2016.

Connable, Ben, *Embracing the Fog of War: Assessment and Metrics in Counterinsurgency.* Santa Monica, CA: RAND Corporation, 2012.

———. *An Enduring American Commitment in Iraq: Shaping a Long-Term Strategy with Iraqi Army Partners.* Santa Monica, CA: RAND Corporation, 2020.

———. *Iraqi Army Will to Fight: A Will-to-Fight Case Study with Lessons for Western Security Force Assistance.* Santa Monica, CA: RAND Corporation, 2022.

———. *Warrior-Maverick Culture: The Evolution of Adaptability in the U.S. Marine Corps.* Thesis, King's College London, 2016.

Connable, Ben, Michael J. McNerney, William Marcellino, Aaron Frank, Henry Hargrove, Marek N. Posard, S. Rebecca Zimmerman, Natasha Lander, Jasen J. Castillo, and James Sladden. *Will to Fight: Analyzing, Modeling, and Simulating the Will to Fight of Military Units.* Santa Monica, CA: RAND Corporation, 2018.

Connable, Ben, Walter L. Perry, Abby Doll, Natasha Lander, and Dan Madden. *Modeling, Simulation, and Operations Analysis in Afghanistan and Iraq: Operational Vignettes, Lessons Learned, and a Survey of Selected Efforts.* Santa Monica, CA: RAND Corporation, 2014.

Cooper, Tom, and Adrien Fontanellaz. *War and Insurgencies of Uganda, 1971–1994.* West Midlands, UK: Helion, 2015. https://www.amazon.com/Wars-Insurgencies-Uganda-1971-1994-Africa-ebook.

Coram, Robert. *Boyd: The Fighter Pilot Who Changed the Art of War.* New York: Hachette, 2002.

Cornish, Paul. *Machine Guns and the Great War.* South Yorkshire, UK: Pen & Sword Military, 2009.

Corum, James S. *The Roots of Blitzkrieg: Hans von Seeckt and German Military Reform.* Lawrence: University of Kansas Press, 1992.

Cox, Samuel J. "H021–1: *Fritz-X*—The Dawn of Precision-Guided Warfare." Online article. Naval History and Heritage Command, September 2018.

Daddis, Gregory A. "Review Essay on Lewis Sorley's Westmoreland: The General Who Lost Vietnam." *Parameters* 41, no. 3 (2011): 99–105.

Dake, Terrence R., and Charles E. Wilhelm. "Reduce the Risk to National Security: Abandon 'Force Design 2030.'" *The Hill*, December 21, 2022.

Darack, Ed. "A Brief History of Quadrotors." *Air & Space Magazine*, May 19, 2017; "The Story behind Draganfly [sic] Innovations." Online commercial brochure with timeline, December 12, 2016.

Daston, Lorraine. "The Coup d'Oeil: On a Mode of Understanding." *Critical Inquiry* 45, no. 2 (Winter 2019): 307–331.

Dastrup, Boyd L. *King of Battle: A Branch History of the U.S. Army's Field Artillery.* Fort Monroe, VA: U.S. Army Training and Doctrine Command, 1992.

Davidson, Janine. "The U.S. 'Pivot to Asia.'" *American Journal of Chinese Studies* 21, special issue (June 2014): 77–82.

Delbrück, Hans. *The Dawn of Modern Warfare.* Translated by Walter J. Renfroe Jr. Westport, CT: Greenwood Press, 1985.

Deptula, David A. *Effects-Based Operations: Change in the Nature of Warfare.* Arlington, VA: Aerospace Education Foundation, 2001.

Dietrich, Steve E., and Bruce R. Pimie. *Developing the Armored Force: Experiences and Visions.* Washington, DC: U.S. Army Center of Military History, December 1989.

Dodenhoff, George H. "A Historical Perspective of Mercenaries." *Naval War College Review* 21, no. 7 (1969): 91–109.

Doughty, Robert A. "Myth of the Blitzkrieg." In *Challenging the United States Symmetrically and Asymmetrically: Can America Be Defeated?*, edited by Lloyd J. Matthews. Carlisle Barracks, PA: Strategic Studies Institute, July 1998, 57–79.

Douhet, Giulio, *The Command of the Air.* Translated by Dino Ferrari. Maxwell Air Force Base, AL: Air University Press, 1921/2019.

du Picq, Ardent. *Battle Studies: Ancient and Modern Battle.* Translated by John N. Greely. New York: Macmillan, 1921.

Dunford, Joseph F. "The Character of War and Strategic Landscape Have Changed." *Joint Forces Quarterly* no. 8 (2018): 2–3.

Dunlap, Charles J. "Joint Vision 2010: A Red Team Assessment." *Joint Forces Quarterly,* no. 17 (Autumn-Winter 1997–1998): 47–49.

Dunlap, Charles J., Jr. "Kosovo, Casualty Aversion, and the American Military Ethos: A Perspective." *Journal of Legal Studies* no. 10 (2000): 95–107.

Dunphie, Christopher. *The Pendulum of Battle: Operation Goodwood-July 1944.* South Yorkshire, UK: Leo Cooper, 2004.

Dunstan, Simon. *The Yom Kippur War 1973 (2): The Sinai.* Oxford, UK: Osprey, 2003.

Dunstan, Simon, and Tony Bryan. *Challenger 2 Main Battle Tank 1987–2006.* Oxford, UK: Osprey, 2006.

Dupuy, Trevor N. "Technology and the Human Factor in War." *International TNDM Newsletter,* August 1997.

Dupuy, Trevor N., Grace P. Hayes, C. Curtiss Johnson, Charles R. Smith, Brian Bader, Edward Oppenheimer, and Arnold Dupuy. *Analysis of Factors That Have Influenced*

Outcomes of Battles and Wars: A Data Base of Battles and Engagements. Dunn Loring, VA: Historical Evaluation and Research Organization, 1984.

Eastwood, Brent M. "A Main Battle Tank the US Hasn't Used in 30 Years Is Still Fighting Wars across the Middle East." *Business Insider*, December 17, 2021.

Echevarria II, Antulio J. *Clausewitz and Contemporary War.* Oxford, UK: Oxford University Press, 2007.

———. "Jomini, Modern War, and Strategy: The Triumph of the Essential." In *The New Makers of Modern Strategy*, edited by Hal Brands, 145–168. Princeton, NJ: Princeton University Press, 2023.

———. "War's Changing Character and Varying Nature: A Closer Look at Clausewitz's Trinity." *Infinity Journal* 5, no. 4 (Summer 2017): 15–20.

Ehrhard, Thomas P. *Air Force UAVs: The Secret History.* Arlington, VA: Mitchell Institute Press, July 2010.

Elsbury, Will. "The Machine Gun: Its History, Development and Use: A Resource Guide." Washington, DC: U.S. Library of Congress, 2022.

Englehardt, Joseph P. *Desert Shield and Desert Storm: A Chronology and Troop List for the 1990–1991 Persian Gulf Crisis.* Carlisle Barracks, PA: Strategic Studies Institute, 1991.

Erickson, John. "Détente, Deterrence, and 'Military Superiority': A Soviet Dilemma." *World Today* 21, no. 8 (August 1965): 337–345.

Everett, H. R. *Unmanned Systems of World Wars I and II.* Cambridge, MA: MIT Press, 2015.

Ezov, Amiram. *Crossing: Suez, 1973.* ContentoNow, 2016. https://www.amazon.com/Crossing-Suez-1973-point-view-ebook.

Fearon, James D., and David D. Laitin. "Ethnicity, Insurgency, and Civil War." *American Political Science Review* 97, no. 1, February 2003, 75–90.

Feickert, Andrew. *Army and Marine Corps Active Protection System (APS) Efforts.* Washington, DC: Congressional Research Service, August 30, 2016.

———. *The Army's Future Combat System (FCS): Background and Issues for Congress.* Washington, DC: Congressional Research Service, 2009.

———. *The Army's Ground Combat Vehicle (GCV) Program: Background and Issues for Congress.* Washington, DC: Congressional Research Service, March 14, 2014.

———. *The Marine Corps' Amphibious Combat Vehicle (ACV).* Washington, DC: Congressional Research Service, March 13, 2023.

FitzGerald, Mary C. *The Impact of the Military-Technical Revolution on Russian Military Affairs: Volume I.* Washington, DC: Hudson Institute, August 20, 1993.

———. *Marshal Ogarkov and the New Revolution in Soviet Military Affairs.* Alexandria, VA: Center for Naval Analyses, 1987.

Fitzsimmons, Matt. "The M47 Dragon Antitank Guided Missile System." *On Point* 24, no. 1 (Summer 2018): 14–17.

Fitzsimonds, James R., and Jan M. van Tol. "Revolutions in Military Affairs." *Joint Forces Quarterly*, no. 4, Spring 1994, 24–31.

Fletcher, David. *Churchill Crocodile Flamethrower.* Oxford, UK: New Vanguard, 2007.

Fontanellez, Adrien, and Tom Cooper. *Ethiopian-Eritrean Wars: Volume I, Eritrean War of Independence, 1961–1988.* West Midlands, UK: Helion, 2018.

Forczyk, Robert. *Case White: The Invasion of Poland, 1939.* Oxford, UK: Osprey, 2019.

Förster, Jürgen. "From 'Blitzkrieg' to 'Total War': Germany's War in Europe." In *A World at Total War: Global Conflict and the Politics of Destruction, 1937–1945*, edited by

Roger Chickering, Stig Förster, Bernd Griener, Christof Mauch, and David Lazar. Cambridge, UK: Cambridge University Press, 2004, 89–107.

Forsyth, Frederick. *The Biafra Story: The Making of an African Legend*. New York: Penguin Books, 1977.

Forsyth, Robert. *Mistel: German Composite Aircraft and Operations 1942–1945*. Manchester, UK: Crecy, 2021.

Foss, Christopher F. "Longer Range, Greater Accuracy." *Asian Military Review*, March 11, 2022.

Francis, Paul L. *Defense Acquisitions: The Army's Future Combat Systems' Features, Risks, and Alternatives*. Testimony, April 1, 2004.

Frank, Benis M. *U.S. Marines in Lebanon 1982–1984*. Washington, DC: History and Museums Division, Headquarters, U.S. Marine Corps, 1987.

Freedman, Lawrence. *The Future of War: A History*. New York: Public Affairs, 2017.

Fuller, J. F. C. "Warfare and the Future." *Armor*. March–April 1953, 42–48.

Fuller, Stephen M., and Graham A. Cosmas. *Marines in the Dominican Republic 1916–1924*. Washington, DC: History and Museums Division, Headquarters, U.S. Marine Corps, 1974.

Gabel, Christopher R. *The 4th Armored Division in the Encirclement of Nancy*. Fort Leavenworth, KS: Combat Studies Institute, April 1986.

Gady, Franz-Stefan, "Useful, but Not Decisive: UAVs in Libya's Civil War." *International Institute of Strategic Studies*, November 22, 2019.

Gardiner, Ian. *In the Service of the Sultan: A First Hand Account of the Dhofar Insurgency*. South Yorkshire, UK: Pen & Sword Military, 2006. Kindle.

Garland, Chad. "'Marines Make Excellent Soldiers': Over Half a Marine Tank Company Just Joined the Army National Guard." *Stars and Stripes*, September 16, 2020.

Gawrych, George W. *The 1973 Arab-Israeli War: The Albatross of Decisive Victory*. Fort Leavenworth, KS: Combat Studies Institute, 1996.

———. "Attack Helicopters in Lebanon." Chapter in *Combined Arms in Battle Since 1939*, edited by Roger J. Spiller. Fort Leavenworth, KS: U.S. Army Command and General Staff College Press, 1992, 35–42.

Gelpi, Christopher, Peter D. Feaver, and Jason Reifler. *The Human Costs of War: American Public Opinion and Casualties in Military Conflicts*. Princeton, NJ: Princeton University Press, 2009.

Gentile, Gian, Michael Shurkin, Alexandra T. Evans, Michelle Grise, Mark Hvizda, and Rebecca Jensen. *A History of the Third Offset, 2014–2018*. Santa Monica, CA: RAND Corporation, 2021.

Gentry, Chris. "Use of Machine Guns in First Army during World War I." *Over There*, no. 8 (March 2018).

Geyer, Michael. "Restorative Elites, German Society, and the Nazi Pursuit of War." In *Fascist Italy and Nazi Germany: Comparisons and Contrasts*, edited by Richard Bessel. Cambridge, UK: Cambridge University Press, 1996, 134–164.

Gilbert, James L., and John P. Finnegan, eds. *U.S. Army Signals Intelligence in World War II: A Documentary History*. Washington, DC: U.S. Army Center of Military History, 1993.

Goerlitz, Walter. *History of the German General Staff, 1657–1945*. Translated by Brian Battershaw. Lucknow Books, 2015/1953. https://www.amazon.com/History-German-General-1657-1945-Illustrated-ebook.

Gordon, Yefim. *Soviet/Russian Unmanned Aerial Vehicles*. Midland, Mich: Midland Publishing Ltd. 2005.

Gouré, Dan. "Force Design 2030: USMC Innovation or Dissolution?" *Defense.info*, April 2, 2020.

Grand-Clement, Sarah, and Theo Bajon. *Uncrewed Ground Systems: A Primer*. United Nations Institute for Disarmament Research, 2022.

Grau, Lester W., and Charles K. Bartles. *The Russian Reconnaissance Fire Complex Comes of Age*. Oxford, UK: University of Oxford Changing Character of War Centre, May 2018.

Gray, Colin S. *Strategy for Chaos: Revolutions in Military Affairs and the Evidence of History*. London: Frank Cass, 2002.

Gray, Colin S., and Jeffrey G. Barlow. "Inexcusable Restraint: The Decline of American Military Power in the 1970s." *International Security* 10, no. 2 (1985): 27–69.

Green, Michael. *American Artillery from 1775 to the Present Day*. South Yorkshire, UK: Pen & Sword Military, 2021.

Griffith, Paddy. *Battle Tactics of the Western Front: The British Army's Art of Attack 1916–1918*. New Haven, CT: Yale University Press, 1994.

Grissom, Adam. "The Future of Military Innovation Studies." *Journal of Strategic Studies* 29, no. 5 (2006): 905–935.

Grossman, Elaine M. "Unintended Lesson of Millennium Challenge?" *Inside Missile Defense* 8, no. 20 (October 2002): 3–5.

Grunden, Walter E. "No Retaliation in Kind: Japanese Chemical Warfare Policy in World War II." In *One Hundred Years of Chemical Warfare: Research, Deployment, Consequences*, edited by Bretislav Friedrich, Dieter Hoffmann, Jürgen Renn, Florian Schmaltz, and Martin Wolf. Springer Open, 2017, 259–288. https://www.amazon.com/One-Hundred-Years-Chemical-Warfare-ebook.

Guardia, Mike. *Crusader: General Donn Starry and the Army of His Times*. Havertown, PA: Casemate, 2018.

Gudmundsson, Bruce I. *Stormtroop Tactics: Innovation in the German Army, 1914–1918*. New York: Praeger, 1989.

Guistozzi, Antonio. *War, Politics, and Society in Afghanistan*. Washington, DC: Georgetown University Press, 2000.

Guillemin, Jeanne. "The 1925 Geneva Protocol: China's CBW Charges against Japan at the Tokyo War Crimes Tribunal." In *One Hundred Years of Chemical Warfare: Research, Deployment, Consequences*, edited by Bretislav Friedrich, Dieter Hoffmann, Jürgen Renn, Florian Schmaltz, and Martin Wolf. Springer Open, 2017. https://www.amazon.com/One-Hundred-Years-Chemical-Warfare-ebook.

Gurtov, Melvin, and Konrad Kellen. *Vietnam: Lessons Learned and Mislearned*. Santa Monica, CA: RAND Corporation, 1969.

Hadley, Kevin, Savannah Spencer, and Justin Martens. *How the Army 2030 Divisions Fight*. Fort Leavenworth, KS: U.S. Army Training and Doctrine Command, February 2, 2023.

Haka, Andreas T. "Thermography." Chapter in *Between Making and Knowing: Tools in the History of Materials Research*, edited by Joseph D. Martin and Cyrus C. M. Mody. Singapore: World Scientific, 2020, 539–552.

Hammes, T. X. "The Democratization of Airpower: The Insurgent and the Drone." *War on the Rocks*, October 18, 2016.

Hanna, Mark. *Task Force XXI: The Army's Digital Experiment*. Washington, DC: National Defense University, 1997.

Harley, Jeffrey S. *Reading the Enemy's Mail: Origins and Development of U.S. Army Tactical Radio Intelligence in World War II, European Theater of Operations*. Thesis, U.S. Army Command and General Staff College, 1993.

Harper, Jon. "Just In: Army Struggling to Simulate All-Domain Warfare." *National Defense*, October 18, 2021.

Harriman, Bill. *The Mosin-Nagant Rifle*. Oxford, UK: Osprey, 2016.

Harrison, Mark, ed. *The Economics of World War II: Six Great Powers in International Comparison*. Cambridge, UK: Cambridge University Press, 1998.

Hasik, James. "Precision Weapons Revolution Changes Everything." Center for European Policy Analysis, February 17, 2023.

Haulman, Daniel L. *U.S. Unmanned Aerial Vehicles in Combat, 1991–2003*. Maxwell Air Force Base, AL: Air Force Historical Research Agency, June 9, 2003.

Hecht, Eado. "Drones in the Nagorno-Karabakh War: Analyzing the Data." *Military Strategy Magazine* 7, no. 4 (Winter 2022): 31–37.

Helmer-Hirschberg, Olaf. *Analysis of the Future: The Delphi Method*. Santa Monica, CA: RAND Corporation, 1967.

Heuser, Beatrice. *Reading Clausewitz*. London: Pimlico, 2002.

Hilner, Eric P. "The Third Offset Strategy and the Army Modernization Process." Center for Army Lessons Learned, May 2019.

Ho, Ben. "The Second Nagorno-Karabakh War: Takeaways for Singapore's Ground-Based Air Defense." *Journal of Indo-Pacific Affairs*, August 25, 2021.

Hoeffding, Oleg. *Soviet Interdiction Operations, 1941–1945*. Santa Monica, CA: RAND Corporation, 1970.

Hooton, E. R. *War over the Steppes: The Air Campaigns on the Eastern Front, 1941–45*. Oxford, UK: Osprey, 2016.

Horowitz, Michael C., and Shira Pindyck. "What Is a Military Innovation and Why It Matters." *Journal of Strategic Studies* 46, no. 1 (2022): 1–220.

Horton, Francis. "The Lost Lesson of Millennium Challenge 2002, the Pentagon's Embarrassing Post-9/11 War Game." *Task & Purpose*, November 6, 2019.

Howard, Michael. "The Use and Abuse of Military History." *Parameters* 11, no. 1 (1981): 9–14.

Hundley, Richard O. *Past Revolutions, Future Transformations*. Santa Monica, CA: RAND Corporation, 1999.

Ichaso, Rafael. "Russian Air Force's Performance in Ukraine, Air Operations: The Fall of a Myth." *Journal of the Joint Air and Space Power Competence Centre*, no. 35 (Winter 2022–2023): 14–25.

An Instructor. *Complete Guide to the Hotchkiss Machine Gun*. London: Gale and Polden, n.d.

Jacobs, Harry A. "The Army's Flying Truck." *Ordnance* 39, no. 210 (May–June 1955): 887–890.

Jalali, Ali Ahmad, and Lester W. Grau. *The Other Side of the Mountain: Mujahideen Tactics in the Soviet-Afghan War*. Fort Leavenworth, KS: Foreign Military Studies Office, 1999.

James N. Mattis. "USJFCOM Commander's Guidance for Effects-based Operations." *Parameters*, no. 3 (Autumn 2008): 18–25.

Jeffcoat, Rachael. "Army Conducts 1st RIMPAC Joint Live-Fire Sinking Exercise as Multi-Domain Task Force." U.S. Indo-Pacific Command, July 25, 2018.

Jensen, Benjamin. "The Rest of the Story: Evaluating the U.S. Marine Corps Force Design 2030." *War on the Rocks*, April 27, 2020.

Jerchel, Michael. *Leopard 2 Main Battle Tank 1979–98*. Oxford, UK: Osprey, 1998.

Johnson, David E. *Fast Tanks and Heavy Bombers: Innovation in the U.S. Army, 1917–1945*. Ithaca, NY: Cornell University Press, 2013.

Johnson, Edward C., with Graham A. Cosmas, ed. *Marine Corps Aviation: The Early Years 1912–1940*. Washington, DC: History and Museums Division, Headquarters, U.S. Marine Corps, 1977.

Johnson, Rob. "What Is War Today?" Online article. Oxford, UK: Changing Character of War Centre, n.d.

Johnson, Robert A. "Predicting Future War," *Parameters* 44, no. 1 (Spring 2014): 65–76.

Jomini, Antoine Henri. *The Art of War*, with G. H. Mendell and W. P. Craighill, trans. West Point, NY: U.S. Military Academy, 1862.

Jowett, Philip S. *The Biafran Army 1967–1970: Build-Up and Downfall of the Secessionist Military*. West Midlands, UK: Helion, 2020.

Kagan, Frederick W. *Finding the Target: The Transformation of American Military Policy*. New York: Encounter Books, 2006.

Kalashnikov, Mikhail, and Elena Joly. *The Gun That Changed the World*. Translated by Andrew Brown. Cambridge, UK: Polity, 2006.

Kania, Elsa, *The PLA's Unmanned Aerial Systems: New Capabilities for a 'New Era' of Chinese Military Power*. Montgomery, AL: China Aerospace Studies Institute, 2018.

Katz, Amrom H. *Some Notes on the History of Aerial Reconnaissance (Part I)*. Santa Monica, CA: RAND Corporation, April 1966.

Kearney, Thomas A., and Eliot A. Cohen. *Gulf War Air Power Survey: Summary Report*. Washington, DC: U.S. Department of the Air Force, 1993.

Kedzior, Richard W. *Evolution and Endurance: The U.S. Army Division in the Twentieth Century*. Santa Monica, CA: RAND Corporation, 2000.

Keefer, Edward C. *Harold Brown: Offsetting the Soviet Military Challenge, 1977–1981*. Washington, DC: Office of the Secretary of Defense, 2017.

Kempinski, Bernard, and Christopher Murphy. *Technical Challenges of the U.S. Army's Ground Combat Vehicle Program*. Washington, DC: Congressional Budget Office, 2012.

Kennedy, Donald R. *History of the Shaped Charge Effect: The First 100 Years*. Presentation at the 100th Anniversary of the Discovery of the Shaped Charge Effect by Max Von Foerster, Schrobenhausen, West Germany, September 20–22, 1983.

Khurshudyan, Isabelle, and Alex Horton. "Russian Jamming Leaves Some High-Tech U.S. Weapons Ineffective in Ukraine." *Washington Post*. May 24, 2024.

Kipp, Jacob W. *The Methodology of Foresight and Forecasting in Soviet Military Affairs*. Fort Leavenworth, KS: Soviet Army Studies Office, 1987.

Kitamura, Shuhui. *World Historical Battles Database Version 1.1*. Research paper, n.d.

Knox, MacGregor, and Williamson Murray. *The Dynamics of Military Revolution, 1300–2050*. New York: Cambridge University Press, 2001.

Kreis, John F. "Unmanned Aircraft in Israeli Air Operations." *Air Power History* 37, no. 4 (Winter 1990): 46–50.

Krepinevich, Andrew, and Barry Watts. *The Last Warrior: Andrew Marshall and the Shaping of Modern American Defense Strategy*. New York: Basic Books, 2015.

Krepinevich, Andrew, Barry Watts, and Robert Work. *Meeting the Anti-Access and Area-Denial Challenge*. Washington, DC: Center for Strategic and Budgetary Assessments, 2003.

Krepinevich, Andrew, and Robert O. Work. *A New Global Defense Posture for the Second Transoceanic Era*. Washington, DC: Center for Strategic and Budgetary Assessments, 2007.

Krepinevich, Andrew F., Jr. *The Military-Technical Revolution: A Preliminary Assessment*. Washington, DC: Center for Strategic and Budgetary Analysis, 1992.

———. *The Origins of Victory: How Disruptive Military Innovation Determines the Fates of Great Powers*. New Haven, CT: Yale University Press, 2023.

———. *Why AirSea Battle?* Washington, DC: Center for Strategic and Budgetary Analysis, 2010.

Krulak, Charles, and Anthony Zinni. "Vision 2035: Global Response in the Age of Precision Munitions." *National Interest*, December 16, 2022.

Kuo, Kendrick. "Dangerous Changes: When Military Innovation Harms Combat Effectiveness." *International Security* 47, no. 2 (Fall 2022): 48–87.

Lacina, Bethany, and Nils Petter Gleditsch. "Monitoring Trends in Global Combat: A New Dataset of Battle Deaths." *European Journal of Population*, no. 21 (2005): 145–166.

Lacquement, Richard A., Jr. "The Casualty-Aversion Myth." *Naval War College Review* 57, no. 1 (Winter 2004).

Laffin, John. *Brassey's Dictionary of Battles: 3,500 Years of Conflict, Campaigns, and Wars*. New York: Barnes & Noble, 1986.

Leishman, J. Gordon. "The Breguet-Richet Quad-Rotor Helicopter of 1907." *Vertiflite* 47, no. 3 (2002): 58–60.

———. *A History of Helicopter Flight*. Online paper, derived from J. Gordon Leishman. https://www.aviatorsdatabase.com/wp-content/uploads/2013/07/A-History-of-Helicopter-Flight-.pdf.

———. *Principles of Helicopter Aerodynamics*. New York: Cambridge University Press, 2000.

LePore, Herbert P. "Eyes in the Sky: A History of Liaison Aircraft and Their Use in World War II." *Army History*, no. 17 (Winter 1990–1991): 30–39.

Lewis, S. J. *Forgotten Legions: German Army Infantry Policy 1918–1941*. New York: Praeger, 1985.

Liddell Hart, Basil Henry. *Paris—or—The Future of War*. New York: E. P. Dutton, 1926.

Liddell Hart, B. H. *The Revolution in Warfare*. London: Faber and Faber, 1947.

Lieberthal, Kenneth G. "The Pivot to Asia." Brookings Institution, December 21, 2011.

Lind, William S. *Maneuver Warfare Handbook*. New York: Routledge, 1985.

Luttwak, Edward N. "Toward Post-Heroic Warfare," *Foreign Affairs* 74, no. 3 (May–June 1995): 109–122.

Lythgoe, Trent. "Our Risk Averse Army: How We Got Here and How to Overcome It." *Modern War Institute*, May 9, 2019.

MacGarrigle, George L. *Taking the Offensive: October 1966 to October 1967*. Washington, DC: U.S. Army Center of Military History, 1988.

Mackie, Will. "Soldiers of Fortune: Why U.S. Mercenaries Should Not Be Legal." *War on the Rocks*. August 26, 2021.

Major, Richard. *RQ-2 Pioneer: The Flawed System That Redefined US Unmanned Aviation*. Thesis, Air Command and Staff College, 2012.

Malovany, Pesach. *Wars of Modern Babylon: A History of the Iraqi Army from 1921 to 2003*. Lexington: University Press of Kentucky, 2017.

Mandel, David R., and Alan Barnes. "Accuracy of Forecasts in Strategic Intelligence." *Proceedings of the National Academy of Sciences* 111, no. 30 (July 29, 2014): 10984–10989.

Manucy, Albert. *Artillery through the Ages.* January 30, 2007. https://www.amazon.com/Artillery-Through-Ages-Illustrated-Emphasizing-ebook.

Marshal Foch. *The Principles of War.* Translated by Hilaire Belloc. New York: Henry Holt, 1920.

Martin, Donald H. *Communication Satellites: 1958–1992.* El Segundo, CA: The Aerospace Corporation, December 31, 1991.

Matsumura, John M., Randall Steeb, and John Gordon IV. *The Army's Next Self-Propelled Howitzer and Resupply Vehicle.* Santa Monica, CA: RAND Corporation, 1998.

Matsumura, John, Randall Steeb, Thomas Herbert, Scot Eisenhard, John Gordon, Mark Lees, and Gail Halverson. *The Army after Next: Exploring New Concepts and Technologies for the Light Battle Force.* Santa Monica, CA: RAND Corporation, n.d.

Matthews, Miriam, Christopher Paul, David Schulker, and David Stebbins. *Frameworks for Assessing USEUCOM Efforts to Inform, Influence, and Persuade.* Santa Monica, CA: RAND Corporation, 2020.

McConville, James C. *Army Multi-Domain Transformation: Ready to Win in Competition and Conflict.* Chief of Staff Paper #1. Washington, DC: Headquarters, Department of the Army, March 16, 2021.

McGrath, John J. *The Brigade: A History, Its Organization and Employment in the US Army.* Fort Leavenworth, KS: Combat Studies Institute Press, 2004.

McNab, Chris. *Sagger Anti-Tank Missile vs M60 Main Battle Tank: Yom Kippur War 1973.* Oxford, UK: Osprey, 2018. https://www.amazon.com/Sagger-Anti-Tank-Missile-Main-Battle-ebook.

Mead, Peter W. *Eye in the Air: History of Air Observation and Reconnaissance for the Army 1785–1945.* London: HMSO, 1983.

Meleca, Vincenzo. "Afabet, March 1988: The Decisive Battle for Eritrean Independence." Online article. https://www.ilcornodafrica.it/afabet-march-1988-the-decisive-battle-for-eritrean-indipendence/

Michel, Arthur Holland. *Counter-Drone Systems,* 2nd ed. Annandale-on-Hudson, NY: The Center for the Study of the Drone at Bard College, December 2019.

Milley, Mark A., "Strategic Inflection Point: The Most Historically Significant and Fundamental Change in the Character of War Is Happening Now—While the Future Is Clouded in Mist and Uncertainty." *Joint Forces Quarterly,* no. 110 (3rd Quarter 2023, 2023): 6–15.

Mizokami, Kyle. "Sweden's 'S-Tank' Had a Super Strange—but Not Stupid—Design." *Popular Mechanics,* April 4, 2016.

Monaghan, Andrew. "Kennan Cable No. 75: Victory, Defeat, and Russian Ways in War." Wilson Center, March 2022.

Moorhouse, Roger. *Poland 1939: The Outbreak of World War II.* New York: Basic Books, 2020.

Morris, Douglas. "The Development and Use of Helicopters." Presentation to the Royal United Services Institute in London, on November 23, 1966.

Mortensen, Daniel R. *A Pattern for Joint Operations: World War II Close Air Support in North Africa.* Washington, DC: Center of Military History, 1987.

Mountcastle, John W. *Flame On: U.S. Incendiary Weapons, 1918–1945.* Mechanicsburg, PA: Stackpole Books, 1999.

Mroczkowski, Dennis P. *With the 2d Marine Division in Desert Shield and Desert Storm: U.S. Marines in the Persian Gulf, 1990–1991.* Washington, DC: History and Museums Division, Headquarters, U.S. Marine Corps, 1993.

Mueller, Karl P., ed. *Precision and Purpose: Airpower in the Libyan Civil War.* Santa Monica, CA: RAND Corporation, 2015.

Murray, Williamson. "Thinking about Revolutions in Military Affairs." *Joint Forces Quarterly*, no. 16 (Summer 1997): 69–76.

Nalty, Bernard C. *Air Power and the Fight for Khe Sanh.* Washington, DC: U.S. Air Force Office of Air Force History, 1986.

Newcome, Laurence R. *Unmanned Aviation: A Brief History of Unmanned Aerial Vehicles.* Reston, VA: American Institute of Aeronautics and Astronautics, 2004.

Ney, Virgil. *Evolution of the U.S. Army Infantry Battalion: 1939–1968.* Fort Belvoir, VA: Technical Operations, Incorporated Combat Operations Research Group, October 1968.

North Atlantic Treaty Organization. *NATO Warfighting Capstone Concept.* Norfolk, VA: Allied Transformation Command, n.d.

Nwazor, Nkolika O., and Stella I. Orakwue. "A Review of Night Vision Technology." *Australian Journal of Science and Technology* 4, no. 1 (March 2020): 265–269.

O'Hanlon, Michael E., "Beware the 'RMA'nia!'" Brookings Institution, September 9, 1998.

———. "How Big an Army Does the United States Need?" Brookings Institution, November 15, 2013.

Oman, C. W. C. *The Art of War in the Middle Ages*, with John H. Beeler, ed. Ithaca, NY: Cornell University Press, 1898/1953.

Orkaby, Asher. *Beyond the Arab Cold War: The International History of the Yemen Civil War, 1962–68.* Oxford, UK: Oxford University Press, 2019.

Orkland, Bob, and Lyman Duryea. *Misfire: The Tragic Failure of the M16 in Vietnam.* Mechanicsburg, PA: Stackpole Books, 2019.

Osinga, Frans. *Science, Strategy and War: The Strategic Theory of John Boyd.* Delft, The Netherlands: Eburon Academic, 2005.

Owens, Bill, and Ed Offley. *Lifting the Fog of War.* Baltimore: Johns Hopkins University Press, 2000.

Paul, Christopher, Jessica Yeats, Colin P. Clarke, Miriam Matthews, and Lauren Skrabala. *Assessing and Evaluating Department of Defense Efforts to Inform, Influence, and Persuade: Handbook for Practitioners.* Santa Monica, CA: RAND Corporation, 2015.

Peck, Jakub. "New Precision-Guided Shells Are Giving Ukraine an Edge over Russia in Their Grinding Artillery Battle." *Business Insider*, October 3, 2022.

Pernin, Christopher G., Elliot Axelband, Jeffrey A. Drezner, Brian B. Dille, John Gordon IV, Bruce J. Held, K. Scott McMahon, Walter L. Perry, Christopher Rizzi, Akhil R. Shah, Peter A. Wilson, and Jerry M. Sollinger. *Lessons from the Army's Future Combat Systems Program.* Santa Monica, CA: RAND Corporation, 2012.

Pietrucha, Mike. "Airpower Orphans, Part II: Whatever Happened to Liaison Aircraft?" *War on the Rocks*, August 26, 2019.

Pinder, John D. *Reactive Armor Tiles for Army and Marine Corps Armored Vehicles: An Independent Report to the Department of Defense and the United States Congress.* Santa Monica, CA: RAND Corporation, 1999.

Pollack, Kenneth M. "Air Power in the Six Day War." *Journal of Strategic Studies* 28, no. 3 (2005): 471–503.

———. *Arabs at War: Military Effectiveness, 1948–1991.* Lincoln: University of Nebraska Press, 2002.

Polmar, Norman. "Historic Aircraft—The Pioneering Pioneer." *Naval History Magazine* 27, no. 5 (September 2013).

Praun, Albert. *German Radio Intelligence.* U.S. Department of the Army, Office of the Chief of Military History, 1950.

Price, Alfred. *Instruments of Darkness: The History of Electronic Warfare 1939–1945.* Yorkshire, UK: Frontline Books, 2022/1967.

Quilter, Charles J., II. *U.S. Marines in the Persian Gulf, 1990–1991: With the I Marine Expeditionary Force in Desert Shield and Desert Storm.* Washington, DC: History and Museums Division, Headquarters, U.S. Marine Corps, 1993.

Raach, George T. *A Withering Fire: American Machine Gun Battalions in World War I.* Booklocker.com, 2015. https://www.amazon.com/Withering-Fire-American-Machine-Battalions-ebook.

Raines, Edgar F., Jr. *Eyes of Artillery: The Origins of Modern U.S. Army Aviation in World War II.* Washington, DC: U.S. Army Center of Military History, 2000.

Rawlins, Eugene W. *Marines and Helicopters: 1946–1962.* Washington, DC: History and Museums Division, Headquarters, U.S. Marine Corps, 1976.

Reach, Clint, Alyssa Demus, Eugeniu Han, Bilyana Lilly, Krystyna Marcinek, and Yuliya Shokh. *Russian Military Forecasting and Analysis: The Military-Political Situation and Military Potential in Strategic Planning.* Santa Monica, CA: RAND Corporation, 2022.

Rempfer, Kyle. "More Than Meets the Eye: Army Selects Next-Gen Camouflage System." *Army Times*, November 7, 2018.

Robinson, Stephen. *The Blind Strategist: John Boyd and the American Art of War.* Dunedin, New Zealand: Exisle, 2021.

Roblin, Sebastien. "Czech Super T-72M4 Tanks Seen Headed to Poland—Ukraine Border." *Forbes*, October 28, 2022.

Rogers, Clifford J. "The Military Revolutions of the Hundred Years' War." *Journal of Military History* 57, no. 2 (April 1993): 241–278.

Romjue, John L. *From Active Defense to AirLand Battle: The Development of Army Doctrine 1973–1982.* Fort Monroe, VA: U.S. Army Training and Doctrine Command, June 1984.

Roncolato, Gerard. "The Character of War Is Constantly Changing." *Proceedings* 148, no. 5 (May 2022).

Rothfels, Hans. "Clausewitz," in *Makers of Modern Strategy*, edited by Edward Meade Earle. New York: Atheneum Press, 1969.

Rottman, Gordon L. *The Bazooka.* Oxford, UK: Osprey, 2012.

———. *World War II US Armored Infantry Tactics.* Oxford, UK: Osprey, 2011.

Roush, Gary. "Helicopter Losses during the Vietnam War." VHPA website, n.d.

Rubin, Michael. "A Short History of the Iranian Drone Program." Online article. American Enterprise Institute, 2020.

Rubin, Uzi. "The Second Nagorno-Karabakh War: A Milestone in Military Affairs." The Begin-Sadat Center for Strategic Studies, December 16, 2020.

Rumsfeld, Donald H. "Transforming the Military." *Foreign Affairs* 81, no. 3 (May–June 2002): 20–32.

Ryan, Mick. *War Transformed: The Future of Twenty-First Century Great Power Competition and Conflict.* Annapolis, MD: Naval Institute Press, 2022.

Sanders, Gold V. "Why Our Tanks Can Score Hits on the Run." *Popular Science* 145, no. 3 (1944): 82–85.

Saney, Isaac. "African Stalingrad: The Cuban Revolution, Internationalism, and the End of Apartheid." *Latin American Perspectives* 33, no. 5 (September 2006): 81–117.

Sasso, Claude R. *Soviet Night Operations in World War II*. Fort Leavenworth, KS: Combat Studies Institute, 1982.

Scales, Robert H. "Forecasting the Future of Warfare." *War on the Rocks*, April 9, 2018.

Scales, Robert H., Jr. *Certain Victory: United States Army in the Gulf War*. Washington, DC: U.S. Government Printing Office, 1993.

Schmidt, Dana Adams. *Yemen: The Unknown War*. New York: Holt, Rinehart, and Winston, 1968.

Schneider, Wolfgang. *Panzer Tactics: German Small-Unit Armor Tactics in World War II*. Guilford, CT: Stackpole Books, 2000.

Setzekorn, Eric. "Taiwan and the U.S. Army: New Opportunities amid Increasing Threats." *Military Review*, September–October 2020, 44–53.

Shachtman, Noah. "First Armed Robots on Patrol in Iraq (Updated)." *Wired*, August 2, 2007.

Shaikh, Shaan, and Wes Rumbaugh. "The Air and Missile War in Nagorno-Karabakh: Lessons for the Future of Strike and Defense." Center for Strategic and International Studies, December 8, 2020.

Sheehan, John J., and James Amos. "Former Marine Generals: 'Our Concerns with Force Design 2030.'" *National Interest*, December 12, 2022.

Shore, Moyers S., II. *The Battle for Khe Sanh*. Washington, DC: History and Museums Division, Headquarters, U.S. Marine Corps, 1969.

Shulimson, Jack. *U.S. Marines in Vietnam: An Expanding War, 1966*. Washington, DC: History and Museums Division, Headquarters, U.S. Marine Corps, 1982.

Silvasy, Stephen, Jr. "AirLand Battle Future: The Tactical Battlefield." *Military Review* 71, no. 2 (1991): 2–12.

Simpson, Michael P., Adam R. Grissom, Christopher A. Mouton, John P. Godges, and Russell Hanson. *Road to Damascus: The Russian Air Campaign in Syria, 2015–2018*. Santa Monica, CA: RAND Corporation, 2022.

Singer, Noah. "Military Robots and the Laws of War." Brookings Institution, February 11, 2009.

Sladden, James, Liam Collins, and Ben Connable. *The Battle of Irpin River*, British Army Review Special Edition. London: Centre for Historical Analysis and Conflict Research, February 2024.

Smith, Rupert. *The Utility of Force: The Art of War in the Modern World*. New York: Alfred A. Knopf, 2007.

The Smithsonian. *Tank: The Definitive Visual History of Armored Vehicles*. London: DK, 2017.

Sokolovakiy, V., and M. Cherednichenko. "Revolution in Military Science, Its Importance and Consequences, Military Art on a New Stage." *Krasnaya Zvezda*, no. 203 (1964): 2–3, translated and published by the U.S. Air Force Systems Command, Wright-Patterson Air Force Base, Ohio, 1964.

Sorley, Lewis. *Westmoreland: The General Who Lost Vietnam*. New York: Houghton Mifflin Harcourt, 2011.

Sorley, Lewis, ed. *Press On! Selected Works of General Donn A. Starry, Volume I*. Fort Leavenworth, KS: Combat Studies Institute Press, 2009.

Soviet General Staff. *The Berlin Operation 1945*. Edited and translated by Richard W. Harrison. West Midlands, UK: Helion, 2016.

Spink, Lauren, and Matt Wells. *Under Fire: The July 2016 Violence in Juba and UN Response*. Center for Civilians in Conflict. Online report, 2016.

Stanley, Elizabeth A. *Evolutionary Technology in the Current Revolution in Military Affairs: The Army Tactical Command and Control System*. Carlisle Barracks, PA: Strategic Studies Institute, 1998.

Stevens, David, "Naval Gunfire Support at Gallipoli." Online article. Royal Australian Artillery History Organization, n.d. https://www.artilleryhistory.org/history_seminar_series/seminar_no_1_13_may_2015/seminar_1_documents/david_stevens_naval_gunfire_support_at_gallipoli.pdf.

Strachan, Hew. "The Elusive Meaning and Enduring Relevance of Clausewitz." In *The New Makers of Modern Strategy*, edited by Hal Brands. Princeton, NJ: Princeton University Press, 2023, 116–144.

Strachan, Hew, and Sibylle Scheipers, eds. *The Changing Character of War*. Oxford, UK: Oxford University Press, 2011.

Strickland, Frank. "The Early Evolution of the Predator Drone." *Studies in Intelligence* 57, no. 1 (March 2013).

Stronell, Alexander. "Learning the Lessons of Nagorno-Karabakh the Russian Way." *IISS*, March 10, 2021

Sun Tzŭ, *The Art of War*. Translated by Lionel Giles. 1910. Attributed to Sun Tzŭ in approximately fifth century BCE. N.p.

———. *The Art of War*. Translated by Roger T. Ames. 1993. In *The Book of War: Sun-Tzu The Art of Warfare & Karl von Clausewitz On War*, edited by Caleb Carr. New York: Random House, 2000.

Taylor, Austin B. *Counter-Unmanned Aerial Vehicles Study: Shipboard Laser Weapon System Engagement Strategies for Countering Drone Swarm Threats in the Maritime Environment*. Thesis, Monterey, CA: Naval Postgraduate School, December 2021.

Terriff, Terry. "'Innovate or Die': Organisational Culture and the Origins of Maneuver Warfare in the United States Marine Corps." *Journal of Strategic Studies* 29, no. 3 (2006): 475–503.

Tetlock, Philip E. *Expert Political Judgment: How Good Is It? How Can We Know?* Princeton, NJ: Princeton University Press, 2006.

Tetlock, Philip E., and Dan Gardner. *Superforecasting: The Art and Science of Prediction*. New York: Random House, 2015.

Thomas, Nicole, Matt Jamison, Kendall Gomber, and Derek Walton. "What the United States Military Can Learn from the Nagorno-Karabakh War." *Small Wars Journal*, April 4, 2021.

Thomas, Timothy L. "Russian Forecasts of Future War." *Military Review*, May–June 2019, 84–93.

Thompson, George Raynor, and Dixie R. Harris. *The Signal Corps: The Outcome (Mid-1943 through 1945)*. Washington, DC: U.S. Army Center of Military History, 1991.

Tincopa, Amaru, *Air Wars between Ecuador and Peru: Aerial Operations over the Condor Mountain Range, 1995*. Warwick, UK: Helion, 2021.

Tong, Michael, "M60 Patton: 'Stopgap' Tank Clocks Up a Half-Century in Service." International Institute for Strategic Studies, July 22, 2019.

Transue, J. R. *Assessment of the Weapons and Tactics Used in the October 1973 Middle East War*. Declassified intelligence analysis, Arlington, VA: Weapons Systems Evaluation Group, 1974.

Turner, Paul E. *Precision Fires Rocket and Missile Systems: New and Evolving Armaments and Subsystems for Future Conflicts.* U.S. Army Precision Fires Rocket & Missile Systems Project Office, April 27, 2016.

U.S. Army. *Army Multi-Domain Transformation: Ready to Win in Competition and Conflict.* Washington, DC: Chief of Staff of the Army, March 16, 2021.

———. *Concepts of the Army Objective Force.* White paper, Washington, DC: Department of the Army, 2001.

———. *Ground Combat Vehicle (GCV) Analysis of Alternatives.* December 17, 2010.

———. *Gun Stabilization Systems (Vehicular).* Aberdeen Proving Ground, MD: U.S. Army Test and Evaluation Command, 1983.

———. *Infantry Battalion.* Technical publication, ATP 3–21.20. Washington, DC: Headquarters, Department of the Army, December 2017.

———. *Javelin—Close Combat Missile System, Medium.* Technical manual, TC 3–22.37. Washington, DC: Headquarters, Department of the Army, August 2013.

———. *M60A1, M60A1 RISE, and M60A1 RISE (Passive) Series Tanks Combat Full-Tracked 105-mm Gun Update System Assessment.* Warren, MI: Logistic Management Division, PMO M60 Tanks, May 1980.

———. *The Operational Environment and the Changing Character of Warfare.* Fort Eustis, VA: Training and Doctrine Command, October 7, 2019.

———. *Operations.* ADP 3–0. Washington, DC: Headquarters, Department of the Army, November 2016.

———. *Operations.* ADP 3–0. Washington, DC: Headquarters, Department of the Army, October 2017.

———. *Operations.* Field Manual 100–5. Washington, DC: Headquarters, U.S. Army, 1982.

———. *Operations.* FM 3–0. Washington, DC: Headquarters, Department of the Army, October 2022.

———. *People's Liberation Army "Ground Forces" Quick Reference Guide.* Fort Leavenworth, KS: Training and Doctrine Command, 2020.

———. *The United States Army in Somalia 1992–1994.* Washington, DC: U.S. Army Center of Military History, n.d.

———. *The U.S. Army in Multi-Domain Operations 2028.* Fort Leavenworth, KS: U.S. Army Training and Doctrine Command, December 6, 2018.

———. *U.S. Army Unmanned Aircraft Systems Roadmap 2010–2035.* Fort Rucker, AL: U.S. Army UAS Center of Excellence, 2010.

U.S. Central Intelligence Agency. *Soviet Artillery Precision-Guided Munitions: A Conventional Weapons Initiative.* Declassified intelligence report, Langley, VA: Directorate of Intelligence, September 1986.

U.S. Congress. *The Army's Future Combat Systems Program and Alternatives.* Washington, DC: Congressional Budget Office, 2006.

U.S. Defense Intelligence Agency. *China Military Power: Modernizing a Force to Fight and Win.* Anacostia, MD: Directorate of Analysis, 2019.

———. *Russia Military Power: Building a Military to Support Great Power Aspirations,* Anacostia, MD: Directorate of Intelligence, 2017.

U.S. Department of Defense. *Abrams M1A2 System Enhancement Packages (SEPs) Main Battle Tank (MBT) and Trophy Active Protection System.* Washington, DC: Office of Testing and Evaluation, 2020.

———. *Acquisition of the Advanced Antitank Weapon System-Medium.* Official audit, Report 92–023. Washington, DC: Office of the Inspector General, December 17, 1991.

———. *DOD Dictionary of Military and Associated Terms*. Electronic manual, November 2021.

———. *Excalibur Precision 155mm Projectiles*, 2015.

———. *Excalibur Precision 155mm Projectiles (Excalibur)*. Selected acquisition report, Picatinny Arsenal. NJ: Defense Acquisition Management Information Retrieval, March 21, 2016.

———. *Military and Security Developments Involving the People's Republic of China 2022*. Washington, DC: Office of the Secretary of Defense, 2022.

———. *Mobile Protected Firepower (MPF)*. Washington, DC: Director, Operational Test and Evaluation, 2022.

———. *Summary of the 2018 National Defense Strategy of the United States of America*. Washington, DC, 2018.

———. *Unmanned Aircraft Systems Roadmap 2005–2030*. Washington, DC: Office of the Secretary of Defense, August 2005.

U.S. Department of Homeland Security. "Counter-Unmanned Aircraft Systems (C-UAS)." Article and video, DHS Science and Technology, n.d.

U.S. Department of State. *A Reordering of Soviet Military Priorities*. Memorandum from George P. Shultz to Caspar W. Weinberger, William J. Casey, and Robert C. McFarlane, July 2, 1984.

U.S. Director of National Intelligence. *The Future of the Battlefield*. MacLean, VA: April 2021.

U.S. General Accounting Office. *Army Armored Systems: Meeting Crusader Requirements Will Be a Technical Challenge*. Washington, DC: National Security and International Affairs Division, June 1997.

U.S. Government. *A Tradecraft Primer: Structured Analytic Techniques for Improving Intelligence Analysis*, March 2009.

U.S. Government Accountability Office. *Unmanned Aerial Vehicles: DoD's Acquisition Efforts*. Congressional testimony, April 9, 1997.

U.S. Joint Chief of Staff. *Dictionary of Military and Associated Terms*. Washington, DC: Joint Staff, November 2021.

———. *Doctrine for the Armed Forces of the United States*. Joint Publication 1. Washington, DC: Chairman of the Joint Chiefs of Staff, 2017.

———. *Joint Vision 2010*. Washington, DC, 1998.

———. *Joint Vision 2020*. Washington, DC, 2000.

———. *Joint Warfighting*. Joint Publication 1, Volume 1. Washington, DC, August 27, 2023.

———. *Strategy*. Joint Doctrine Note 1–18. Washington, DC, April 25, 2018.

U.S. Joint Forces Command, *MC02 Final Report*, Norfolk, VA, 2002.

U.S. Marine Corps. *Advanced Base Operations in Micronesia*. Fleet Marine Force Reference Publication 12–46. Washington, DC: Headquarters, U.S. Marine Corps, 1992.

———. *An Annotated Bibliography of the United States Marine Corps' Concept of Close Air Support*. Washington, DC: Headquarters, U.S. Marine Corps Historical Branch, 1968.

———. *Campaigning*. MCDP 1–2. Washington, DC: Headquarters, U.S. Marine Corps, August 1997.

———. Company "B" (Rein), 4th Tank Battalion, 4th Marine Division. Operation Desert Storm Command Chronology excerpt, n.d.

———. *A Concept for Stand-in Forces.* Washington, DC: Headquarters, U.S. Marine Corps, December 2021.

———. *Expeditionary Force 21.* Concept paper. Washington, DC: Headquarters, U.S. Marine Corps, 2014.

———. *Force Design 2030: Annual Update.* Washington, DC: Headquarters, U.S. Marine Corps, April 2021.

———. *Force Design 2030 Annual Update.* Washington, DC: Headquarters, U.S. Marine Corps, May 2022.

———. *Force Design 2030: Annual Update.* Washington, DC: Headquarters, U.S. Marine Corps, June 2023.

———. *MAGTF Ground Operations.* MCWP 3–10. Washington, DC: Headquarters, U.S. Marine Corps, April 2018.

———. *Strategy.* MCDP 1–1. Washington, DC: Headquarters, U.S. Marine Corps, November 1997.

———. *Tactics.* MCDP 1–3. Washington, DC: Headquarters, U.S. Marine Corps, July 1997.

———. *Warfighting.* MCDP-1. Washington, DC: Headquarters, U.S. Marine Corps, 1997.

U.S. War Department. *240-mm Howitzers M1918M1 and M1918M1A1, 240-mm Howitzer Carriage 1918A2, and Transport Wagons M4 and M5.* TM 9–340, April 6, 1944.

———. *Basic Field Manual, U.S. Rifle, Caliber .30, M1.* Washington, DC: Government Printing Office, 1940.

———. *German and Japanese Solid-Fuel Rocket Weapons.* Washington, DC: Military Intelligence Division, n.d.

———. *Handbook on German Military Forces.* TM-E 30–451. Washington, DC, March 1945.

———. *Infantry Battalion.* Field manual, FM 7–20. Washington, DC: U.S. Government Printing Office, October 1, 1944.

———. *Soldier's Guide to the Japanese Army.* Washington, DC: Military Intelligence Service, 1944.

Uebe, D. Klaus. *Russian Reactions to German Airpower in World War II.* Captured military document, Maxwell Air Force Base, AL: Aerospace Studies Institute, July 1964.

UK Army, *Army Doctrine Primer.* Wiltshire, UK: Development, Concepts and Doctrine Centre, 2011.

———. *Land Operations.* Army Doctrine Publication AC 71940. Wiltshire, UK: Land Warfare Development Centre, 2017.

UK Ministry of Defence. *UK Land Power.* Joint Doctrine Publication 0–20, 6th ed. Shrivenham, UK: Development, Concepts and Doctrine Centre, 2023.

van Dijk, Anthonie. "The Mysterious Floating Batteries of the Royal Netherlands Navy." *Warship International* 25, no. 3 (1998): 229–238.

Van Riper, Paul K.. "The Marine Corps' Plan to Redesign the Force Will Only End Up Breaking It." *Task & Purpose,* April 20, 2022.

van Tol, Jan, Mark Gunzinger, Andrew Krepinevich, and Jim Thomas. *AirSea Battle: A Point-of-Departure Operational Concept.* Washington, DC: Center for Strategic and Budgetary Analysis, 2010.

Van Wyck, David W. "Beyond the Burn: Studies on the Psychological Effects of Flamethrowers during World War II." *Military Medical Research* 7, no. 8 (2020): 1–8.

Vego, Milan. *Recce-Strike Complexes in Soviet Theory and Practice.* Fort Leavenworth, KS: Soviet Army Studies Office, 1990.

Ventner, Al J. *Battle for Angola: The End of the Cold War in Africa c1975–1989*. West Midlands, UK: Helion, 2016. https://www.amazon.com/Battle-Angola-Cold-Africa-1975-89-ebook.

von Clausewitz, Carl, *On War*. Translated by J. J. Graham, 1873.

———. *On War*. Translated and edited by Michael Howard and Peter Paret. Princeton, NJ: Princeton University Press, 1976.

———. *On War*. Translated by O. J. Matthijs Jolles, 1943. In *The Book of War: Sun-Tzu The Art of Warfare & Karl von Clausewitz On War*, edited by Caleb Carr. New York: Random House, 2000.

von Schlieffen, Alfred. *Cannae*. Fort Leavenworth, KS: Command and General Staff School Press, 1931.

Wallach, Jehuda L. *The Dogma of the Battle of Annihilation: The Theories of Clausewitz and Schlieffen and Their Impact on the German Conduct of Two World Wars*. Westport, CT: Greenwood Press, 1986

Watling, Jack, and Nick Reynolds. *Meatgrinder: Russian Tactics in the Second Year of Its Invasion of Ukraine*. London: Royal United Services Institute, May 19, 2023.

Webb, Jim. "The Future of the U.S. Marine Corps." *National Interest*, May 8, 2020.

Weller, Donald M. *Naval Gunfire Support of Amphibious Operations: Past, Present, and Future*. Arlington, VA: Universal Systems, 1977.

Wells, Linton. "Thoughts for the 2001 Quadrennial Defense Review." Memorandum, Washington, DC, April 12, 2001.

Wendel, Robert F. *Casualty Aversion in the Post-Cold War Era: Defined and Analyzed through the Logic of Clausewitz*. Thesis, Quantico, VA: U.S. Marine Corps Command and Staff College, 2001.

Werrell, Kenneth P. *Archie to SAM: A Short Operational History of Ground-Based Air Defense*, Maxwell Air Force Base, AL: Air University Press, 2005.

———. *The Evolution of the Cruise Missile*. Maxwell Air Force Base, AL: Air University Press, 1985.

Westmoreland, William C. "New Developments in Ground Warfare," Congressional testimony. In U.S. Senate, Volume 115 of the Congressional Record, Part 22, October 16, 1969, 30348–30349.

———. *Report of the Chief of Staff of the United States Army, 1 July 1968 to 30 June 1972*. Washington, DC: Department of the Army, 1977.

———. *A Soldier Reports*. Garden City, NY: Doubleday, 1974.

Whiting, Kenneth R. "Soviet Air-Ground Coordination, 1941–1945." In *Case Studies in the Development of Close Air Supports*, edited by Franklin Benjamin Cooling. Washington, DC: U.S. Air Force Office of Air Force History, 1990, 115–142.

Whittle, Richard. *Predator: The Secret Origins of the Drone Revolution*. New York: Henry Holt, 2014.

Wilcock, Paul. "The Armoury of His Grace the Duke of Buccleuch and Queensberry." *Armour* 9, no. 2 (2013): 181–205.

Wilson, Gary, William A. Woods, and Michael D. Wyly. "Exchanging a Force-in-Readiness for a Force-in-Waiting." *Fabius Maximus*, September 18, 2022.

Wilson, G. I., Michael D. Wyly, William S. Lind, and Bernard E. Trainor. "The 'Maneuver Warfare' Concept." *Marine Corps Gazette* 65, no. 4 (1981): 49–54.

Wilson, John B. *The Evolution of Divisions and Separate Brigades*. Washington, DC: Center of Military History, 1998.

———. *Maneuver and Firepower: The Evolution of Divisions and Separate Brigades.* Washington, DC: U.S. Army Center of Military History, 1998.

Windrow, Martin. *The French Foreign Légionnaire versus Viet Minh Insurgent.* Oxford, UK: Osprey, 2018.

Wolfe, Thomas W. *Evolution of Soviet Military Policy.* Santa Monica, CA: RAND Corporation, 1968.

Woods, Kevin M., David D. Palkki, and Mark E. Stout. *The Saddam Tapes: The Inner Workings of a Tyrant's Regime, 1978–2001.* New York: Cambridge University Press, 2011.

Woods, Kevin M., Williamson Murray, Elizabeth A. Nathan, Laila Sabara, and Ana M. Venegas. *Saddam's Generals: Perspectives of the Iran-Iraq War.* Alexandria, VA: Institute for Defense Analysis, 2011.

Woods, Kevin M., Williamson Murray, and Thomas Holaday. *Saddam's War: An Iraqi Military Perspective of the Iran-Iraq War.* Washington, DC: National Defense University Institute for Strategic Studies, March 2009.

Work, Robert. "Marine Force Design: Changes Overdue Despite Critics' Claims." *Texas National Security Review* 6, no. 3 (Summer 2023).

Work, Robert, James A. Winnefeld Jr., and Stephanie O'Sullivan. "Steering in the Right Direction in the Military-Technical Revolution." *War on the Rocks,* March 23, 2021.

Work, Robert O., and Shawn Brimley. *20YY: Preparing for War in the Robotic Age.* Washington, DC: Center for New American Security, January 2014.

———. "Remarks by Deputy Secretary Work on Third Offset Strategy." Transcript from a speech delivered in Brussels, Belgium, on April 28, 2016, U.S. Department of Defense.

———. quoted in "On the Future of the Marine Corps: Assessing Force Design 2030," transcript of an online event held on May 16, 2022, Washington, DC: *Center for Strategic and International Studies.*

Yeap, Samuel, Konstantinos P. Baevanakis, and Anish Roy. "A Study on the Effectiveness of Explosive Reactive Armour against the Penetration of Long-Rod Projectiles." *Journal of Mechanical Engineering Science* 236, no. 15 (2022): 8462–8471.

Yoshihara, Toshi. "Sun Zi and the Search for a Timeless Logic of Strategy." In *The New Makers of Modern Strategy,* edited by Hal Brands. Princeton, NJ: Princeton University Press, 2023, 67–90.

Zaloga, Steven J. *M7 Priest 105mm Howitzer Motor Carriage.* Oxford, UK: Osprey, 2013.

———. *Poland 1939: The Birth of Blitzkrieg.* Oxford, UK: Osprey, 2002.

———. *T-34-85 vs M26 Pershing, Korea 1950.* Oxford, UK: Osprey, 2010.

———. *US Anti-Tank Artillery 1941–1945.* Oxford, UK: Osprey, 2005.

Zasloff, J. J. *The Role of the Sanctuary in Insurgency: Communist China's Support to the Vietminh, 1946–1954.* Santa Monica, CA: RAND Corporation, 1967.

Zenko, Micah. "Millennium Challenge: The Real Story of a Corrupted Military Exercise and Its Legacy." *War on the Rocks,* November 5, 2015.

INDEX

A2/AD. *See* anti-access/area-denial
AAA. *See* antiaircraft artillery
Abkhazia, 166
ACV. *See* Amphibious Combat Vehicle
Adrar des Ifoghas-Ametettai, 183
Afghanistan, xiv, 28, 31–35, 104, 122, 142, 155, 156, 159, 161–66, 175, 182, 188, 191, 194–95, 206, 213, 215–16, 219, 227, 233–34, 238, 241–43, 245, 262, 273, 286
aircraft, manned, fixed-wing, xiii, 9, 24, 29, 38, 40, 60, 65, 67–68, 70, 85–87, 89, 90–92, 103, 112–13, 117–18, 134, 137–38, 142–44, 156–57, 161–62, 170–71, 174, 176, 184, 188–90, 196–97, 201, 203, 205, 216, 227, 232, 233–37, 241, 243–45, 257, 262–64; A-10 Thunderbolt II, 117, 143, 263; A-29, 233; A-37, 110, 121; AC-30, 156–57, 233–34; AV-8B, 263; B-25, 60, 133; BAC 167 Strikemaster, 134; C-119, 110; C-130, 201; C-17, 266; CP-140, 171; D4Y Suisei, 92; F-117, 137–138; F-15, 195; F4-variant Corsair, 86; IL-2 Sturmovik, 70, 86, 235–236; Kfir, 121; L-4, 92; L-39, 82, 197, 233; Mi(g)-23, 233; Mi-29, 161, 172, 195; MV-22, 267; OV-10, 138, 233, 235, 262; P-38 Lightning, 68–69; P-47 Thunderbolt, 143; Po-2, 92; Su-22, 233; Su-24, 236; Su-25, 139, 161, 167, 206; Su-34, 236; Tornado, 195, 227; Typhoon, 195
air defense, 92, 112, 116, 190, 203, 204–205, 235. *See also* antiaircraft artillery *and* antiaircraft missile
Air Force, U.S., 137, 144, 258, 262
AirLand Battle, 23, 24, 27, 41, 82, 142
AirSea Battle, 33–35, 38
Al-Faw (Faw), 104–5, 113–15, 156–57, 221
Al-Hudaydah City, 195–96
Al-Mellah Farms-Castello Road, 189–90
Al-Nusra Front, 189, 173
Al-Ramadi (Ramadi), 32, 157–58, 184, 187–88, 267
Al-Shabaab, 199, 215, 226
amphibious, 24, 34, 37–38, 57, 60–61, 64, 71, 91, 105–06, 109, 114, 135–36, 155–56, 161, 164, 188, 221, 271–72, 274
Amphibious Combat Vehicle, 272
Ansar Allah, 161, 215, 226. *See also* Houthi
anti-access/area-denial, 33–35, 37
antiaircraft artillery, 67, 69, 92, 108, 116, 121–22, 130, 133, 145, 159, 163, 174, 197–98; 12.7 mm, 168, 235; 20 mm, 68, 80; 23 mm, 229, 235; 25 mm, 68, 118; .50 caliber, 110, 143, 223, 234, 267; 57 mm, 174, 235; 88 mm, 72–73
antiaircraft missile, 116, 136, 195, 197, 235; Buk M1-2, 190; Pantsir S1, 197; SA-7 (9K38 Igla), 116, 136, 174; SA-8, 116, 136; Stinger (FIM-92 Stinger); 116, 235
antitank gun, 88 mm, 72–73; 90 mm, 134; MT-12, 139
antitank guided missile, BILL, 143; HOT, 112; Javelin, xiv, 31, 83, 143, 156, 220, 222–23, 271; Konkurs, 198; Kornet, 83, 85, 198; M47, 222;

Malyutka, 4, 83, 134; Metis, 185; Milan, 24, 83, 157, 183; TOW, 22, 83, 118, 138, 189; ZT3, 115
antitank rocket, AT-4, 141–42, 223; M72 LAAW, 22, 121, 141–43, 220, 223; NLAW, 83, 143, 202; Panzerschreck (Raketenpanzerbuchse), 73, 83; PIAT, 59, 64, 66, 83; RPG-7, 83, 121, 134, 139, 169–70, 172, 174, 224; RPG-26, 143; RPG-30, 282; Type 4, 98
Arab-Israeli War of 1967, 103, 133, 286
Armed Forces of the Democratic Republic of the Congo, 172
Armenia, 119–20, 190–91, 194, 198–99, 204–05
armored personnel carrier(s), 72, 81, 106, 112, 120, 133, 157, 161, 168, 185, 229, 231; Achzarit, 143, 160; BMD-series, 202; BTR-series, 115, 120, 133, 138–39, 161, 163, 203–29; Kangaroo, 72; LAV III, 243; LVT series, 106; M113, 112, 143, 160, 162, 168, 185, 192, 231; MTLB, 174; Ratel, 221; V-150, 192; YPR-series, 162. *See also* infantry fighting vehicles
Army, U.S., 5, 11, 23, 25, 30, 38, 61, 65, 78–81, 83, 87, 89, 94, 105–7, 117, 132, 140, 142, 221–24, 253, 255, 264–65, 267, 270, 273, 275
army-level organizations, Chinese 6th, 60; Japanese 11th, 60; Japanese First Area, 69–70; Soviet 1st Red Banner, 69–70; Soviet (Red Army) Fifth, 69
Army Multi-Domain Transformation (McConville), 36
Army of the Republic of Vietnam, 110–11
Army Tactical Missile System, 31, 225
artillery systems, 75 mm, 71–72, 106, 109, 225; 85 mm, 170, 198, 225; 105 mm, 62, 85, 107, 116, 121, 137, 192, 267; 122 mm, 119, 121, 133, 139, 159, 161, 168, 173, 183, 185–86, 189, 190, 201, 225; 130 mm, 133, 139, 161, 168, 225; 152 mm, 132, 168, 185, 190, 198–99, 225; 155 mm, 112, 132, 160, 162, 183–84, 196, 225, 272–23; 203 mm, 112, 185, 225; 240 mm, 62, 67, 84, 185; M7, 85, 94; cannon, xiii, 38, 59, 60, 63, 65–66, 68, 94, 105, 106, 109, 112, 114, 118, 171–72, 175, 185, 189, 194, 198, 202, 205, 219, 224–27, 262–64, 271–74; Excalibur round, 227–28; G5, 116; PzH2000, 162; self-propelled artillery, 70, 85, 162, 267; SH5, 269
Artsakh, 190, 198, 204–05
ARVN. *See* Army of the Republic of Vietnam
assault gun, 66–67, 72–73, 80, 82; StuG-43, 72–73; Sturm-variant guns, 66; Su-76, 69
ATGM. *See* anti-tank guided missile
Australia, 67–69, 155, 235
Azerbaijan, 119–20, 190, 194, 198, 204–5, 225

Baghdad, Iraq, xiii, 32, 156, 161, 218
balloon, 32, 91, 227, 262
Base 46, 173–74
battalions, Democratic Karen Buddhist Army 906, 169; Democratic Republic of Vietnam 7th, 107; DRV 8th, 108; DRV 9th, 107; DRV 66th, 107–108; Japanese 455th, 67; Netherlands 42 Armoured Infantry, 162; U.S. 1/7, 107; U.S. 2/5, 107; U.S. 2/7, 107; U.S. 2/28, 132
Battle of 73 Easting, 119, 266
Belgium, 58, 63–64
Beni, 157–58, 217
Beqa'a Valley, 104, 105, 111–13, 136, 159
Berger, David H., 37–39, 41–42, 205, 271–74
Biddle, Stephen, xiii, 4–6, 25, 139, 275, 286
Bint Jbeil, 159–60
Blitzkrieg, 23, 26–30, 33, 40, 80
Bloch, I.S., 256–58, 260

Boko Haram, 186–87, 199
bomb, FAB-500, 263; Fritz-X, 90; GB-4, 90; glide, 87–88, 90, 237; laser-guided, 22, 24, 157; unguided, 85–86, 135, 144, 161, 172, 236, 245
Borneo, 58, 57–58
Bosnia-Herzegovina, 104, 139, 144
brigade, Australian 26th, 67; Indian 202nd and 304th, 108; Iraqi 37th Armored, 118; Israeli 35th Paratroop, 160; Israeli 51st Reserve, 160; Kachin Independence Army 252nd, 240; Pakistani 205th Infantry, 108; Russian 40th Naval Infantry, 203; Russian 155th Naval Infantry, 202–3; Syrian 80th, 173; UK 3 Commando and UK 5 Commando, 70; UK 43rd, 70; Ukrainian 72nd, 202–3; Ukrainian 93rd and 95th, 185; United Nations Force Intervention, 197; U.S. 3rd Infantry, 63, 117
Britain, 1, 5, 29, 70–72, 83–85, 87, 91–92, 94–95, 130–132, 134, 136, 141, 155, 176, 204, 233, 235, 254–56, 265, 269; British Army, 1, 254–55, 269
Bukavu, 164, 221
bunker, 63, 65, 68–69, 85, 89, 93, 109, 113, 116, 117–18, 121, 136, 142, 157, 163–64, 171, 190, 194, 203, 235, 240, 242–43, 263. *See also* bunkers
Bzura River, 30

camouflage, 145, 183, 191
Canada, 57–59, 63–64, 80, 159, 235, 243
Cannae, 29
CAS. *See* close-air support
CDB90, 285, 287. *See also* Land Warfare Database
Cenapa Valley, 104–5, 139
Center for Strategic and Budgetary Assessment, 32–34
Chad, 104, 133, 156, 159, 164–65, 166, 170, 175, 182–83, 186, 194–95, 199
Chaffee, Jr., Adna R., 81
Changde, 57–58, 60–61, 93, 95, 288
Changing Character of War Centre, 5, 253
character of war, the, xi, xii, 1–6, 8, 12–13, 36–39, 87, 95, 116, 201, 204, 252–55, 259–61, 268–71, 274
chemical and biological warfare, 60, 62, 93, 114–15, 136, 213, 243, 266, 277
Chernihiv, 245
China, 22, 32–38, 58, 60–61, 69–70, 103–4, 130, 216, 269–71, 273
Chora, 161–63
Chuyev, Yuri, 6
civilians, presence on battlefields, 67, 93, 130, 159–60, 173, 192, 241–42
Clausewitz, Karl Von, xi, 8, 11, 23, 27–29, 40, 218, 252–53, 268
close-air support, 60, 65–66, 85–86, 105, 110, 112, 116, 131, 133, 136, 138, 142–44, 157, 162–63, 168, 183, 217, 233, 235–36, 264
Cohen, Eliot, 31
Cold War, 37, 103, 116, 130–31, 141, 144, 193, 201, 276
combat effectiveness, 12–13, 268–69
combat power, 12, 22, 29, 30, 33, 35, 38, 107, 117, 119, 131, 200, 204, 235, 264, 267–72, 274
combined arms, 1, 10–11, 14, 28, 31, 56–59, 61, 65, 72–73, 78–79, 86, 94, 103–4, 106–7, 111, 116, 120, 121–22, 129–36, 139, 142, 155, 157–58, 160–62, 164–69, 171, 173–74, 184, 186–87, 193, 196, 198, 213, 245, 262, 269, 272–74, 286
company, 72, 78–79, 107, 162, 198–99, 222, 271
conventional war, 10, 32, 94, 130
Correlates of War database, 285
counterattack, 30, 58–60, 62–63, 65–66, 68–71, 81, 91, 105–6, 109–11, 114–15, 118, 120, 135, 138, 142, 157, 160, 163, 169, 171–72, 183, 186, 189, 191, 197, 199–200, 202–3, 266

counter-drone, 205, 239–40
coup d'oeil, 8
CSBA. *See* Center for Strategic and Budgetary Assessment
Cuito Cuanavale, 103–5, 115–17, 136
cyber, 213, 239, 241, 270

Democratic Karen Buddhist Army, 169
Democratic People's Republic of Korea, 105–6
Democratic Republic of the Congo, 165, 172–73, 181, 221
Department of Defense, U.S., 27–27, 36, 40, 103
Dien Bien Phu, 104, 130–31
Deptula, David A., 137–38, 258
division, Canadian 1st Infantry, 58; Canadian 3rd Infantry, 63; Chinese 3rd, 10th, and 57th, 60; Chinese 52nd, 129; Democratic Republic of Vietnam (DRV) 6th, 7th, and 341st, 110; German 1st Parachute, 58; German 3rd Panzergrenadier, 81; German 4th Parachute, 61, 72; German 64th Infantry, 63; German 90th Panzergrenadier, 58–59; Iraqi 3rd Mechanized Tawakalna, 117; Iraqi 10th and 12th Armored, 117–118; Iraqi 26th Infantry, 113–114; Israeli 36th Armored, 162nd Infantry and 643rd Territorial, 184; Japanese 14th Infantry, 64; Japanese 54th, 71; Pakistani 7th, 9th, and 14th, 168; Russian 106th Airborne, 202; Syrian 1st Armored, 111; U.S. 1st Armored and U.S. 3rd Infantry, 117; U.S. 4th Armored Infantry, 81, 85; U.S. 81st Infantry, 65; U.S. 85th Infantry and 91st Infantry, 61; U.S. First Marine, xiii, 64, 105
DKBA. *See* Democratic Karen Buddhist Army
doctrine, 1, 2, 11, 23, 25, 33, 85, 92, 116, 131, 139, 141–42, 167, 181, 193, 205, 222, 268–69
DoD. *See* Department of Defense
Donetsk Airport, 184–86, 193
Douhet, Giulio, 256–58, 260
DPRK. *See* Democratic People's Republic of Korea
DRC. *See* Democratic Republic of the Congo
drones, Ababil, 136; Borgward, 88; Breguet-Richet Gyroplane, 261; Chukar, 113; Crocco Telebomb, 87–88; Firebee, 113, 144, 261; Global Hawk, 237–38; Goliath, 67, 88–89; ground drones, 66–67, 87–89, 144, 221, 241; Harfang, 184; Heron, 221; Hunter, 238; Kettering Bug, 87–88, 94, 261; Lancet, 203; Larynx, 87; Mavic 3, 221, 261–62; Mistel, 88–89; Mohajer, 136, 194; Orbiter-3, 197; Orlan, 168, 203; PB4Y Liberator, 87; Pioneer RQ-2, 113, 238; Pointer, 238; Predator MQ-1, 144, 157, 238–39, 261; Raven, 223–24; Reaper MQ-9, 94, 194, 221, 238, 263; Seeker, 90, 116, 136, 144; Shadow, 238; Sparviero SM-79, 87; Spike Firefly, 198; TB-2, 197, 240, 261, 263; TDR-1, 89, 94, 261; Wing Loong II, 195, 197, 269. *See also* counter-drone
Dyck Advisory Group, 199–200

Echevarria II, Antulio J., 253
effects-based operations, 258
El Alamein, 94–95
electronic warfare, 23, 31, 38, 91, 112, 115–16, 187, 205, 213, 241
Ellis, Earl H., 3, 4, 42
ENDF. *See* Ethiopian National Defense Force
epistemology, xii, 95, 278
ERA. *See* explosive reactive armor
Ethiopia, 3, 28, 133, 135, 139, 159, 191, 194, 200–01, 204–06, 236, 242, 289–90
Ethiopian National Defense Force, 194, 200

Ethiopia-Tigray War, 198, 201, 205–06, 289–90
Europe, 23, 35, 37, 78, 82–83, 90, 131, 135, 138, 213, 235, 256, 265, 275, 290
Expeditionary Advanced Base Operations (EABO), 37
explosive reactive armor, 140, 167, 171, 231

Falkland Islands, 24, 104, 136, 218
FARDC. *See* Armed Forces of the Democratic Republic of the Congo
FCS. *See* Future Combat System
FD 2030. *See* Force Design 2030
flame weapons, 59, 63–66, 68–69, 92–94, 106
Force Design 2030, 4, 13, 21–23, 25, 27, 32–33, 37–39, 41, 204, 252, 270–75
forecasting, xii, 1, 3, 6–8, 20, 23, 25, 28, 32, 35, 37, 39–41, 242, 246, 255–56, 273, 274–76. *See also* forecast
Forecasting in Military Affairs (Chuyev and Mikhaylov), 6–7, 275
forecast time, 7, 8, 41, 275
France, 58, 80, 182–183; French, 26, 29–30, 81, 83, 91, 130–31, 136, 170, 183–84, 216, 229, 233, 240, 261, 265
Freedman, Lawrence, 255–56, 258, 275
Free Syrian Army, 173, 189, 193, 216, 219, 225
FSA. *See* Free Syrian Army
Fuller, J.F.C., 256
Future Combat System, 32, 34, 41, 265–66

Gaza, xiv, 166, 182, 184–85, 231, 277
GCD-V1. *See* Ground Combat Database, Version 1
GCV. *See* Ground Combat Vehicle
Georgia, 167
Germany, 27, 29–30, 58, 61, 63, 66, 72, 89–90; German(s), 26–27, 29–30, 33, 57–59, 61–64, 66–67, 72–73, 80–92, 95, 144, 218, 226, 252–53, 256, 262, 265, 270
Geyer, Michael, 29
Global Positioning System, 22, 91, 143, 145, 167, 175–176, 227–28
GNA. *See* Government of National Accord
Goma, 171–73
Goose Green, 104, 136
Government of National Accord, 196–97, 269
GPS. *See* Global Positioning System
Gray, Colin S., 6, 41, 259–60
Grenada, 137, 273
Grenade, hand, 71, 160, 219, 223–24, 262; launcher, 11, 121–22, 137, 223–24
Griffith, Paddy, xii, 260, 277
Ground Combat Database, Version 1, xiv, 8, 295
Ground Combat Vehicle, 264–65. *See also* GCV
Grozny, 104, 138–39
Gulf War, the, xii–xiii, 4, 24, 40, 94, 113, 117, 118–19, 137–38, 227, 232, 258, 266, 273, 286

hand-to-hand, 59, 64, 66, 73, 109, 111
Harasta, 216
Hecht, Eado, 205
Hejlij-Pandthau, 171–72
helicopters, 21, 33, 92, 107, 112–15, 121–23, 133, 136–41, 143–45, 157–58, 160–61, 167–68, 172, 175, 183, 185, 190, 195–96, 199, 233–36, 245, 262, 264, 266–67; AH-1 Cobra, 112, 138, 168, 234; AH-64, 137, 195–96, 234; CH-47, 234; Eurocopter Tiger, 183; Gazelle, 112, 136, 233; MD-500, 262; MG-520, 235; Mi-8, 123, 158, 161, 199, 233; Mi-24, 139, 185, 195, 199–200, 233; Mi-35, 139, 195; UH-1, 107, 123; UH-60, 234
Heuser, Beatrice, 253
Hezb'allah, 160, 189, 218

Hill 170, 57–58, 70–72, 74, 95
Hilli-Bogra, 104–105, 108–9
Hitler, Adolf, 27, 29
Horenka, 201–2
horses, 30, 59–61, 129, 256, 288
Houthi, 161–62, 188, 195–96, 215, 226, 243. *See also* Ansar Allah
Howard, Michael, 5, 275
human shield, 188, 192, 242
Hussein, Saddam, 137, 215

Ia Drang Valley, 104–5, 107–8
IED. *See* improvised explosive device
improvised explosive device, 32, 160, 185, 192, 220, 243; suicide-vehicle-borne improvised explosive device, 243
Inayat Qilla-Bai Cheena, 168, 218
Inchon-Seoul, 104–6, 168
indirect fire, 11, 65, 72, 78–79, 83–85, 105, 111, 116, 121, 122, 134, 141, 159, 161–62, 173, 185, 188, 190, 192, 201–2, 215, 218, 221, 224–28, 242–44, 255, 274, 277
Indonesia, 134
infantry, dismounted, 109, 118, 129; infantry-armor teaming, 58, 65, 69–70, 73, 80, 82, 105–6, 109, 114, 117, 136, 157, 168, 184, 189, 219, 231, 272; mechanized infantry, xiv, 72, 81–82, 112, 114–16, 118–19, 157, 160, 163, 167–68, 182, 184, 188, 203, 220, 242, 257; motorized infantry, 81, 171–72, 197, 231
Infantry Battalion (U.S. Army), 222
infantry fighting vehicle, 81, 106, 117, 120, 133, 135, 161–70, 173–85, 188, 195, 198, 229; BMP-series, 117–18, 120, 133, 135, 138–39, 143, 161, 163, 170, 172–74, 185, 195, 198, 202–3, 229, 242; M2/M3 Bradley, 117–18, 138, 143, 229, 264–65, 267; XM30, 267–68
information operations, 241
innovation, xii, 3–4, 12–13, 20–22, 26, 30–32, 36, 82, 84, 204, 255, 259–60, 264, 276–78
Iran, 103, 113–14, 122, 135–36, 170, 181, 186, 194–95, 227, 286
Iran-Iraq War, 103, 113–14, 122, 135, 227, 286
Iraq, xii, xiv, 3–4, 10–11, 24, 31–32, 34–35, 40, 94, 103–5, 113–15, 117–18, 122, 132, 135–38, 142, 155–58, 161, 164–66, 170, 175, 181–82, 187–88, 191, 200, 206, 213, 215–18, 220–22, 227–29, 231–35, 237–39, 241–45, 262, 266–67, 270, 273, 286
Irpin River, xv, 201–2
irregular war, 103, 173, 187, 217, 273
Islamic State, 11, 181–82, 184, 187–88, 191–93, 196, 198–99, 213, 215, 224, 226, 235, 237, 239, 242–43, 288
Israel, 4, 103, 111–13, 133–34, 136, 143–44, 159–60, 166, 184–85, 190, 204–5, 218, 221, 229, 231–33, 261, 286

Japan(ese), 3–4, 26, 42, 57–58, 60–61, 64–73, 80, 83, 87, 90, 91–95, 130, 262
JDAM. *See* Joint Direct Attack Munition
Joint Direct Attack Munition, 31
Jomini, Antoine-Henri, 8, 31, 253

Kangaw, 70–71
Knox, MacGregor, 20, 259, 275
Korea(n), 34, 92, 103–6, 122, 130, 258, 273
Korean War, 92, 103–4, 122–30, 273
Krepinevich, Andrew, 24–27, 30–31, 33–36, 42, 259–60
Krulak, Charles, 27, 271

Lacquement, Jr., Richard A., 140–41
Land Operations (British Army), 254
land war, 1–4, 6, 8–9, 12, 20–24, 26–27, 31–33, 35–37, 41–42, 56, 73, 103–4, 130–31, 138, 155, 165, 171, 188–90,

194, 218, 242, 246, 254, 260, 268, 273–74, 277, 285–86, 290, 292
Lan Jian-B, 269
lead interval, 7–8, 275
Leopold Canal, 57–58, 63–64
Liberation Tigers of Tamil Eelam, 163–64, 215, 226, 243
Libya, 3, 35, 135, 165–66, 170–71, 174–75, 183, 184, 188, 191–92, 194–98, 214–15, 225, 223, 235–36, 243, 262–64, 269
Libyan National Army, 196–97
Liddell Hart, B.H., 27, 256–58, 260
Lifting the Fog of War (Owens), 28, 31
Lind, William S., 26–27
LNA. *See* Libyan National Army
LTTE. *See* Liberation Tamil Tigers of Eelam
LVT, 106. *See also* Landing Vehicle, Tracked

M23, 172–73, 224
machinegun, 7.62 mm, 135, 223; 12.7 mm, 168, 235; KPV 14.5 mm, 139; M2, 222–23, 234, 267, 271; M240, 223, 271; M250, 223
magazine depth, 117, 228, 272
Maiduguri, 186–87
Mali, 28, 35, 165–66, 171, 181–84, 233
Malvinas. *See* Falkland Islands
maneuver warfare, 23, 25–28, 36, 41, 142, 159, 271
MANPAD. *See* anti-aircraft missile(s)
Manucy, Albert, 84–85, 141
Marawi, 181, 191–92, 235
Mariupol, 221
Marshall, Andrew W., 24–27, 256
Mataghis-Sugovushan-Talish, 198, 205
Mattis, James N., 36–37
MC2002. *See* Millennium Challenge 2002
McConville, James, C., 35–37
MDO. *See* multi-domain operations
Medicina, 57–58, 72–73, 92
MENA. *See* Middle East-North Africa
methodology, 9, 14, 276, 285–93
micro-terrain, 62, 202, 218
Middle East, 32–34, 130, 133, 135, 139, 165, 170, 174, 181, 213, 215, 227, 229, 231
Mikhaylov, Yuri, 6
Military Power (Biddle), xiii, 4, 25, 286
military-technical revolution, 20, 22, 24–28, 32, 35–37, 41, 78, 81–82, 84, 94, 112, 118, 132, 137, 141, 274
Military-Technical Revolution (Krepinevich), 25
Millennium Challenge 2002, 40, 271
Milley, Mark A., 35–37, 42, 205
Mines, 58, 59, 61, 68, 88–89, 108, 110–11, 116, 121–22, 136, 142–43, 160, 163–64, 185, 196, 203, 205, 226, 231, 242–43, 245, 265
missile, surface-to-surface, 136, 156, 170, 195, 218, 225, 264
mobile protected firepower, 80, 82, 113, 140, 267, 272
Mogadishu, 138, 140, 159–60, 171, 267
Molotov cocktail, 66, 109
Monte Altuzzo, 57–58, 61–62, 218
mortar, xiii, 11, 32, 57–59, 61–69, 71–72, 78–79, 84, 86, 94, 106–9, 114, 117–18, 121–22, 130, 132–35, 137, 139, 142, 157–64, 168–70, 172–75, 183–92, 194, 196–97, 199–202, 221–26, 240, 242–45, 271, 273, 288
Moshchun, 201–2, 289–90
Mount Longdon, 218
Mozambique (Mozambican), 122, 194–95, 199–200, 233
Muhamalai, 161, 243
multi-domain operations, 34–36, 40–41
multiple-launch rocket system(s), 69, 84, 116, 120–21, 133, 139, 156, 161, 168, 170, 171, 173, 187, 189–90, 197–98, 225; 107 mm, 162, 171, 225; 122 mm, 119, 121, 135, 161, 169, 173, 185, 189, 198, 225; 220 mm, 190, 225; 300 mm,

multiple-launch rocket system(s), (*cont.*) 198; HIMARS, 227–28, 272–73; Nebelwerfer, 58–66; Valkiri, 116
Murray, Williamson, 20, 256, 259–60, 275
Mutanchiang, 57–58, 69–70, 80, 186
Myanmar, 35, 165–66, 168–70, 175, 182, 188, 194–95, 205–6, 216, 236, 239, 293
Myawaddy-Three Pagodas Pass, 169

Nagorno-Karabakh, xiv, 3, 28, 104–5, 119, 120, 135, 182, 190–91, 194–95, 198–99, 204–5, 214, 232–33
Nancy, battle of, 81–82
National Movement for the Liberation of Awzad, 224, 172–73
National Transitional Council, 170
National Union for the Total Independence of Angola, 115–16, 136
NATO. *See* North Atlantic Treaty Organization
nature of war, 3–4, 10–11, 23, 25–26, 31, 41, 137, 253, 258–59, 261
naval fires, 68, 90–92, 105, 139, 157, 165, 167, 184, 191, 192, 195, 216, 243
Navy, U.S., 22, 32–34, 40, 64, 87, 89, 94, 105, 157, 191
Nepal, 156–59, 217
Niger, 133, 182, 186, 195–97
Nigeria, 133, 182, 186–87, 195, 235–36, 240, 269
North Atlantic Treaty Organization, xi, 25, 86, 103, 140, 142, 165, 170–71, 175, 205, 216, 223, 243, 255, 263, 269
NTC. *See* National Transitional Council

Obama, Barack H., 33
Objective Force, U.S. Army, 27, 32
observation interval, 7–8, 74, 275–76
obstacles, 68, 88–89, 108, 111, 114, 202
Offset, Third, 33, 35–36, 38
Ogarkov, Nikolai, 256
Oman, 134
On War (Clausewitz), 8, 11, 23, 29, 253
Operation Barbarossa, 26–27
Ortona, 57–59, 61, 63–64, 80
Oryx, 204, 232
Owens, William, 28, 30–31, 35–36, 41–42, 258, 262, 264

Pakistan, 28, 108–9, 111, 155–57, 165–68, 175, 182, 188, 218, 225, 235, 238, 240, 269
Palestine Liberation Organization, 112
Palestinian Islamic Jihad, 184–85
Palma, 199–200, 203
Panama, 136–37, 273
Pavlivka-Vuhledar, 201, 203, 263
Peleliu, 57–58, 64–66, 82, 106, 183
People's Liberation Army, China, 129, 269
People's Liberation Army, Nepal, 158
PGM. *See* precision-guided munitions
Philippines, 134, 181–82, 188, 191–92, 206, 233, 240, 242, 262, 273
pillbox, 61, 68–69, 82
PLA. *See* People's Liberation Army
PLAF. *See* People's Liberation Armed Forces
platoon, 10–11, 57, 62–63, 78–79, 95, 105, 107, 119, 122, 131, 134, 162, 169, 198, 219, 221–22, 231, 269, 286
PLO. *See* Palestine Liberation Organization
PMC. *See* private military company
Poland, 29–30, 57–58, 66–67, 72, 83, 288
pontoon bridge, 202
precision-guided munitions, xii, 9, 21–22, 25, 89, 167, 192, 228, 236, 245, 258
private military company, 199

RAAM. *See* Remote Anti-Armor Mine
radio, 85–86, 88–93, 105, 176, 262, 264
Rally for Congolese Democracy, 164, 221
RAND Corporation, xiii, 12, 41, 291, 319
RDC. *See* Rally for Congolese Democracy

ReARMM. *See* Regionally Aligned Readiness Modernization Model
recoilless rifle, 105–7, 109, 133–34, 137, 139, 162, 171, 173–75, 185, 189, 196–97, 220
recon-strike complex, 24–25, 90, 236, 245. *See also* reconnaissance-strike complex
Red Army, 29–30, 69, 86
regiment, 62, 65, 78–79, 107–10, 117, 118, 131–32; Commonwealth 6th Gurkha Rifles, 72; Democratic Republic of Vietnam 66th, 107–8; Indian 69th Armored, 109; Syrian 46th, 173; U.S. 2nd Armored Cavalry, 117; U.S. 28th Infantry, 132; U.S. 7th Marine, 132; U.S. Seventh Air Cavalry, 107; U.S. 7th Cavalry, 118; U.S. First Marine, 65
Regionally Aligned Readiness Modernization Model, 37, 267
Remote Anti-Armor Mine, 203
Revolution in Military Affairs, 4–5, 23–26, 28, 31–34, 36, 40–42, 252, 258, 260, 270
RGF. *See* Russian Ground Force(s)
rifles, xii, 11, 13, 30, 59, 61, 64–66, 71–72, 79, 82–84, 93–95, 106–9, 121, 130–39, 141–45, 155–56, 158–62, 169–75, 183, 185, 189, 191, 196–97, 199, 202, 205, 219–24, 242–43, 245, 264, 266, 271, 288
risk aversion, 27, 140–41, 263–66, 267–68
RMA. *See* Revolution in Military Affairs
RSTA. *See* reconnaissance-surveillance-targeting-acquisition
Russia, xiii, xiv, 28, 29, 32–33, 35–37, 81, 93, 138–40, 165–67, 169–71, 174–75, 181–82, 184–86, 188–94, 197–98, 201–6, 215–16, 221, 224–25, 227–29, 231–33, 235–37, 239–40, 245, 263, 266, 270
Russian Ground Forces, 202, 224
Rwanda, 171–72

SAA. *See* Syrian Arab Army
Sa'ada, 161–62
satellite, xii, 22, 91, 94, 118–19, 121, 123, 145, 176, 213, 241
Saudi Arabia, 132, 137–38, 194, 196, 269
Scheipers, Sibylle, 5
Scheldt Estuary, 63–64
scopes, 90, 93, 138, 145, 155, 176, 222, 262
Seelow Heights, 84–85, 228
Shusha, 104–5, 119–20, 139, 191, 205
Sirt, 170–71, 188
skirmish, 1–2, 9, 21, 59, 74, 78, 94–95, 103, 115, 119, 121–22, 129–30, 134–35, 137, 159–61, 170, 174–75, 191, 196, 245, 254, 285–86
Smith, Rupert, 3, 8
smoke, obscuring or signaling, xiii, 24, 62, 71, 73, 86, 114, 117, 138, 145, 165, 187, 191
snipers, 59, 66, 90, 121
Somalia, 28, 35, 138, 140, 156, 159, 161, 164, 166, 170–71, 175, 182, 191, 194–96, 199, 215, 225, 236, 243, 267, 273, 293
Somme, The, 84–85
South Asia, 32, 165
South Ossetia, 166–67
South Sudan, 35, 171–72, 175, 182, 188, 191
special operations forces, 42, 114, 121, 137, 162, 167, 184, 191, 220, 236, 269
Sri Lanka, 3, 28, 155–56, 158, 161, 163–64, 166, 175, 213, 215, 217, 238, 243
Starry, Donn A., 22–25, 27, 33, 37, 41
stealth, 22, 24, 38, 94, 123, 137–38, 156, 213, 241, 258, 277
Sternberg, Fritz, 29
Strachan, Hew, 5, 275

strategy, xi, 1, 2, 6, 20–21, 28–29, 33–37, 58, 73, 89, 93, 132, 140, 253–54, 259, 276, 277–78
Sudan, 166, 171–72, 175, 243
Sun Tzu, 8, 27, 40
SVBIED. *See* improvised explosive device, suicide-vehicle-borne
Swat Valley, 168–69, 235, 269
Syria, 3, 11, 35, 111–13, 135–36, 165–66, 173–75, 181–82, 184, 187–96, 200, 206, 213, 215–17, 219, 225, 228–29, 231–33, 236, 239, 242–43, 262, 272–73, 292–93
Syrian Arab Army, 111, 173–74, 182, 189, 193, 219, 239
Syrian Civil War, 181, 193, 293

Taliban, Afghan, 139, 159, 162–63, 165, 199, 216, 219, 225, 238
Talish-Lalatepe Heights, 190–91, 198–99, 205
Tamil Tigers. *See* Liberation Tigers of Tamil Eelam
tank, Abrams M1 variants, 4, 117–18, 138, 142, 188, 195, 229–230, 242, 265–66, 272; Carro Armato L6/40, 80; Churchill variants, 83, 93–94; KV-85, 80; Leclerc, 195, 265–66; Leopard variants, 229, 265; M-10, 267–68; M48, 132; M551, 137; M60, 142, 229; Mark I, 94; Mark III Panzer, 59; Mark IV Panzer, 80; Matilda, 80; MBT-70, 265; Merkava, 112–13, 160, 184–85, 229; Olifant, 116; PT-76, 109–110; Sherman M4, 59, 62, 65, 71–73, 80, 142; T-34, 70, 80, 105–6, 141, 229; T-54, 110, 132–33, 139, 229; T-55, 109–110, 115–16, 135, 141–42, 156–57, 161, 163, 168, 170–71, 173–74, 189, 196–97, 201, 229, 243; T-62, 133, 161, 170, 173–74, 189, 201, 229; T-64, 140, 185, 229; T-72, 112, 117–19, 142, 156, 171, 185, 189–90, 198–99, 203, 229, 242–43, 263, 266; T-80, 203, 229; T-90, 139–41, 229; tank destroyer, 62; Tiger II, 80; Type 59, 133; Type 69, 163, 168; Type-95 light, 65; Type 97, 80; Type 99, 229
Tanzania, 135, 199
Tarakan, 57–58, 67–68
Tatmadaw, 169, 188, 239–240
Tawakalna, Battle of the, 104–5, 117–18, 137, 139
technophilia, xi–xiv, 24, 205, 264, 266–68, 277
technophobia, xi, 277
Tehrik-e-Taliban Pakistani, 167–68, 218
Tembien-Agbe-Abiy Addy, 194, 200–201, 242
Tigrayan People's Liberation Force, 194, 200–201, 242
TPLF. *See* Tigrayan People's Liberation Force
trench, xiv, 61–63, 68–69, 71, 84–85, 89, 93, 110–111, 113, 115–16, 118, 129–30, 136, 138, 142, 156, 163, 171, 187, 189–90, 194, 196, 198, 202–3, 231, 240, 242–43, 245, 262–63
Tripoli, 170, 196–97, 269
Trophy system, 185, 231
Tskhinvali-Gori, 166–67
TTP. *See* Tehrik-e-Taliban Pakistani
Turkey, 91, 193, 197, 204–5, 229, 261, 263

Uganda, 22, 135, 225
UK. *See* United Kingdom
Ukraine, xiii–xv, 3, 25, 33, 35, 37, 80, 83, 90, 135, 140, 154, 166, 181–82, 184–86, 188, 191, 193–95, 197, 200–206, 213, 215, 221, 224–29, 231–33, 235–36, 239–41, 243–45, 261–63, 266, 273, 277, 289–90, 292. *See also* Ukraine War
UNITA. *See* National Union for the Total Independence of Angola
United Kingdom, 24, 57, 72–73 144, 156–157, 193, 221, 270, 275

urban, 57, 59–61, 67, 70, 73–74, 89, 106, 109, 111, 113, 138, 156, 159, 166, 170, 176, 184–188, 191–94, 196–97, 203, 217–19, 272
U.S. Marine Corps, xii, xv, 3–5, 10–11, 13, 20–21, 25–28, 32–42, 64–65, 79, 86, 94, 105–6, 131–132, 137, 145, 155, 168, 191–92, 204, 219, 233–35, 252–53, 255, 267, 270–75. *See also* United States Marine Corps, USMC, Marine(s)

Van Riper, Paul K., 27, 39–40, 271, 274
van Tol, Jan, 33–34
Viet Minh, 130–31
Vietnam, 13, 21–22, 32, 34, 104–5, 107–8, 110–11, 113, 122, 129–34, 137, 139–41, 224, 227, 262, 266, 269, 273. *See also* Vietnam War
Vom Krieg (Clausewitz), 11. See also *On War* (Clausewitz)
von Seeckt, Hans, 29–30

Wadi al-Hujair Wadi al-Saluki, 159–218
Wallace, Ben, 204
Warfighting (U.S. Marine Corps), 253
wargame, 41
Warsaw, 57–58, 66–67, 89
Warsaw Pact, 103, 131
Watts, Barry, 26, 33, 260
Wehraboo, 33
Wehrmacht, 26–30, 66–67, 81, 83, 88
Westmoreland, William C., 20, 21–22, 24, 27–28, 31, 35, 37, 41–42, 132, 256, 260, 262
wet gap, 73, 114, 117, 134
will to fight, 11–12, 30, 66–68, 80, 120, 138, 140, 167, 173, 201, 225, 227–27, 233, 268–69, 286
Work, Robert O., 33, 35–36, 39, 41–42, 205, 260, 262, 264, 274, 276
World Historical Battles Database, 285–87
World War I, 21, 26, 29, 78–79, 82, 84–85, 87–88, 90–94, 106, 136, 233, 256–58, 262, 273, 286

Xuan Loc, 104–105, 110–111, 132–134

Yemen, 3, 35, 103, 132, 135, 156, 159, 161–62, 164–66, 170–71, 174–75, 182, 184, 188, 194–96, 200, 206, 215, 217, 229, 233, 235, 243, 272
Yom Kippur War, 4, 113, 133–34, 144, 227, 232, 286

Zinni, Anthony, 39

ABOUT THE AUTHOR

Ben Connable is a retired U.S. Marine and an independent research leader and adjunct professor at Georgetown University. He has over thirty-five years of combined military and research experience working across the Middle East, North Africa, Asia, and Europe. Ben is the author or coauthor of numerous monographs on warfare including *How Insurgencies End* and *Embracing the Fog of War*. He co-led the RAND Corporation's ongoing research on the will to fight in war.